AF754660

FOREIGN OBJECTS

EDITED BY
CRAIG N. CIPOLLA

FOREIGN OBJECTS

Rethinking Indigenous Consumption in American Archaeology

THE UNIVERSITY OF ARIZONA PRESS
TUCSON

The University of Arizona Press
www.uapress.arizona.edu

© 2017 by The Arizona Board of Regents
All rights reserved. Published 2017

Printed in the United States of America
22 21 20 19 18 17 6 5 4 3 2 1
ISBN-13: 978-0-8165-3191-2 (cloth)

Cover design by Leigh McDonald
Cover image: *Mother Tongue* [detail] by Brian Jungen. Image courtesy of Catriona Jeffries, Vancouver. Photo by SITE Photography.

Library of Congress Cataloging-in-Publication Data
Names: Cipolla, Craig N., 1978– editor.
Title: Foreign objects : rethinking indigenous consumption in American archaeology / edited by Craig N. Cipolla.
Description: Tucson : The University of Arizona Press, 2017. | Includes bibliographical references and index.
Identifiers: LCCN 2016039009 | ISBN 9780816531912 (cloth : alk. paper)
Subjects: LCSH: Indians of North America—Antiquities. | Indians of North America—Material culture. | Indians of North America—Foreign influences. | Consumption (Economics)
Classification: LCC E77.9 .F67 2017 | DDC 970.004/97—dc23 LC record available at https://lccn.loc.gov/2016039009

This paper meets the requirements of ANSI/NISO Z39.48-1992 (Permanence of Paper).

CONTENTS

Acknowledgments vii

Introduction: Indigenous People and Foreign Objects: Rethinking Consumption in American Archaeology 3
CRAIG N. CIPOLLA

Extending Consumption

1. **Approaching an Archaeology of Choice: Consumption, Resistance, and Religion in the Prehispanic Southwest** 29
LEWIS BORCK AND BARBARA J. MILLS

2. **A Tale of Two Settlements: Consumption and the Historical Archaeology of Natives and Newcomers in the 19th-Century Great Lakes Region** 44
MATTHEW A. BEAUDOIN

Defining Bodies and Persons

3. **Beyond Representation: Indigenous Economies of Affect in the Northeast Woodlands** 59
JOHN L. CREESE

4. **Powhatan Sovereignty and Consumer Politics in the Algonquian Chesapeake** 80
CHRISTOPHER SHEPHARD AND MARTIN GALLIVAN

5. Christian Symbols in Native Lives: Medals and Crucifixes in the Tunica Region of French Colonial Louisiana 94
DIANA DIPAOLO LOREN

6. Our Strange Garments: Cloth and Clothing among Native Elites in 17th-Century New England 110
KATHLEEN J. BRAGDON

Negotiating Political and Spiritual Worlds

7. The Olive Jar in the Shrine: Situating Spanish Objects within a 15th- to 17th-Century Maya Worldview 127
MAXINE OLAND

8. Cosmic Debt and Relational Consumption 143
CHARLES R. COBB AND KEITH D. STEPHENSON

9. Sympathetic Magic and Indigenous Consumption of Kettles during Early Colonial Encounter in the Northeast 162
MEGHAN C. L. HOWEY

Resisting and Enduring

10. Indigenous Vaqueros in Colonial California: Labor, Identity, and Autonomy 187
LEE M. PANICH

11. Archaeologies of Native Production and Marketing in 19th-Century New England 204
PATRICIA E. RUBERTONE

Postscript: Postcolonial Archaeology in the Age of Things 222
CRAIG N. CIPOLLA

References Cited *231*
Contributors *285*
Index *289*

ACKNOWLEDGMENTS

THIS VOLUME IS BASED ON A SYMPOSIUM that I organized for the 79th annual Society for American Archaeology meetings in Austin, Texas. Titled "Indigenous People and Foreign Things: Archaeologies of Consumption in the Americas," our symposium was sponsored by the American Anthropological Association Archaeology Division and took place on Sunday morning, April 27, 2014. The original presenters included all of the volume's contributors in addition to Kevin McBride (who coauthored a paper with me), Stephen Silliman, and Matthew Liebmann. Paul Mullins and Rosemary Joyce served as our discussants and provided thought-provoking comments that certainly helped us improve the final product.

In the two years following the symposium, contributors worked very hard, reading one another's papers, exchanging feedback, revising their respective chapters, and—of course—putting up with my constant barrage of nagging emails. I thank each and every one of them for sticking with the project, staying open to feedback, and, for the most part, keeping up with all of my deadlines.

Thanks are also due to Kelly Ferguson, who provided the initial copyediting, compiled the first draft of our master bibliography, and helped with the index; a Marie Skłodowska-Curie actions research fellowship (number 333909) provided the funding for her work. I am grateful to Allyson Carter at the University of Arizona Press, who expressed interest in this project from the very beginning and provided support throughout. This volume clearly benefited from the critical feedback of four reviewers: two readers who commented on the proposal and two who offered extensive feedback on the completed volume. My own contributions—and views on these topics—have grown immensely through my conversations with Kelly Ferguson, Ollie Harris, Kat Hayes, Rosemary Joyce, Jay Levy, Diana Loren, Kevin McBride, Steve Mrozowski, Paul Mullins, Bob Preucel, James Quinn, and Steve Silliman. I am forever thankful for my family who made this volume possible and who also helped me survive the trials and tribulations of yet another transatlantic move while finishing this project. Thanks to Kelly, Maya, Siany, and Pete for the love and support.

During the final stages of this project, I lost an old friend. I dedicate this work to him. Burton Morris (1986–2016), you are sorely missed.

—Craig Cipolla, Toronto, ON

FOREIGN OBJECTS

Introduction

INDIGENOUS PEOPLE AND FOREIGN OBJECTS

Rethinking Consumption in American Archaeology

CRAIG N. CIPOLLA

SAMPLING THE LONG-TERM HISTORY OF FOREIGN OBJECTS IN CONNECTICUT: AN INTRODUCTION

ON AT LEAST A FEW OCCASIONS DURING THE WOODLAND PERIOD, raw materials or finished goods that originated with Adena culture(s) situated in and around the Ohio River drainage made their way to present-day Connecticut. All known examples of these movements are associated with mortuary contexts (Lavin 2013:162). These rare burials include items such as block-end tube pipes, boatstones, and projectile points made of "foreign" lithic materials, copper beads likely from the Great Lakes region, and/or *Olivella* shells from the American Southeast (Cooke 1989; Cooke and Jordan 1972; Grayson 1970; Nadeau and Bellantoni 2004; Ritchie and Dragoo 1959; see also Lavin 2013). The archaeologists writing about these phenomena usually discuss them in one of two related ways. In all instances, archaeologists see the presence of these unexpected materials as evidence for contact and interaction between indigenous peoples of Connecticut and Adena peoples. In at least one case (Nadeau and Bellantoni 2004), archaeologists also consider the possibility that the burials in question were those of actual Adena peoples who came to the region for trade and died while in Connecticut. In either case, much less attention is paid to precisely how "local" indigenous peoples of Connecticut might have viewed, valued, used, or even repurposed these foreign objects.

Jumping ahead to the 16th and 17th centuries A.D., we witness the start of a new era of foreign objects on indigenous sites in Connecticut. As European presence in the area increased, so did local indigenous groups' use of European-made goods along with raw materials that originated in the Old World. Archaeological contexts from this period include an impressive breadth of items ranging from clay smoking pipes to copper kettles, from refined earthenware ceramics to glass trade beads. All of these items originated thousands of miles away from across the Atlantic Ocean. Such items are useful for placing assemblages into a relative chronology and for discussing hotly debated topics such as identity and cultural transformation. Similar to the ways in which the Adena assemblages were originally valued, archaeologists writing about indigenous sites in colonial Connecticut once focused mainly on the ways in which introduced items stood as evidence for cross-cultural interaction and exchange. Most attention remained on freezing the moment of acquisition in time and squeezing it for all its interpretive worth.

Over the last few decades, Connecticut archaeologists have moved beyond this "frigid" gaze to ask questions about how foreign objects operated in their new indigenous contexts (Cipolla 2013a; McBride 1990; Silliman 2005, 2009; Silliman and Witt 2010; see Vesa-Pekka and Nurmi 2009 for similar examples in a European context). For example, Kevin McBride (2008) reports on a fascinating medicine bundle assemblage recovered from a 17th-century Pequot grave. In a remarkable case of preservation, the bundle included a page torn from the King James Bible, along with an unidentified chunk of corroded iron and the articulated claw of a bear. The Bible page mentions the "hand of god," suggesting not only that 17th-century Pequots had the means to understand the written English language but that they also resocialized the page, the language, and possibly the religion that it described using their own cultural conventions, a creative and transformative process, a *becoming*.

From pots-equal-people studies of diffusion to the recent posthumanist turn toward things, the discipline of archaeology boasts a deep and varied history of studying foreign objects such as the shells, lithic materials, Bible page, and animal parts discussed here. In this sense, the present collection of essays is far from revolutionary. What is new about this book is that it brings a diverse set of archaeologies into dialogue with one another regarding how we as archaeologists make sense of—and use—*the foreign* in our interpretations of indigenous history.* The question remains

* This "foreign" status qualifies the artifacts discussed in this volume as *objects* rather than *things*. A recent volume edited by Rosemary A. Joyce and Susan D. Gillespie (2015) makes a similar distinction. As the editors describe in the first chapter of the volume, objects "arrest our attention" (Joyce and Gillespie 2015:4), while things often do their work under our radar. Perhaps, following Joyce and Gillespie, the foreign objects become more thing-like through the processes of consumption and resocialization, fading into the background but still "working behind the scenes," so to speak. This notion shares similarities with Daniel Miller's (1987, 2005a) notion of the "humility of things."

as to whether the two examples juxtaposed above represent "consumption" of fundamentally different kinds. The answer, of course, depends on whom one asks. While maintaining careful focus on the differences that exist between various eras of prehistory and colonial history, we in this book argue that there is great potential for a broadly cross-temporal consideration of indigenous consumption of foreign objects. Likewise, we feel that such studies are excellent venues for exploring current debates concerning material culture, ontologies, and the turn toward things.

WHY CONSUMPTION?

Given the temporal breadth of the volume and its inclusion of noncapitalist contexts, why use consumption as a unifying theme? It is plausible to frame the volume as a study of trade networks or the general acquisition of things, so how precisely is this book about consumption? Is it even possible to cleave away consumption from the contexts of capitalism and Eurocentrism with which it is often associated? In addressing these important questions, I first establish some basic terminology and explain how it relates to this project's twin goals. The first of these, of course, is to bring consumption studies into closer dialogue with indigenous contexts. The second is to extend these frameworks back into the realm of ancient history, typically labeled "prehistoric." I argue that these two objectives, taken together, are vital steps toward decolonizing American archaeology (see also the postscript, this volume).

Consumption studies often concentrate on the acquisition of *commodities* and on people's increasing dependence on objects and things *made by others* (Miller 1995, 2005a, 2005b, 2006a, 2006b; Mullins 2011a, 2011b).[†] On the very first page of *Capital,* Marx (1990[1867]:41) provides a bare-bones definition for the commodity as "an object outside of us, a thing that by its properties satisfies human wants of some sort or another." He goes on, however, to present a much more specific definition for the term as it relates to capitalism. In such contexts, commodities are things whose value is obscured in a very specific manner (Matthews 2010). A thing's "use value"—its inherent useful quality for people—is glossed over in favor of its "exchange value," ultimately associated with its cost in abstract human labor. While use value is inherent in the object and thus material, exchange value is symbolic and immaterial. It is

[†] Though consumption applies to a number of time periods and regions, *consumerism* is typically thought of as associated with modernity and perhaps late capitalism. Consumerism involves mass distribution and mass consumption, by which consumers have access to a seemingly limitless array of commodities (Majewski and Schiffer 2009:192). While all the case studies explored in this book concern consumption, only a few potentially concern consumerism.

abstract, allowing people to equate and exchange seemingly disparate, unrelated entities. Exchange value allows us to quantify how much waterfront property an electric tea kettle is worth or to calculate the relative worth of an antique steam engine compared with a West Highland white terrier pup. *Commodity fetishism* refers to an extreme version of this exchange system, perhaps unique to capitalist contexts, where objects come to stand in for people (Matthews 2010:3) and where a commodity's conditions of production are obscured from the consumer (Miller 2006a). A central concern for Marx was the story of how people came to rely upon objects that they did not—could not—produce themselves (Miller 1995:154). Put succinctly by Miller, Marx saw humanity as "the product of its capacity to transform the material world in production, in the mirror of which we create ourselves. Capitalism is condemned above all for interrupting this virtuous cycle by which we create the objects that in turn create our understanding of who we can be" (2005a:2).

What I take from these concepts is a strong association between notions of consumption and "foreign" raw materials or objects, ranging from objects made by outsiders to materials that simply originated elsewhere. Considering consumption in situations of culture contact or colonialism complicates these matters significantly. We are indebted to postcolonial theorists like Homi Bhabha who provide frameworks for analyzing the inequalities and admixtures that pervade colonial interaction and domination. Bhabha's work (e.g., 1994) on cultural appropriation, mimicry, and hybridity in colonial contexts proves particularly valuable for understanding exchange and blurring between the "cultures" of colonist and colonized (Lydon and Rizvi 2010; Silliman 2015; van Dommelen 2011). A postcolonial lens affords fresh perspectives on colonial exchange that move beyond the strictly Eurocentric frameworks of capitalism briefly outlined above in my discussion of Marx.

In cases of cross-cultural exchange, a slightly different version of *fetishism* emerges. Miller (2006b) discusses this in terms of colonial European perspectives on indigenous peoples' regard for foreign—often European-produced—objects. As the foreign became familiar, indigenous groups often valued and used trade objects in ways that were unfamiliar to Europeans (Keane 2001a). Indigenous "fetish" of foreign objects challenged European conventions, including their sense of exchange value. According to European observers, European-made objects were frequently misused or misunderstood by their new indigenous owners and users. This book pays particular attention to these processes of translation and transformation, seeking to challenge Eurocentric assumptions about exchange and consumption in colonial contexts. Beginning with the chapters that deal with time periods that most would associate with some form of capitalist exchange (Beaudoin, Loren, Bragdon, Oland, Howey, Panich, Rubertone), we open up new spaces for identifying and exploring topics that are relatively new for consumption studies, particularly those studies situated under the banner of historical archaeology. These new topics include considerations of the relationship between consumption and the nature of bodies, personhood, spirits, and colonial resistance and survivance. Engaging these issues helps further decolonize studies of consumption. The studies in this volume place new emphasis on indigenous peoples as consumers with their own agencies, sensibilities, and ontologies that may or may not have overlapped with Western notions of consumption and capitalism more broadly. For instance, considering the above quotation from Marx, we present challenges in this book to his dualistic (Western) framing of subject–object. In this sense, we embark on a quest to explore "multiple modernities" (Taylor 2003) rather than just singular accounts of Western capitalist exchange in which notions of value are assumed to be homogeneous and shared between different exchange partners.

In *The Archaeology of American Capitalism* (2010), Christopher Matthews critically considers the ways in which select Native American groups became ensnared in capitalism through the fur trade. He argues that this particular form of exchange created a common ground for colonial (capitalists) and indigenous individuals and groups (Matthews 2010:27–56). This new ground typified people on each side of the exchange as representatives of radically different cultures. In perpetuating these forms of cultural *alterity*, participants made it possible for indigenous producers and consumers to take part in exchange relations while remaining on the outside (or at least on the fringe) of capitalist society. This external or marginal position offered immediate benefits for both groups. For colonists, the recognition of cultural alterity offered a high-ground perspective on their indigenous exchange partners as culturally inferior, thus providing further justification for colonization. These differences also meant that colonists had little accountability for the welfare of their indigenous trade partners. For indigenous participants who had yet to become dependent on colonists, their contradictory inside–outside status offered opportunities to preserve their own traditions and to maintain the political autonomy of their group for a time.

Matthews (2010) focuses specifically on the ways in which indigenous peoples of 17th-century Rhode Island and 18th-century upstate New York characterized their exchange relations with members of colonial populations. A fatal miscalculation, according to Matthews, came in the form of misplaced blame and self-deceit on the part of indigenous participants in the trade. While indigenous peoples' unequal position in the fur trade's division of labor was the real culprit, they often chalked negative results up to general cultural differences between them and their colonial exchange partners. Matthews considers the ways in which Indians constructed cultural difference through the material world. These constructed differences cloaked and concealed the fact that Native peoples were in the process of becoming (or had already become) commodities. He explains that even when some participants denied their place within capitalism through material discourse, "all persons in capitalism live in a system wherein their life is conceived and defined as a commodity within the market at least in some way" (Matthews 2010:55).

Matthews's work offers a valuable perspective on the complex interrelations and dependencies that characterize the history of capitalism. While, as implied by the title of his book, he focuses largely on the capitalist system, material discourses within that system, and the system's binding together of various groups, contributors in this volume largely focus on indigenous communities and their respective cultural milieus. The volume demonstrates that there are other ways to see and analyze indigenous consumption in capitalist contexts. We take seriously the exploration of what colonists might have written off as indigenous fetish. In recognizing the ways in which various indigenous groups added their own color to exchange and consumption in colonial contexts, we simultaneously raise an important question about the prehistory–history divide. If, following Charles Taylor (2003), there are multiple modernities, what does this mean for the periods that came before? If, as the volume demonstrates, indigenous ontologies shaped the ways in which foreign objects were socialized in colonial and capitalist settings, then what is the "prehistory" of these processes and modes of existence? This question dovetails with the second challenge presented in this book: we ask if it is possible to meaningfully compare indigenous consumption before and after the start of European colonialism. Is this application of consumption simply anachronistic? Recognizing the many problems with the artificial divide between prehistory–history, I do not see the extension of consumption into indigenous contexts dating to time periods preceding the presence of Europeans or capitalism in the New World as anachronistic whatsoever. Since the general themes discussed so far are not unique to capitalism, "the transformation of any society should be revealed by the changing relations of person to objects within it" (Comaroff and Comaroff 1990:196).

We take John and Jean Comaroff's claim to heart in this volume. With case studies ranging geographically from present-day Ontario to Belize and from California to the East Coast (Figure 0.1), this book explores how a general framework of consumption sheds new light on foreign objects in a variety of contexts. In the spirit of the two brief examples of consumption in Connecticut introduced above, and complementing the geographic breadth of this volume, is an equally broad temporal span. Contributors consider case examples dating from the 11th to the 19th century. Here we apply consumption as a general term, defined as the acquisition and use of material culture, or what Paul Mullins (2011b; see also Miller 1987, 1995) recently framed as the socialization of material goods. As described in this introduction, I base this generalized use of the term on ideas from thinkers like Arjun Appadurai (1986), Nicholas Thomas (1991), Bruce Trigger (1976), and a number of historical archaeologists interested in the study of capitalism.

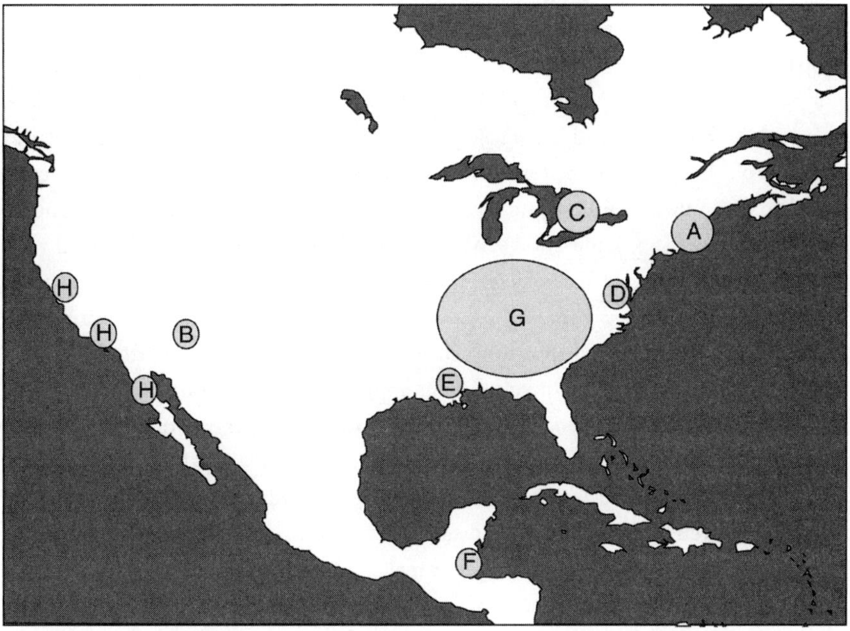

FIGURE 0.1. Map showing the locations of case studies in this volume: A (introduction, Chapters 6, 9, 11); B (Chapter 1); C (Chapters 2, 3), D (Chapter 4); E (Chapter 5); F (Chapter 6); G (Chapter 8); and H (Chapter 9).

The approach laid out in this volume is meant to reiterate the general notion that consumption involves choice (Hamilton and Nicholson 2007) or some degree of power and agency on the part of consumers, a fact that archaeologists have glossed over—or at least minimized—for a sizeable chunk of the discipline's history. On the one hand, the last three decades of archaeological theory have challenged and enriched understandings of "subaltern" agency and practice. On the other hand, several archaeologists problematize the ways in which practice theory and ideas of agency are employed in consumption studies on the grounds that "consumer choice" is a highly variable term that is often poorly contextualized (Wurst and McGuire 1999; Silliman and Witt 2010; Panich, this volume). Taking this point into account, case studies in this volume prioritize context. This entails viewing the foreign objects we find as more than just *standing for* diffusion, cultural exchange, acculturation, or any of the other related terms. Instead, when possible, we attempt to understand how these new materials became part of indigenous worlds (Alberti et al. 2011), some of them shared with European newcomers, of course. In some cases, new items led to drastically novel cultural forms, while in other cases indigenous ontologies rewrought foreign objects in dramatic ways. Rather than focusing on how Adena goods in indigenous burials of Connecticut prove culture contact and exchange, we could take the analysis a step further by asking how the *Olivella* shells or the Ohio smoking pipes became "entangled" (Hodder 2012; Jordan 2009; Thomas 1991; Stahl 2002; see also Smith 2007) in their new contexts, or how a page from the King James Bible—in relation to the humans and nonhumans around it—became Pequot in a 17th-century medicine bundle (McBride 2008). We ask if and how this new set of material relations begot new ways of being Pequot. In his study of ancient Greek colonization, Michael Dietler (2010:57) recently asked what social conditions, opportunities, cultural values, and cultural dispositions informed indigenous consumption of Greek materials. We in this volume take a similar approach to indigenous consumption in the Americas. Such an approach urges us to consider all of the options available to consumers as often as we can (Silliman and Witt 2010), while also forcing us to think critically about consumption as a diachronic process, with long-term outcomes that often endure well beyond the actual instance of acquisition. These facets of consumption and more constitute the main subject matter of this introduction.

More curious than the general concept of consumption that I lay out below are the two shifters (*sensu* Silverstein 1976) in the title of this introduction and at the heart of the volume: "indigenous" and "foreign." Following the recent work of Katherine Hayes (2015), in which she scrutinizes the ways in which the terms "indigenous" and "diasporic" are used within archaeologies of colonialism, I see the concept of indigeneity as inseparable from our current political context and history, especially in American archaeology. Similar to Hayes, I see this notion as relational, as a reaction and resistance to European colonialism. Today it relates directly to federal Indian law in the United States. This is to say that indigeneity now has much to do with *not* being a colonist, settler, or descendant thereof. With the prehistoric examples in this volume, indigeneity ties to a specific location, but again, it is usually thought of in a relational sense (see also Lilley 2004, 2006). For now, these basic notions provide a common ground on which to begin to build our arguments. While discussions of indigenous and Native American identity and authenticity are important and interesting topics of debate (Cipolla 2013b) that do, in fact, present themselves in several chapters (Beaudoin, Rubertone, postscript), these tensions lie largely beyond the scope of the project as a whole.

The "foreign" objects explored in this volume include sundry items ranging from teawares to projectile points, olive jars to boot spurs, and medicine bottles to medicine bundles. These are all defined as foreign in the sense that they resulted from intercommunal exchanges or came from far-off places. Indeed, many chapters consider patterns of exchange between white colonists and indigenous groups (Beaudoin, Oland, Howey, Loren, Panich, Bragdon, Rubertone), while others consider modes of exchange between different indigenous groups (Borck and Mills, Creese, Shephard and Gallivan, Cobb and Stephenson). A few chapters simply consider the presence of "exotics" in indigenous communities (Shephard and Gallivan, Cobb and Stephenson). In these cases, though the presence of exotics does not necessarily imply intercommunal exchange, the authors demonstrate that the items in question originated from places possibly conceived of in the past as nonlocal. We could also conceptualize "foreign" here in the sense of nonhuman, a point to which I return below. For now, it is worth noting that archaeologists have come to recognize that "artifacts," "material culture," or "things" serve as much more than people's "extrasomatic means of adaptation" (Binford 1962; White 1959). This is evinced in several chapters that challenge these Western assumptions about bodies and their boundaries, personhood, and materiality.

By bringing the two shifters (indigenous and foreign) into dialogue, or juxtaposition, with one another, we evoke shades of Bruno Latour's insightful discussion of scale (2005; see also Cipolla 2015), which appears as part of his description of Actor-Network-Theory.[†] Though we do not endorse a singular approach to materiality or scale in this volume, Latour's thoughts on the latter do apply to all chapters herein and, in my opinion, should appeal to most archaeologists, a group that often begins thinking locally at sites about "bigger" issues. Latour reminds us that "there exists no place that can be said to be 'non-local.' If something is to be 'delocalized,' it means that it is being sent from one place to some *other* place, not from one place to *no* place" (2005:179). Here he draws attention to connections that are often ignored, undetected, or downplayed. I recognize this succinct point in my own considerations of indigeneity and foreignness (Cipolla 2015). We must ask how these classifications are "assembled" in the contexts we discuss, of course, including ourselves as key ingredients in the assembly. Latour's argument relates to his attempt to "localize the global" by tracing the way in which macroscale and global processes are always assembled locally. For the anthropologist, perhaps this is most obvious in the ways that linguistic grammar works: the shared rules cannot exist without everyday use. There are numerous assumptions tied to scalar problems in archaeological interpretation, not the least of which is placing abstractions like "capitalism" or "tradition" on a scale that is fundamentally different from the experience of everyday life. For Latour, the idea of different scales is really a question of the number and nature of connections that entities share with other entities. So we might ask how the local events of consumption highlighted in this volume reproduced, challenged, and transformed (or assembled) what

[†] I am indebted to Kat Hayes for initially suggesting this connection.

we typically conceive of as "bigger" categories or classifications (e.g., communal identities, indigeneity, foreignness, social ranks) while also keeping an eye on the ways in which we assemble and connect these categories.

THINGS AND THE LONG TERM

How and why does a broad focus on consumption help to shed new light on the specific historical circumstances investigated in each case study? It places value on a key set of characteristics that are sometimes undervalued or even overlooked by archaeologists:

- socialization of foreign things (how the foreign becomes familiar; how things become localized)
- holism (various social relations tied to acts of consumption; diachronic perspectives on consumptive choices)
- dynamism of material things
- consumer choice (power and agency)
- cross-cultural perspectives (regimes of value)

These new focal points encourage fresh interpretations of indigenous culture, materiality, and cultural dynamism. Through its exploration of these angles, this book pushes the idea of consumption into "foreign territory." As iterated above, it applies frameworks of consumption to non-Western and heterogeneous colonial contexts of the Americas. The results are a rich and diverse set of archaeological histories of consumption. What is evident from these cases is that indigenous history is vibrant, dynamic, and complex whether it involves stone tool technologies or mass-produced ceramics. This alone is an important new direction for consumption studies.

A core theme of the volume is the study of objects and nonhuman "agency." In their seminal volume on consumer goods, *The World of Goods*, Mary Douglas and Baron Isherwood argued that "instead of supposing that goods are primarily needed for subsistence plus competitive display, let us assume that they are needed for making visible and stable the categories of culture" (1979:38). Over the last two decades, archaeologists have immersed themselves in debates over materiality, things, and the ways in which nonhumans exert agency. More so than Douglas and Isherwood, who took a structural-inspired approach to material culture, we now recognize that things do more than represent, reflect, or simply reify culture. For example, Nicholas Thomas (1991) called attention to this point in his discussion of the "promiscuity of objects." He began to look at consumed things as types of actors and agents.

For some thinkers, objects possess a distinct type of agency bestowed upon them by humans (Gell 1998), while for others, agency originates among networks of relations between *actants*, which could be humans, nonhumans, or some hybrid combination thereof (Latour 2005; Hodder 2012). This means that we cannot and should not privilege or even distinguish one from the other, a priori. The latter group of scholars takes influence from the writings of Bruno Latour (e.g., 1993, 2005) and often uses phrases like "symmetrical archaeology" "new materialisms," "posthuman approaches," "the turn toward things," or "archaeology after interpretation" (e.g., Olsen 2010; Olsen et al. 2012; Harris 2014; Witmore 2007).[§] Some rally behind the idea that "things are us!" (Webmoor and Witmore 2008), which is a nuanced point about the long-term coevolution and amalgamation of humans and nonhumans in relation to one another. As Ian Hodder (2012) recently described, there is a complex entanglement of "dependences" and "dependencies" between humans and nonhumans that boasts a deep and ancient history. As the narrative goes, humans are so entangled with things that it is problematic to make assumptions about categories of human and nonhuman and their potential influence over one another in different contexts. Notwithstanding this point, the slogan "things are us!" has the potential to strike fear into the heart of any archaeologist dealing with a strong intellectual or public legacy of "pots equal people" or acculturation theory (discussed in the next section). Here we must use caution to avoid a new "pots equal people" scenario (Bauer 2013). As a volume, we do not endorse a singular and unified approach to these problems, but we do recognize the importance of such questions for our interpretations of consumption. Authors certainly take such arguments under consideration in their engagements with indigenous understanding and incorporation of foreign objects. In order to understand the multiple and competing "regimes of value" discussed in the next section, contributors pay special attention to their specific contexts, trying to understand indigenous ontologies that might challenge Western sensibilities. This is evident in the attention we place on context-specific notions of bodies, personhood, spirit worlds, and colonial tensions.

As a result of the broad temporal breadth of the volume, time and temporality represent another core theme. We join a recent flourish of publications that strive toward more complete understandings of long-term indigenous histories. We can trace this general theme back to Kent Lightfoot's (1995) critique of the relationship between prehistoric archaeology and historical archaeology in American academic practice. Two volumes (Scheiber and Mitchell 2010; Oland et al. 2012) recently took up this critique and challenged these temporal dividing lines by studying the relationships

[§] This is not to imply that all of these approaches are the same. See cited sources for more detailed descriptions of the differences.

between later prehistory and history, paying special attention to prehistoric-historic transitions in various contexts (see also Arnn 2012; Hantman 1990; Lucas 2005:121–126; Rubertone 2000; Silliman 2009). We have read of the "violence" that the label "prehistory" does (Wobst 2005) and even heard of the "death of prehistory" (Schmidt and Mrozowski 2013), though these arguments do not necessarily mean that the study of prehistoric contexts is unwell in some way. In contrast, these critiques have much more to do with *our* relationships with indigenous and other descendant communities that are impacted by our work (Cipolla and Hayes 2015). These critiques are epistemological in the sense that they challenge historical archaeology's sometimes uncritical embrace of false divides between prehistory and history. Thus, we must ask how the history of prehistory shaped colonial formations while also taking into account the political contexts that frame our interpretations and classifications of chronology and history (see Lightfoot et al. 2013).

The history of American archaeology is far from a holistic study of long-term indigenous history. There is a clear predilection for studying only certain eras of the indigenous past. The study of prehistory once dominated the discipline to the point that historical archaeology and the archaeology of colonialism were seen primarily as stepping-stones (i.e., means to an end) leading back in time via the direct historical approach (Rubertone 2000). The Columbian Quincentenary ushered in an increased interest in the study of culture contact and early colonial interactions, along with new consideration of the historical archaeology of Native Americans in colonial contexts (e.g., Cobb 2003; Gosden 2004; Jordan 2009; Lightfoot 1995; Panich and Schneider 2014; Rothschild 2003; Silliman 2005, 2009). In spite of these developments, later colonial contexts of the 18th through 20th century remain understudied. By bringing case studies from various eras of prehistoric, early colonial, and later colonial contexts together, this book breaks with—or at least challenges—the myopic scholarly traditions described by the likes of Bernard Fontana (1965) and Robert L. Schuyler (1970) in the early days of American historical archaeology. This point should not be taken as an argument for dissolving historical archaeology or the study of any specific era of indigenous history. Nor should it be read as a denial of the violent, disruptive, and inhumane nature of European colonialism for indigenous peoples of the post-Columbian Americas. Instead, I argue for further cross-fertilization between the study of different time periods while recognizing the many differences between eras and regions. The general approach to consumption described below provides a means of linking the case studies in useful ways.

One could argue that the 18th- and 19th-century contexts explored in this book (Beaudoin, Loren, Panich, Rubertone) lend themselves most naturally to the study of consumption as it has been applied in archaeology up to this point. However, as several scholars point out (Cipolla 2015; Rubertone 2000; Silliman and Witt 2010), archaeologists rarely approach indigenous contexts from this period in terms of consumption. Similarly, the early colonial case examples in this volume (Creese, Bragdon, Oland, Howey) are not typically considered in terms of consumption practices either. Instead, archaeologists studying these periods and contexts often use foreign goods recovered from indigenous sites for telling time and, until fairly recently in our discipline's history, for measuring cultural loss. Finally, the prehistoric examples in this volume (Borck and Mills, Shephard and Gallivan, Cobb and Stephenson) represent contexts in which consumption is rarely considered, despite the fact that there is a strong scholarly tradition of studying prehistoric trade networks (Bell 1947; Lapham and Johnson 2002; Lattanzi 2007; Nichols et al. 2009; Vehik 2002). As discussed with the brief Adena example given above, we see a predominant focus on the *presence* of foreign goods rather than a strong interest in the ways in which they were socialized in new contexts.

CONTEXTUALIZING INDIGENOUS CONSUMPTION

Archaeological studies of consumption are certainly on the rise. Nearly 20 years ago, Daniel Miller noted this general shift in anthropology. He predicted that consumption would eventually replace kinship as the core focal point of the discipline: "Mass commodities and mass consumption predate the emergence of modern anthropology, which was developed in clear but usually implicit alterity, originally drawing its students mostly to societies defined by the absence of such goods" (Miller 1995:142; see also Fowles 2010b for a discussion of absence). Miller noted the ways in which the anthropological gaze had come to focus on the mass-produced rather than the locally made while also turning attention to the "potentially active role of consumers in *resocializing* commodities" (1995:143, my emphasis) rather than treating consumption as a culturally homogenizing process. For Paul Mullins (2011b), the archaeology of consumption has yet to fully realize its potential despite its unique perspectives on materiality and everyday life. This volume joins a growing body of literature on the archaeology of consumption in hopes of applying the idea to a new set of case studies and moving toward archaeology's "natural" capacity to study processes of consumption and the resocialization of consumed goods.

One of the main tensions in the history of consumption studies is that between production and consumption, supply and demand. These and other problematic binaries listed below often impede archaeologies of indigenous consumption. They reduce the complexity of exchange, interaction, and cultural admixture by glossing over the middle ground between categories. In this volume, we treat these categories as differences of degree rather than as differences of kind.

- Production–consumption
- Gift–commodity
- European–indigenous
- Change–continuity
- Individual–collective
- Accommodation–resistance

For instance, in the archaeology of colonialism, in which considerable power differences often existed between indigenous consumers and colonial producers, practitioners sometimes struggled to understand the complicated relationship between forces of production and consumption, often treating this relationship as a duality. Too much emphasis on the production end of the spectrum in this case might lead the researcher to overlook instances where indigenous consumer preferences actually influenced colonial production. For example, Bruce Trigger (1976:242) once noted the presence of an iron celt that resembled a Huron-made stone celt. He saw this object as an indication that Huron preferences and sensibilities had led Europeans—either on ships or back in their home country—to produce such items specifically for Huron consumption. Similarly, Christopher Miller and George Hamell (1986) focused on the interconnections between colonial production and consumption with their discussion of Native American interests in certain colors of trade bead, relating consumer choice and indigenous symbolism to European production of trade goods.

This tension extends to the different participants in trade and exchange and their cultural perspectives on those transactions. We now know that participation in capitalist modes of exchange does not necessarily imply a simple sharing of values and expectations by all participants (Douglas and Isherwood 1979). In this regard, *The Social Life of Things: Commodities in Cultural Perspective* (Appadurai, ed. 1986) broke new ground for anthropologists studying exchange and value. The volume significantly broadened the field of analysis for consumption studies by creating an interpretive framework that integrated ideas on gift exchange (Mauss 1990[1954]) and alienable commodities (Marx 1990[1867]). In the introductory chapter, Arjun Appadurai (1986) argued for a new approach to the study of commodities that would define them as anything intended for exchange. Mauss's gift and Marx's commodity coexist comfortably in Appadurai's notion of regimes of value, which "does not imply that every act of commodity exchange presupposes a complete cultural sharing of assumptions, but rather that the degree of value coherence may be highly variable from situation to situation, and from commodity to commodity" (1986:15; see also Comaroff and Comaroff 1990; Comaroff and Comaroff 2006; Meskell 2004:57 [for a critique]; Turgeon 2006).

Appadurai also insists on the dynamic nature of commodities: "Commodities, like persons, have social lives" (1986:3). He points out that material culture shifts in and out of the commodity state depending on the contexts in which it circulates. Likewise, Igor Kopytoff's (1986) discussion of the cultural biography of things, which appeared in the same volume, looks at the dynamic life history of objects (see Joyce and Gillespie 2015 for a recent critique of this approach). The approach that Kopytoff laid out has since inspired a number of archaeological approaches (Gosden and Marshall 1999; Peers 1999), including those in this volume.

Nicholas Thomas's (1991) study of indigenous-colonial contexts in the Pacific broke new ground for material culture research and anthropologies of colonialism. Similar to Appadurai and his colleagues, Thomas insisted on studying the social life of things that only comes into focus when the analysis moves beyond thinking of exchange primarily in terms of capitalism and abstract exchange value. Thomas discussed exchange between Westerners and indigenous populations as opportunities for cultural transformation on both sides of the interaction rather than framing them as impositions of the "West upon the rest" (1991:83), a point reiterated in Chris Gosden's (2004) later work on the archaeology of colonialism (see also Dietler 2010). As I point out in my discussion of archaeologics of trade and exchange below, this "two-way street" model represented a revolutionary idea for those early scholars of culture contact who relied too heavily upon uncritical uses of the acculturation concept. As Thomas noted, "This sort of account can appear in works which convey a sympathetic attitude to the people colonized, but the fundamental implication is that their 'loss' of their own cultural and political autonomy is the result of the fatal attraction of European goods: the people are innocent but hopelessly greedy" (1991:85). Thomas used the term "entanglement" to refer to the complicated cultural intersections that were part of many such exchanges. That is, when viewed diachronically and in terms of cultural implications, consumption often results in new cultural and social formations.

Thomas's work provides interesting new perspectives on the ways in which indigenous societies appropriated "foreign" objects, demonstrating that the functionality and form of artifacts, their use value, are far from deterministic. He illustrates this basic point with a number of examples. Most striking is his discussion of the transformation of rifles and iron hatchets traded by Europeans to Pacific Islanders. As these objects changed hands, indigenous ideas and preconceptions redefined them. Like war clubs in the Solomon Islands, newly introduced rifles and hatchets were decorated with inlaid shell patterns (Thomas 1991:103–106), but, more importantly, they were also reconceptualized as objects. In this regard, social structure, including cultural convention (or ontology, more broadly), served to familiarize the foreign and transform it, as is the case with many of the examples discussed in this volume. It is important to note, however, that American archaeologists have come to focus on artifacts that represent clear processes of cultural admixture, such as copper trade kettles clipped into tinkling cones (e.g., Howey, this volume). Thomas reminds us that physical modification of trade objects was likely the exception rather than the norm in such exchanges. For instance, in my own work on 18th- and 19th-century Native American contexts, I have used this point to argue for the study of mundane objects that do not appear to be modified physically, such as European-made ceramics and professionally carved gravestones (Cipolla 2013a, 2015; see also Beaudoin, this volume).

ARCHAEOLOGIES OF PREHISTORIC CONSUMPTION

Although the term "consumption" is not prominent in the archaeological literature on the pre-Columbian Americas, the ways in which it has been used provide an interesting set of comparisons for the study of post-Columbian contexts. Perhaps prehistorians' reluctance to discuss consumption relates to a general uneasiness with the possibility of uncritically mapping our own contemporary sensibilities of consumerism onto the people of the past. This pattern also likely ties to an epistemological issue raised in Borck and Mills's chapter: the lack of other lines of evidence to help identify and further contextualize consumption practices in deeper periods of prehistory. When the term "consumption" is employed in such contexts, it is typically used in one of three ways. First, archaeologists use the term to discuss prehistoric foodways and subsistence strategies (e.g., Emerson et al. 2005; Fish and Donaldson 1991), a subject that fits within the scope of the present volume, though none of the chapters herein actually deal primarily with subsistence practices (however, see Cobb and Stephenson, this volume). Second, consumption is occasionally used as a means of studying social ranks and ranking (Taché 2011). For example, Gary M. Feinman, Linda M. Nicholas, and Helen R. Haines (2006) consider the use of nonlocal goods for creating and displaying social status. Third, researchers discuss the consumption of foreign objects in the context of ritual and ceremonial practices (Bayman 1996; Mathien 2001; Vaughn 2004; Wilson 1999). Such studies typically interpret exotic, nonlocal items in terms of the parts that they played in these practices (Cobb and Stephenson, this volume). For example, Colin Renfrew (2001) considers production and consumption in noneconomically "rational" terms in order to interpret spiritual and religious meanings and practices, including pilgrimages, at Chaco Canyon (but see Fowles 2013 for a critique of this general approach). Only some of these studies concern intracommunal trade relations similar to those that existed between indigenous consumers and colonial producers, but these prehistoric consumption studies *do* provide an excellent reminder that not all acts of foreign consumption need denote cultural loss in the sense of the acculturation problem addressed next.

ARCHAEOLOGIES OF EARLY COLONIAL CONSUMPTION

Archaeological studies of trade and exchange between indigenous peoples and European colonists first focused on foreign goods: (1) in terms of their diagnostic value for dating archaeological assemblages (Kidd 1953, 1954; Quimby 1960b; Sprague 1985; Whitthoft 1967; Woodward 1978[1937]); (2) as chronicles of trade relations between Natives and newcomers; and/or (3) as barometers of acculturative change (Redfield et al. 1936) or, later, cultural loss. In contrast to the prehistoric studies summarized above, nearly all of these approaches failed to delve very deeply into precisely *how* foreign objects were socialized after indigenous peoples acquired them. This is a mistake of scale. Harking back to Thomas's (1991) critique of anthropologies of indigenous consumption, this approach is Eurocentric. The allure and transformative potential of European-made trade items are assumed rather than observed. Local acts of consumption and socialization of foreign goods are framed as subservient to the global, the powerful, the European. If we attempt to "localize the global" (à la Latour 2005), a different picture emerges.

Most studies of culture contact and early colonial exchange up to the 1970s were influenced by George Quimby and Alexander Spoehr's (1951) "Acculturation and Material Culture" (Rubertone 2000). In this seminal work, the authors classified objects in the Chicago Natural History Museum in terms of different combinations of indigenous and foreign influence and origin. They presented a rigid typology for understanding cultural hybridity as manifest in the material culture record. Of course, we now see such studies as problematic in their use of simple binaries (indigenous versus foreign, change versus continuity). Also embodied in later archaeological applications of acculturation theory is an assumed reflective relationship between cultural identity and material culture. Unfortunately, some archaeologists applied Quimby and Spoehr's work uncritically as a "Rosetta stone" for decoding complex cultural interactions and exchanges, where material culture assemblages simply *stood for* cultural authenticity (a form of purity) or lack thereof (e.g., White 1975).

Much like the specter of "culture" that these artifacts were said to reflect, the acculturation narratives highlighted here still continue to haunt us in certain ways discussed in the postscript of this volume. For now, it is important to point out that thinkers like Robert Redfield, Ralph Linton, and Melville J. Herskovits (1936) and Quimby and Spoehr (1951) did *not* actually see material culture as simply reflective of cultural identity (Rubertone 2000). This idea is evinced in the later writing of George

Quimby. For instance, in a discussion of the Great Lakes Region, Quimby noted the replacement and/or transformation of indigenous-made material culture: "In addition to their old-style dwellings, the Indians made use of log cabins and similarly shaped houses covered with bark. Household utensils included brass kettles; pewter and silver spoons; wooden ladles and bowls; various kinds of glass bottles; Chinese blue and white porcelain and later Staffordshire pottery of similar shapes and decoration; glass mirrors; iron strike-a-lights for starting fires; and many other items that were also part of the material culture of contemporary white men" (1960a:148). He went on to note that cultural change went both ways, stating that, despite the observed material transformations, "Indians were still Indians" (1960a:148). The ways in which Indians stayed Indian despite changes in material culture must be considered in terms of indigenous ontologies. I point to the positive aspects of such studies in order to avoid displacing the baby with the bathwater.

For instance, Bruce Trigger's (1976) *The Children of Aataentsic* represents an exemplary study of the archaeology and ethnohistory of Huron consumption, though he did not use that term. The book focuses on the Huron Indian Confederacy up to 1660. Like his contemporaries, Trigger placed considerable emphasis on the absence or presence of European-made trade goods at Huron sites. Referencing the foundational work of archaeologists like Kenneth Kidd (1954) and George Quimby (1960a, 1960b), Trigger compared Huron sites in terms of their relative frequencies of foreign goods. As Kidd (1954) noted earlier, such goods provided an excellent line of data for establishing relative chronological relationships between sites. Trigger further explored Huron–French trade relations via ethnohistorical accounts, often focusing more on the analysis of lists of trade goods rather than on the goods themselves. In many instances, he emphasized functional interpretations of European goods (á la Marx's use value) recovered from Huron sites. For example, metal cutting implements were more efficient than stone cutting implements, as were copper kettles as compared to indigenous-produced ceramics in the area (Trigger 1976:360, 410–411). But Trigger also took indigenous symbolism into account. In a discussion of kettles, for instance, he states that they sometimes held prestige and supernatural powers for the Huron (Trigger 1976:410–411), perhaps in ways similar to those discussed by Howey in this volume.

As implied by Trigger's interpretation of Huron kettles, functionality is only one type of material culture meaning, one that was likely not distributed evenly between producers and consumers in this case. This example speaks to distinct regimes of value within single interactions and exchanges. It also offers a critique of Western claims of indigenous fetish. Trigger recognized Huron perspectives and agency in these encounters, noting, for example, that the Huron referred to the French as Agnonha, which glossed as "metal people" (1976:360). In other words, the Huron literally defined the French in terms of the foreign objects that the Huron sought most, similar to Bragdon's discussion of "Coatmen" in 17th-century New England (this volume; see also Bragdon 2009). Trigger also noted the impacts that French-made goods had within and between different Native communities, a general theme explored further in this volume (Shepherd and Gallivan, Cobb and Stephenson). Finally, Trigger showed that foreign objects impacted indigenous groups in a variety of manners, in some instances leading to the replacement of "traditional" material culture, while in others complementing it (Krauss 1944; Quimby 1960b). More precise understandings of the ways in which "Indians stayed Indian" despite their consumption of foreign objects began to emerge at this time. We continue to follow the same thread in this volume.

In the same year that Appadurai's volume came out, Miller and Hamell (1986) argued for increased attention to indigenous choice and symbolism in Indian–white colonial exchange in northeastern North America. Similar to Appadurai, Miller and Hamell recognized the cultural variability that framed colonial exchange, critiquing simplistic notions of acculturation by teasing out the ways in which indigenous cultural practices and symbolic conventions served to redefine "white" artifacts. Ultimately the authors made the point that indigenous peoples involved in trade did not see European-made trade goods as completely foreign but rather fit them into their respective cultural frameworks (see also Scaramelli and Tarble De Scaramelli 2005; Silliman 2005, 2009). In a similar way, Constance Crosby (1988) used the Algonquian concept of *manit* (Creese, Shephard and Gallivan, Howey, this volume) to interpret grave assemblages in colonial New England. Represented in Crosby's work is a distinct commitment to look beyond issues of functionality and economic–adaptive rationality when it comes to consumer choice. Here also we see a commitment to considering indigenous philosophies and the ways that they influenced consumption practices.

ARCHAEOLOGIES OF CAPITALIST CONSUMPTION

Compared to the archaeological approaches summarized thus far, historical archaeology boasts a deeper history of consumption studies (for recent examples, see Hodge 2014; Mullins 2011a; Mullins and Jeffries 2012). The dualistic tensions between studying production and consumption mentioned above also played out in historical archaeology. Early studies of consumption began with a focus on socioeconomic status (Spencer-Wood 1987). Like the acculturation problems discussed above, such studies employed somewhat uncritical interpretations of material culture as reflective of certain aspects of social identity or character. We now recognize that consumed objects are "not mirrors for 'real' identities," and thus it is "infeasible, on the one hand to reduce objects simply to reflective or mimetic mechanisms or, on the other, to accord them absolute power to forge identity" (Mullins 1999:29). Having noted these interpretive problems, it is important to point out that this earlier work on the historical archaeology of consumption yielded new and valuable understandings of historic material culture (Miller et al. 2000), especially its cost (Miller 1980, 1991).

In the 1990s the pendulum swung the opposite way by drawing on Douglas and Isherwood's (1979) approach to consumer goods. This work, along with a general turn toward practice theory at the time, inspired some historical archaeologists to shift focus from production to consumption and individual choice. As historical archaeologists came to embrace practice theory and questions of agency, they also came to rethink power as diffuse rather than as a top-down phenomenon (Certeau 1984). This approach frames consumption practices as both *structured* and *structuring* (Bourdieu 1977, 1990). These studies framed "shopping" as a selective, creative, and symbolic process (Cook et al. 1996; Crook 2000; see also Rubertone 2000 for a similar argument). Consumer practice and agency took center stage alongside issues of power and inequality. This meant that even "subalterns" had roles to play in negotiating inequality and class structures through their consumptive choices (Cessford 2012; Mullins 1999; Mullins and Ylimaunu 2015; Sweitz 2012). These interpretations recognize possibilities for resistance (in varying degrees of consciousness) among subaltern populations. For instance, Paul Mullins's (1999) study of African American consumption in Annapolis, Maryland, demonstrates the ways in which acts of consumption allowed African Americans to navigate complicated structures of race, racism, and inequality.

These new orientations to consumption sometimes lost touch with the relationships of production that enabled consumption. LouAnn Wurst and Randall H. McGuire (1999) pointed to this imbalance and took issue with the ways in which consumer agency approaches glossed over the exploitative relations of production that enabled consumer agency. They saw these approaches as ideologies of modern capitalism in the sense that they masked social inequalities both in the past and in the present. For Wurst and McGuire, the focus of such studies should be on processes of social reproduction as a whole, allowing researchers to better understand the relationship between production and consumption (e.g., Hodge 2013; Mullins 2009). As an example of this problem, we can trace the ways in which our smartphones relate to our identity and our seemingly autonomous personhood. In a few quick clicks, we can post photos of our elaborate breakfast or our vacation trip to Holland. If we choose to do so, however, we can also easily trace the connections between these aspects of our own "individuality" to the exploitative and inhumane factory conditions in China, where some of our phones are mass-produced in the most cost-effective way.

These connections are surely important for researchers when they think about consumption, but how does this point relate to the majority of the cases explored in this volume? In many cases, the authors are not dealing with mass production and extreme inequalities between producers and consumers. Surely we could link Beaudoin's analysis of Mohawk teawares to the conditions of labor in ceramic factories at Stoke-on-Trent, England, but what about the other cases? The point is to focus on as many connections as possible when it comes to interpreting consumption practices and to maintain a focus on the modes of production, origin of materials, and object trajectories or "itineraries" (Joyce and Gillespie, eds. 2015).

When we begin to pay serious attention to the connections that lead up to moments of acquisition, we find that consumer choice is highly variable. Not everyone has the same degree of choice when it comes to acquiring goods (Wurst and McGuire 1999). This point is emphasized in the work of Stephen W. Silliman and Thomas A. Witt (2010) in their analysis of 18th-century consumption practices on the Eastern Pequot Reservation in Connecticut. The authors highlight the importance of contextualizing indigenous choice and the structures that gave it shape. The Eastern Pequot individuals in question did not have the ability to acquire any and all goods. In fact, they acquired items such as European-produced ceramics in distinct ways compared to other consumers in the area. In this volume, Panich (see also Panich 2013, 2014) also critically considers contexts of acquisition, discussing the ways in which several indigenous Californian groups gained access to horses and the material culture associated with them, leading to the emergence of indigenous *vaqueros*, or "cowboys."

In contexts such as these, we see evidence for mixed economies in the sense that indigenous consumers might have maintained distinct regimes of value compared to their exchange partners, usually individuals and groups linked to them through capitalism (Cipolla 2013a, 2015; Mann 2008; Pezzarossi 2014; Schwartz and Green 2013). Like Thomas (1991), several authors in this volume are sensitive to the fact that they may be dealing with mixed or plural economies of exchange in which different parties understood exchange in disparate manners. Seth Mallios's (2006) analysis of 17th-century exchange relations in the Chesapeake involving indigenous communities, English colonists, and Jesuit missionaries illustrates just how complicated it can be to understand diverse regimes of value. Mallios argues convincingly that violence in this area stemmed directly from different cultural understandings and expectations for cross-cultural trade and exchange.

ORGANIZATION OF THE VOLUME

The volume consists of four parts. The first, "Extending Consumption," is composed of two chapters that highlight the epistemological challenges and benefits of considering consumption in relatively new archaeological contexts. Though all chapters in the volume deal with archaeological epistemologies to some degree, Borck and Mills (Chapter 1) and Beaudoin (Chapter 2) highlight the differences that frameworks of consumption make for the study of their respective time periods and regions. Borck and Mills wrestle with the difficulties of extending frameworks of consumption into deeper time with their study of the spread of "Salado" polychrome ceramics and associated feasting practices in prehistoric Arizona. Beaudoin (Chapter 2) uses consumption to investigate and challenge epistemological divides between historical archaeology and the archaeology of colonialism. He analyzes two 19th-century Mohawk assemblages from Ontario, revealing the complexities of Mohawk consumption and identity construction in the modern era.

Four chapters make up the second part of the volume, "Defining Bodies and Persons." Authors present examples of consumed foreign objects that—in their new contexts—became "extensions" of bodies and persons. Creese (Chapter 3) discusses 17th-century Wendat consumption of foreign smoking pipes, marine shell, and kettles in the Great Lakes region. His analysis of Wendat ontologies challenges taken-for-granted Western categories such as "human," "identity," and "person." Shephard and Gallivan (Chapter 4) focus on foreign shell and copper objects in Algonquian societies of the precolonial Middle Atlantic region. They concentrate on sovereignty as it related to the constant interaction of bodies and items of bodily adornment. Loren (Chapter 5) analyzes Tunica consumption of Catholic symbols and material culture in 18th-century French colonial Louisiana. She considers the subtleties of Tunica concepts of body and soul as they relate to dress and fashion. Bragdon (Chapter 6) looks at indigenous consumption of English-made cloth and clothing in 17th-century coastal New England. She argues that these foreign objects contributed to new understandings of personhood, social status, and health and well-being during uncertain times.

The third part of the volume, "Negotiating Political and Spiritual Worlds," includes three chapters that view consumed foreign objects as important for maintaining political and/or spiritual balance. Oland (Chapter 7) considers Maya consumption of Spanish-made goods in colonial Belize. She argues that elite and ritual use of these foreign objects continued a set of Mayan practices with an ancient genealogy, further challenging our disciplinary divides between prehistory and history. Cobb and Stephenson (Chapter 8) use frameworks of consumption and notions of the foreign to rethink Mississippian feasting in the late prehistoric American Southeast. They view feasting as more than political, demonstrating the ways in which feasting and consumption of foreign and local goods allowed participants to maintain a "cosmic" balance. Howey (Chapter 9) examines indigenous consumption of copper kettles in the Northeast. She revisits data from mortuary practices in the region, rethinking copper in terms of the part it played in sympathetic magic.

Part 4, "Resisting and Enduring," considers emergent and hybridized social categories that built upon and transformed foreign materials and practices. Panich (Chapter 10) considers indigenous vaqueros in Spanish California. He examines shifting and varied relationships between indigenous peoples and several foreign entities related to vaquero status, ranging from actual horses to spurs and other horse-related hardware. Rubertone (Chapter 11) reverses the gaze on consumption provided in all other chapters. Her analysis of 19th-century Providence, Rhode Island, focuses on an indigenous person as both a producer and a marketer of goods for white consumption.

In the postscript, I provide thoughts on future research concerning indigenous peoples and foreign objects, particularly as it relates to two key moves in our discipline: the rise of postcolonialism and the posthuman "turn toward things."

EXTENDING CONSUMPTION

1

APPROACHING AN ARCHAEOLOGY OF CHOICE

Consumption, Resistance, and Religion in the Prehispanic Southwest

LEWIS BORCK AND BARBARA J. MILLS

And we could not live with ourselves if our archaeology produced accounts of individuals, cultures, and societies that left no space for individuality, freedom of choice, will, self-determination, creativity, innovation, and resistance.

MOORE (2000:260–261)

IN THIS CHAPTER, we present a model that can help archaeologists move beyond the modern dichotomy of indigenous and colonizer (see in this volume Cipolla, introduction; Creese; Shephard and Gallivan; Cobb and Stephenson), a binary that can also be understood as nonstate versus state. Since states dominate the documentary record, interpreting the past often occurs within an implicit statist framework (Flexner 2014:83–84). To overcome this deficiency, we explore a way of examining themes often reserved for periods with written documents in a manner that archaeologists working in pretextual contexts can use. We situate this method within a consumption framework that allows archaeologists to examine decisions archaeologically. In doing so, we hope to create a two-way bridge that crosses the "great divide" between precolonial and colonial inquiries—between "historic" and "prehistoric"—with clear applicability in other regions that predate modern colonialism.

We view consumption as a continuum that includes production, use, and discard. This perspective differs from that of other object-oriented paradigms that parallel consumerist theories (e.g., object biography) by focusing on human agency instead of on object agency (i.e., Gosden and Marshall 1999). As a continuum, consumption emerges as more than a simple yes–no choice in human-object interactions. Along this continuum, human decisions dialectically interact at every moment with the material world. This recursive process generates the space in which material and humans create and affect each other (*sensu* Hodder 2012; Latour 2005; Mullins 2011b).

When we view consumption as a continuum starting prior to production and continuing through final discard and archaeological recovery, the choices made become encapsulated within the material objects embedded in that continuum. Each item, such as a ceramic vessel, becomes a repository for the decisions of each group, household, or person that interacted with it in the past. Material things represent choices, and assemblages of things are considered as aggregated choices through time. It is here that an archaeology of choice emerges (*sensu* Brumfiel 2000).

An archaeology of choice—revealed through consumption patterns—recognizes that decisions are involved at every step along the consumption continuum. In an archaeology of choice, ceramics, for example, are liminal objects that transition the archaeological record from one of things to one of acts, decisions, and experiences. Ceramics are evidence of historical choices. Each pot moves beyond the corporeal field of the material and into the incorporeal field of human history.

When contextualized within the literature on enculturation (e.g., LeVine 1990; Netting 1993), specifically high-visibility attributes from Carr's (1995a, 1995b) unified theory of artifact design (see also Clark 2001), these consumption patterns indicate people's choices in terms of what they wished to transmit to household members, community members, and even other communities. Patterns of consumption also demonstrate structural restrictions on where and when people can act, serving to minimize potential overstatements of individual agency. In archaeology, the enculturation literature is often used to examine low-visibility attributes (e.g., Clark 2001) to get at underlying issues of group identity and communities of practice. Yet by focusing on the high-visibility attributes, such as painted decorations on ceramics, these consumption patterns might indicate decisions made by individuals about the groups in which they sought to signify—or avoid signifying—their membership. By examining the consumption of these highly visible attributes, archaeologists are able to draw connections between artifacts and historical choices.

To play with a tired phrase, pots are not people, but they *are* choices. While discussing consumers' conscious symbolic agency, Mullins noted that "people actively define the meaning of things, often in opposition to dominant ideology" (2011b:134). In this chapter, we use the framework of consumption to analyze whether opposition to a new spreading ideology was present in the U.S. Southwest between A.D. 1300 and 1450. The material culture associated with this ideology (labeled "Salado") has proven difficult for archaeologists to interpret. However, research over the last 20 years demonstrated that Salado was an emergent religious cult with an inclusive nature (Clark et al. 2013) centered on public feasting (e.g., Crown 1994). We present a model in which knowledge and attitude, modified by topographic cost distance, combine to determine the integration of—or opposition to—foreign social practices. We apply our model to the Salado case study of the U.S. Southwest.

CONSUMPTION AS VIEWED THROUGH DIFFUSION

We argue that changing patterns of ceramic consumption indicate shifts in people's affiliations, both conscious and unconscious. When pottery carried clear ideological meanings and was used in public feasting, as Salado polychromes were (Crown 1994; Mills 2007), the consumption of these ideologically charged ceramic vessels may be one way to demonstrate how people chose to express their alignment to particular ideologies. These alignments, or lack thereof, may be especially visible when looking at assemblages diachronically or across large distances of space. Prior to engaging the temporal component, however, the process of transmitting technology and ideas warrants further examination.

Sociologists studying the spread of ideas primarily use the related diffusion of innovation and contagion theories (Burt 1987; Golub and Jackson 2012; Marsden 1998; Qi 2013; Rogers 2003; Ugander et al. 2012; Valente 1996a, 1996b). Investigations into the diffusion of innovation started during the 1930s and 1940s as sociologists examined the variability in uptake of new agricultural technology among farmers (e.g., Ryan and Gross 1943). Such studies discussed a logistic, or S-shaped curve, in terms of cumulative adoption and argued that interpersonal relationships are fundamental to understanding diffusion. Knowledge alone was not enough to convince people to adopt; they also needed someone they knew, often someone with high prestige, to have adopted. There are other modifiers to technology uptake as well. For instance, cultural ontologies appear to predispose certain adoptions of foreign technology and ideas (see Howey, this volume).*

In 1973, Everett Rogers noted that the perception of advantage or disadvantage for a new idea or technology could determine how successful it was in spreading. He used the term "knowledge-attitude-practice (KAP) gap" to describe differences in uptake of new innovations based on people's reactions to them. Rogers revisited social theory in use since the 1940s (e.g., Hyman and Sheatsley 1947; Tichenor et al. 1970) that had shown a gap in how different socioeconomic classes received new ideas. He expanded this theory so that it took into account individuals' changing attitudes toward innovations.

Simply knowing about something new is not enough to convince someone to use it. Attitudes, modified by culture and society, play a role as well. Through time, knowledge of an innovation is followed by an attitude toward that innovation (either negative

* "Foreign" is described here as ideas or material culture that originated outside of the indigenous material culture and ideology of the extant local groups, often from within migrant communities or the later communities that emerged as migrants and locals intermarried.

or positive) and then eventual adoption (or rejection) of the innovation. This draws on previous research by Bryce Ryan and Neal C. Gross (1943) that showed that adopters could be meaningfully divided based on the time it took them to adopt new ideas or materials (seen in their relative positions along the curve). The horizontal distance between knowledge and adoption is the gap, and the size of this gap will vary through time. Rogers identified several factors that affected this gap, including perceived advantage, compatibility, complexity of use, trialability, and the social field of performance. The KAP gap is important in understanding how attitude affects the diffusion process. It also suggests that diffusion could stall based on negative reactions (as discussed below).

The KAP is limited, however, in that it only treats attitude as a dichotomy of positive or negative; we will overcome this dichotomy by examining attitude as a continuum with positive on one end, negative on the other, and neutral in the middle. KAP also fails to consider the role of space in the diffusion process. Understanding how environment and space affect the transmission of ideas is key to understanding social and technological transmissions (Barash 2011:15).

The diffusion of ideas—often associated with the investigation of the diffusion of innovations by sociologists—has been of limited interest to archaeologists, who have primarily focused on the diffusion of technologies and distance decay models (e.g., Hodder 1980; Renfrew 1975; although see Cameron n.d.). While sociologists rarely incorporate spatial considerations into the spread of ideas and instead rely upon social and structural relationships within networks, archaeologists tend to favor spatial distributions of materials, population size and distribution, and environmental constraints. Despite this shortcoming, sociological investigations into diffusion that examine how ideas spread based on the structure of a network (i.e., network topology) composed of nodes (individuals) and edges (their relationships) can be useful to archaeologists.

The position of nodes within the structure of the network is important, particularly if nodes are in locations that enhance the transmission of information and technologies (Mills and Peeples n.d.). We argue that a geosocial approach that combines a relational approach (network topology) with a spatial approach (materials, population, and regional topography) can help researchers gain a more holistic method for understanding how changing patterns of consumption are driven by the diffusion of goods and their associated ideas.

RECOGNIZING RESISTANCE USING NONTEXTUAL DATA AND MODELS OF DIFFUSION

Resistance piqued the interests of anthropologists and archaeologists during the poststructural paradigm shift in the 1980s and 1990s. Much of the resulting research had roots in Antonio Gramsci's (1971) ideas on how subordinate groups resist a dominant group's ideology, in Marxist understandings of power struggles, and within Nietzsche's (2007[1887]) and then Foucault's (1981, 1995) Genealogies.

While offering valuable insights, studies of resistance in anthropology have sustained substantial criticism. Anthropologists have been accused of romanticizing resistance (Ortner 1995:177) and often oversimplifying a complex process (Scarry 2001: 55) by creating a dichotomy of dominant–subordinate (Sakamoto 1996). Michael F. Brown (1991:389–406; see also Mattingly 2013) argues that this oversimplification fails to recognize that instances of resistance can also entail rejection of the current political structure of subordinate groups. In essence, marginalized groups still actively create the societies they live in (Gosden 2004). However, this focus on the agentive and creative ways in which less powerful groups navigate social and political situations has also received criticism for downplaying massive inequalities in privilege and power (González-Ruibal 2014).

Further critiques include the uncritical application of a range of theories forged within a postcolonial paradigm to periods lacking the colonizer–colonized dynamic. These critiques have been given short shrift by researchers such as Marshall Sahlins (1999:52) and Brown (1991). For example, Sahlins notes that resistance and cultural subversion are intrinsic to the nature of intercultural relations, as these relations involve a change in cultural context of "external forms and forces" (1999:52). This change alters the values placed on familiar categories and relations. In this context, resistance theories are integral for understanding cultural contact and power relations in all times, not just during the period of Western imperialism.

Another critique of the resistance literature is that researchers often fail to effectively use available data (Ortner 1995) and too often rely on textual data instead of available ethnographic data. This can be overcome by incorporating archaeological data. Material culture, which can be a bridge between the deep history of archaeology, the textual past, and the ethnographic present, is another line of evidence that should be mobilized to understand power dynamics in the past and present.

Archaeologists have observed forms of resistance in the archaeological record in a number of ways. Ceramics have been examined to show how rural enslaved Africans created household place and a material culture that did not reinforce their position in the dominant ideology's hierarchy (Ferguson 1991:260–268). Researchers have also studied style and iconography to identify resistance in the past (Emerson and Pauketat 2002; Kelley 1992; Schurr 2010; Webster 1999), as well as using ceramic distributions to examine resistance at the boundary of empires (Anders 1989:7–9).

In the U.S. Southwest literature, resistance seems most obvious at the spatial boundaries of dominant cultures (e.g., Borck 2012, 2017; Fowles 2010a; Mills 2008) and more subdued closer to the centers of power (Liebmann 2002; Mobley-Tanaka

2002; Spielmann et al. 2006; Wilcox 2009). Resistance might also have a strong spatial component. This can take the form of maintaining earlier forms of dispersed settlement patterns, or patterns of mobility as resistance to centralization and increasing hierarchy. "Subverting domination through separation" (Sassaman 2001:227) can lead to cultural and social persistence of subaltern groups. This pattern is also seen during the colonial period in the U.S. Southwest (Ferguson 2002).

Based on the above literature, a spatial component, along with social networks, should be applied to any archaeological investigation of resistance—especially when using models of diffusion to understand and explore resistance. The study of how space affects social transmission is an important, yet unresolved, question in our understanding of how ideas are transmitted (Barash 2011:15) and resisted. The study of how social connections affect the spatial distribution of technology is equally important and equally unresolved. In 1992 John E. Douglas and Carol Kramer highlighted the notion that both social and spatial measures needed to be taken into account when examining the spread of technology, the movement of people, and consumption and production practices. While little has been done to look at how these two measures interact, much has been done on them individually (see Borck 2016a for an overview of geosocial research; see also Bernardini and Peeples 2015; Coward 2013; Hill et al. 2015; Mills, Clark, et al. 2013 for recent syntheses of social network and spatial analyses).

Is it possible, then, to recognize resistance in nontextual assemblages? We argue that beyond being possible, in some instances it might even be preferred to rely on nondocumentary data to identify ancient acts and processes of resistance when text-based evidence is missing, erratic, not present, or biased. However, this preference should be coupled with the recognition that the material record also comes with its own set of biases and assumptions.

In our particular case study, we follow ideas of power that infuse the work of Pierre Bourdieu and Michel Foucault, specifically that "power works best when it is invisible. When power becomes visible . . . it provokes resistance" (Hoy 2004:15). To recognize resistance without the textual record, we integrate inferential tools developed by postcolonial researchers examining historically neglected groups with a social network model in which knowledge and adoption of foreign objects are considered separate historical events. The adoption of new consumption practices is an agentive process where simple knowledge of foreign objects is not sufficient to explain their adoption. Attitude, pivotal to the model, is multivocal and governs future interactions. This model demonstrates how and why consumptive practices are affected by culture contact and shows how archaeological and historical data can be operationalized to approach the adoption of foreign objects and practices at multiple social and spatial scales (see Cipolla, introduction, this volume).

WHAT IS SALADO? AN IDEOLOGICALLY DRIVEN SOCIAL MOVEMENT

A substantial part of the Colorado Plateau was depopulated during the A.D. 1200s, setting off a demographic cascade that affected much of the U.S. Southwest. At least some of the migrants, especially those from northeastern Arizona, were instrumental in founding a new religious practice that was adopted throughout the southern Southwest (Clark 2001; Clark and Lyons 2012; Crown 1994; Lyons and Lindsay 2006; Mills, Clark, et al. 2013). Our discussion focuses on the prehispanic depopulation of northeastern Arizona and subsequent movement of those groups into populated areas in southern Arizona (Figure 1.1; see Borck 2016; Borck et al. 2015; Mills, Clark, et al. 2013; Mills et al. 2015 for an examination of the regional impacts during this period). An emergent religious movement, termed "Salado," resulted from this culture contact.

Salado is an archaeological concept that has been debated for decades in terms of both its origin (Dean 2000; DiPeso 1958; Doyel and Haury 1976; Gladwin and Gladwin 1935; Haury 1945; Nelson and LeBlanc 1986) and its ideological and organizational meaning (Crown 1994). More recent research indicates that much of what is now called "the Salado phenomenon" is likely related to an ideology that spread from northern Pueblo migrant networks to their neighbors in their new southern homes (Crown 1994; McGuire 2012; Mills, Roberts, et al. 2013; Mills, Clark, et al. 2013). Salado incorporated new consumptive practices, including decentralized production of polychrome ceramics and large-scale feasting using these polychrome ceramics (Figure 1.2) as serving vessels (Crown 1994; Mills 2007). This shared ideology has been proposed as a way to ease intergroup tensions among migrants and locals and facilitate migrant integration (Crown 1994; Clark and Lyons 2012), as well as a way to maintain a shared identity in diaspora (Clark et al. 2013; Clark and Lyons 2012; Lyons and Clark 2011; Lyons et al. 2008; Lyons and Lindsay 2006; Mills 2011). Religion does not simply integrate, though. The picture is always much more complicated than that, and conflict between—even within—communities engaged in different religious practices is common through all points in time (see Borck 2016, 2017 and Dungan 2015 for recent examples of southwestern research into how religion divides).

Early researchers posited that Salado originated in the Tonto Basin, which they labeled the "Salado Heartland" (Doyel 1976; Haury 1945). However, Roosevelt Red Ware, which is the broader term for Salado polychromes and related bichrome ceramics, occurs in large amounts in areas as disparate as the San Pedro Valley and the Transition Zone of Arizona (Clark 2001). It now appears that the ware originated in the Silver Creek area in the late 13th century (Mills et al. 1999) before being adopted throughout the central and southern Southwest.

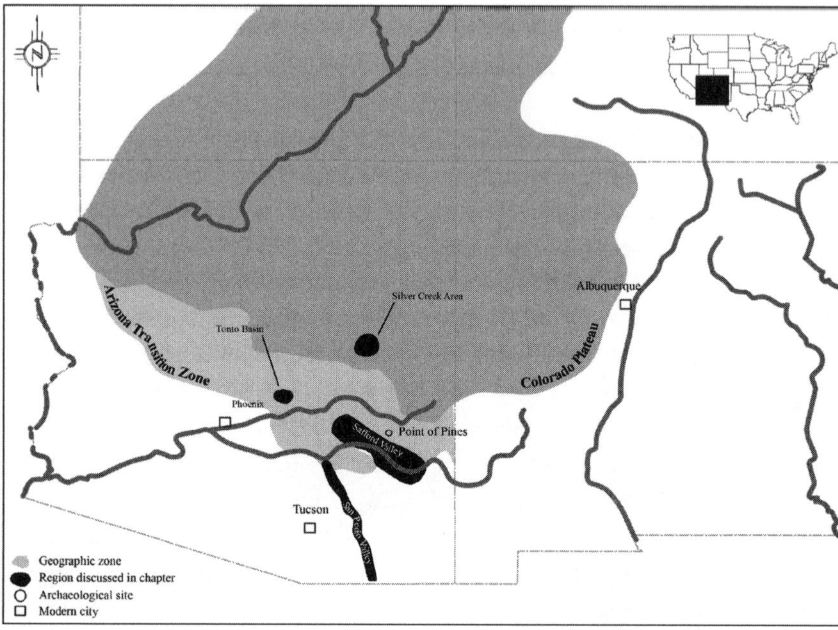

FIGURE 1.1. Overview map.

In many areas, the initial arrival of these migrants was fraught with competition and conflict. The lower San Pedro Valley (Wallace and Doelle 2001), where the locals aggregated into walled villages and constructed platform mounds, demonstrates this tense social situation. Social conflict was also present in the Point of Pines region, where a migrant enclave of at least 20 rooms was burned in the A.D. 1280s (Haury 1958, 1989).

Patricia Crown (1994) provides much of the background research on the Salado; she examines a number of models that could explain how Salado polychromes were adopted. These explanations include (1) elite exchange, (2) indicators of economic alliances, (3) ceramics as objects associated with the spread of a religious ideology, and (4) ceramics as markers of migrant ethnicity (Crown 1994:191–210). Since Salado polychromes are sourced to most areas where they are found (i.e., locally produced), Crown concludes that they were likely associated with the spread of ideas and not material exchange. Additionally, because the artistic content of the ceramics often revolves around images associated with fertility such as stylized clouds and horned serpents, she further proposes that these ceramic vessels were material indicators of the spread of a cult or ideology—a conclusion with which we agree.

However, Crown presents this conclusion while rejecting alternative explanations, including that of migrant ethnicity. While ethnicity may not be the correct term, the association of Salado ceramics with migrant identities in diaspora is consistent with the ideological interpretation of the content of the designs (Clark et al. 2013). In addition, Randall H. McGuire (2012) points out that there is no need to reject a political explanation for the process; feasting and the production of these symbolically charged ceramics were important venues for the establishment and maintenance of power in the southern Southwest. Thus, while originally framed as alternatives, Crown's hypotheses can be viewed as intersectional processes.

By about A.D. 1350, as settlement clusters within the Salado influence aggregated, and after 50–100 years of influence from migrants from the north and their descendants, many settlements displayed an intricate range of Pueblo immigrant and local attributes (Clark and Lyons 2012). Within just a few generations, then, a range of time in which these changes would have been clearly visible to adults in the population, Salado came to signify both an inclusive ideology that emerged out of contact with locals and northerners from the Colorado Plateau and an interfused cultural identity

FIGURE 1.2. Gila Polychrome (Salado Polychrome / Roosevelt Red Ware) ceramic vessel. Image courtesy of Eastern Arizona College, photo by Mathew A. Devitt.

spread across a vast region of the Southwest (Clark et al. 2013). The Salado identity that was probably something shared by migrants in diaspora during the late 13th and early 14th centuries became a widespread religious tradition that was adopted by thousands of people living in multiethnic communities. There were, however, many living in relatively close proximity to those who adopted this set of religious practices who did not adopt them. The disjuncture between those who participated in this ideologically driven social movement and those who did not raises two interrelated questions. First, why did the hosts of migrants in many areas adopt the foreign objects represented by Salado ceramics? Second, why did others abstain?

McGuire (2012) argues that Salado polychromes may also be evidence of control within the inequalities of the Classic period (A.D. 1050/1150–1450) social landscape of southern Arizona. This is likely true in the few areas where Salado polychromes were imported by elites and were not created by locals. It does not appear to be true, however, throughout the majority of the region in which Salado polychromes were present (see Borck 2016).

Regardless of whether Salado is viewed as an inclusive ideology or an ideology used for political control by a few elites, interpreting the diffusion of this ideology relies on an understanding of the acceptance or resistance of the social movement termed "Salado." This also highlights one of the difficulties mentioned earlier when examining resistance in the past. Power relationships are complex. Resistance, if it was occurring, was likely happening in multiple directions. For instance, elites in some regions may have resisted the spread of this new, decentralized ideology by co-opting its material culture at the same time that groups in other regions that were participating in the elite platform mound ideology were resisting the dissemination of Salado ideology by restricting the spread of the polychromes (and their associated power and ideas) into their communities. All of this would likely have happened while other groups resisted the platform mound elites' hierarchical control of ritual knowledge by participating in this new decentralized and accessible religious practice (see also Borck 2016a).

TOPOLOGY, TOPOGRAPHY, AND RESISTANCE TO FOREIGN OBJECTS

Networks are constructed of nodes and edges. Nodes are the actors, often individuals or communities, in these networks. Edges are the relationships, or connections, between the nodes. Diffusion operates through networks in two ways. The first is through direct interactions between individuals. In this view, the nodes labeled 1 in Figure 1.3 will be the first to adopt a new practice or idea from the source node since

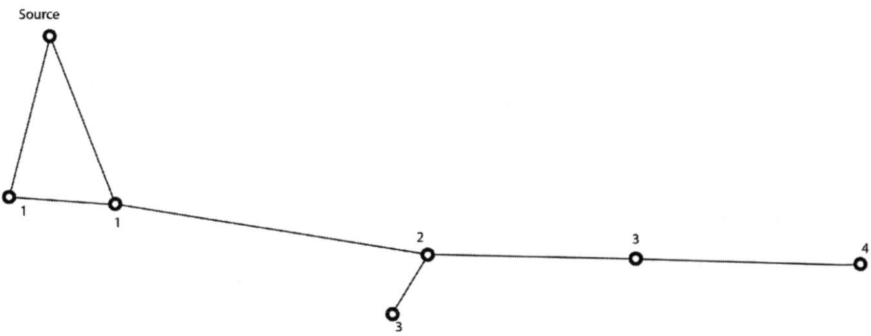

FIGURE 1.3. Network topology. Diffusion can, at its most basic, be modeled as moving along paths throughout the network structure. Node labels indicate path distance, or the number of nodal connections, from source.

they interact directly with the source. The second form is through structural equivalence. For instance, both of the nodes labeled 3 would be likely to adopt a new practice or accept a new idea because of their similar relationship with the broker of that idea (here, the node labeled 2). The shared likelihood of their adoption has nothing to do with their relationship with each other.

A central aspect of diffusion through structural equivalence is that it requires weak spots, or structural holes (in our case, the area between nodes 1 and 2 in Figure 1.3 is a structural hole). Brokers (nodes 1 and 2) bridge these holes. Brokers and bridging ties are very important in disseminating new ideas and technology to otherwise unattached groups (see Burt 1992 for an in-depth discussion of brokerage and Peeples and Haas 2013 for an application in archaeology). For example, recent archaeological applications of network theory have shown that brokers or "weak ties" bridge different groups and are often in intermediate areas (Peeples and Mills 2016). Here we extend this idea to areas in the southern Southwest to look at other factors that influenced the adoption and resistance to Salado ideology and material culture. We would like to highlight that one important but overlooked reversal is that these brokers are also important for stopping or slowing the spread of information.

In the simplified example in Figure 1.3, each node is labeled with a number indicating the shortest distance between it and the source node. The number represents how quickly new material spreads through the network through both positional and direct interaction. It is easy to see how much power the node labeled 2 has in controlling the distribution of new material. If this node decides that there is something wrong with the foreign objects, no other members of their group will have knowledge of it. Assuming that they pass it along, though, it would only take four steps in this

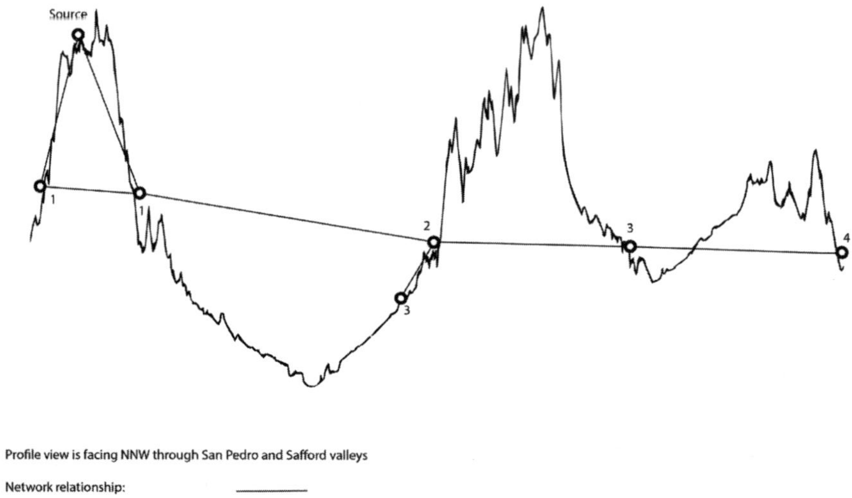

FIGURE 1.4. Topology and topography. Viewed horizontally, and spatially in context, a network's topology is intersected by the topographic features within which the social network resides.

example (i.e., path distance) to get to the most distant member or four steps to spread through two groups. If we do not see the foreign objects at the node labeled 4 and the attached node labeled 3 but do see it at the lower node at path distance 3, is it safe to assume that the last two nodes without the foreign objects were rejecting or actively resisting the inclusion of these objects into the social practices?

Figure 1.4 takes our network example and overlays it on the contours for the San Pedro and Safford Valleys in southern Arizona. These two valleys contained both local and immigrant populations, and in them Salado material culture, and thus its associated ideas, moved at variable rates through time. In these two valleys, the Salado polychromes had become the most common decorated ware at all sites by A.D. 1350.

What becomes clear in Figure 1.4 is that topography and topology can have a complicated relationship. We know that groups often follow the law of spatial propinquity and are often formed from interactions with spatially proximal neighbors. In the Southwest, however, we also know that interactions can span large distances and multiple environments (Mills, Clark, et al. 2013). For example, Mills, Clark, et al. (2013) found that spatial propinquity and material culture similarities were only weakly correlated. Moreover, they found that the correlation was weakest in the southern Southwest, where Salado polychrome ceramics were most frequent.

Therefore, to understand how goods moved through a social network, we *must* consider how that social network is situated in space. Figure 1.5 gives us a clearer idea

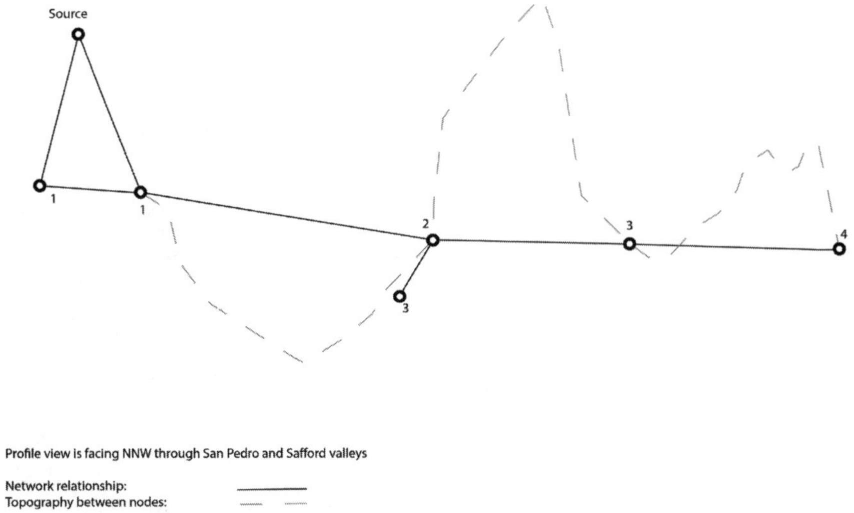

FIGURE 1.5. With the topographic contours removed, it is easy to see how network topology interacts with spatial topography to modify how quickly or slowly foreign objects or the knowledge of foreign objects might travel.

of the modifying influence that topography can have on topology. The dashed gray line is the path of interaction incorporating topography. When we reexamine the first example, where the nodes at path distance three and four did not show evidence of new consumption practices, we can see that instead of an act of resistance to new ideas and new practices, the low amount of Salado polychromes could be a product of the local geography. Thus, the first step is to understand the effects of both topography and social networks (or geosocial effects) on the consumption of objects at the regional scale.

DISCUSSION AND CONCLUSIONS

Modeling relationships between social and spatial data can provide insights into the adoption of—and resistance to—material culture. Models of consumption that are applied at the regional scale may not be able to identify resistance without taking into account cost distance between localities. Here we have also introduced the importance of considering the structure and position of actors within the network as a hypothetical way of integrating the two approaches. In previous research the combination of spatial and social networks has shown that neither is explanatory on its own (e.g., Mills, Clark, et al. 2013).

In addition to modeling spatial distributions vis-à-vis social relationships within a network, we also suggest returning to some of the insights of Rogers and others who have looked at the diffusion of innovations within social networks. Rogers (2003) suggested that perceived advantage, compatibility, complexity of use, trialability, and the social field of performance are all factors in the KAP gap. With respect to resistance, which of these factors might be operative in the diffusion of the ideology attached to Salado polychromes? Perceived *disadvantages* of adopting Salado polychromes include the responsibilities for hosting feasts associated with religious activities and obligations to others within the network.

The advantages, though, seem to be primarily political. The Hohokam world during the 14th century was full of settlements with platform mounds. Although the exact functions of these mounds seem to be variable, they are associated with higher than usual evidence for feasting, as well as the consumption of higher-valued material goods such as obsidian, turquoise, and shell by elites (see Shephard and Gallivan; Oland; and Cobb and Stephenson in this volume for descriptions of similar processes). For these reasons, as well as the cross-cultural data on the use of elevated mounds, many archaeologists working in the Southwest have interpreted these mounds as evidence for intracommunity inequality (e.g., Elson 1998). For those who are not in a position to participate, adopting Salado polychromes and other Roosevelt Red Ware ceramics may have been a way of resisting inequalities and social obligations that were extant in other areas of the southern Southwest.

Salado may, in fact, be best characterized as a populist social movement rather than one with a high degree of secrecy and control of ritual knowledge, which was more the case for the northern Southwest's kiva religion (e.g., Brandt 1994). Thus, it is the social and political disadvantages of participating in the Salado social network that we think merit the greatest attention in why they might have been resisted.

Consumption patterns of foreign objects can tell us a great deal about ideology and resistance in a prehispanic and precolonial setting. In these patterns we can see relative differences in the pace by which different groups adopted foreign objects. These patterns can shed new light on why various groups did or did not adopt new innovations by facilitating the creation of static models, in our case diffusion models, to test against.

Most diffusion models—both sociological and archaeological—work on rates of adoption curves. By incorporating both network topology and spatial topography, the adoption curves can be modified to be more holistic and to allow for more accurate interpretations of the social processes that determine whether new material practices and their associated ideologies are incorporated into the sociological and ideological practices of a particular group. Moreover, life is not composed of the decision to singularly accept or reject one idea or new material object at a time. It is a set of interlocking variables where accepting one new idea can dramatically change how individuals interact with foreign objects and ideas.

In the U.S. Southwest around A.D. 1300, Salado technology and its associated ideologies were introduced to new areas in a series of successive stages. Yet at the same time people were also interacting with ceramics from groups much farther south, ceramics that were encoded with a different set of social cues. These cues can help to determine a group's *attitude* to new ideas after they gain *knowledge* of them.

Consumption practices of ideologically charged material items, specifically the Salado polychrome ceramics, can reveal how migrant groups in diaspora may have utilized ideology to integrate themselves into the social fabric of new regions. This approach helps to answer why this integration was so effective that in many regions within just a few generations the first-comers and the guests merged historically precedented local traits with newer traits into an interfusion that archaeologists label "Salado."

Consumption practices of ideologically charged materials can also uncover how religious practices may have created fissures within ideological landscapes. These fissures create choices. By examining these fissures through resistance theories and diffusion of innovations, researchers can uncover whether groups in adjacent areas may have been specifically resisting the spread and incorporation of a new ideology. This is one of the many reasons a consumption framework is an effective means of examining an archaeology of choice. Consumption studies take into account agentic ability to choose between alternatives while recognizing that these decisions are structured within a geosocial setting (*sensu* Brumfiel 2000).

This choice to resist seems to have been made in the Coyote Mountains to the southwest of modern Tucson, where platform mound communities with almost no Salado ceramics were located relatively close to communities in the Tucson Basin and San Pedro Valleys that consumed many Salado polychromes. To understand if communities such as those in the Coyote Mountains were actively resisting the dissemination of Salado ideology, though, we need to understand how space and sociality interact. In this chapter, we have set out a conceptual guide to researchers looking to understand how people interact with new ideas in deep history and the material choices that result. We used this approach to examine a variety of acts of resistance versus acts of isolation, but the concept can be used to model any synchronic or diachronic analyses of consumption. It allows researchers to compare models derived from textual data with those derived from material goods. Such models will undoubtedly serve to create new dialogue between historical and nontextual archaeologists, a theme highlighted throughout this volume.

2

A TALE OF TWO SETTLEMENTS

Consumption and the Historical Archaeology of Natives and Newcomers in the 19th-Century Great Lakes Region

MATTHEW A. BEAUDOIN

CONTEMPORARY HISTORICAL ARCHAEOLOGY arguably divides into two related fields of study: the archaeology of the colonized (or the "archaeology of colonialism") and the archaeology of the colonizer (or general historical archaeology). The archaeology of colonialism generally focuses on the experiences of the colonized within the colonial process (in North America, "colonized" most often refers to Indigenous peoples), while general historical archaeology focuses on the experiences of Europeans and/or people of European descent (in North America, often framed as Euro-Canadians or Euro-Americans). Despite repeated assertions that this dichotomy is more complicated and problematic (e.g., Lightfoot et al. 1998; Silliman 2005, 2009; Voss 2008), the archaeologies of the colonizer and the colonized continue to privilege differing datasets, interpretations, and discourses, which in turn reify the a priori differences between them. This creates a continuous conceptual framework and discourse where there is something essentially different between the archaeology of the colonizer and the archaeology of the colonized, which in turn replicates the colonial tensions of the past within the archaeological present (Harrison 2014; Oliver 2014; Rubertone, this volume). Shadows and vestiges of this dichotomy remain within the discipline. The underlying assumption remains that colonizers and colonized are essentially different and can be contrasted to search for and explain why they are different.

Undoubtedly differences do exist, as between any two defined groups of people, but should being defined as one side or the other of the colonial process wholly dictate how one's experiences then become framed? Embedding the archaeology of historic Indigenous peoples almost exclusively within the archaeology of colonialism simultaneously privileges Eurocentric experiences within historical archaeology and continuously emphasizes the experiences of the colonized as "othered" (Rubertone 2000; Loren, this volume). The experiences of the colonized are thus enclaved within their own thematic subdiscipline, which can be understood as a continuing colonization of the past. Instead of relegating the experiences of the colonized to their own narratives, they should be brought into dialogue with historical archaeology to create discourses that can be understood as integral to the experiences of everyone in the past regardless of being labeled as "colonizer" or "colonized." This bridging would have the twofold effect of incorporating the experiences of the colonized into the main discussion, accompanying some popular conceptualizations of identity formation and maintenance (e.g., survivance and residence), as well as allowing for the archaeology of the colonized to place more emphasis on foci traditionally explored within the archaeology of the colonizer (e.g., class and capitalism).

The rubric of consumption—as framed by Paul Mullins (2011a) and Michael Dietler (2010)—is a valuable framework to help fill the gap mentioned above, similar to the way that it can assist in bridging the prehistoric and historic periods (Cipolla, Bragdon, Howey, Loren, Oland, Panich, Rubertone, and Shephard and Gallivan, this volume). In a broad sense, consumption encompasses the acquisition and use of objects by peoples. Where consumption may differ from other conceptualizations is that it emphasizes the simultaneous consideration of individual choices within the lived experience of the broader social context. By emphasizing the contextual specifics alongside the more general patterning, consumption encourages archaeologists studying colonial contexts to directly engage with the broader social patterns within which these past peoples were embedded. As such, it is a conceptual, rather than methodological, framework that can challenge often unspoken disciplinary assumption. This chapter examines two 19th-century Mohawk communities in southwestern Ontario (Mohawk Village and the Davisville settlement) to consider the strengths of this integrated approach.

Consumption is an especially useful conceptualization when analyzing the 19th century in North America. By that time, goods were often commoditized, and trade networks had been firmly established to promote a level of consistency in the access to goods. These factors belie interpretations based on whether many goods are considered "foreign" or "local," as the importance of the objects is based more on the local understandings rather than original areas of production. For example, the majority of the ceramic vessels purchased in 19th-century Ontario, by colonizer and colonized peoples alike, were produced in England (Kenyon and Kenyon 1982). As such, the ceramics could be understood as "foreign" to both groups. Instead, the importance of these goods is derived from the interplay of local social, colonial, and economic factors that influence people's purchasing choices (see Cipolla's discussion of "localizing the global" in the introduction to this volume).

In recent years there has been a significant amount of research addressing and deconstructing this arbitrary binary. Unfortunately, the colonial binary was long entrenched within archaeological interpretation. This means that vestiges of it remain that insidiously act to perpetuate it, even as we act to deconstruct it (Oliver 2014). For example, the archaeology of capitalism was long upheld as a means to bridge the colonial divide (Orser 1996, 2012); others advocated that the people's engagement with the capitalist system was able to go beyond other identity categories (Wilkie and Bartoy 2000). But these thinkers were simultaneously describing how the capitalist structure is an inherently Eurocentric construction. As such, various others could only differentially participate with the capitalist system, which replicates the colonial dichotomy within the capitalist structure. This conceptualization of historical archaeology is embedded within modern European colonialism, which implies that there is something inherently and essentially different between the rise of European capitalism and everything prior. In a very real sense, the rise of capitalism as a mainstay of historical archaeology ends up being a means to isolate modern European colonialism and global history from other times and contexts. This isolation creates a model of the recent past that privileges a colonizer-centric narrative within which various colonial others can only be seen—and engaged with—through that colonizer lens. The assumption is that the capitalist endeavor subsumes other forms of identity in a manner that places varied groups on a "more equal ground" for comparison, homogenizing them into a European sensibility (Thomas 1991).

This is what I see as one of the strengths of the idea of consumption within the archaeology of colonialism: it is an effort to consider how Indigenous peoples in the past engaged with the market economy without "losing" their identity (Silliman and Witt 2010). In consumption's initial conceptualization and application within historic archaeology, many of the same Eurocentric critiques of capitalism can be applied to consumption; however, consumption's broader framing can allow for discourses that transcend its Eurocentric framings. Consumption emphasizes the presence of a social structure of etiquettes and dispositions that inform action and behavior with which *all* participants are differentially engaged, as well as the agency to allow individuals to navigate the specifics of their local context (Dietler 2010:57). The choices people made in acquiring, ignoring, or eschewing objects are framed by social and cultural logics of the specific time and place. Furthermore, consumption emphasizes the roles individuals or communities played in navigating these logics. People's practices could reinforce, subvert, adapt, or ignore dominant structural frameworks; however, these practices must be understood within the specifics of the local contexts.

The archaeology of consumption embraces the complexity of the choices that people make in a manner that aims to correct Eurocentric framings within capitalist contexts while still allowing for the contextually specific meanings of local contexts. Such a project has the potential to create an engaged dialogue where fractured identities such as colonizer–colonized or Indigenous are facets of lived existence but do not define the entirety of the process.

The North American context is implicitly understood as an emergent colonial landscape where individuals of European descent simultaneously adapted, and were adapted by, the local context. Changes in colonizer practices become innovative adaptations to their contexts, whereas changes in colonized practices become losses of identity (Cipolla 2013b; Liebmann 2012). For example, changes in the diets of Europeans have been framed as a result of other forms of variation, such as differences in social class (Cheek 1998; Peres 2008) or changes across urban–rural divides (Landon 1996, 2008), but rarely as a loss of European foodways and identity. Instead these changes are celebrated as evidence for overcoming struggles. In these discussions, the choices of the colonized to use or eschew European goods instead become framed as a political or social choice where their Indigenous (i.e., traditional) dispositions are confronted, combated, and perhaps "lost" at an essential level simply by the presence of these goods within their domestic material life.

The archaeology of the colonized is framed within the dominant discourse of static tradition and looking back to the past, whereas the archaeology of the colonizer is framed within the dominant discourse of dynamic modernity, forever adapting. It is assumed that Indigenous people in the past could not engage with structures or practices that are perceived as "Euro-Canadian" without losing some aspect of their essential identity. This conceptual divide implicitly reifies the colonizer–colonized bifurcation by creating differing discourses and methods of meaning making; this in itself continues to perpetuate the idea that there is something essentially different between the two. Euro-Canadians are modern and adaptable, which therefore led to their colonization of the modern world. In contrast, First Peoples are traditionalists and stagnant, which means they are enclaved "others" who cannot embrace modernity without losing some essential part of their identity.

The combination of a consumption framework that emphasizes personal choice with the concepts of survivance and residence, as recently championed by Stephen Silliman (2001, 2014), becomes a valuable conceptual framework for bringing the archaeology of the colonizer and colonized into dialogue. Survivance is best summed up as meaning "survival with attitude, implying activity rather than passivity, using aggressive means not only to stay alive but to flourish" (Velie 2008:147 in Silliman 2014:59). The concept situates individuals as surviving through the best means they see with the ability to incorporate and change their materials and dispositions without losing essential connections to identities, communities, or their respective pasts. When combined with residence, the concept that people inhabited an actual real world in a manner that emphasizes daily dispositions in lieu of purposeful and confrontational resistance (Silliman 2014:61–62), survivance gives archaeologists a new set of approaches that change the narrative of colonized identities. This is not to say that the colonized had freedom to operate beyond European colonizers but rather that the colonized still navigated their dispositions within the tangible dimensions and understandings of the world in which they lived. The strength of this approach is demonstrated next with analysis of two 19th-century Mohawk assemblages from southwestern Ontario.

A TALE OF TWO MOHAWK SETTLEMENTS IN CANADA

The Mohawk Nation is a Haudenosaunee group that comprises part of the Six Nations (formerly Five Nations) Confederacy of the Iroquois. During the American Revolution, the Confederacy of the Iroquois was temporarily disbanded because the nations could not come to a consensus on how to navigate the conflict between Great Britain and the American colonies (Graymont 1991; Mackenzie 1896; Snow 1994; Taylor 2002). In general, the Mohawk, Seneca, Onondaga, and Cayuga supported Great Britain, while the Tuscarora and Oneida supported the American colonists. The Loyalist Iroquois nations were forced to cede their land and relocate north of the U.S. border, while those that sided with the United States chose to remain. In the years following the American Revolution, Capt. Joseph Brant (Thayendanegea), understanding that the American government would look negatively upon the political alliance between the Iroquois and the British, led well over 1,800 Iroquois Loyalists from New York State to lands along the Grand River. They settled along the Grand River in the winter and spring of 1784 and 1785, with the Mohawk (along with the Upper Cayuga, Tutelo, Oneida, and Tuscarora) occupying villages near what is now Brantford (Johnston 1994:170; Weaver 1978:525). The Six Nations reserve was established in Tuscarora Township in 1847.

Mohawk Village, established around 1784, is situated at an oxbow of the Grand River and overlooked extensive floodplains (Ferris 2009). A framed Anglican church, schoolhouse, and Joseph Brant's residence were some of the important community structures at Mohawk Village that made it an administrative center and external "face" for the Anglicized Six Nations inhabiting the upper portion of the Grand River prior to 1805 (Kelsay 1984). As such, many prominent people passed through the community and recorded numerous descriptions of Mohawk Village (e.g., Cruikshank 1929; Gray 1954; Johnston 1964; Kelsay 1984) that contribute to "a greater descriptive legacy than for any other Iroquois settlement on the Grand" (Ferris 2006:244). The social and political history of Mohawk Village allowed for its residents to gain relative prosperity and elite status within the local community.

Excavations at Mohawk Village focused on two areas associated with multiple generations of the Powless family; the early features date between roughly 1800 and 1830, and the later features date roughly between 1830 and 1860 (Ferris 2009:146; Kenyon and Ferris 1984:24). Both the early and late features are focused around the possible cellars of two houses that were occupied sequentially by two generations of the Powless family—likely Paulus Sah-oh-wad-i and his family in the earlier home, with Paulus's son, Peter Powless, becoming the patriarch of the early household late in its existence. Peter Powless's family resided in the later household past his death in the 1850s. Subsequently, in the 1860s, his wife, Elizabeth, relocated to the Tuscarora reserve (Ferris 2009:143, 145; Kenyon and Ferris 1984:32). Substantial archaeological assemblages were recovered from both household features. The residents of the Powless households were primarily consuming domesticated animals supplemented with wild game and were also inhabiting substantial residential structures that would not have been out of place in any contemporary community in southwestern Ontario.

Davisville, also known as Davis's Hamlet and River Bend, based on its geographic location on the Grand River (Luard 1966:19), was named for Thomas Davis (Tehowagherengaraghkwen), a highly regarded Mohawk war chief of the Wolf Clan who fought in the Revolutionary War and the War of 1812 (Sharpe 2003:165; Grand River Heritage Mines Society 2003:24). Davis was also a cousin of Joseph Brant. The Davisville settlement was established as a response to Davis's negative perception of Mohawk who followed the Church of England (Hosmer 1864:93–96; Smith 1987). Davis and his followers were most troubled by the excessive consumption of alcohol and social changes associated with navigating political and colonial circumstances. In contrast to Mohawk Village, the Davisville settlement embraced the teachings of Methodism, most notably alcohol abstinence, the importance of education, and an emphasis on living a moral life (Playter 1862:229–230; Semple 1996:154–155; West 1827:280–281).

The excavations at the Davisville settlement targeted four separate cabin sites (Horsfall and Warrick 2003; Timmins Martelle Heritage Consultants, Inc. 2009; Warrick 2002a, 2002b, 2004), including two earlier sites that date roughly 1800–1820 (Davisville 1 and 2) and two later sites that date roughly 1830–1860 (Davisville 7 and 8). Davisville 1 and 2 have been the focus of a greater amount of archaeological investigation; however, all four sites have generated roughly similarly sized archaeological assemblages. The sites could not be directly tied to any specific community members or families; however, the patterns at Davisville 1 and 7 and at 2 and 8 are relatively similar. This would suggest that there is some level of continuity between these groupings of sites. The Davisville inhabitants were primarily consuming wild game supplemented with domesticates. The houses that the Davisville inhabitants lived in were primarily wooden cabins with glass windows, and some or most had wooden floors and subsurface cellars, but they lacked many of the more overt signs of European sensibility at that time (e.g., plaster or mortar).

The two settlements were close to one another, with Davisville roughly five kilometers upstream from Mohawk Village, and there was regular contact back and forth. For example, Joseph Brant specifically brought many travelers of the region to Thomas Davis's house for visits (Burwell 1833; Hosmer 1864; Johnston 1964; West 1827). This suggests that the residents of both communities would have been well aware of the happenings and trends within each community, and they even had similar opportunities for acquiring commodities. For example, the annual presents from the British Crown (King's Gift) were distributed from a central hub, which was Mohawk Village for the Brantford area. In order to receive these items, members of the Davisville settlement would have had to travel to Mohawk Village (Kenyon and Ferris 1984:36). The same limitations of access occur with the purchase of commodities from merchants. The closest merchants would have been the same for both communities (Kenyon and Ferris 1984:38–40).

The patterns at Six Nations sites in Ontario have long been contrasted against a generalized Euro-Canadian pattern and sensibility to emphasize their differences (Kenyon and Kenyon 1982, 1986; Kenyon 1985, 1987, 1997). The established pattern demonstrated that there were essential differences between Six Nations and Euro-Canadian sites that reproduced a colonizer–colonized binary. However, several assumptions within the patterning, along with the fact that limited efforts have been made to update the pattern since the 1980s, reflect the archaeological sensibilities of the time, rather than concrete differences between Six Nations and Euro-Canadian sites (Beaudoin, 2016). To critically reevaluate the established patterning in light of new data and modern archaeological sensibilities, site data were collected and standardized from published sources, cultural resource management (CRM) reports, and gray literature from 19th-century Six Nations and Euro-Canadian sites from the southwestern Ontario region (Beaudoin 2013).

Comparing a series of ceramic vessel forms from 19th-century Euro-Canadian and Six Nations sites in southwestern Ontario (Figures 2.1 and 2.2), the most obvious finding is that the colonizer and colonized sites do not immediately separate into clusters. Within the percentage of plates, bowls, and tea sets (hereafter referred to as "teas"), there does appear to be some polarization of the Euro-Canadian and Six Nations sites based primarily on the percentages of bowls; however, the majority of the sites

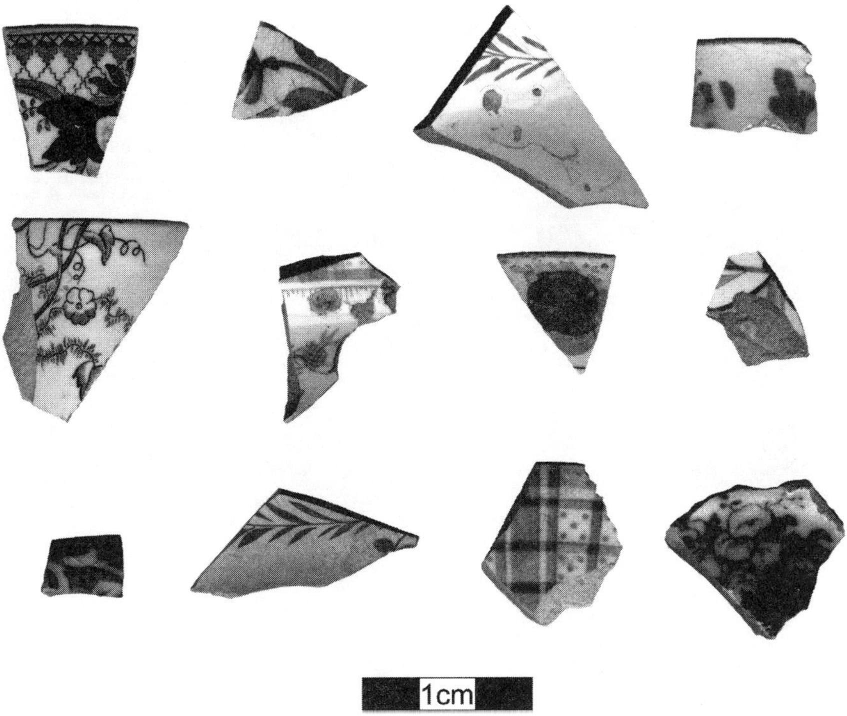

FIGURE 2.1. Sample of the 19th-century ceramics from Davisville 8. Photo by the author.

are clustered together within the approximate center of the distribution limits. This suggests that there is a point of convergence within representations of 19th-century Ontario vessel forms as documented in archaeological assemblages. All households, whether occupied by Euro-Canadians or Indigenous peoples, were using plates, bowls, and teas within their meal conventions; no household was avoiding plates, bowls, or teas altogether. There is some flexibility within the specific percentages; however, these are subtle variations resulting from a confluence of factors, rather than an essentialist colonial or capitalist division. The aforementioned polarization based on bowls is an example of this subtle variation. For a variety of factors (such as tradition), some Six Nations sites tend to have a greater percentage of bowls than many Euro-Canadian sites. But this is not a universal for either the Six Nations or Euro-Canadian sites, and the subtle variation precludes using vessel form as a gross means to differentiate the two. The subtleties of the variation could be further explored to understand what they might signify. Such an analysis would show that *some* Six Nations sites do not match up with general 19th-century patterns, indicating that the people at those sites were

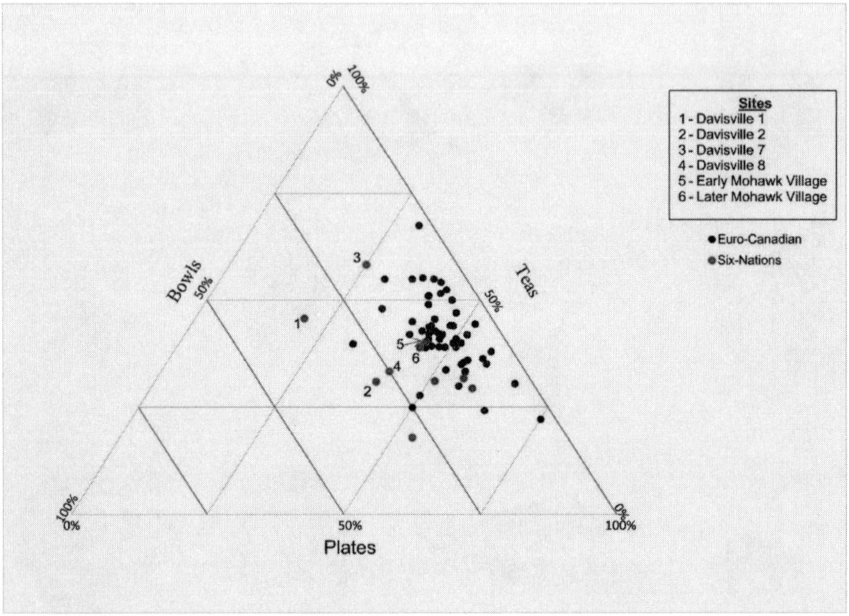

FIGURE 2.2. Percentages of plates, bowls, and teas at 19th-century sites in Ontario.

perhaps differentially engaged, materially, with the colonial world they were a part of. However, the same could be observed in the archaeological patterns of *some* Euro-Canadian sites.

What these patterns do indicate is that the use of plates, teas, and bowls is a commonality of existence during the 19th century. Archaeologists would be hard-pressed to find a 19th-century domestic site that did not have examples of these three vessel forms; if they could find such a collection, they would be forced to explain why these vessels were absent. Everyone in the 19th century was using these vessel forms, which belies arguments of acculturation or identity loss. This is the structure of consumption with which people are differentially engaged. As such, we should not be searching to explain why these vessel forms are present at non-European sites (e.g., Adams and Boling 1989; Burley 2000). Throughout the 19th century, consumerism in southern Ontario (in all its iterations of choice, acquisition, economic differential, etc.) emerged as a commonality of everyday life. Within these distinctions, it could be tempting to frame differences as the result of a single differing identity, and these singular differences may apply to any particular subset or social context; however, an overemphasis of singular identities produces simplistic, one-dimensional framing of difference instead of a nuanced confluence of everyday life. We need to think differently about how we approach these data and accept that all identities (ethnic, social, colonial, gender) are simultaneously expressed, contested, denied, and revealed in daily choices.

A comparison of ceramic data from Mohawk Village and the Davisville settlement to a generalized 19th-century pattern indicates that residents of Mohawk Village tended to follow a generalized 19th-century pattern while residents of Davisville did not. The patterns at the Davisville settlement indicate that the inhabitants were using more bowls than at the other sites examined. While it would be tempting to interpret the higher percentage of bowls at the Davisville settlement as a connection to the inhabitants' Mohawk heritage, we need to consider the local and temporal context (Oland, Panich, this volume). If we were to situate Davisville as more traditionally Mohawk, this inadvertently shifts Mohawk Village to being more acculturated to the 19th-century patterning or practicing inauthentic Mohawk traditions. The mistake here would be situating 19th-century patterns as European patterns instead of patterns with which everyone is differentially engaged. Instead of framing Mohawk Village as showing a loss of Indigenous practice because it is similar to the 19th-century norm, we should be exploring why the pattern of Davisville differs from the 19th-century norm. We could argue that it is "Mohawk culture," but that further reifies the concept that there is something essentially different about Mohawk heritage that sets it apart from the 19th-century norm, thus fixing that identity in the past. Instead, I choose to emphasize the specifics of the relationship between Mohawk Village and the Davisville settlement.

If we consider the differences between the Davisville settlement and Mohawk Village within Silliman's (2014) framework of residence and survivance, an interesting interpretation emerges. The residents of early Davisville sites had contemporaneous and past connections to Mohawk Village and were undoubtedly continuously engaged with the community. They had at least seen, if not lived in, the houses at Mohawk Village, shared meals there, and observed how people were clothed there. Davis was vocal about contesting the lifeways of the inhabitants of Mohawk Village, decrying the excessive alcohol consumption and renouncing their practice of Anglican religion. As such, it seems likely accurate to frame the Davisville settlement in the process of survivance in contrast to Mohawk Village rather than directly or solely against Euro-Canadian encroachment or creeping colonialism.

Davis and the other residents of Davisville chose to move away from Mohawk Village because they perceived the emergence of an "Upper Canadian elite" identity as a crisis for the Mohawk peoples. This ran counter to what they saw as Mohawk. A similar process has been noted in other contexts, such as Mark Wagner's (2010) description of the rise of the Nativist movement among the Shawnee, where communities coalesced around a leader who decried the actions of a related community as being "inauthentic" or "not true" to what it meant to be of the community. In Wagner's example, the movement was a response to the perceived negative adoption of European lifeways and loss of Indigenous sensibilities and identities. At Davisville, residents rejected the urbane, cosmopolitan sensibilities embodied historically in the aims and values of Joseph Brant and those who shared his views. This is seen archaeologically in the material dispositions of such an elite sensibility reflected in the Mohawk Village assemblages. Unlike Wagner's example, Davisville was not about a rejection of contemporary material lifeways and an attempt to return to a pre-European time; instead, it was a selective rejection of elite excesses and Christian values while still fully engaged in the broader material lifeways of 19th-century southern Ontario.

Adapting and continuing the process of identity formation and maintenance in residence requires a foil to delineate what is a part of, and apart from, an identity. To make sense of their conceptualizations and practices, especially when contested, people need to be able to point to something, in their present or past, to say "we are that" or "we are not that." Whether it is the Mohawk Village residents pointing to the Euro-Canadians and saying "we are that plus . . ." or the Davisville residents pointing to Mohawk Village and saying "we are not that," the process provides individuals with a "signpost" to navigate what their identities mean to them. These "signposts" can be overt or subliminal, real or perceived, and they all function as signifiers providing meaning in daily life. This can be accomplished through active defiance, like Davis's rejection of the Mohawk Village sensibilities, or through more mundane choices, such as what ceramics to buy. The selection of plates over bowls and the role and importance of each vessel are given meaning by individuals because, within constraints of time and place, they are exercising their choice. I am not arguing for a rigid them–us bifurcation of identity, but rather for a more nuanced contrast between various groups. Identity formation is not a simple "I am colonizer and you are colonized," but it is the intersection of innumerable "me–you us–them" perceptions that serve to coalesce people's own meaning of their own pluralistic identities.

With this understanding, I think it is inaccurate to frame the Davisville inhabitants as simply "differently Christian" than those of Mohawk Village. While they railed against certain aspects of 19th-century everyday life being exhibited at Mohawk Village, other aspects that the Davisville inhabitants did not find problematic were retained. For example, most of the archaeological analysis suggests that the Davisville inhabitants did not attempt a return to pre-European ways of residence. The Davisville inhabitants lived in houses that were the same basic forms of residence as at Mohawk Village. However, the lack of evidence of walls suggests that one of the more visibly conspicuous aspects of the Powless residences is missing. Another point of interest is that the Davisville inhabitants embraced Methodism in lieu of Anglicanism. This suggests that Christian denominations—their emphasis on differing social values and the association of a particular denomination with perhaps differing class conceptions and self-identity—played into broader definitions of identity and the implications of belonging to one or another denomination.

If we accept the premise that people constantly construct, adapt, and come to terms with their own senses of identity, a more nuanced dialogue is required. All residents of these sites were simultaneously and continuously renegotiating their own senses of being Mohawk, being Iroquois, being in the 19th century, and being in the emergent colonialism of southern Ontario, all based on their own perceptions, understandings, and contexts. This framework can help explain why there appear to be two groups within the Davisville settlement (Davisville 1 and 7, Davisville 2 and 8). Each group was negotiating what it meant to be Mohawk at least in part through an awareness of and contrast against Mohawk Village, arriving at their own conclusions. Both material patterns laid down during the occupation of these locales represent the results of groups within the Davisville settlement navigating their own sets of dining etiquettes based in the past, negotiated in the present, and oriented to the future. Allowing for these possibilities is one of the strengths of purposefully approaching this context as survivance.

CONCLUSIONS

I am emphasizing the strengths of a complex engagement with consumption within Indigenous archaeologies. It allows for a conceptual structure that can bring colonizer and colonized dialogues into direct conversation that encourages a more nuanced discourse. By framing the contemporaneous commonalities of existence as being a reality of everyday life in their time, instead of a Eurocentric frame with which various "others" cannot participate, we can nurture dialogues that explore the specifics of how people navigated daily life within their own logics and structures. By situating the patterns at the Davisville settlement and Mohawk Village against the backdrop of the general 19th-century patterns *and* the contextual specifics of each community, a narrative emerges that greatly differs from those that would have emerged from either side of the conventional debate; neither community demonstrates an acculturation of traditional identity toward Eurocentric norms, nor do they draw the entirety of their identity from the past. Instead, both communities are navigating the complex contextual specifics of their time in a manner that is based in *their* own pasts, navigated through *their* presents, with a vision toward *their* future to create the patterns we are interpreting in our present. By framing our interpretations in such a way and attempting to remove our own preexisting biases and assumptions, new narratives emerge. This is not to say that there were no restrictions of access and discriminatory practices in the past, but rather that we need to explore how they were enacted, perceived, and navigated within the specifics of the local times and contexts, instead of imposed onto the past from our present-day logics. I see further explorations of consumption in both Indigenous and non-Indigenous archaeology as a valuable step in decolonizing the discipline.

ACKNOWLEDGMENTS

I would like to thank Neal Ferris for his support and guidance during this research. I would also like to thank Holly Martelle and Peter Timmins from Timmins Martelle Heritage Consultants, Inc., and Gary Warrick for providing access to the collections. Finally, I would like to thank Craig Cipolla, Charlie Cobb, and Maxine Oland for their insightful feedback on earlier drafts of this chapter.

DEFINING BODIES AND PERSONS

3

BEYOND REPRESENTATION

Indigenous Economies of Affect in the Northeast Woodlands

JOHN L. CREESE

ACCULTURATION THEORY has cast a long shadow over academic and popular thinking about the passage of foreign things into indigenous hands, particularly in the era of early modern globalization (Ferris 2009; Loren 2008; Nassaney 2004; Rubertone 2000; Silliman 2009). In the archaeology of the Great Lakes region, its lingering chill has been difficult to shake off. In his popular 1981 synthesis of regional archaeology, Ronald Mason mused: "It is hard for us at this distance removed from the events to appreciate properly what must have been the seductive appeal that the ocean crossers' wares held for people *whose own technology they themselves almost instantly and universally concluded to be inferior*" (2002:376, emphasis added). Although archaeologists have generally moved away from such overtly Eurocentric language, many of the basic assumptions about material culture and identity that guided this tradition of scholarship continue to dog contemporary academic thinking (e.g., Brose et al. 2001). Some of these assumptions pertain to matters of fact and are easily checked against the archaeological record. Others, however, cut to the heart of how archaeologists habitually think about the relationship between material things and subjects. These assumptions often remain implicit in archaeological reasoning, and so the object of this chapter is to make some of them explicit by way of comparison with indigenous Wendat alternatives.

The wider implications of this comparison, beyond highlighting different cultural experiences of person-thing relations, are epistemological. They remind us that the material record is formed not only by people's operation within ontologically distinct cultural worlds but also from the very practices through which those worlds were continually contested, negotiated, and reproduced. European-sourced and foreign indigenous goods were inevitably caught up in a diversity of local social projects in which the rich possibilities for refining or redistributing subject–object relations were never fully closed. Consequently, a person's decisions about how to engage with foreign things, however apparently traditional or novel, were always creative and multifaceted acts of social reproduction.

BEYOND REPRESENTATION

A first-line strategy of postcolonial critique is to tackle the factual evidence supporting claims of inevitable Native American cultural loss in the face of foreign things. Most simply and immediately, we can ask whether the material record actually supports the thesis that indigenous people abandoned existing crafts in favor of European functional analogues wherever and whenever they were available. By focusing on consumption and consumer choice in this context, aboriginal ways of incorporating foreign things into local practices can be highlighted to counter simplistic notions of material replacement and consequent assimilation. Invariably, this kind of work has given the lie to the image of the credulous Native, overawed by and covetous of European technical mastery. In the Northeast, many aboriginal ceramic, lithic, and bone-tool industries continued to evolve and flourish during the first century of routine trade with Europeans (ca. A.D. 1580–1680) (Goodby 1998; Handsman 1988; Kuhn 1986; Martelle 2002; Nassaney 2004; Ramsden 1990; Snow 1995; Wright 1981). At the same time, European goods were frequently repurposed or recycled to suit preexisting needs and indigenous cultural imperatives (e.g., Bradley 1987; Bragdon, this volume).

As a decolonizing strategy, however, this approach only takes us so far. It is limited because it leaves to one side (or even reinforces) the issue of equating consumption choices with self-representation (Cipolla, introduction, this volume). The impetus for this chapter springs from a growing uneasiness I feel about decolonizing strategies that counter acculturation theory by emphasizing individual consumer choice as a means of constructing personal identity. It is important to stress that this line of thought has been and continues to be quite stimulating and productive for the field (e.g., Casella and Fowler 2005; Loren 2010b; White 2009). Its strengths come to the fore in case studies where consumer choice, subjectivities, and identity are richly contextualized (e.g., Beranek 2009; Loren 2009).

Nevertheless, the lurking danger is that we come to uncritically reproduce a popular mode of identity discourse that is narrowly *representationalist*. In this mode, identity is spoken of as an object of performance to be actively deployed, resisted, or appropriated through various forms of material consumption and display. Here, agents are triumphantly declared the strategic producers and consumers of identities. The unnerving aspect of this discourse is that it draws its major idioms quite directly from the broader late capitalist conditions within which most of us daily operate (cf. Wurst and McGuire 1999). In the "selfie era," mass media and cultural theorists alike posit consumption as a vehicle for creative self-expression in contemporary life, and I wonder if it is not becoming difficult for us to imagine other possibilities.

How, then, can we begin to productively rethink the relationship between consumption and identity? Marilyn Strathern's (1999) Melanesian ethnography provides an important departure point. She observes that in Mt. Hagen, New Guinea, the performance of individual identity in men's public dances is not communicated through obvious material distinctions of their movements or regalia. Rather, a dancer's appearance indexes (*sensu* Hoopes 1991) a complex network of relationships: "It is in the relationships that a man gathers to himself that his individuality lies; the accomplishments that bring a person a 'name' come from holding persons together" (Strathern 1999:39). According to Strathern, identification in Mt. Hagen depends on reading the feather regalia as a document of the wearer's enabling relationships. For the Hagener, the self is realized, amplified, and extended through those relationships (cf. Brittain and Harris 2010; Chapman 2000; Fowler 2004). So the basic operation of identity at work in Mt. Hagen is not self-*expression* but self-*assembly* via materially mediated social relationships (cf. Hoskins 2006; Knappett and Malafouris 2008; Tilley 2006). This mode of identification can be called *relational-affective* in view of its emphasis on the emergent generation of subjectivities in emotionally resonant material engagements (cf. Tarlow 2000).

Such a relational-affective model of identification is in keeping with current post-structuralist theories of agency, personhood, and materiality (Bennett 2005; DeLanda 2006; Harris 2014; Hodder 2012; Latour 2005; Robb 2010), as well as a growing interest in the archaeological study of emotion (Tarlow 2000, 2012; Harris and Sorensen 2010; Harris 2014). Thus, the model can be productively generalized beyond the New Guinea case to illuminate some important characteristics of identity and consumption that appear cross-culturally. In principle, relational-affective identification depends on the premise that persons and things are defined foremost by their relationships, so that the affective quality of those relationships becomes a major area of concern and attention for actors (Creese 2016a). By working on developing good feelings, trust, friendship, esteem, indebtedness, and so on, subjects reciprocally assemble themselves, achieving good names for their respective houses or kin groups (cf. Munn 1986). To the extent that durable goods are recruited in these efforts, the emphasis is on the role of objects in making and sustaining relationships of various kinds, rather than on consumption as an end in itself. In the Wendat case explored further below, certain foreign goods were valued precisely for their ability to positively affect the mental and bodily health of exchange partners, that is, for the vital emotion-work (*sensu* Hochschild 1979) they accomplished.

Before going any further, it will be helpful to define our key terms: *consumption*, *consumer*, and *foreign*. For present purposes, I define consumption broadly, with Paul Mullins (2011b), as the socialization of material goods. We can correspondingly define a consumer as a culturally competent and creative agent of this socialization process. Foreign goods can be defined as those that exist in a state of social pluripotency. Foreign things are ideal consumables precisely because they await local resocialization and revaluation. Although it is important to distinguish between European-made (e.g., copper and brass kettles) and indigenous nonlocal things (e.g., wampum), I believe this distinction has sometimes been overplayed on the assumption that European-made goods came with an automatic aura of value. At least in the Wendat case, however, it was arguably the unique socialization potential of things from elsewhere that really mattered. A corollary is that the nature of consumption in a given historical situation is to a significant degree shaped by the wider system of identification and, hence, value in which it operates. This way of framing consumption, consumer, and foreignness is especially useful because it makes room for indigenous and non-Western alternatives to the dominant capitalist paradigm of consumption (Cipolla, introduction, this volume). Of course, one might be tempted to ask why we should bother attempting to rescue the language of "consumption" and "consumer" from its contextual moorings in contemporary Western thought. Why not instead just speak of people making, acquiring, and using things? My answer would be that consumption is a particularly salient general description of the process in which material goods become effectively transformed, internalized, and incorporated into the social body of individuals and groups. As we shall see, Wendat people played on the metaphor of consumption themselves, symbolically collecting, transforming, and incorporating trade goods into the body politic using the image of "the kettle."

With these definitions in mind, we can draw some systematic connections between the two models of identification outlined above (representational vs. relational-affective) and patterns of consumption. Here we plow headlong into the long-standing dichotomy between Mauss's gift and Marx's commodity (Cipolla, introduction, this volume). If we follow Marcel Mauss's (1990[1954]) formulation, gift exchange is the ideal form of consumption in a relational-affective mode. The Maori gift (*taonga*), according to Mauss, is in an important sense inalienable from its giver. The spirit of the gift (*hau*) compels its return in the form of a countergift: "The obligation attached to a gift itself is not inert. Even when abandoned by the giver, it still forms a part of him. Through it he has a hold over the recipient" (Mauss 1990[1954]:9). According to this line of thought, gift exchange extends and distributes the agency of the subject (cf. Gell 1998), binding persons together in a series of reciprocal obligations and social interdependencies through which they exert a hold over each other. In a gift economy, consumption serves exchange and the affective relations it enables, rather than the other way around. Through gift exchange, subjects assemble personal identities at the same moment and, by the same motion, tie themselves to others. In this sense, the power of the gift lies in its tendency to behave like a subject or person, which, as Igor Kopytoff (1986) has noted, is related to its singularity and resistance to commensuration.

On the other hand, commodity exchange depends on a notion of the social alienation and commensurability of goods. For Kopytoff, "a commodity is a thing that has use value and that can be exchanged in a discrete transaction for a counterpart, the very fact of exchange indicating that the counterpart has, in the immediate context, an equivalent value" (1986:68). Freed of relational-affective moorings, the ideal commodity is primarily subject to and serves representational modes of valuation and identification. The pure case of this is money, which works according to a strictly arbitrary representational logic, but the same principle underlies consumer choice as a form of self-representation. The consumption of commodities in late capitalism accordingly serves as the primary vehicle for identification in a representational mode. Here, exchange serves consumption, and the power of the commodity lies in its ability to be objectified. In this way, the commodity, unlike the gift, enters the social universe of the consumer with (apparently) "no strings attached."

OBJECT BIOGRAPHIES AND ONTOLOGICAL PLURALISM

Representational–commoditized and relational-affective–gift modes of identification and value are presented here as idealized and therefore fictive polar types. As such, they provide tools for thinking about how patterns of exchange and consumption may articulate with culturally particular ontologies of personhood, body, and identity. We must not make the mistake of thinking that cultures or communities are characterized by ontological purity with respect to these heuristic terms. As Oliver Harris and John Robb (2012) have recently illustrated, ontological pluralism with respect to cultural understandings of the body was commonplace at most times in European history, a phenomenon they have termed "multimodality." Multimodality in this sense refers to the way in which different and at times contradictory understandings of the body (e.g., as a source of both sinful corruption and magical healing) may be present within the same society and for the same observer. Multimodality should also be expected when it comes to how objects of exchange are valued and consumed. One can readily find examples of both representational and relational-affective identity at work in contemporary public culture. Indeed, Arjun Appadurai (1986) notes that the purist Marxian view of the commodity as inherently impersonal and anticultural is not empirically well supported, as Marx's own discussion of commodity fetishism reveals. There is no particular reason to suppose that noncapitalist societies should be any less heterodox in this respect.

Of particular interest, then, is the changing socialization of goods as they move from person to person, context to context, and culture to culture, with attendant modal shifting between frameworks of value and constructions of personal identity vis-à-vis consumption. The "foreign" status of goods that enter a local system of exchange from outside is particularly relevant, since this passage gives them possibilities for revaluation that locally produced goods may not have. Here we can productively build on Appadurai's (1986) concept of regimes of value. According to Appadurai, the commodity should not be seen as a particular fixed class of thing. Instead, with Kopytoff (1986), he proposes to view commodification as a process (Cipolla, introduction, this volume). From this perspective an object socially transforms as it moves between distinct spheres of exchange (or, indeed, exists within different spheres for different subjects at the same time). This observation is critical for understanding the movement, socialization, and resocialization of foreign things both between groups (e.g., European and indigenous) and within them. Importantly, the concept of regimes of value makes room for the multimodality, ambiguity, and openness of forms of exchange, consumption, and identification in which an object or class of objects may move. As we shall see, gift–commodity and relational–representational multimodal shifting was an essential part of the life histories of foreign things as they moved into and within indigenous contexts of consumption in the lower Great Lakes.

ECONOMIES OF AFFECT

A reconsideration of consumption in relational-affective terms for the Wendat (or Huron) people of 17th-century eastern Canada leads me to propose a model of indigenous economies of affect. Understood as a regime of value, this model helps to explain aboriginal demand for foreign things in a way that I hope more adequately historicizes Native experiences of consumption, personhood, and embodiment. In the 17th century, the Wendat practiced swidden horticulture, fished, hunted, and traded in present-day south-central Ontario (Ramsden 1990; Trigger 1976; Warrick 2000). Wendat long-distance trade came to involve far-flung indigenous and European trading partners toward the close of the 16th century (Latta 1976). This trade fed into local village-based systems of gift exchange and prestation that were overwhelmingly concerned with moderating the bodily and emotional states of participants, constituting a distinctive economy of affect. Importantly, this regime of value incorporated a good deal of ontological pluralism in which foreign things cycled between poses of inalienability and alienation, singularization and commensuration.

WENDAT HISTORY AND THE EARLY FUR TRADE

Archaeological work in southern Ontario over the past century demonstrates that ancestral Wendat people lived in the region for at least seven centuries prior to the arrival of Europeans (Bamann et al. 1992; Creese 2012; Wright 1966). Like other Iroquoian-speaking groups in the lower Great Lakes, the Wendat lived in large, densely occupied agricultural villages, often surrounded by substantial wooden fortifications (Birch 2012). The subsistence economy was based around the cultivation of maize, beans, and squash, supplemented by fishing and hunting, in a shifting swidden regime (Hart 2001; Monckton 1990). Women worked the fields, and their dominant position in food production was associated with high social status (Trigger 1976). Men were involved in hunting, fishing, trade, diplomacy, and warfare, exploits that periodically took them great distances from the home village (Bamann et al. 1992; Warrick 2000). From 1300, Wendat villages in southern Ontario expanded significantly in size from populations in the low hundreds to the low thousands (Creese 2011). This process involved both demographic growth (Warrick 2008) and community aggregation or coalescence (Birch 2012), which culminated in the early 1500s at the immediate cusp of indirect trade with Europeans. As communities grew, they moved into local clusters separated by increasingly large buffer zones, ultimately contracting into a small but densely inhabited territory in present-day Simcoe County, Ontario (Ramsden 1990). This settlement process reflects the increasing scale of intertribal warfare and political integration during this period (Birch 2010). Thus, the centuries immediately preceding the development of the fur trade were characterized by rapid changes in the scale and political organization of Wendat communities.

From the 1530s, a trickle of objects of European origin made their way via Algonquian and Iroquoian middlemen into southern Ontario (Fitzgerald and Ramsden 1988; Latta 1976). However, large quantities of European-made goods, such as iron axes, copper and brass kettles, and glass beads, did not begin to flow into Wendat villages until after 1580 (Kenyon and Fitzgerald 1986; Michelaki et al. 2013). Sometime around 1600, Wendat traders began to travel down to Quebec to trade directly with European ships. French colonists and missionaries operating from New France were early allies and trading partners of the Wendat, a situation that resulted in voluminous historical records related to Wendat culture and society during the first half of the 17th century. A formal alliance was concluded at Quebec between the Wendat leader Atironta and the French in 1609 (Trigger 1976:246). From the 1620s, an ill-fated series of missions to the Wendat by members of the Recollect and later Jesuit orders influenced the nature of subsequent trade. Christian converts were given preferential access to items such as firearms, and Jesuits sought to shelter Wendat people from the morally corrupting influence of French settlers and traders (Trigger 1976). European-introduced epidemic diseases and warfare with the Iroquois, or Haudenosaunee (backed by their Dutch allies in New York), led to the dispersal of Wendat people from southern Ontario between 1648 and 1651. Bruce Trigger has written in detail of the tremendous economic and political upheavals of this period (1976, 1985). The focus here is the period of peak trade, from 1580 to 1650.

WENDAT PERSONS AND THINGS

Before we can adequately answer questions about why foreign things were locally consumed in particular ways, we'll need to consider how Wendat people thought about the relationship between persons and things in general. Jesuit missionaries during the 17th century struggled with a multitude of Wendat terms they translated as "body," "mind," or "soul" but that in practice refused to cleave easily along familiar ontological planes. For instance, the term closest to the French *corps* (body), *,aata* or *yaata*, was also variously translated as "substance" (1693), *entité* (entity) (1693), *chose vivante* (living thing) (1751), and *personne* (person) (1697) (Pomedli 1991). Jesuit linguists were generally perceptive, especially in theological matters, so this ambiguity is not likely to reflect poor comprehension. Rather, the polyvalence of the ,aata concept is strongly implied by the Jesuits' use of it to explain the divine "persons" of the Christian Trinity (Pomedli 1991). Arguably, ,aata conveyed a holistic notion of body-person-substance that was critical to Wendat involvement with and use of material things.

On the flip side of the corporeal, missionaries found a bewildering plurality of terms that might be glossed as "soul" (*khiondec8i, endionrra, gonennoncwal*), "demon" (*oki*), "ghost/bones" (*esken/atisken*), and so forth. From the missionaries' early modern perspective, these ideas seemed hopelessly mired in the material world. In his 1636 relation, for instance, Father Jean de Brébeuf condescended that the Wendat "give to it [the soul] even a head, arms, legs—in short, a body; and to put them in great perplexity it is only necessary to ask them by what exit the soul departs at death, if it be really corporeal . . . for to that they have no reply" (Thwaites 1896–1901, vol. 10:140–141). Materiality and substance, then, were not opposed to immateriality and essence in Wendat thought, a perspective that the Jesuits found extremely difficult to counter when discussing issues such as the nature of the afterlife.

One Wendat term, *gonennoncwal*, is particularly revealing about the nature of the relationship between persons and things. Gonennoncwal was the soul, "in so far as it bears affection to any object; whence it happens that they often say *ondayee ihaton onennoncwat*, 'That is what my heart says to me, that is what my appetite desires'" (Thwaites 1896–1901, vol. 10:140). This "affectionate soul" was closely linked to Wendat disease theory. Unfulfilled desires of the gonennoncwal were identified as the root cause of physical or mental illness. These desires were revealed in dreams that called for the provision of sick persons with large numbers of gifts: things such as wampum, brass kettles, canoes, knives, pipes, as well as feasts, games, and dances. In the *Ononharoia*, or dream-guessing rite, participants announced that they had dreamed and, going from house to house, took what they pleased. Brébeuf recounts that "those of the cabin guess what it is, and present it to the band [of dreamers], who refuse nothing until the right thing is guessed. You see them come out with hatchets, kettles, porcelain [wampum], and like presents hung around their necks, after their fashion. When they have found what they sought . . . the sick man begins to get better" (Thwaites 1896–1901, vol. 10:175–176). Emotional distress presaged physical illness, and both were generally symptomatic of unfulfilled longings for persons or things (Thwaites 1896–1901, vol. 10:220; Wrong 1939:118). A contemporary Recollect missionary observer speculated that what began as a "mental caprice" was somehow converted into a bodily disease (Wrong 1939:201).

Within this milieu, objects performed vital "emotion-work" (see Hochschild 1979), assuaging grief and fulfilling deep desires. Gifts were not simply tokens of affection—they acted powerfully on the mental and physical states of givers and recipients, adding to or diminishing an individual's body-person-substance, ,aata. Thus, the most potent gifts were those that were intimately associated with the body—such as smoking pipes, combs, glass and marine-shell beads, and copper ornaments recycled from trade kettles. For instance, in the Iroquois story of the founding of the Haudenosaunee confederacy, an evil-minded witch (Tadodaho), with snakes for his hair, is healed by the power of a magic comb. His negative affect is transformed, and he becomes a founding chief of the confederacy (Snow 1994). Excavated antler combs from the 17th century are often decoratively carved, suggesting that they were made to be worn in the hair (see Bradley 2007). A curative role, however, is also indicated in graves of the Attiwandaron people, where they were routinely interred with turtle-shell rattles and bone "sucking tubes" (Kenyon 1982:47, 95, 204)—artifacts associated with healing.

PERSONS AND COLLECTIVES

The intimate histories that certain objects developed through their contributions to an individual's ,aata seem to have established a metonymic relationship between person

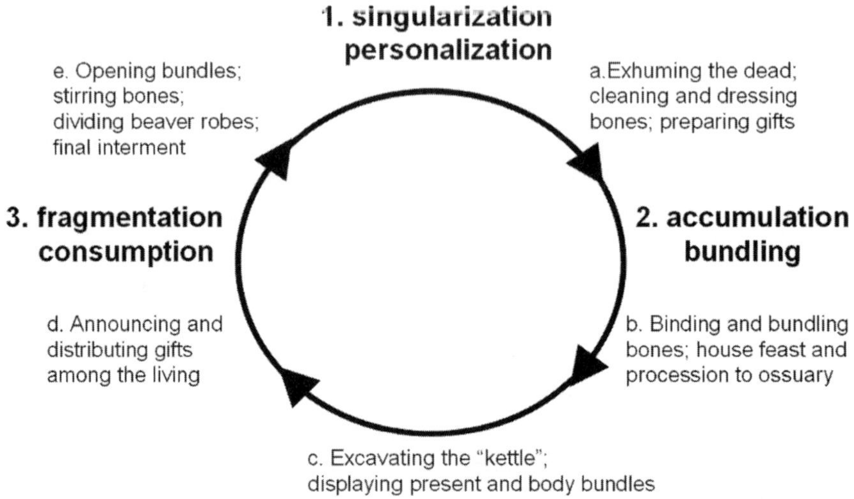

FIGURE 3.1. Structural model of the flow of goods and bodies within the Feast of the Dead. The movement of gifts and bodies between stages of singularization, bundling, and fragmentation is mirrored by the circulation of smoking pipes, wampum, and copper within the wider Wendat economy of affect.

and thing that was the basis for desire and longing (cf. Stewart 1991). Materials became desirable for their affective and life-sustaining connections to absent friends, kin, and the dead. Consequently, gift exchanges at a whole series of scales took place within Wendat society, ranging from the informal to the highly ritualized. The specific contexts for these exchanges are difficult to identify archaeologically, with the exception of those associated with mortuary programs. They are, however, well attested ethnographically and include routine acts of hospitality, feasts, dream imperatives, curing rituals, mortuary rites, reparation payments, intertribal diplomacy, and gambling, which was an occasion for significant redistribution of wealth between kin groups and also, following the principle of emotion-work, a source of healing power for persons afflicted by soul-desires.

The flow of goods within this economy of affect can be visualized as a cycle that moved from stages of bodily and material accumulation to fragmentation and dispersal (Figure 3.1; cf. Chapman 2000; Knappett 2006). In keeping with the premise of multimodality, objects moving through this system shifted character as they occupied relatively individualizing versus collectivizing poles within the overall cycle. As objects changed hands, things that were intimate personal possessions associated with a particular named individual were bundled into potent collective assemblages associated with larger corporate entities (houses, clans, villages) in which their metonymic associations with former owners were downplayed or subsumed to the collective.

This cycle took its most conspicuous and dramatic form in the bodily transformations and elaborate prestations associated with the Feast of the Dead (Seeman 2011). In it, the bodies of village members who had died since the last such feast (generally a period of some ten years) were exhumed and brought into houses for careful disarticulation, defleshing, dressing, and bundling in fresh mats and beaver robes (Thwaites 1896–1901, vol. 10:264–313). The mat and robe were particularly symbolic here as archetypal personal belongings (Steckley 1987:26). Other personal objects such as bracelets, council sticks, and wampum strings were used to dress the body, and the "souls" were assembled for a feast at which the living house chief sang the personal song of the deceased chief. This stage (stage 1, Figure 3.1) emphasized the lived bodily connections between an individual and his or her personal possessions. The next stage (stage 2, Figure 3.1) involved a gathering of the entire tribal community. Visitors from surrounding villages flowed into the host village, carrying with them bundled bodies and presents—kettles, iron axes, beads, beaver robes, and the like. A burial pit, referred to as the "kettle," was excavated, and bundled presents furnished by each family were suspended on poles on a large scaffold surrounding the pit. These were displayed for a period of time before being replaced by the body bundles of the dead. At this point (stage 3, Figure 3.1) the presents were announced and distributed in the name of the deceased persons whose body bundles replaced the presents. Later, the bodies were placed in the pit along with a minority of the presents and the whole interred as a single mass grave. In this process, body bundles were opened and permitted to commingle. Brébeuf observed that the robes that had been used to bundle the bones were cut into small pieces and thrown to onlookers, who scrambled to snatch them (Thwaites 1896–1901, vol. 10:213).

The pointed structural equation of present bundles with body bundles and the subsequent fragmentation and dispersal of both effectively traced out a movement from individual to collective (and back again) that mirrored, in microcosm, the wider Wendat economy of affect. Objects shifted value at different points in the cycle. Momentarily singular and inalienable personal possessions were later precisely alienated from the singularized bodies of their former owners in the name of a wider collective body. The "hold" that the dead may have had over the living recipients of these gifts was perhaps thereby loosened, making room for new relational-affective connections among the living. This can be understood as a kind of disarticulation and resocialization process that was ideally suited to managing the dangerous potency of the foreign goods that flooded into Wendat communities at the time. Foreign things, like gifts from the dead, came with unknown strings attached. One way of dealing with this was to figuratively cut those strings in order to clear the way for new ones.

WENDAT CONSUMPTION OF FOREIGN THINGS

With all this in view, we can begin to make sense of how foreign things were consumed within Wendat communities. I briefly consider three classes of such things that have been studied archaeologically: one of panregional indigenous manufacture (smoking pipes), one of foreign indigenous manufacture (wampum), and a third of European origin that underwent substantial local repurposing (brass and copper kettles).

SMOKING PIPES

Smoking pipes have a deep history in the Eastern Woodlands, dating back to at least 1000 B.C. (Rafferty 2004). For much of this time they were relatively rare objects, but from approximately A.D. 1300 they became ubiquitous on ancestral Wendat and other sites in the lower Great Lakes (Smith 1992). Most Wendat pipes were probably of local manufacture, but they can also be seen as panregional intercultural objects in important ways. They quickly became associated with social exchanges at a range of scales and were an important feature of intertribal and diplomatic rituals at the time of contact. In the 17th century, Wendat ceramic and ground-stone smoking pipes were shared in routine gestures of hospitality among friends and in shamanic activities (Braun 2012; von Gernet and Timmins 1987). These practices emphasized idioms of shared bodily substance—especially of blood and breath—that connected smokers to each other and to other-than-human persons. Gabriel Sagard, Recollect friar and missionary to the Wendat in the 1620s (1639:197 in Wrong 1939), for instance, reported that Wendat men repaired broken pipes using blood drawn from their arms. Tobacco was critical in shaping the affective character of these relationships, since, as Brébeuf put it, "they believe that there is nothing so suitable as tobacco to appease the passions" (Thwaites 1896–1901, vol. 10:218). Pipe effigy figures typically faced the smoker, and popular 17th-century Wendat types such as the "pinch-face" style depicted a blowing or sucking action that may have been associated with shamanic healing practices (Figure 3.2; Kearsley 1997; Mathews 1976). Interestingly, these respiratory themes became popular on Wendat sites following the severe epidemics of the 1630s and 1640s, supporting the hypothesis that they were associated with healing (Mathews 1976). In these practices, the body, and particularly the face and its orifices, seems to have become a focus for affective work aimed at promoting emotional and physical well-being (Creese 2016a).

As objects for performing healing emotion-work, smoking pipes were ideally suited to mediating larger political and ritual exchanges between social factions or collectives (Drooker 2004; Kuhn and Sempowski 2001). Pipes, for instance, were presented as

FIGURE 3.2. A "pinch-face"-style ceramic effigy-smoking pipe from the Thomson-Walker site (ca. A.D. 1625–1649) shown in profile and from the smoker's perspective (*center*). Photo courtesy of Royal Ontario Museum Images.

gifts in political exchanges. Once again, the theme of shared breath is evident. As one giver reportedly expressed, "'My brothers,' said he, 'these two tobacco-pipes are yours. We must in the future have only one breath and a single respiration, since we have only one and the same soul'" (Thwaites 1896–1901, vol. 40:206). Such practices were likely widespread in eastern North America as part of shared protocols for intergroup interaction and alliance building. Archaeological evidence confirms that the exchange of pipes was widespread among northeastern peoples during this period (Drooker 2004; Kuhn 1987). Penelope Drooker has documented the interregional distribution of specific pipe styles across the Northeast and Midwest. Iroquoian types, for instance, have been recovered from Fort Ancient sites in Ohio, while Oneota-style disk pipes, likely originating in the Upper Mississippi, have been recovered from Wendat sites (Figure 3.3; Fox 2002).

These patterns suggest that smoking pipes performed vital emotion-work for social assemblages of various scales. Paralleling the flow of goods and bodies at the Feast of the Dead, pipes apparently operated in both intimate interpersonal contexts and economic transactions attending the fur trade (Mann 2004). In this respect, it is fascinating to note that, like the bodies and presents accumulated at the Feast of the Dead, Wendat smoking pipes were also routinely fragmented—intentionally defaced and broken (cf. Kearsley 1997) or cut and ground to form beads and pendants (Creese 2016b). Recent analysis of artifact collections at the 17th-century Forget and Thomson-Walker sites by the author, for instance, has documented effigy figures that, having been broken or otherwise removed from pipes, were drilled for suspension

FIGURE 3.3. An Oneota-style stone disk pipe recovered from the Wendat Thomson-Walker site (ca. A.D. 1625–1649). Pipes of this form are associated with groups in the upper Mississippi region of Wisconsin and Minnesota. Photo courtesy of Royal Ontario Museum Images.

(Figure 3.4). Beads were also made by grooving and snapping pipe stems (Figure 3.5), a pattern that dates back at least to the 15th century at the Keffer site (Creese 2016b). As objects of personal adornment, pipe fragments worn about the neck or woven onto clothing would have metonymically referenced the once-whole pipe in a manner that paralleled the relationship between the body of the wearer and the wider social collectives that the wearer was caught up in.

In this respect, it is intriguing to note that Wendat people seem to have had little or no interest in acquiring European-manufactured white ball clay pipes. While the Wendat people were eager to purchase tobacco from the French, European pipe fragments are rarely found on 17th-century Wendat sites (Evans 2002; Latta 1976). This lack of interest may be related to the fact that European pipes were mass-produced, relatively interchangeable in appearance, and easily broken. They were, in fact, commodities par excellence. Accordingly, they stand out as an example of a class of foreign thing that was rejected by Wendat consumers because they lacked attributes that would have made them amenable to resocialization within a relational-affective regime of value.

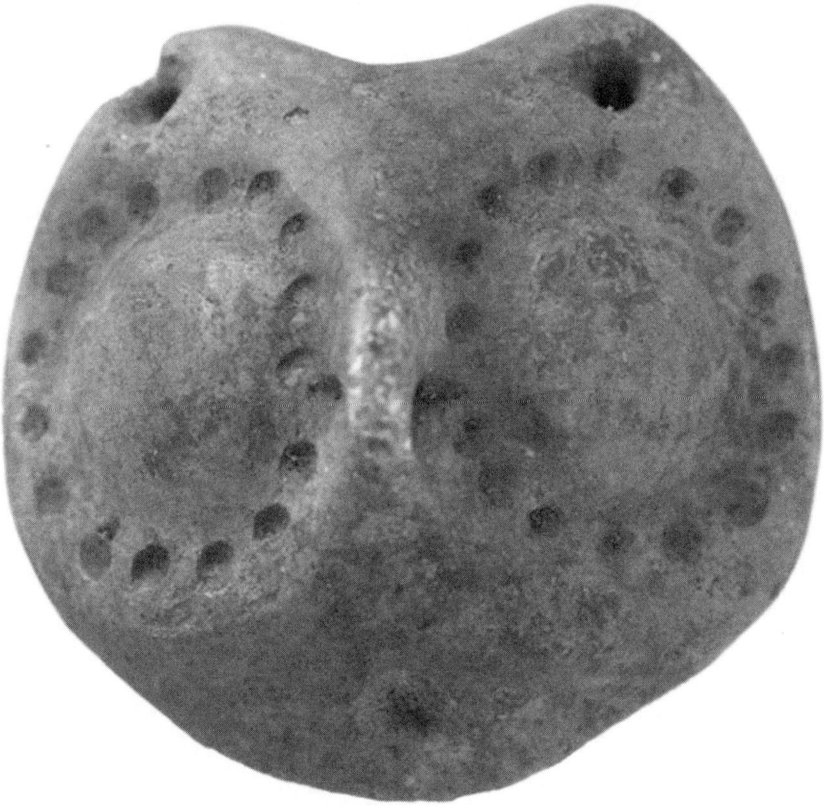

FIGURE 3.4. Owl effigy pendant (ceramic) made from a recycled effigy pipe, Thomson-Walker site (ca. A.D. 1625–1649). Photo courtesy of Royal Ontario Museum Images.

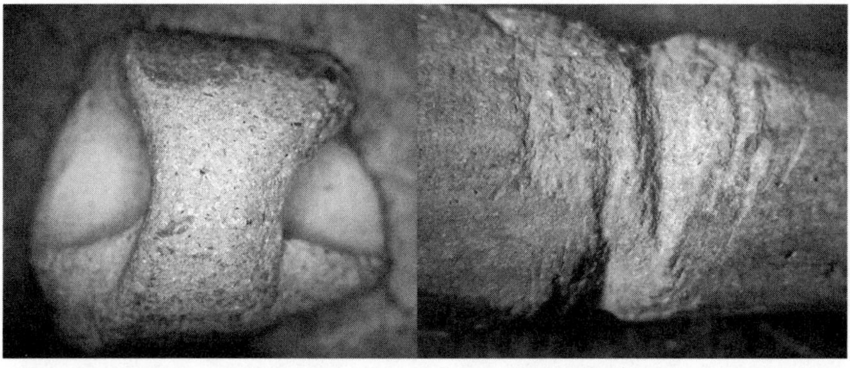

FIGURE 3.5. Bead made from a ceramic pipe-stem fragment (*left*) and pipe stem showing scoring typical of the bead-making process (*right*), Keffer site (ca. A.D. 1450–1500). Photos by the author.

WAMPUM

Marine-shell beads known as wampum (Figure 3.6) were important vehicles for complex cross-cultural entanglements during the 17th century (Beauchamp 1901; Ceci 1982; Snyder 1999). While marine-shell beads of various forms had circulated for millennia before contact, wampum *sensu stricto*, of a relatively standard shape and size (averaging 360 beads to the Dutch fathom in 1626 [Peña 2001:158]), sometimes called "true wampum," is best seen as a product of intercultural interactions during the emerging fur trade (Peña 2001; Snyder 1999). Toward the end of the 16th century, tubular white and purple beads were manufactured in large quantities from the quahog (*Mercenaria mercenaria*) and less often the common whelk (*Buccinum undatum*) by coastal Algonquians who traded with Europeans for a variety of cloth and metal goods (cf. Bragdon, this volume). European traders then used these beads to buy furs from Iroquoian groups to be shipped back to Europe and sold for a handsome profit (Ceci 1982:98). Because of currency shortages and the high value placed on wampum by indigenous consumers, wampum was used as cash money in New Netherland and was legal tender in New England until 1662 (Peña 2001:159).

Reasons for the demand for wampum among interior Iroquoian peoples are complex and have been explored in different ways by a number of authors (Snyderman 1954). While wampum's commodity (and limited currency) status for Europeans is well documented, explanations for its value and meaning among indigenous consumers are more variable. The focus in recent years has been on its symbolic significance in mortuary practices (Snyder 1999), mythology (Ceci 1982), and forest diplomacy (Foster 1985). George Hamell (1992), for instance, has written eloquently about the ideological value of wampum and the semantic associations of whiteness with life and light.

Building on this, we can add that wampum had important affective value. As was the case for smoking pipes, wampum transactions worked at multiple nested social scales, articulating personal identities in the form of bodily adornments, as well as wider collective entities in the form of mnemonic strings and treaty belts (Figure 3.6). Sagard describes Wendat women wearing wampum necklaces "three and a half feet or more" in circumference, as well as strings adorning their ears, hips, arms, and hair (Wrong 1939:144). Not simply decorative, however, wampum performed vital emotion-work. For instance, it formed the primary transactional substance in emotionally fraught murder reparation rituals, as well as the "resuscitations" of adoption and condolence rites (Snow 1994; Tehanetorens 1972:27, 34–35). In Brébeuf's account of one such exchange, some sixty strings of wampum were given in order to "[wipe] away the blood"; "to console them [the relatives] in their affliction and to wipe away their tears"; "to give a drink to the mother of the deceased, to heal her as being seriously sick on

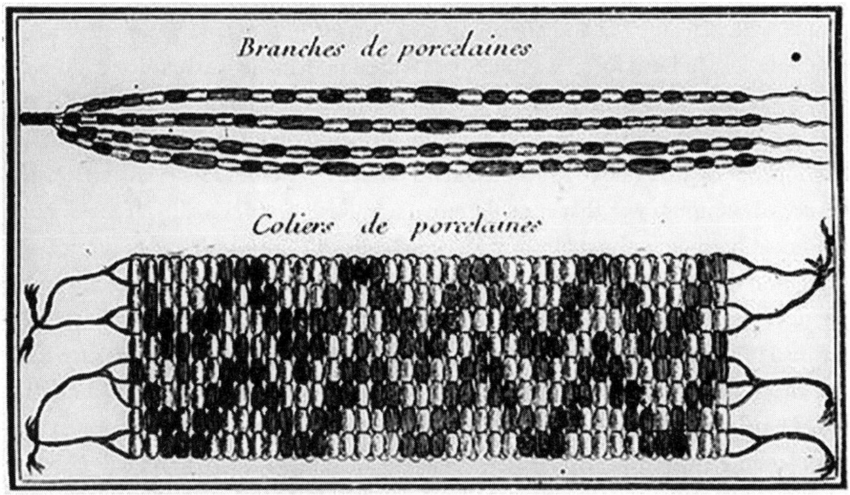

FIGURE 3.6. Illustration of Iroquois wampum belt (*below*) and strings (*above*), from Claude-Charles Le Roy Bacqueville de La Potherie's *Histoire de l'Amérique septentrionale* (Paris: Nion et Didot, 1722).

account of the death of her son"; "to place and stretch a mat for her" (Thwaites 1896–1901, vol. 10:216–220). Thus, wampum was a substance that worked on people, assuaging grief and promoting well-being. As the contemporary Haudenosaunee writer Tehanetorens puts it, the purpose of condolence wampum is "to encourage and cheer up their downcast spirits" (1972:35).

Wampum beads were also woven into large belts to be exchanged in diplomatic contexts and treaty negotiations (Bradley 2007; Ceci 1982; Foster 1985). The iconography of many such belts depicts the "linking of hands" that typified the positive affective relations they were intended to condition (Foster 1985:109; Tehanetorens 1972). As Michael Foster (1985) has argued, wampum exchanges were not simply records and ratifications of treaty proceedings. The entire structure of council protocol was organized around the "prospective" quality of wampum prestations. That is, wampum was exchanged in order to *achieve* desired qualities of interchange and communication between the parties. The large numbers of beads needed for making these belts would have required amassing them from many hands within the community. In this way, treaty belts can be seen as collective social projects, objects that materialized corporate interests through the active networking and accumulation of persons and their data. As with the pipes, then, a parallel metonymic relation was established between beads and belts, persons and social collectives, through the cyclical accumulation and fragmentation of these affecting things.

Notwithstanding these relational-affective values, Wendat and other northeastern people were well aware of and arguably active partners in promoting wampum's use as a commodity. In bead form, wampum was widely in demand, standardized, durable, and interchangeable with others of its kind—an ideal candidate for currency status (Synder 1999). This aspect of wampum's life history cannot have been lost on indigenous people, who came to expect standard exchange rates for furs (Peña 2001). The beauty of wampum was that it could move seamlessly and reversibly between commodity and gift states and between personal and collective scales of prestation. As wampum operated in a relational-affective regime of value, it was socialized by being physically and metaphorically connected with the body and its emotional health. It was also physically singularized by being used as a component in unique artifacts such as articles of clothing, implements such as inlaid war clubs (Bradley 2007), and diplomatic belts. In this way, it could be flexibly (but not irreversibly) transformed into singular and inalienable objects that could circulate as gifts. Later, if need be, beads could easily reenter a commodity state.

COPPER AND BRASS KETTLES

European metals were extremely rare in Wendat country during the mid-16th century and appear mainly in the form of tiny pieces of scrap copper, although some iron implements are known (Fitzgerald 1990; Noble 1971). By 1580 Basque and Breton traders were bringing copper kettles to the maritime region of Canada in large numbers, and this is likely the source for early "red" copper in Wendat assemblages (Fitzgerald 1990; Turgeon 1997). In the first quarter of the 17th century, metals, often in the form of rolled tubular copper beads, became much more common in southern Ontario. Contrary to acculturationist expectations, European brass and copper kettles were not immediately seen as superior—or even very suitable—functional replacements for Native-made ceramic vessels. Certainly, their thermal characteristics may have made traditional cuisine a challenge (cf. Frink and Harry 2008). Instead, they were largely used as a source of raw material for an array of small implements and ornaments, from bracelets, to bangles, to rings, to tinkling cones—a pattern that is widespread across the entire Northeast and northern Midwest (Anselmi et al. 1997; Bradley 1987; Ehrhardt 2005; Evans 2002; Latta 1976). Copper scrap on early 17th-century sites in Ontario demonstrates the systematic processing of kettles to make tools and ornaments (Evans 2002; Michelaki et al. 2013). Whole or nearly complete kettles are almost unknown from Wendat sites, with the important exception of ossuary burials (Latta 1976:229). The majority of metal artifacts at the Wendat Ball village site (ca. 1600), for instance, took the form of copper and brass debitage resulting from the processing of an estimated two or three dozen kettles (Michelaki et al. 2013).

One influential interpretation of these practices is that indigenous demand for copper was, like wampum, motivated by color symbolism and cosmology. In their efforts to explain the fabrication of copper spirals and hoops by Iroquoian peoples in the Finger Lakes and Susquehanna areas, for instance, James Bradley and S. Terry Childs (2007) argue that Native metalworking was motivated by indigenous understandings of Europeans as returning underworld culture heroes. We can perhaps add to this interpretation by suggesting a more active and instrumental role for copper within the wider value regime of an affective economy. The potent healing power of copper is attested in 19th-century sources (Bradley and Childs 2007:304), and this medical understanding of copper can be linked to the wider logic of emotion-work and relational-affective exchange described above. It is therefore not surprising that the focus of aboriginal efforts at resocializing copper involved the creation of bodily adornments. Worn on the body, copper would have been most efficacious in fulfilling dream desires and performing healing emotion-work.

Also in broad parallel with pipes and shell beads, the relationship between kettle parts and wholes was used to establish connections between persons and wider social collectives. Whole kettles were conspicuous additions to Wendat ossuary burials in the early 17th century (parallel to practices examined by Howey in the maritime Northeast, this volume). In the mortuary arena, the metonymic relation between these whole kettles and copper ornaments was explicitly cited by the deposition of whole kettles at the center of ossuaries (Kenyon 1982; Kidd 1953) that were themselves referred to as metaphoric "kettles" (Seeman 2011). Unlike those discussed by Meghan Howey, these do not appear to have been deliberately broken. As described earlier, the part-whole relationship between kettles and kettle fragments was mirrored by the ritual structure of the Feast of the Dead, with its cyclical accumulation and dispersal of bodies and presents (Johnston 1979; Pfeiffer 1980; Williamson and Steiss 2003). As with smoking pipes and marine shell, then, European metal flowed into indigenous gift economies, where its exchange and consumption performed healing emotion-work, weaving together individual and collective ,aata in cycles of fragmentation and accumulation.

DISCUSSION

For heuristic reasons, I have drawn a strong distinction between relational-affective social assembly and commodity transactions as though they were mutually exclusive alternatives. But if this were so, the energy driving much of the work to which Wendat people put things would be inexplicable. In reality, representation and relationality are two sides of the same coin, and both are active in person-thing relations. Within the wider Wendat economy of affect, multimodal shifts in the primacy of representation versus relationality are evident in the movement of goods between relatively personal to relatively corporate contexts (and back again).

In order for wampum, copper, or smoking pipes to work as gifts that bound persons to others, first they had to be identified with specific individuals and bodies. Because foreign goods entered the community without clearly defined relational-affective ties, the establishment of an intimate biographical connection between these goods and particular bodies was a necessary preliminary to the wider cycle of exchange. This stage emphasized, in Kopytoff's (1986) terms, the singularity of both the thing and the person who owned it, establishing a metonymic relation between the two. This imperative helps explain the rejection of fragile mass-produced European smoking pipes by Wendat consumers, since these objects were neither singular nor sufficiently durable to invite biographical connection with their owners. It also explains why copper and brass kettles were used primarily as raw material for making objects of bodily adornment. Once such bodily connections had been established, pipes, shell beads, and copper ornaments were ideal candidates for exchanges that knit persons together. However, as these items were assembled to materialize and mediate alliances of wider social collectives, they were physically transformed (or conspicuously *not* transformed, in the case of kettles) in ways that loosened their connections to individual bodies and emphasized some aspects of commonness, alienability, and exchangeability. The desire to make bodily and emotional connections via gift exchanges appears to have been balanced at times by efforts to disentangle objects from their relational-affective histories in order to clear the way for new ones. Wampum was the ideal medium for such shifts in value, since its particulate form allowed it to move fluidly between commoditized transactions with Europeans, relational-affective bodily ornamentation, and collective representations as treaty and diplomatic belts. Interestingly, in its collective pose, amassed to form reparation payments between clans or as binding contracts between parties to an alliance, wampum in effect became more currency-like as its affective distance from individual persons increased. Acts of intentional fragmentation (of kettles, smoking pipes, beaver robes, and body bundles) and assembly (of wampum belts, bones in mass graves, or people in smoking ceremonies) therefore played on the thematic tensions and contradictions between individuation and collectivization, inalienability and alienation, gift and commodity inherent to such exchanges.

CONCLUSION

This account shifts the study of indigenous consumption, materiality, and identity away from acculturationist narratives of technological superiority and cultural loss. At the same time, it also helps avoid limiting indigenous agency in the early fur trade to a thin account of identity construction via consumption that overlooks precisely what was different and important about these practices. The Wendat economy of affect depended on relational-affective understandings about how objects—especially items of bodily adornment—might be used to act on bodies and minds in order to cultivate and extend life-sustaining social relationships. Its characteristic cycles of accumulation and fragmentation bound persons and things into wider "affective fields" (cf. Harris and Sorensen 2010; Harris 2014) through a continuous ebb and flow of goods.

What does the Wendat case have to tell us about archaeological approaches to indigenous ways of acquiring and consuming foreign things? On one level, it is clear that Wendat relational-affective modes of identification differed profoundly from the representational paradigm that undergirds much archaeological thinking about how people use things to constitute the social. In that sense, it provides a reminder that in order to adequately study the role of foreign goods as they made their way into indigenous hands, we must take ontological alterity seriously. At yet a deeper level, however, the vigorous entanglement of material things and persons in the assembly of Wendat social relations reflects anything but the actions of people slavishly conforming to a rule-bound worldview. Rather, it reveals the creative labor that was involved in establishing an order in which material things were desirable because of their ability to cultivate and nurture social relationships. In the unprecedented flood of durable material culture occasioned by the fur trade, foreign things were conscripted into dynamic and ultimately novel projects of subject formation, where objects reached out to entangle others principally as signs of relations, rather than by describing social boundaries.

4

POWHATAN SOVEREIGNTY AND CONSUMER POLITICS IN THE ALGONQUIAN CHESAPEAKE

CHRISTOPHER SHEPHARD AND MARTIN GALLIVAN

IN MAY 1614 English colonist Ralph Hamor met with Wahunsenacawh, paramount chief of the Powhatan, at a village along the Pamunkey River. Hamor had traveled to the village of Werowocomoco to arrange a marriage between the governor of the Virginia colony, Thomas Dale, and a daughter of the chief. When Wahunsenacawh met Hamor he abruptly grabbed him by the neck, an act that Hamor saw as an attempt on his life (Hamor et al. 1615:38). Releasing Hamor, the great chief demanded to see the "chaine of pearle," a gift he had given Governor Dale earlier in the year with specific instructions to send it with any men seeking to hold a council with him. In a later account Hamor wrote that the pearl necklace was simply a marker of his political relationship with the governor of the Virginia colonies and proof that he was able to make political decisions on the governor's behalf (Hamor et al. 1615:39).

Although Wahunsenacawh authorized violent acts against various foes, he rarely carried them out with his own hands. His response to Hamor's affront, we believe, hints at a decidedly Powhatan notion of sovereignty, one that centers on control over the human body and the movement of objects that animated political relationships. With this line of thought we join a growing scholarship that considers sovereignty not as the uniform effect of unlimited power but as a "political order produced by an assemblage of administrative strategies" (Ong 2006:98). In the colonial Chesapeake, these strategies responded directly to an intrusive European population that (1) introduced large volumes of objects despite the fact that they existed outside of the indigenous political order and (2) threatened to disrupt a complicated and fragile political landscape of graduated sovereignty, where authoritative agents exerted power over populations at varying political scales. We argue that the most potent objects exchanged, displayed, and retained among the coastal Algonquian did not simply reflect underlying notions of prestige or power but embodied Algonquian perceptions of manitou, an active and animate class of persons, objects, and practices that independently influenced the world. The changing materiality of authority during the early 17th century, we suggest, created economic opportunities previously unavailable to large segments of the population and fundamentally changed the way in which politically charged objects were consumed throughout the region.

The Algonquian desire for foreign objects—shell and copper ornamentation—occurred at the nexus of broad structural political processes and individual agency. As Paul Mullins suggests, consumption is a "continual albeit largely unexpressed process of self-definition and collective identification" (2011b:135). Objects not only were central to practices that reproduced Chesapeake Algonquian political structures but also mediated chiefly strategies of domination and the diverse ways in which subjection was defined and experienced over the *longue durée* (Braudel 1980). Recent scholarship has claimed the human body as the site where sovereignty is defined and the object upon which notions of authority and subjection are performed (Agamben 1998; Smith 2011). As an extension of the body, adornment—through its acquisition, display, circulation, and retention—mediated political relationships but also acted as a tool for resisting structures of political domination that sought to imprint chiefly (or European colonial) rule onto the bodies of indigenous people (Hansen and Stepputat 2006:297). Instead of indexing acculturation, foreign objects were actively redefined and put to use in ways that concretely impacted human relationships (Rubertone 2000:432).

By "foreign" objects we reference a particular set of materials produced outside of the Powhatan political geography through methods largely unknown to the Native inhabitants of the coastal southern Middle Atlantic. While these societies relied on shellfish as a staple of their diet, there is little evidence of local shell ornament production prior to the last quarter of the 17th century (Shephard 2015). The closest copper sources were located west of the Chesapeake in the Blue Ridge Mountains, a territory held by the Monacan, a Siouan-speaking group that held tenuous relations with the Powhatan despite the maintenance of formal trade relations between the groups in the early 17th century (Hantman 1990:685). Early colonial accounts indicate that copper and shell ornamentation flowed through chiefly lineages and that, although particularly powerful corporate groups controlled their acquisition and distribution, these objects were available, at least in small quantities, to the entirety of the Powhatan population (Smith 1986a; Strachey 1953[1612]; Spelman 1998[1609]). While we consider all Powhatan as possible consumers of "foreign" wealth objects, intrasocietal differentiation based on kinship and achievement likely dictated greater access to particular segments of the populace—regulatory structures that were fundamentally disrupted by unrestricted trade with Europeans in the early 17th century.

Although we touch on the "indigenization" of European objects during the early colonial period, our chapter diverges from others in this volume in that we seek to contextualize the consumption of "foreign" objects prior to the arrival of Europeans and prior to the development of a global market economy. Transcending traditional historic and prehistoric temporal boundaries and focusing on long-term culture change within the region allow us to foreground colonial interactions and evaluate the full range of influences that shaped the postcolonial political landscape (Lightfoot 1995). Focusing on the deep history of political interaction within the region shifts the frame of reference from an uncritical reading of English-authored accounts toward a perspective that is inclusive of Algonquian worldviews and culturally specific ways of engaging with the material world. Although we recognize that uncritical use of the term *culture contact* can whitewash the power inequities, violence, and oppression of colonialism (Silliman 2005), we believe interactions prior to the First Anglo-Powhatan War (1610–1614) were influenced, in large part, by a desire to qualify political relationships in a time when colonial dynamics were not yet in place. There was hostility, especially from the Paspahegh, whose hunting territory the Jamestown colonists had chosen to settle in without seeking consent, but Wahunsenacawh, with the manpower to destroy the unauthorized settlement, instead attempted to incorporate the newcomers and make them Powhatan (Hantman 1990).

MANITOU AND THE MATERIAL WORLD

First-contact narratives that are overwhelmingly laced with themes of apotheosis have complicated our understandings of the relationship between indigenous people, Europeans, and their objects. From Africa to the Pacific and the North Atlantic coast, indigenous people are said to have mistaken "white men" for gods and to have marveled at the technologies that they brought with them (Haefeli 2007; Sahlins 1985). Of the Algonquian speakers of the Carolina Sound, Thomas Hariot writes in 1585 that the "thinges that wee had, were so straunge vnto them, and so farre exceeded their capacities to comprehend the reason and meanes how they should be made and done, that they thought they were rather the works of gods then [*sic*] of men" (1588:39). Hariot's interpretation of the indigenous fascination with European-made objects, however, stands as a misreading of Algonquian ontology, as their ideas about the nature of being and the kinds of things that had existence differed starkly from an Elizabethan understanding of the world.

Coastal people of the southern Middle Atlantic, like their linguistic counterparts to the north, appear not to have recognized divisions between the *natural* and *supernatural* or the *secular* and *religious*. Irving Hallowell's fieldwork among the Ojibwe revealed that a whole host of Ojibwe Algonquian nouns, including tree, sun, moon, thunder, stones, and objects of material culture like pipe and kettle, were linguistically classified as animate (1960:22). In their world, many reified other-than-human "person-objects" existed with the same ontological status as human beings and were organized into the same "linguistic class" (Hallowell 1960:24). Active elements, both seen and unseen, were behind all worldly action, orchestrating outcomes, both positive and negative, through their personal relationship with others. Outward appearance, in other words, was only an incidental attribute of sentience and being (Hallowell 1960:34).

While there are some indications of differences in the ways eastern Algonquians understood the concept, manitou generally referred to the way in which power was distributed throughout the universe and its impact on the ability for human and other-than-human actors to actively influence the lived world (Crosby 1988). Potencies could be moral, psychological, spiritual, or technological, but they were always expressed in the world and attainable by human beings (Haefeli 2007:421). In his famous 1643 *A Key into the Language of America*, Roger Williams translates manitou among the Algonquians of southern New England as "god," yet his description of its context and usage suggests that indigenous understandings of the concept may have been significantly more complex. He writes that it is a "general Custome amongst them, at the apprehension of any Excellency in Men, Women, Birds, Beasts, Fish . . . to cry out Manitóo . . . as thus if they see one man excel others in Wisdome, Valour, strength, Activity . . . of the English ships, and great buildings, of the plowing of their Fields" (1997[1643]:126). In other words, confronting manitou was a part of everyday life, as its potency or power was unevenly distributed across persons, animals, objects, places, and practices. Political authority came from harnessing this power and connecting with manitou in sophisticated ways—Wahunsenacawh's title of *mammanitowick* directly referenced his inseparability from manitou, which distinguished him from lower-level *weroances* (chiefs). As Kathleen Bragdon has noted among New England Algonquians, the control and acquisition of powerful objects was not solely personal but promoted "community well-being, making the social and the sacred a seamless whole" (1996:199). Where the God of Christians was seen as separated from the worldly plain, manitou was the unseen spirit that inhabited entities and enabled them to elicit action in the world.

The potency of manitou, however, was unpredictable and could bring misfortune as easily as prosperity. Virginia planter Robert Beverly wrote in 1705 that if Tidewater

Algonquians "did not pacify the Evil Spirit, and make him propitious, he wou'd take away, or spoil their Health, their Peace and their Plenty, by sending War, Plague and Famine among them; for . . . this Evil Spirit, is always busying himself with . . . [their] affairs, and frequently visiting . . . [them], being present in the Air, in the Thunder, and in the Storms" (Beverley and Wright 1947[1705]:201). The fear of manitou—of crop failure, of infertility, of attacks from outsiders, and ultimately of death—motivated human interaction *with* and manipulations *of* the material world. Individuals were in constant danger of failing to perform rituals correctly, of giving inappropriate gifts, of not respecting the correct social or spiritual order, and so of losing manitou or having it turn against them (Haefeli 2007:422).

For the Chesapeake Algonquian, then, it was the fear of creating imbalance between a diverse world of potentially active social entities (material and immaterial) that both animated transformations of the material world and shaped its consumption. An array of material forms, including the food and drink consumed at feasting events, beads of copper and shell that adorned clothing, ceremonial pipes, specialized ceramic vessels, and even architectural features like palisades, were *products of* and *instruments for* establishing, maintaining, and manipulating political authority (Gallivan 2007; Hantman and Gold 2002; Shephard 2009). Foreign objects were incorporated into social practices that allowed individuals to acquire spiritual power—practices that spanned the pre- and postcolonial periods (Crosby 1988). The development of the Powhatan paramount chiefdom, in fact, appears to have resulted directly from the expansion of material possibilities for authorities to successfully manipulate manitou for the benefit of their communities. From an original inheritance of six districts, which likely occurred in the 1560s (Rountree 2006:39), Wahunsenacawh expanded his domain southeastward across the James and York River peninsulas to the Atlantic coast. The coast offered a bounty of subsistence resources, including productive agricultural land, wide brackish rivers, and expansive marshlands hosting a wide variety of flora and fauna (Binford 1983; Smith 1971; Turner 1992). But perhaps even more appealing was the potential for subjugating those societies on the Eastern Shore who specialized in shell bead production and controlled their distribution (Smith 1986a:168).

MOVEMENT, SINGULARITY, AND SACRIFICE

The coastal Algonquian worldview placed objects, people, and even practices and events within a relational network through which potencies flowed. The most influential objects—those imbued with manitou—were set apart from others in their potential to retain history, achieve singularity (lacking any equivalent), and forge indelible links to powerful persons and corporate groups. Particularly potent objects may have also played a role in imposing social forms onto individuals, triggering the capacity to receive social information and representing active elements in processes of human socialization (Rubertone 2001:143–144).

During the Late Woodland period (A.D. 900–1607), fewer but more ritually significant objects were being moved over long distances compared to earlier periods (Stewart 1989). *Marginella* shell beads, clamshell discs, whelk columella barrel beads, and gorgets entered the region as early as the 11th century A.D., with consumption increasing through the 17th century (Klein and Sanford 2004:56). Although copper has been recovered from sites in the Delaware Valley dating to as early as the Late Archaic period (Lattanzi 2007), it appears not to have entered the Chesapeake, at least in any significant amount, until the 14th century. By the establishment of the Roanoke Colony in 1585, however, copper had superseded shell in terms of consumer demand (Klein and Sanford 2004:60).

For the Powhatan, objects produced at the village level generally flowed through multiple tiered political orders as tribute (Potter 2006). Colonist William Strachey wrote in 1612 that all weroances beholden to Wahunsenacawh were required to provide in tribute eight parts in ten of all "the Commodities which their Country yeildeth, as of wheat, pease, beans . . . of dying roots . . . of skyns and furrs" (Strachey 1953[1612]:87). As in most societies, Algonquian objects were ranked on a continuum (Graeber 2001:34), with the majority having little chance of acquiring manitou. Commodities produced at the household level, including maize, meats, shellfish, nuts, basketry, ceramics, stone tools, and skins, were set apart from nonlocal objects that were distinguished by the long-distance exchange routes that brought them into the region, their control by a minority elite, and the distinctive social settings in which their exchange took place (Klein and Sanford 2004:53; Rountree 1993). While commodities were mutually exchangeable with a whole host of other objects in discrete transactions, singular preciosities had no exchangeable counterparts and were often locked in human relationships of debt and obligation (Kopytoff 1986; Mauss 1990[1954]).

The unique Algonquian relationship between objects and people was little understood by the English. They frequently offended their indigenous exchange partners, whose notion of value was wrapped up in negotiations of authority, identity, and status (Mallios 2006). In January 1608 John Smith and his compatriots visited Wahunsenacawh's capital village of Werowocomoco, hoping to obtain enough maize to get the struggling colony through the winter. He writes that Wahunsunacock "desired to see all our Hatchets and Copper together, for which he would give us corne. . . . [H]is offer I refused, offering first to see what hee would give for one piece. Hee seeming to despise the nature of a Merchant, did scorne to sell, but we freely should give him, and he liberally would requite us" (Smith 1986d:71). Smith's approach to this particular transaction was one of pure Western economics, definitively asking Wahunsenacawh the requisite equivalency value of corn to hatchets (see Cipolla's discussion of exchange value in the introduction). Commodities were not foreign to the Powhatan, but the political relationship between the Natives and the English had yet to be qualified, and thus the English desire to deal in equivalencies was met with indignation. Here, maize was a product of Wahunsenacawh's authority through the labor of his subjects, the fertility of chiefly fields, and the positive manipulation of manitou through the distribution of white beads—foreign objects—during spring planting ceremonies (Spelman 1998[1609]:493). Maize in this situation acted as a node in Wahunsenacawh's extensive social network, and the English effort to treat it like a commodity was an assault on his generosity and his ability to give to them a piece of himself, with all of the debt and obligations that it entailed.

Indeed, part of the creation of value and the socialization of objects within the indigenous Chesapeake involved the bundling or binding of objects to other objects, persons, or practices, the combining of which produced entities with the ability to influence increasingly larger networks of relationships (Pauketat 2012:39). Objects bestowed by the hands of particularly potent individuals—those endowed with manitou—could take on and retain the essence of the giver, transforming its relative value and its ability to influence worldly action (Mauss 1990[1954]). English interpreter Henry Spelman witnessed an event that occurred after Powhatan laborers had spent the day planting maize in Wahunsenacawh's personal fields. The workers gathered around the great chief, who had a copper crown placed on his head given to him by King James I of England the same year. Spelman writes that the laborers always faced the king, "expecting when he should fling some beads among them, which his custom is at that time to do, making those which had wrought to scramble for them" (1998[1609]:493). Margaret Williamson interprets Wahunsenacawh's distribution of beads on his newly planted field as an assurance of fertility and the symbolic distribution of his semen to his subjects and workers (2003:157). While we agree that the beads served as an extension of his biological body, his lineage, and the sovereign political order that expanded across 34 political districts, we argue that these objects actively opposed the imbalance potentially created by not providing the proper offerings to powerful otherworldly beings. At the same time, the beads, when bestowed upon the laborers, expanded their potential to manipulate manitou in an attempt to ensure the fertility of their own fields and influenced forms of partible personhood that renewed the relationship of overt domination between authority and subject (Creese, this volume; Fowler 2004; Strathern 1988).

No rigid ritual schedule appears to have been observed by the Powhatan, with offerings being bestowed on an "as-needed" basis or at the enactment of events such as the first corn harvest of the season (Rountree 1989:137). Offerings took various forms and were enacted in social settings based on individual sociopolitical status, personal relationships with divine beings, and the vicinity of individuals to cosmologically charged places (Williamson 2003:236). According to John Smith, in an effort to quell violent storms, conjurers (chiefly spiritual advisors) would "cast Tobacco, Copper, [and] Pocones . . . into the water to pacifie that God whome they thinke to be very angry" (1986b:171). Without a distinction between the natural and supernatural, all worldly action was a result of an animate actor, seen or unseen, whose displeasure could be assuaged through offerings and sacrifice (Brown 2006). When in the presence of powerful places, such as Uttamussack, the principal "temple" of the Pamunkey, all but *quiyoughcosoughs* (priests) and weroances (chiefs) would cast offerings of copper, white beads, or maize into the river in fear that the god Oke would be offended and seek revenge (Smith 1986b:169–170). Offertory practices were likely motivated by broader Algonquian concepts of destruction and renewal, influencing the nature and frequency of sacrifice and backed by the belief that "the greater the sacrifice, the greater the social gain" (Bragdon 1996:240).

The most concrete evidence of offerings in the archaeological record is in objects purposefully placed on or around the bodies or bones of the deceased during burial ceremonies. In situ strands of ornamentation excavated in precolonial burial contexts suggest that they were worn in various configurations on the head and neck, through the ears, in the hair, and around the waist, wrists, and ankles (Blanton et al. 1999; Fesler et al. 2001; Painter 1980). Archaeological fieldwork at the Paspahegh site, the location of a Powhatan village just up the James River from the English settlement at Jamestown, yielded several burials, both ossuaries and single interments (Luccketti et al. 1994:232). A strand of interspersed shell and copper beads, associated with bundle 1F55 within a larger ossuary, revealed notching of the shell beads to dovetail with the copper, whose excurvate blanks created V-shaped gaps in each end of the bead after it was rolled. Sheet copper pendants from another burial at the site revealed the purposeful cutting of larger pendants and the reconfiguration of the pieces on strands to highlight specific parts of the body (Luccketti et al. 1994:230). In each case, individual beads and pendants were modified from their original form in order to create new and potentially recognizable entities—perhaps evidence for the movement of these objects from commodities (readily exchangeable objects) toward singularity, or incomparable objects lacking exchange value (Kopytoff 1986:68–69). As John Creese suggests (this volume), the fragmentation of larger objects may have referenced relationships between individuals and the broader social collectives within which they were engaged.

Shell and copper beading also adorned Native bodies in life and likely took an active role in performative events that reproduced regional sociopolitical structures.

Depending on the season, 17th-century Algonquians dressed in skins: a loincloth-type garment for men and fringed skirt for women, with mantels or matchcoats covering their upper bodies during the winter months (Strachey 1953[1612]:71–72). These garments were often decorated with a modest amount of shell or copper beading but were also emblazoned with drawings of "beasts, fowle, tortoyses, or other such like Imagery" (Strachey 1953[1612]:72). Instead of specialized clothing, ceremonial dress generally involved adding ornaments in the form of long strands of beads thrown over the shoulder, bracelets, earrings, and various types of head garments (Rountree 1989:69). Beadwork and strung jewelry involved in ritual performances likely entered the archaeological record unintentionally as the result of loss or breakage. Groups of beads have been found commingled with food refuse, in and around hearth features, and in exterior floor areas within village settlements (Blanton and Hudgins n.d.; Harmon 1999; Jirikowic 1999). Recent excavations at the Powhatan village of Kiskiak along the York River, for instance, have yielded both shell beads and sheet copper within dense shell midden deposits. Comprised primarily of oyster shells and clamshells, animal bone, charcoal, fire-cracked rock, and Roanoke simple-stamped ceramic sherds, these remains likely represent waste from intensive feasting events. Shell beads from the Hughes site located along the Potomac River were recovered from a large basin-shaped pit feature in the central portion of a palisaded settlement (Jirikowic 1999). The location of the feature was interpreted as an area reserved for more restricted and, potentially, ceremonial activities, in contrast to the domestic work, raw material processing, and burial of the dead that occurred in close proximity to the palisade walls in the exterior portions of the site.

FOREIGN OBJECTS AND CULTURAL METAPHORS

In part, shell and copper were particularly powerful among Chesapeake Algonquian societies because of their uncanny origin. Webb Keane (2001a) describes valuables among the Sumba of eastern Indonesia as transcending "the physical labor of the body" and therefore invoking a transcendental source of value. In other words, the value of "foreign" objects "lies not in local control over the means of production but perhaps in the promise of an escape from the demands of production altogether, and in its capacity to supplement physical labor" (Keane 2001b:83). Copper-sourcing studies suggest that these Chesapeake Algonquian ornaments were produced in areas of modern-day Pennsylvania, New Jersey, and New York and may have entered the region through trade with the Monacan, a Siouan-speaking group residing in the western Piedmont (Hantman 1990; Lattanzi 2007; Stevenson et al. n.d.). Sites yielding evidence of shell bead production almost exclusively occur at the margins of the

Powhatan and Piscataway political territories (Shephard 2015). Shell ornamentation was likely made by artisans who were considered "outsiders" and who lived within a dynamic zone of political, cultural, and social interaction (a "frontier" *sensu* Lightfoot and Martinez 1995) that developed over the previous century as a direct result of the centralization of political authority within the region (Gallivan et al. 2008).

Foreign objects, through their sensuous qualities, linked the body to broader cultural metaphors related to region-wide political structures, the complicated relationship between power and authority, and social–spiritual action. George Hamell (1992) and others have well established the cross-cultural significance of white, black, and red throughout the Eastern Woodlands, where Algonquian, Iroquoian, and Siouan groups shared at least some practices and principles associated with these colors. For the Powhatan, white and red together often appeared in opposition to black. The white of shell beads and pearls represented life and renewal or rebirth—the mundane as opposed to the spiritual (Williamson 2003:253). Wahunsenacawh threw white beads to those who labored in his fields in the early spring, thus renewing and restoring their subjugation while at the same time legitimizing his authority. The redness of copper and of puccoon (a body paint) made these materials the most animate and energetic elements within the Powhatan world. Paint adorned the bodies of dancers, priests, and warriors entering battle, and copper was often the gift to allies just prior to a raid. Red represented power and thus social action, as opposed to black, the color of authority (Williamson 2003:253). The Huskenaw, a rite of passage that turned boys into eligible priests and weroances, culminated in painting the initiates black, mourning their social death, and sending them into the woods (Smith 1986b:171–172). Black referenced not only the permanence of death and authority but also the desire for spiritual guidance and blessings (Bragdon 1996; Williamson 2003:253).

Few examples of iconography exist in the archaeological record of the Chesapeake region, likely related to the poor preservation of organic materials due to the acidity of coastal plain soils. However, Powhatan's mantle (Figure 4.1), housed at the Ashmolean Museum at the University of Oxford, is a prime example of an object that was actively engaged in the negotiation and legitimization of indigenous authoritative structures (see Bragdon's chapter, this volume, for a discussion of the connection between elite identities and bodily adornment in early colonial New England). Constructed of four deerskins sewed together, the mantle is adorned with thousands of marine shell beads (Figure 4.1). A human-like figure is depicted in the central portion of the garment, flanked on either side by a feline and a large mammal, likely a white-tailed deer. Around these figures are sewed thirty-four roundlets of *Marginella* shell. The precise history of the piece is unknown, but it may represent a gift from Wahunsenacawh to King James I in 1609 (Waselkov 2006:455). Christian Feest (1983) has argued that the size of the piece would have made it unwieldy, and it was more likely

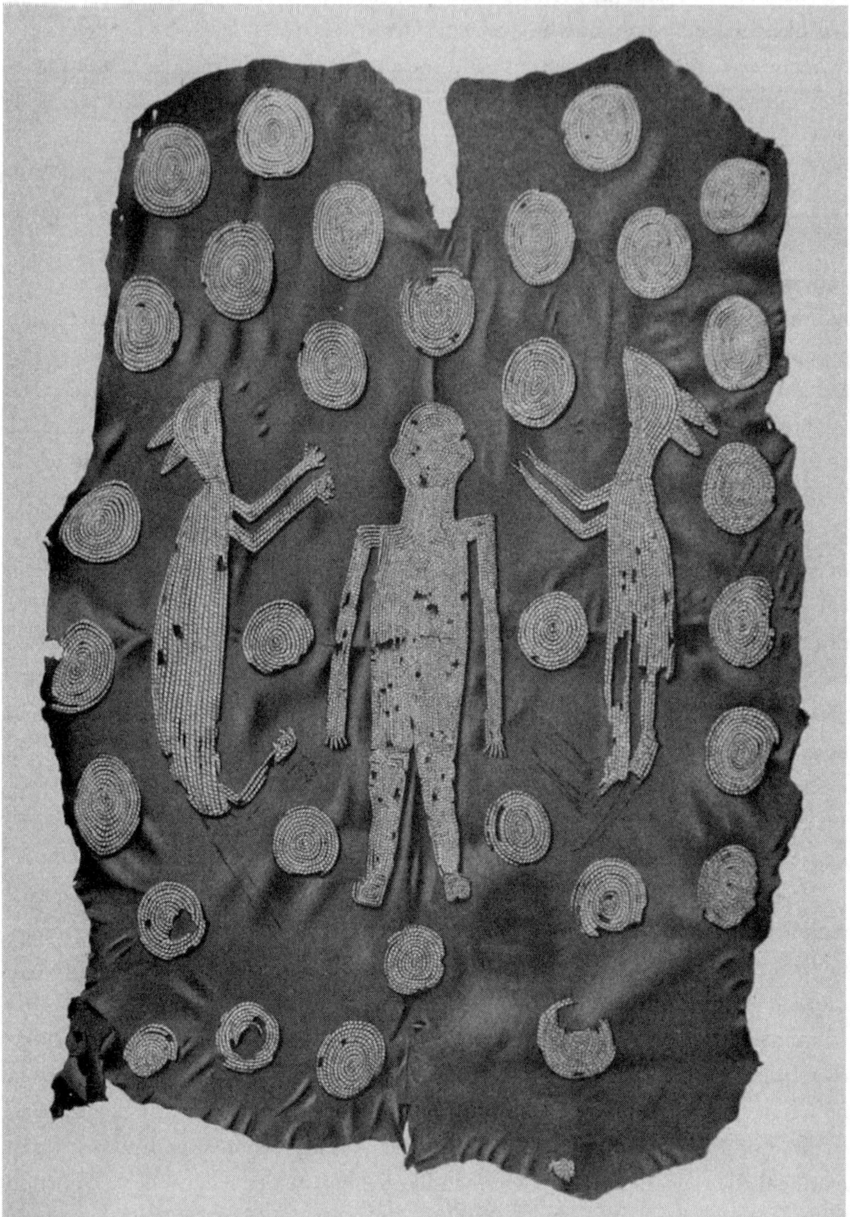

FIGURE 4.1. Powhatan's mantle (by E. T. Shelton, photograph, ca. 1888; P. W. M. Trap; lithography, ca. 1888; public domain via Wikimedia Commons).

a wall hanging rather than a cloak-like vestment, adorning the interior of a *quioccasin*, or temple accessible only to priests and chiefs. The discussion of its function, however, fails to recognize its historical biography, one that may have included it as an object transferred between individuals and groups, displayed at public ceremonies, worn routinely, or hidden from general display and cherished as an "inalienable object" that rarely changed hands (Weiner 1992).

The imagery depicted on Powhatan's mantle presented the past and present as a unified whole. The feline (a cougar or other large cat) and the deer may have represented the coming together of two clans and the birth of the political alliance that Wahunsenacawh inherited sometime during the 16th century (Gallivan, 2016). John Smith describes similar figures—a bear, a dragon, a leopard, and a "giant-like man" depicted in each of the four corners of a temple outside of Orapakes, a remote settlement in the swamps surrounding the Chickahominy River, that housed "[t]reasure . . . skinnes, copper, pearle and beades" (Smith 1986b:173–174). Bundles that visually referenced clan affiliations may actually have been inhabited by the souls of ancestors, materializing the immaterial as a means of socializing foreign objects, accessing and controlling manitou, and legitimizing Powhatan political authority. In contrast, the 34 roundlets (or elliptical figures) depicted on the mantle may portray the contemporary 17th-century political landscape (Turner 1976:133–134), indexing the discrete societies subject to Wahunsenacawh's authority. Such an interpretation is validated in the words of colonist William Strachey, who wrote in 1612 that Wahunsenacawh's "petty Weroances in all, may be in number, about three and fower and thirty, all which have their precincts, and bowndes, proper" (1953:63). Elliptical shapes are repeated throughout the coastal Algonquian world in the architectural layout of palisades, ditches, or dirt tracks associated with rites of passage ceremonies, the footprints of houses, and cut copper pendants and shell gorgets (Atkins et al. 2010). Ellipses linked powerful people and places—themselves possessing well-established historical biographies—with the bodies, materials, and practices of everyday life.

Like the *Marginella* shells that adorn Powhatan's mantle, objects introduced into the region by Europeans exhibited sensuous qualities not unlike those embodied by foreign objects that had circulated throughout the region centuries before the first English ships sailed into the Chesapeake Bay. These objects fit well into an indigenous semiotic framework that structured a political and cosmological world that already relied on the constant flow of nonlocal objects. The small amounts of sheet copper, kettles, and metal tools gifted to Wahunsenacawh and some of the lesser chiefs in the first months following the establishment of the Jamestown colony mirrored Algonquian means of establishing relations between sovereign polities. In January 1608 a number of resupply ships entered the Chesapeake Bay. Of the sailors on these ships, John Smith writes, "We gave them liberty to truck or trade at their pleasures.

But in short time, it followed, that could not be had for a pound of copper, which could before was sold for an ounce. Thus ambition, and sufferance, cut the throat of our trade" (1986c:215). Unrestricted access to copper—and thus manitou—likely appealed to Powhatan consumers in part because the Englishmen existed outside of the indigenous political order and had more modest and immediate expectations of reciprocity. Later in the year, when the English sought to exchange copper for maize, Wahunsenacawh told them that he valued a basket of corn more precious than a basket of copper, as he could eat the corn but not the metal (Smith 1986a:194).

The material foundation of indigenous authority had been threatened. Seeing this process unfold, Wahunsenacawh attempted to redefine the bounds of Powhatan sovereignty by conducting a ceremony aimed at "indigenizing" John Smith—an effort to reroute English goods by incorporating the English into the tributary economy that he controlled. He ordered a mixed group of Powhatan men to take John Smith captive, moving him from village to village for a month along the outskirts of Powhatania. While Smith was at the village of Pamunkey, a group of priests enacted a ceremony centered on a material rendering of the Powhatan world. Around a fire the priests laid down ground corn in a circle and then whole corn kernels, followed by sticks and finally more whole corn kernels. According to Smith, "The circle of meal signified their country, the circles of corn the bounds of the sea," and the sticks represented the English homeland (1986a:149–150). Although Smith interpreted the event as a "divination" ceremony, it is more likely that the creation of a diagram of Tsenacommacah (the Powhatan homeland) was not merely a static representation of their world but instead actively affected the universe, redefining the relationship between the Powhatan and English (Gallivan 2007:94; Gleach 1997). The Powhatan themselves were represented by ground corn, culturally processed and materially distinct from the sticks (or the English), which existed completely outside of the system. However, the sea—materialized by unprocessed corn—bounded both worlds, actively bridging the gap between the two realms (Gleach 1997:115). The ritual brought the English into the Powhatan world, allowing Wahunsenacawh to redefine the bounds of English sovereignty—a point made clear the next year when he announced that Smith was now his son and the colonists were no longer Tassentasses (strangers) or Paspaheghs (the people who lived in the territory surrounding Jamestown) but "Powhatans" (Smith 1986d:67).

CONCLUSION

During the decade following the founding of Jamestown colony, the processes surrounding the importation, socialization, and redistribution of copper within the

Algonquian southeast went through significant transformation. The illicit and unregulated importation of British scrap copper weakened its association with manitou and forever altered the political landscape (Hantman 1990; Mallios and Emmett 2004; Potter 2006). Wahunsenacawh and his successors never fully regained control over the movement of preciosities throughout the region as sovereignty during the postcolonial era became increasingly fragmented—distributed among multiple, overlapping, informal, and localized authorities (Hansen and Stepputat 2006). Despite the importation of large quantities of glass beads into the region, archaeological evidence suggests that Algonquian demand for these objects had waned by the middle 17th century (Miller et al. 1983:143). Sites bearing evidence of shell bead production, however, prove to be more numerous during this period than in all previous centuries combined. There is even evidence that indigenous laborers at Jamestown were producing beads for use by the colonists (Kelso et al. 2012). Shell beads produced in the 17th century were indistinguishable from those produced five hundred years or so earlier and, for a short time, became the medium of intercultural exchange and the battleground for conflicting "regimes of value" (see Cipolla, introduction).

Precolonial Powhatan sovereignty existed within a materiality that centered on control of the body through the circulation of a set of materials that both animated and mediated relationships of authority and subjection. Shell and copper ornamentation allowed for the harnessing of manitou—and a redirecting of its potencies to bolster political legitimacy and maintain balance in the world. The materiality of coastal Algonquian sovereignty remained intact, though, for only a brief period during the early colonial era. As the colonial period progressed, coastal Algonquian sovereignty was increasingly shaped by strategies aimed at dealing with direct and indirect threats to the multitiered political structures that had developed over the previous several hundred years. Although copper and shell continued to play a significant role in political reproduction, a new desire for swords and guns by Powhatan consumers underscored the desperation of authorities (at all political scales) to protect their communities and to maintain their territories. Beyond that, guns provided a reliable means for Native people to engage in an increasingly global world market that valued fur and indigenous knowledge to lead Europeans on hunting and fishing expeditions. It was illegal for a Native person to own or operate a firearm during the colonial period (and really up until the last century). Nonetheless, court records citing Native people for such offenses alongside evidence of guns and bullets at numerous indigenous sites throughout the region suggest that Native consumers continued to acquire "foreign" goods, creating new—and sometimes illicit—markets that undermined the increasingly tight grip of European authority.

5

CHRISTIAN SYMBOLS IN NATIVE LIVES

Medals and Crucifixes in the Tunica Region of French Colonial Louisiana

DIANA DiPAOLO LOREN

IN THIS CHAPTER I explore the concept of ambivalent consumption. I focus on how concerns of body and soul were consumed, embodied, materialized, and ministered in the lives and fashions of Tunica peoples living in 18th-century French Louisiana, particularly through their use of Catholic items. Unlike other items requisitioned for trade with Native Americans, Catholic items (including crucifixes, rosaries, and religious medals) were rarely produced in bulk and were passed to Native Americans through the hands of Jesuit priests as material icons of religious conversion. While not traditionally considered an object of commodity within historical archaeology, Catholic items were meant to be consumed by colonial peoples, embedded in the social and material relationships to be recontextualized and differentially valued (Dietler 2010; Thomas 1991). Archaeological interpretations of religious items on historical sites suggest the variety of ways in which these items were part of the lived experiences of Native Americans as symbols of conversion, resistance, or colonial mimicry (Bhabha 1994; Crossland 2010; Loren 2013a). In this particular colonial context, I put forward that ambivalence, rather than adoption or subversion, is a more appropriate framework for considering this class of artifacts (see Cobb and Sapp 2015). Here, I consider Catholic artifacts from the perspective of ambivalence to consider the nuances of their use and meaning in the Tunica community. In this part of the colonial world, where Tunica people lived alongside Jesuit priests, French settlers, and enslaved Africans, how were religious items incorporated into the dress of Tunica peoples? How was the sacred consumed, and was it materialized or socialized as such?

In this process, ambivalence emerges as a central concern in understanding how "foreign" or European-manufactured material culture made its way into the hands and lives of colonial indigenous peoples. The concept of ambivalence highlights the discursive process of how imperial imaginings intersected with lived experience, the slippages that occurred in colonial categories, and the ways in which colonial peoples structured their world under colonial rule.

COLONIAL LOUISIANA NORTH OF NEW ORLEANS

The French colony of Louisiana was incorporated at the end of the 17th century after several decades of exploration in the Lower Mississippi Valley. When the first permanent settlement at Biloxi was established in 1699, numerous Native American communities had long occupied the Lower Mississippi Valley. By 1720 many households, posts, and concessions (plantations) had been established along the Mississippi River beside Native American communities. The French developed tribal alliances to build a trade network, primarily for fur and salt (Brain 1988; Usner 1992). Enslaved Africans were brought to Louisiana beginning in the 1720s to work on the growing number of French indigo and tobacco concessions (Usner 1992). French émigrés to Louisiana included French noblemen (who were often officials), Jesuit priests, soldiers from a variety of backgrounds, middle-class craftsmen, lower-class laborers and servants (both male and female), freed prisoners (again both male and female), and some elite women (Usner 1992).

The principal Tunica village, Grand Tonicas (also known as the Trudeau site), and satellite villages, known as Petits Tonicas, were located east of the Mississippi River near the mouth of the Yazoo River in present-day Mississippi. A French mission was established during the early part of the 18th century along with a small French settlement and the temporary fort of Lubois (Brain 1988:297–299). By 1726 fewer than 100 French settlers and soldiers lived in the area, and no enslaved Africans were accounted for in the local population census (Usner 1992:48). Army officer Jean-François-Benjamin Dumont de Montigny mapped the community in 1744, detailing the layout of Grand Tonicas, including the temple and the location of the nearby French community (Figure 5.1). Jesuit father Antoine Davion was assigned as the missionary for the Tunica, as well as for neighboring Koroa and Yazoo tribes. Davion was also responsible for ministering to the French population (Brain 1988:297–298). Historical accounts indicate that the Tunica allied with the French in several wars against other neighboring Native Americans, notably the Natchez Revolt in 1729. In June 1731 Tunica

FIGURE 5.1. Jean-François-Benjamin Dumont de Montigny, *Plan du village des Tonicas et fort des Natchez.* From *Poème en vers touchant l'établissement de la province de la Louisiane,* 1744. Courtesy of Bibliothèque Nationale de France.

chief Cahura-Joligo was killed along with numerous other Tunica in a conflict with the Natchez. Shortly following this event, the Tunica moved just a few kilometers south along the east bank of the Mississippi, a location known archaeologically as the Trudeau site. By the beginning of the 19th century, the Tunica had moved again, to Marksville Prairie on the Red River in Louisiana. Today, the Tunica-Biloxi Indian Reservation is located in Marksville, Louisiana.

CONSUMPTION AND MATERIALITY IN COLONIAL LOUISIANA

Contemporary archaeological studies of consumption—studies that approach it as more than just capitalist consumerism—illuminate the opportunities colonial peoples had for shaping identity, meaning, and materiality within New World colonies. Michael Dietler (2010), Paul Mullins (2011b), and Stephen Silliman and Thomas Witt (2010) are some of the recent scholars who highlight material aspects of colonial entanglements and interrogate the ways in which people "socialize" foreign objects. Moving well beyond the assumption that all imported items are desirable and valuable to indigenous peoples (a concept most closely tied to mid-20th-century assimilation models), recent approaches consider degrees and varieties of availability, taste, and use that varied in each local colonial context while highlighting power relationships (Cobb and Sapp 2015; Cipolla 2013a, this volume; Dietler 2010; Ferris 2009; Gosden 2004; Harrison 2004; Jordan 2008, 2015; Loren 2010a, 2015; Mann 2015; Mullins 2011b; Rubertone 2000; Silliman and Witt 2010; Stahl 2010; Voss 2010). These contemporary works remind us of the limits of World Systems Theory in investigating ascribed uses of "foreign" material culture in colonial communities located at some distance from the imperial core (Dietler 1998). Current perspectives on consumption illustrate the uniqueness inherent in colonial communities rather than scripting those communities as naive consumers of the foreign and strange for the purposes of displays of power and wealth. Following Arjun Appadurai (1986:15), the social value of material culture "lies at the complex intersection of temporal, cultural and social factors," all of which are distinct within each colonial context. A simplified definition of colonized and colonizer belies the complexity of the colonial world (Beaudoin, this volume). Consumption of foreign goods in each colonial context was an active process of creative appropriation and manipulation played out by individuals and social groups with a variety of competing interests and strategies of action (Dietler 1998, 2010; Loren 2010a; Gosden 2004; Mullins 2011b; Rubertone 2000; Silliman and Witt 2010; Thomas 1991; Voss 2010).

Materiality was essential in colonial consumption. Objects materialized cultural order, inculcated identity, and enabled people to locate others in their social world (Bourdieu 1984). Strange objects were used with familiar ones to create new meaning, to support and revitalize existing practices, identities, and structures, as well as create new ones (Crossland 2010; Crossley 2001; Gosden 2005; Ingold 2007; Thomas 1991; see also Shephard and Gallivan, this volume; Howey, this volume).

The lived experiences of colonial subjects reveal the ruptures and limitations of colonial boundaries of inclusion and exclusion, implicating colonial concerns regarding mimicry and mockery. In its broadest definition, mimicry is the desire for the colonized to adopt (either forcefully or intentionally) the colonizer's material and cultural habits and values. Building on Jacques Lacan's discussion of mimicry as camouflage (referring to the natural world), Homi Bhabha (1994) describes mimicry as discourse that (in almost the same way but not quite) is generated out of ambivalence but is potentially subversive. When colonial discourse encourages the colonial subject to "mimic" the colonizer, the result is never a simple reproduction of those traits but a blurred copy of the colonizer. Mimicry is at once resemblance and menace. The desire for the colonized to imitate the colonizer also erodes and mocks colonial authority as it continually suggests differences in social and material colonial identities (Bhabha 1994:123).

Bhabha's articulation of mimicry also highlights the ambivalence present in these colonial negotiations between imperial policies and lived experience. He notes that "the discourse of mimicry is constructed around an ambivalence" (Bhabha 1994:86), perhaps threatening to the colonizer but created in the negotiation of colonial boundaries that often only existed in communities as abstract concepts. Imperial concerns of shaping, defining, and maintaining colonial boundaries were meant to distinguish not only colonized from colonizer, but also status, gender, and race among and between different groups (Casella and Voss 2012; Dietler 2010; Lightfoot 2005; Lightfoot and Martinez 1995; Loren 2008; Stoler 1989). This is a more complicated system of boundaries than just the binary distinction that has been commonly used in studies of the colonial world. As Dietler notes, "The boundaries in such processes are always subject to definition within specific contexts and they are always an evolving relational phenomenon" (2010:66). While the colonizer often saw such boundaries as clear, fixed, and distinct, these boundaries were also rapidly changing, being shaped and blurred by social relations in the everyday lived experiences of colonialism (e.g., Ferris et al. 2015; Jordan 2015; Stoler 1989; Stoler and Cooper 1997; Voss 2008). I agree with Jordan that these structural categories are useful "as an entry point for analysis" (2015:110), a way to understand the imperial vision of New World colonies and as a foil by which to understand lived colonialisms in particular historical contexts. Moreover, manipulation of these structural categories by colonial individuals in everyday life implicates ambivalence: how daily practices diverged from imperial visions, the limits of colonial rule, and how colonial individuals fashioned and constituted "self" with material culture.

As Craig Cipolla (introduction, this volume) discusses, colonial consumption was not just about consumer choice or (at times) conscious resistance of foreign goods and ideologies and embodied categories of taste. It was also about availability (see Dietler 2010; Silliman and Witt 2010; Panich, this volume). Within the categories of "trade items" made available for political and social interactions between French and Native American communities in the New World, Catholic items—crucifixes, rosaries, devotional medals—were rarely produced for broad trade but were meant as personal and intimate symbols of devotion and conversion. Historical accounts do not indicate that these were often-requested items, unlike glass beads, wool cloth, and ready-made clothing. Rather, the consumption and use of Catholic items spoke to more personal connections, passed from individual to individual in certain religious and social settings. Not surprisingly, these items are rarely encountered at historical sites in French colonies. Their location in colonial contexts suggests a range of uses far beyond their intended function, however, highlighting diversity of lived colonialism and hinting at colonial ambivalence (see Cipolla's discussion of fetish in the introduction to this volume).

I focus on the body as a place of colonial consumption of religion and religious items. The body was always the site of colonial power. Social hierarchies brought to the New World from the Old were inscribed with early modern notions of race and embodiment, leading to the assertion that any body had the capacity (or not) to be civilized through engagement of the mind and soul (Lindman and Tarter 2001; White 2013). Clothing was a boundary marker: sumptuary laws created by colonial officials mandated certain fashions for colonized and colonizer. In French Louisiana sumptuary laws dictated the attire of noblemen, servants, soldiers, and Jesuit priests while at the same time policing the clothing of Native American and African peoples (Roche 1994:6; White 2003). While the imperial vision of dress visualized colonial schemes of inclusion and exclusion, these boundaries were made fluid by colonial peoples, who often manipulated clothing and adornment to afford social movement (White 2013; see also Panich, this volume). Herein lies an important distinction with regard to imperial boundaries in practice: while dress and adornment were intended to indicate social differences, the population of colonial Louisiana was to be mostly Catholic. Indigenous peoples were to be converted, and efforts were put in place to maintain the faith among the existing Catholic population.

In the 18th-century European world, physical health of the body and soul was as important as dress (Finch 2010:1). Spiritual salvation and physical health were closely connected at the time. Imperial control of indigenous peoples in colonial Louisiana followed a model found in other Catholic colonies: the conversion of Native Americans. The 1724 Louisiana Code Noir, which dictated the behavior of French settlers and Africans in the colony, stated simply that "la Religion Catholique Apostolique & Romaine" was the official religion of Louisiana and that public exercise of any religion other than Roman Catholicism was prohibited (Van Ruymbeke 2005:89). Catholicism was seen as the "true" religion. Any deviation from this in the colony—be it a Native American or a Protestant religion—was viewed as a threat to the colony (Van Ruymbeke 2005:87; White 2013). Catholicism was then visibly manifested in dress (covering naked flesh), adornment (wearing religious medals, crosses, and crucifixes), speech, sexual activities, and comportment (Finch 2010:1).

The colonization of indigenous peoples in colonial Louisiana followed a model found in other Catholic colonies: conversion of Native Americans would enable Europeans to better control the bodies of the colonized. Successful conversion was predicated on healthy bodies and souls. Jesuit priests were charged with tending not only to the spiritual needs of their converted community but also to their medical needs based on the Jesuits' knowledge of the "physick." In the 18th century, knowledge of the body and health was derived from Galenic humoral theory, predicated on the knowledge that the body was composed of four humors: black bile, yellow bile, phlegm, and blood. When the humors were balanced, the body was healthy. Imbalance of the humors, caused by improper diet, thought, or action (sin), resulted in illness. Balance could be restored through ministrations to the physical body and spiritual soul through prayers, bloodletting, and compounds ingested internally and applied externally (Shyrock 1960). Members of the Jesuit orders ministered people in remote regions where access to doctors and surgeons was rare or nonexistent (Stange 2012). In 18th-century Louisiana, most individuals living outside New Orleans (where *the médecin du roi, chiurgien major*, royal hospital, and royal apothecary were located) compounded medicines and dosed themselves or sought treatment through priests, who used a combination of scientific knowledge, botanical ingredients, and prayer (Barnes and Sered 2004; Stange 2012).

French authors in the Lower Mississippi Valley had their own perspectives of Native American religious and healing practices. These perspectives were largely influenced by their own experiences as Catholics and their knowledge of healing according to beliefs about the body and humoral theory. French colonial narratives suggest, however, that religious and healing practice in Lower Mississippi Valley Native American communities were tied to competing forces of good and evil; in turn, these were regulated by balancing forces from Upper World and Underworld through reciprocal gifting (Carson 2005). As James Carson (2005:66–69) suggests, French colonizers were seen as a source of woe because of the imbalance they caused between worlds with the introduction of new materials and diseases. Maintenance of balance, including practices of healing through application and ingestion of herbals, as well as songs and ceremonies, was of long standing in Tunica communities and was often carried out by healers or shamans (Swanton 1911:177–180). Rituals intended to aid individuals, such as those carried out to cure illness and commemorate death, also took place under the supervision of shamans.

Historical accounts of the Tunica in the 18th century provide little information on their specific practices of well-being and health. Jesuit father Jacques Gravier noted in 1700 that the Tunica were "so close-mouthed as to the mysteries of their religion that the missionary [Davion] could not discover anything about it" (Shea 1861:134). Father Davion and other visiting missionaries did not record how the Tunica treated the ill, although Davion did note that the temple located in the center of the community (and depicted in Figure 5.1) was not often used (Swanton 1911:318). However, French authors did note several medical practices and beliefs among other groups in colonial Louisiana (including the Natchez) that provide some insights into indigenous knowledge and ontologies of the body. Notably, both Dumont de Montigny (2012:346) and Antoine S. Le Page du Pratz (1975:215, 226–239) describe practices of bloodletting needed for extracting evil spirits from the body along with the use of cypress, Spanish moss, sweet gum, and other herbal compounds (known to the French as "simples") to counteract swelling, infections, and fevers (see also Stange 2012). Numerous French settlers were so impressed with indigenous "knowledge of simples" that they often sought relief from Native American healers or enslaved Africans rather than traveling to New Orleans to receive treatment (Galloway 1998; Stange 2012:137; Swanton 1911:82–84).

Father Davion ministered to the spiritual and physical needs of the French and Tunica community for nearly two decades during the 18th century (Swanton 1911). His time in the Tunica region was captured in Jesuit accounts, which (unsurprisingly) lauded Davion for his undying efforts in Native conversion. Just one of a handful of Jesuits living in Louisiana, Davion baptized numerous Tunica just before they died of smallpox and other diseases (Swanton 1911:308–309). The practice of baptizing the dying is well documented in historical accounts as early as the late 17th century, when French missionaries were just beginning to explore the Lower Mississippi Valley. For example, in 1698 Father de Motigny noted that "we have not made any great conversion, nevertheless we have the consolation of having baptized several dying children and a very distinguished chief of the Tonicas [*sic*], women we instructed by interpreters. We were surprised to see such a judgment in an Indian and dispositions as Christian as he had. As he was in extremis we baptized him and gave him the name of Paul. He died the next day, after performing acts of religion that greatly edified us" (quoted in Swanton 1911:307–308).

While baptism was common for the dying, Father Davion wrote of his failures in indigenous conversion outside periods of disease (Swanton 1911:309–312). One night, in a fit of frustration, Davion set the central Tunica temple ablaze but was not punished for his act (Stange 2012; Swanton 1911). Other Jesuits and colonial officials described Tunica reactions to Davion's extremist act as distinctly ambivalent. According to Jesuit accounts, the Tunica did not punish Davion for the destruction of the temple, where they performed healing and other religious ceremonies, nor did they rebuild the temple (Stange 2012; Swanton 1911). Rather, they enacted ceremonies without their temple, and Davion remained a member of their community, continuing to proselytize while ministering to the sick and dying alongside Tunica healers. In one Jesuit account, a Tunica chief's son died after being cared for by both a Tunica healer and Father Davion, who baptized the boy at death (Swanton 1911:326). The grief expressed by the Tunica chief over the loss of his son is palpable in this historical account, as he sought any means by which to cure or comfort his dying son. With this historical narrative of ambivalence in mind, I want to turn briefly to the archaeological record.

MATERIALITY

During the 18th century, Catholic missionaries distributed crucifixes and other religious paraphernalia among Native American populations to allow individuals to visually signify conversion through adornment. Historical accounts, namely, *The Jesuit Relations* (Thwaites 1896–1901), indicate that religious artifacts were an integral aspect of Jesuit activities and were used to facilitate conversion through consumption of physical property (see also Mason 2003). Devotional items, often worn as necklaces or attached to clothing, were intended as tangible reminders of faith and religious duty. Distinguished from "trade goods," these items were meant as gifts from Catholic missionaries and priests to the unconverted. When worn, did these items symbolize alliance, a conversion to Christianity, or did they become part of the individual's wardrobe in a way that was ambivalent to religious concerns? Each of these devotional items had a specific function in devotional practice. Rosaries were meant to guide pious exercises of prayer and meditation (Deagan 2002:58). Crucifixes—bearing an image of Christ's body—and crosses had different intended uses for 18th-century Catholics. Crucifixes were used in ceremonies surrounding baptism and death, while crosses (both plain and decorated) were often used as items of jewelry (Deagan 2002:54).

While Jesuit rings are often considered a devotional item, these objects came in bulk lots for trade with indigenous peoples as a "trade good" or, perhaps better phrased, as an item to facilitate alliances and diplomacy. Often sized for children, these rings were intended to be worn as jewelry rather than as a devotional item (Mason 2003). For example, hundreds of Jesuit rings have been recovered from the

La Belle shipwreck site (Bruseth and Turner 2004:107). The *La Belle* was one of the ships in the expedition of René-Robert Cavelier, *sieur* de La Salle, and it carried people and items necessary for establishing a small colony at the mouth of the Mississippi. The *La Belle* sank in the Gulf of Mexico in 1684 prior to reaching its destination and was later excavated in 1995 (Bruseth and Turner 2004). Along with the Jesuit rings, numerous other "trade goods" were excavated at the site, including more than a million glass beads and hundreds of hawk bells. Despite the richness of this assemblage, it only included one crucifix.

When religious ornaments are recovered from colonial period Native American sites, they are commonly interpreted as evidence of missionary activity. Religious objects are often rare in New World colonial contexts, and we archaeologists often fetishize these items because of their uniqueness. Yet the context in which a Christian symbol was worn is crucial; depending on space, community, and placement on the body, it may have simultaneously spoken to other issues such as ethnicity, status, and gender (see Howey, this volume). Crucifixes and religious medals held certain meanings for baptized individuals, but these same items took on new meanings when Native Americans combined them with other objects to purposefully and publicly negotiate self in colonial contexts. And I would argue that ambivalence, rather than conversion, mimicry, or resistance, was an aspect of some of these negotiations of clothing and adornment.

Colonial illustrations provide some insight into how French officials viewed indigenous dress. French military engineer and lieutenant Alexandre de Batz drafted, designed, and illustrated several dozen buildings, plantations, and communities in French Louisiana for the French Crown. De Batz's documentation of the colony also included four watercolors of Native Americans and Africans living in the Lower Mississippi Valley (Loren 2013b). De Batz created an archive of material and corporeal difference through the depiction of clothing, gesture, stance, and tattoos. In the fourth watercolor, *Sauvage matachez en guerrier* (Savage painted as warrior), de Batz illustrated Tunica chief Bride les Boeufs wearing a breechcloth, knife, and powder horn while holding a staff with scalps (Figure 5.2). To his right stand the wife and son of a deceased Tunica chief. The boy, Jacob, is unclothed, while the woman wears a skirt most likely woven of mulberry fibers. In each of these watercolors, de Batz depicted Native Americans and Africans wearing loose and unstructured clothing. Only a few objects of European manufacture—the shirt, knife, and pipe—are illustrated. The majority of the items are of Native American manufacture, and mixed fashions are not present. Both de Batz and his imperial audience would have perceived essential, uncreolized Native American identities through these images, easily distinguished from French colonists, priests, and officials who, in theory, wore ready-made and fitted clothing. This tied into ideological views drawing a sharp division between

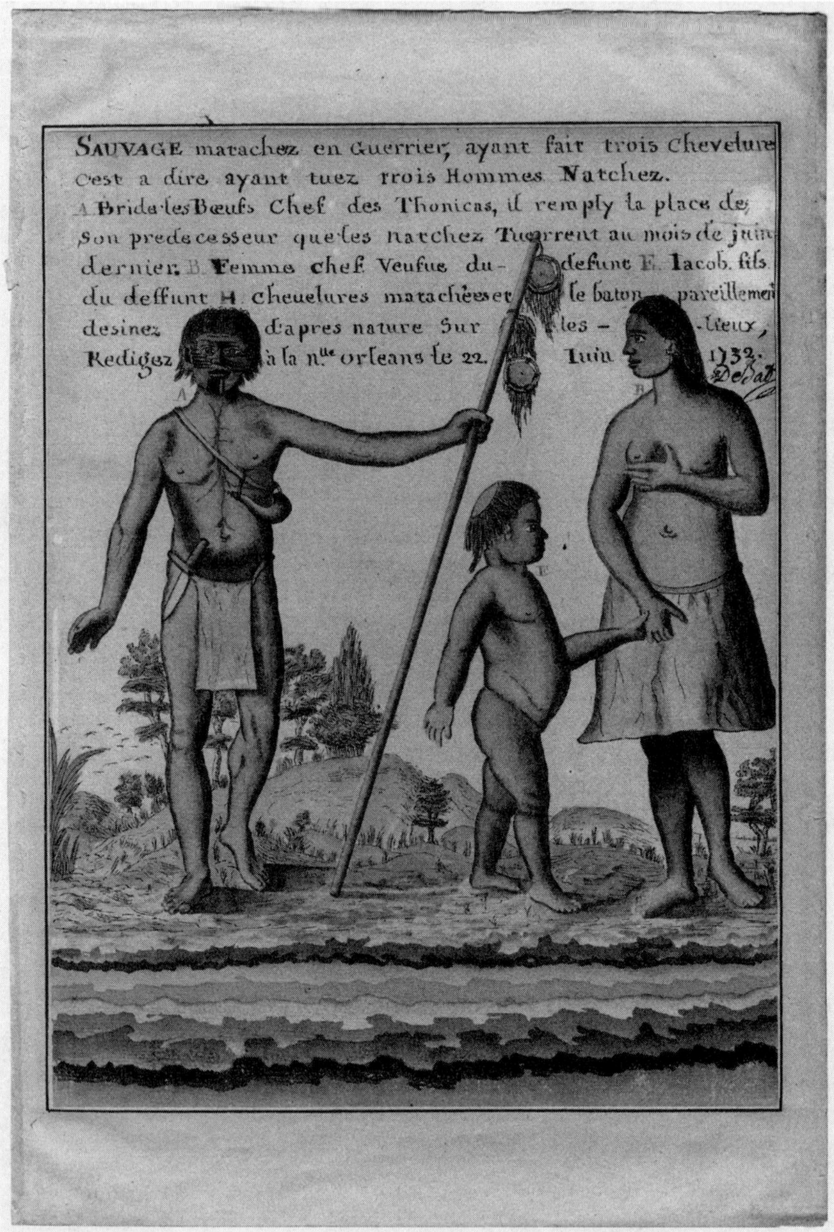

FIGURE 5.2. Alexandre de Batz, *Sauvage matachez en guerrier* (Savage painted as warrior), ca. 1732. Gift of the Estate of Belle J. Bushnell. Courtesy the Peabody Museum of Archaeology and Ethnology, Harvard University, PM #41-72-10/18 (digital file #990020018).

complex, even sophisticated, Europeans from uncovered indigenous peoples living close to what the French conceived of as a "state of nature" (Sayre 1997:145–179; see also White 2013).

In contrast, written accounts suggest a more complicated intersection of material and corporeal. Colonial laws prohibited interethnic marriage and sexual relations in order to enforce boundaries of exclusion. But slippages of boundaries occurred. For example, in December 1721 Father Charlevoix described his meeting with Tunica chief Cahura-Joligo: "The chief received us very politely; he was dressed in the French fashion, and seemed to be not at all uneasy in that habit" (Swanton 1911:312). In 1730 Jesuit missionary Mathurin Le Petit (1730:165–167) noted that among the captives spared in the wake of the Natchez Rebellion were a tailor and several French women because they knew how to sew coats, shirts, and dresses. Archaeological collections also provide a different perspective to that of de Batz.

Colonial period material recovered from the Tunica region was published in two volumes: *Tunica Treasure* (Brain 1979) and *Tunica Archaeology* (Brain 1988). *Tunica Treasure* highlights the artifacts recovered from the Trudeau site by an avocational archaeologist in the late 1960s. The collections then came to Harvard for analysis in the 1970s. Through conversations with the collector and other interested parties, it was revealed that the collections were recovered illegally from private land (see Brain 1979); thus, they lack specific provenience information, although they were likely removed from burial contexts. Following a drawn-out litigious battle, the material that was removed from the Trudeau site was eventually returned to the Tunica-Biloxi Tribe of Louisiana in the late 1970s. The collections are now on view at the Tunica-Biloxi Indian Museum in Marksville, Louisiana.

For the Lower Mississippi Survey (LMS) of the Peabody Museum, Harvard University conducted an archaeological survey of the Tunica region through the late 1970s and 1980s, culminating in the publication of *Tunica Archaeology* (Brain 1988). This volume details archaeological excavations conducted at the Trudeau site, as well as at some of the smaller villages, including those known archaeologically as the Bloodhound and the Haynes Bluff sites. Funerary and domestic contexts were excavated at both of these sites. Funerary objects were repatriated to the Tunica-Biloxi Tribe of Louisiana under NAGPRA, while other nonfunerary collections are currently housed at the Peabody Museum of Archaeology and Ethnology at Harvard University. In the analysis that follows, I draw from Brain's published research on Tunica collections and from artifacts in the Peabody's collections.

Artifacts related to clothing and adornment recovered from Tunica sites (Trudeau, Bloodhound, and Haynes Bluff) include shell ear pins, brass and copper tinkler cones, Jesuit rings, religious medals, bear incisor pendants, one- and two-part coat buttons, brass bells, shoe and belt buckles, and thousands of glass beads (Figure 5.3;

FIGURE 5.3. Brass tinklers, brass pendant, and glass beads from Haynes Bluff. © President and Fellows of Harvard College, Peabody Museum of Archaeology and Ethnology, PM #977-26-10/100579, 977-26-10/100580, 977-26-10/100581, 977-26-10/95895, and 977-26-10/95892 (digital file #99320131).

Brain 1979, 1988). These and other items of clothing and adornment recovered from these sites suggest that the Tunica had a rich and varied wardrobe that was more complicated in practice than a simple, unbuttoned shirt and a necklace of shell beads, as depicted in the de Batz image (Loren 2013a). Large glass beads were most likely worn as necklaces and bracelets or were worn in the hair. The presence of shoe buckles suggests that at least some individuals in the community wore European-manufactured leather shoes. Brass tinkler cones and janglers were worn with brass bells (hung from ankles or waist) and religious and secular jewelry; shell ear pins, brass coils, and silver ear bobs dangled from the ears; coat and sleeve buttons indicate that ready-made coats and shirts were worn close to the body (Brain 1979, 1988). Tools used for making and mending clothing, such as needles, thimbles, scissors, and pins, were also part of these assemblages. The artifacts of clothing and adornment recovered from domestic and midden contexts suggest the mixing of different fashions in practice, while those recovered from burials suggest more purposeful combinations of different fashions. In funerary contexts at Trudeau, Haynes Bluff, and Bloodhound, several adult men and women were buried wearing combinations of European-manufactured clothing (including frock coats and trousers) and adornment (glass beads, brass finger rings, silver earrings), as well as indigenous-made clothing and adornment (shell ear pins and necklaces) (Brain 1988).

Within this varied assemblage of clothing and adornment artifacts there is only a small sample of crucifixes and religious medals. These include several crucifixes, a plain copper cross, three brass crosses with glass stone insets (Figure 5.4), a child's copper-alloy Jesuit ring, and a crucifix embedded in a shell necklace (Brain 1979, 1988). Most of these items were recovered from domestic and midden contexts. Only one funerary context—that of a small boy—included a crucifix, which had been embedded within a shell necklace. Otherwise, religious items were not included in funerary contexts. These diverse locations outside of funerary contexts further suggest

FIGURE 5.4. Brass crucifix with inset blue glass stones from the Trudeau site. Published in Brain (1979:191). © President and Fellows of Harvard College, Peabody Museum of Archaeology and Ethnology, PM #2011.0.26.2 (digital file #99320018).

the ambivalence with which religious items were activated in the daily life of Tunica peoples. Catholic objects may have been part of the wardrobe for Tunica individuals, but these objects were well within the Tunica's own understandings and needs. The Tunica incorporated the familiar and the foreign in a nuanced way: as adornment that had the potential to shift from symbols of Catholic spirituality to simple objects worn on the body, depending on the context and need.

Yet the placement of the crucifix—hung from an elaborate white shell necklace in the burial of the small boy at the Bloodhound site—indicates further nuances in consumption and use, perhaps even Catholic intent through the hands of Father Davion as he sought to minister to the sick and dying. This particular context is reminiscent of the historical account of the chief's son who was cared for by both a Tunica healer and Father Davion. Shell beads were an important aspect of Tunica dress. They were often worn as necklaces and earrings and were woven into the hair. Shell beads continued to be manufactured and used long after the introduction of glass beads. Further, glass and shell beads were often worn together, signifying their continued importance for the Tunica. The attachment of the crucifix (the new) and the shell necklace (the familiar) suggests an act of spiritual care, a way to protect the body and soul of the dying boy through the conscious use of a foreign object, perhaps by the father seeking a way to care for his son as he moved from this world to the next. In this context, different material and social practices for body and soul, familiar and foreign, were intertwined, marking that particular act with ambivalence and grief.

CONCLUSIONS

In 1727 Jesuit missionary Paul du Poisson visited the Tunica chief to inform him of the death of Father Davion in France. Du Poisson noted that while the chief was interested in having another missionary to reside amongst the Tunica, the chief bore "no mark of being a Christian but the name, a medal, and a rosary" (1900:307). Another missionary was not assigned to the community after the departure of Davion, and soon after, in the wake of the Natchez Revolt and other antagonisms among the French settlers and Native Americans living in the colony, the Tunica moved farther south along the Mississippi.

The consumption and use of religious items in the 18th-century Tunica region does not seem to suggest colonial mimicry that tended toward subversion but rather acts of consumption that were marked by ambivalence (Bhabha 1994). Overall, archaeological contexts indicate that there was little distinction made by the Tunica in the consumption and use of religious items in their daily lives. These items were worn alongside other objects of adornment as part of Tunica fashion. But neither were these acts of adornment without meaning. Tunica individuals were well versed in the language of French clothing. For example, chiefs were described as wearing French fashion when meeting with French colonial officials (Loren 2010a, 2011). But at that time, consumption was marked by ambivalence. As suggested by the boy buried with a shell necklace and a brass crucifix, religious items meant to depict devotion and care for the ailing body were part of the language of clothing that Tunica peoples incorporated into their own fashions to care for self and other.

6

OUR STRANGE GARMENTS

Cloth and Clothing among Native Elites in 17th-Century New England

KATHLEEN J. BRAGDON

Like our strange garments, cleave not to their mold
But with the aid of use

WILLIAM SHAKESPEARE, MACBETH, ACT 1, SCENE 3

WILLIAM SHAKESPEARE'S INSIGHT concerning the "aid of use" in making new clothing familiar is the inspiration for this study of the consumption of trade cloth and clothing by Native elites as embodied practice in 17th-century New England. Recent work on dress using this perspective (Loren 2009, 2010a; Entwistle 2000:325) engages concepts linked to the phenomenological theories of Maurice Merleau-Ponty (1981), Thomas Csordas (1990, 1996), and Marcel Mauss (1973), among others, and has been applied usefully to archaeological research as well (Joyce 2005:142–143). Briefly, the phenomenological perspective begins with the body as the source and mediator of perception and seeks to challenge interpretations that rely on the Western conceptual divide between the ideal and the corporeal. Phenomenological approaches also draw our attention away from abstractions such as social structure toward relations among culturally constructed bodies, often manifest in intense concentration on bodily decoration, including tattooing, painting, and dress (Vilaça 2005:447). If consumption can be defined as "the way consumers negotiate, accept, and resist goods' dominant meanings within rich social, global, historical, and cultural contexts" (Mullins 2011b:133), the phenomenological perspective also allows us to see the acquisition and use of foreign-made materials such as cloth and clothing by Native Americans as creative, agentive, and culturally consistent with precolonial materiality and its bodily expression. As a significant minority of Native people in southern New England adopted Christianity in the 17th century, a focus on embodied practice also allows us to consider the contrasts between indigenous and Protestant Christian concepts of materiality. Arguing that "the body [is] simultaneously a physical and a symbolic artifact, . . . both naturally and culturally produced and . . . securely anchored in a historical moment" (Scheper-Hughes and Lock 1987:6), this chapter looks at how 17th-century elites among the historic Wampanoag, Narragansett, and Pequot—chiefly societies occupying what is now southeastern Massachusetts and coastal Rhode Island and Connecticut—engaged material objects through sociocultural practice. I suggest that the social dynamics of such periods of change were reproduced and transformed at the level of bodily practice, specifically through dress, including garments made of European cloth and ready-made cloth coats acquired by Native American elites through trade and gift. Such practices imbued these material forms with cultural value and concretized some southern New England indigenous ideas of "bodiliness." An attention to embodiment and bodiliness allows a "way in" to the dynamic lived experience of Native people in southern New England in the throes of great change.

A focus on embodiment directs our attention to the body as "mindful and relational" and puts the study of the uses made of the body and ideas about it in different societies on par with that of other aspects of cultural life (Csordas 1990:31ff.). Of particular interest in Amerindian ethnography and ethnohistory are the insights this approach provides to an understanding of bodiliness that incorporates a broader conception of personhood than is encompassed in modern Western thought. Irving Hallowell, a student of Ojibwa ontology, remarked, "While in all cultures, 'persons' constitute one of the major classes of objects to which the self must become oriented, this category is by no means limited to human beings" (1960:20). Like the Ojibwa, Native people of southern New England included within their notions of persons the possibility of transformation into other forms and of taking on the perspectives of nonhuman persons, including animals, clearly a distinctive process of "bodily objectification" that sees bodies as "chronically" unstable (Vilaça 2005:452). In many parts of the Americas, this changeable or "unstable" capacity was also impacted by social context, bodily ornamentation, and dress.

Some anthropological writings on embodiment suggest that dress is best understood as an "extension" of the body, a means through which social status may be read and by which social categories are reproduced (Hansen 2004; Entwistle 2000; see also Loren, this volume). Recent work on these topics addresses the active and relational dimensions of identity formation and the role of materiality in this process. Building upon these studies, I focus on mortuary remains and historical images of southern New England Native people clothed and/or in motion, seeking a more dynamic interpretation of the sociality of dress. This approach allows for new understandings of the "lived world" of those long dead (Lesure 2005). The important insights regarding the encultured nature of self-adornment, clothing choice, and other aspects of bodily appearance (Strathern 1979) also underline the complexity of the relationships between personhood and the social order. Marilyn Strathern (1979, 2009), in particular, challenges the universality of the notion of autonomous individuality, upon which much theorizing about clothing and other bodily ornamentation depends (Creese, this volume). This chapter pursues these arguments by a further consideration of the historicity and cultural specificity of the process of bodily objectification, with special focus on the highly fluid conditions of the mid- to late 17th century in southern New England from the point of view of its Native people and the transformative possibilities of clothing. Clothing and other "extensions" of Native elite bodies as we know them from contemporary accounts, public records, and archaeology offer a window into the use of trade items, not as acquisitions alone but as socially mediated signs. As Webb Keane argues, here we can challenge the false contrast between "global material forces" and "local meanings" (2003:409). In this region, traditional social relations seem to have been mediated through the exchange of objects, but these were not different in kind from the use of symbolic tokens such as formal speeches and other "media of circulation of social value" that were important in the region as well (Turner 1995:147). Thus, the clothing-extended bodies of elites, who engaged in and had prominent positions at important rituals, used clothing as "tools" for cultural work during a period of rapid social change. The adoption of imported cloth and clothing by leaders and its public display in significant cultural events allowed expression and interpretation, if not mitigation, of the deeply ambiguous experiences of the period of colonization. It was through this process, rather than through exchange alone, that cloth and clothing acquired their meaning and power within Native societies.

The adoption and subsequent role of cloth and ready-made clothing in Native New England have been interpreted in numerous ways. Some argue that the increasing scarcity of fur-bearing animals in the region led to a need for an appropriate clothing substitute (Thomas 1979).* The changing role of Native people within the colonial economy as day workers, sailors, and domestic servants also sometimes made the wearing of English-style clothing compulsory for Native people. Some scholars have identified Native use of English clothing as subversive or as part of the tactics of war (Lepore 1998; Little 2001). Native converts to Christianity were likewise required to dress in European clothing, a typical form of cultural intervention that was sometimes understood to reflect broader ideational changes (Comaroff and Comaroff 1997). Several scholars also note that a mixture of English and Native clothing elements was likely an ethnic marker as well (Welters 1993). Finally, the use of imported clothing has been interpreted as a status marker, particularly in the earliest period of

* Other studies have looked at the importance of trade cloth as a medium of exchange in the fur and deerskin trade in the Atlantic world and the links it provided between manufacturing hubs in Britain and Europe and the slave trade in Africa, the Caribbean, and the New World (Bailyn 1955). Still other research focuses on the detrimental effects of the fur trade on Native societies in New England and the problematics of the substitution of cloth for Native textiles and skin clothing as the supply of fur-bearing animals dwindled throughout the 17th century (Thomas 1979).

colonization (Brenner 1988). By the late 17th century, a combination of these factors appears to have "diluted" the semiotic significance of imported clothing, as the forces listed above came to be more significant and as Native sovereignty was undermined. Additionally, as the frontier moved west, trading protocol required that Native intermediaries always wear "trade coats" as a badge of office (Johnson 2009). But that European-made coats and other textiles (such as blankets) became features of a generalized "American" frontier dress (Baumgarten 2002:68) in the 18th century should not distract us from their different and culturally revealing role in the early period of colonization, when the outcome of conflict between Natives and newcomers had not yet been determined.

In its focus on how "strange" garments figured in the "work of culture" that was bodily practice among Native people of southern New England in the 17th century, however, the approach employed here differs from earlier studies of the consumption of imported cloth and clothing that understand them as one category among many kinds of trade goods (Dillon 1980; Johnson 2004), as data in the history of textiles (Baumgarten 1975), as cultural critique (Lepore 1998; Little 2001), as reflecting ethnicity (Welters 1993), or even as continuity of Native practices of dress (Becker 2005). Instead, this chapter looks at the complexity of the adoption of clothing and cloth, their "value" within Native society, and their role in the "work" of reproducing cultural forms while mediating transformation in the middle decades of the 17th century. Part of this work was incorporating new objects and substances, such as garments and cloth, while making them explicable in Native terms. For this, it is useful to recognize that Wampanoag ontology included a theory of "chronically unstable bodies" (Vilaça 2005), that is, the understanding that the body was changeable and nondelimited, and that other people, objects, and surroundings gave the body "shape." This "perspectivist" approach allows us to understand consumption of foreign or introduced material culture without relying on ideas of "mimicry" or "acculturation" but rather understanding it as culturally consistent and agentive. Further, southern New England Native ideas about personhood and health, associated with a broader and more inclusive definition of humanity, also assist in understanding the role of Native cloth and clothing consumption at the time.

SETTLEMENT, EPIDEMICS, AND THE FUR TRADE IN NEW ENGLAND

What is now southern New England was occupied by a number of linguistically related, Algonquian-speaking societies that, beginning at least in the 15th century, were increasingly in contact with European fishing expeditions, exploratory voyages,

FIGURE 6.1. Map of 17th-century New England. (By http://maps.bpl.org; A map of New England and New York; CC BY 2.0 [http://creativecommons.org/licenses/by/2.0], via Wikimedia Commons).

resource extraction, and settlement. Some of these societies, particularly those in coastal regions, were led by hereditary rulers and elite families, as were other chiefly polities in the Northeast. Among these rulers was the Pockanoket or Wampanoag leader Ousamequin, better known as Massasoit (meaning "grand sachem"), a long-time ally of the Pilgrims at Plymouth. The Wampanoag territories extended from the eastern shore of Narragansett Bay east to Cape Cod and north to the Blackstone River, and they included the islands of Martha's Vineyard and Nantucket (Figure 6.1; Bragdon 1996).

This territory, whose Native inhabitants were decimated by a plague introduced into the area in 1617, was subsequently settled by English Separatists at Plymouth in the 1620s, while the area just to its north was claimed and occupied by English Puritans ruling from Boston in the 1630s. To the west were the Narragansett and Pequot, powerful enemies to the Pokanoket (now known as Wampanoag), who had grown "rich" through the fur trade initiated by the Dutch in Narragansett Bay and along the Connecticut River (McBride 1994). These peoples were spared the devastation of the 1617 epidemic but were hard hit by the equally devastating introduced diseases of the early 1630s (Cook 1973; Spiess and Spiess 1987).

Between the late 1620s and the 1660s, the currency of the fur trade was shell beads known as wampum, principally manufactured in and near Narragansett Bay (Bradford 1892:282). It was the fur trade that brought imported cloth and clothing to the region as highly desirable goods that could be exchanged for furs and purchased with wampum (Ceci 1990). Wampum, cloth, and furs were central to the trade and brought wealth to chiefly families in the region who initially served as mediators and directors of trade. Wealth was crucial to the Native people of the region because of its ability to ensure and attract health and well-being for the individual and the community (Simmons 1976). Paradoxically, however, the trade also brought social conflict and disease, serious threats to the indigenous social and political bodies of the region (Starna 1992). As noted above, the introduction of Protestant Christianity to Natives of the region was another factor in the history of the adoption of cloth and clothing by the Native peoples of the region, as missionaries imposed their own ideas of proper dress on their converts, requiring many to adopt English-style (but modest) clothing (Cogley 1999:53). The centrality of cloth to this historically contingent nexus of Native practice, experience, and meaning in the mid-17th century can be further examined through a deeper analysis of Native notions of bodiliness.

Early reports describe the Native peoples of southern England as sparsely dressed. For example, Roger Williams found that both men and women wore only "little aprons" over their "privates" at home. While away from home, they wore mantles, which still struck Williams as leaving much of their persons "all open and naked" (1936[1643]:106). Even sachems and their families were informal in dress in their own homes (Winslow 1910[1624]). Public appearances of the elite (and of warriors), however, were often marked by bodily decoration (tattoos and paint); the use of copper and shell ornaments; and, during the mid-17th century, lavish use of wampum belts, necklaces, headbands, and bandoliers (Willoughby 1905).

In the 1630s Williams implied that imported clothing was evidently still a rarity in Native communities. In fact, Williams also noted that someone wearing clothing was marked by the distinctive term *wautacone*, and Europeans were sometimes referred to as Wautaconâuog, or "Coatmen" (1936[1643]:60). But Williams's association between nakedness with Indianness—as in many early European accounts—was also a recognizable literary trope (Little 2001). To the contrary, other evidence suggests that cloth and clothing were incorporated into Native practice within a decade of the arrival of English settlers in the region. The factors that influenced this change in bodily practice included the development of the fur trade and its subsequent political disruptions in Native societies, rituals of diplomacy, struggles for territory, and the devastation caused by European-introduced disease.

An example of how these factors were embodied and performed cultural work in Native practice comes from the biography of the Wampanoag leader Ousamequin and his son Metacom, or Philip. The earliest descriptions of gifts and payments to Ousamequin from the Pilgrims mention cloth and coats, the first apparently given to him within a year of the establishment of Plymouth in 1620/1621. *Mourt's Relation* records this gift of a red coat trimmed with lace and a gold chain: "Having put the coat on his back and a chain around his neck, he was not a little proud to behold himself, and his men also to see their king so bravely attired" (Heath 1963[1622]:65).*

During the remainder of his life (until ca. 1661), Ousamequin became increasingly insistent on gifts and payments of cloth and clothing in exchange for title to land and other resources. For example, in 1642 the Plymouth Colony court records noted that "John Hassell affirmeth that Ussamequine chose out X fathome of beads at Mr. Williams, and put them in a basket, and affirmed that he was fully satisfied therewith for his lands at Seacunck, but he stood upon it that he would have a coat more, & left the beads with Mr. Williams, & willed him to keepe them until Mr. Hubberd came up" (2:49, in Bangs 2002:251). Several years later, on March 28, 1649, another payment was made: "In consideration of [this] sale of land we . . . Miles Standish, Samuel Nash and Constant Southworth do bind ourselves to pay to . . . Woosamequin . . . 7 coats, a yard and a half in a cote, 9 hatchets, 8 hoes, 20 knives, 4 mooseskins, 16 yards and a half of cotton" (Plymouth Colony 1861, 2:157).

Ousamequin died in 1660 or 1661. After the brief ascension of Wamsutta (known to the English as Alexander), Ousamequin's first son, Metacom, or Philip, assumed the sachemship. The leader of the first organized rebellion against the English, Metacom is frequently described as wearing imported clothing along with elaborate belts, sashes, and headbands of wampum (Figure 6.2; Willoughby 1905:506, 508). He and his allies were also described as leading complex rituals designed to "make" Native soldiers in preparation for war (Church 1827[1716]:92–93). Ousamequin's and other Native leaders' interest in garments and cloth was often interpreted in light of the importance placed on gifts in Native diplomacy, something that British officials recognized and catered to until well into the 18th century (Wicken 1993). In addition, it is likely that Ousamequin and other Native leaders in turn distributed these "gifts" among their followers to reinforce their own authority.

However, it also appears that within the span of Ousamequin's life and that of his son Metacom, some kinds of clothing and cloth came to serve as "extensions" of the

* Although Ousamequin seems in his first encounter with the English to have been given a constructed garment, the term "coat" can also refer to a pieced cloth, often a yard and a half to two yards wide, worn as a cloak or mantle. This kind of garment, as Marshall Becker (2005) observes, represented a form of dress of great longevity that was iconic of Indianness until the 20th century.

FIGURE 6.2. Portrait of King Philip, or Metacom, from Samuel Gardener Drake (public domain, via Wikimedia Commons).

body that took their place alongside other signs of its social construction. They did so through their association with the social significance and political role of their wearers. Clothing indexed leaders' continuing importance as diplomats and directors of trade. At the same time, this garb reinforced and justified their hereditary status and the hierarchical structure of the society they led; their continued significance as the embodied capital of the community; and their health and wealth, which were crucial to those of the communities they represented and led. In their bodies and bodily practices, then, Ousamequin and Metacom were constructed by—and participated in—the transformations of the societies they represented during the middle decades of the 17th century.

Elites were not alone in their interest in and desire for cloth. Many sources document the widespread adoption of coats and mantles as trade items by indigenous peoples in southern New England. Mid-17th-century records of fur traders William and John Pynchon of Springfield, Massachusetts, demonstrate that cloth and ready-made clothing were exchanged for fur and that cloth constituted by far the largest category of trade goods in most traders' inventories (Bailyn 1955; Bridenbaugh 1985; Thomas 1979). Literally tons of cloth and clothing were imported into New England in the 17th and 18th centuries, and, at least at first, much of it came into Native hands. Nonelites also used wampum to pay for cloth and clothing and presumably engaged in a secondary exchange of cloth and clothing, using them in localized gift giving. It is also likely that the Connecticut Valley trade in cloth allowed Native people of the region to serve as middlemen to a trade with Native societies farther to the west during the middle decades of the 17th century. The ubiquitous presence of cloth, however, does not explain its meaning in Native communities nor help us understand how cloth and clothing figured in the changing experiences of Native people or how cloth and clothing came to impact bodily practice.

BODY AND PRACTICE IN NATIVE SOUTHERN NEW ENGLAND

The Native term for "body" in all southern New England languages was *muhhog* (Trumbull 1903:227), although Roger Williams recorded *nohòck* as "my body, myself" (1936[1643]:60). The term has both animate and inanimate-gendered forms. For example, *nuhhog*, "my body," is inanimate, while *wuhogkuh*, "himself," is animate (Goddard and Bragdon 1988:719). A term that linguist James Hammond Trumbull believed was related to the term for "body" was *hogko,o*, "he is clothed (or covered?) with" (1903:235). According to Williams (1936[1643]:60), the Wampanoag, the Narragansett, and their neighbors endowed certain parts of the body with importance, notably the head and hands, and often removed them from their enemies after battle. For example, the captive Mary Rowlandson saw one of Philip's allies wearing a necklace of finger bones (Willoughby 1905:506).

The modern conceptualization of the person as an autonomous individual is unlikely to have been the same for indigenous people of southern New England, whose attribution of animateness endowed "personal" qualities to features of the lived or, in Terrence Turner's (1995) word, "ambient" nonhuman world. Like Amerindians in other regions, personhood was understood as the quality of behaving like a person, something animals, spirits, and even natural phenomena might do (Vilaça 2005). Persons were also likely understood not entirely as separate individuals but as "dividual" persons, defined in terms of—and emergent from—their place within a group (Strathern 1979; Bragdon 2015). Further, "dividuality" among the Natives of southern New England was less likely to be focused on social categories such as age and gender but rather on the human–nonhuman divide.

Native ideas about the body were often misunderstood by newly arrived Europeans whose writings we rely upon to understand the processes of cultural continuity and change (Creese, this volume). It hardly needs saying that most 17th-century European observers misunderstood and condemned the Native beliefs that Europeans interpreted as evidence of ignorance, idolatry, and subjugation to the devil (Simmons 1981:56). Many scholars have noted that the missionary project in southern New England, in addition to achieving the Natives' spiritual conversion, also sought the transformation of Native bodies through control of dress, hairstyles, and sexuality (Plane 2002:51). If we read descriptions of Native practice with these biases in mind, however, Native ideas of the body and its construction and changeability sometimes emerge. For example, the missionary Henry Whitfield recorded this testimony from a 17th-century Martha's Vineyard *powwau*: "One [whose perspective he took on] was like a man which he saw in the Ayre, and this told him that he did know all things upon the island, and what was to be done; and this he said had its residence over his whole body. Another was like a Crow, and did look out sharply to discover mischiefs coming towards him, and had its presence in his head" (1834:186). Powwows could also change Natives' bodies. William Wood wrote of the sachem Passaconaway, "He can make the water burn, the rocks move, the trees dance, and metamorphise himself into a flaming man" (1977:101).

Inextricable from ideas of the body in Native southern New England was the theory of the dual souls thought to be possessed by every human, a common idea in Native America. These souls, which had their seat in the head and heart, partook of many of the characteristics of humanity: they were capable of traveling outside the body, causing harm, and communicating with the living (Simmons 1981:60). The fluidity and mobility of souls mirrored the changeability of bodies and informed bodily practices, including treatments of the body at birth and death and the attention paid to bodily decoration as a feature of social life. Bodily expressions of the social also included hairstyle and the "dress" of children and adults. William Simmons (1970) and Margaret Holmes Williamson (2003) both note the cultural significance of hairstyle as representing various degrees of socialization and antisociality as these were linked to different stages of bodily growth and decay. Young girls and women, wearing "strings" on their legs (Winslow 1910[1624]:273), may have been marked as attaining various degrees of growth toward maturity, as is true in other societies where unclothed bodies were the rule (see Turner 1995:155–156). Similarly, paint and tattooing also indicated specific social statuses and conditions (Willoughby 1905:501).

Another dimension of conceptions of bodiliness among Algonquian-speaking peoples of southern New England was reflected in the Native languages of the region. First, as with all Algonquian languages, nouns are divided into grammatical gender categories known as animate and inanimate. Although gender classes are arbitrary to a large extent, Hallowell (1960) argues that animacy was a sign of attentiveness to the potential of all things to behave "as persons." Animate gendered nouns included human beings, spirits, animals, and "the soul" (Goddard and Bragdon 1988:486). Another grammatical category, that of dependent nouns, marked certain body parts and kin that appeared only in possessed form, so one could say "my brother" but not (grammatically) "a brother" (Bloomfield 1941, 1946:32). Native writings from New England include dependent nouns such as body parts, the term for "body," kin terms, "friends," "neighbors," the term for "house," and "words" (Goddard and Bragdon 1988:499).

Objects such as knives and pipes were similarly treated as "extensions" of the body. In the early to mid-17th century trade cloth and clothing took their place as another kind of bodily extension and signaled a world in which the fur trade, disease, and warfare were part of "lived experience." Some evidence concerning this incorporation comes from word lists and documents written by Native speakers of Wampanoag in the 17th and 18th centuries that include terms for objects of European origin with animate suffixes added (Bragdon 2015; Goddard and Bragdon 1988).

Further understanding of bodiliness in the region concerns Native theories of disease. Shamanic practice in New England often involved the removal of "sickness" that had invaded the body, sometimes through witchcraft, particularly by sucking but sometimes by incision. These practices can be understood as "techniques of the body" that reflect larger ideas about health and disease (Mauss 1973). That sickness itself was understood to be a social condition was reinforced by the fact that these endeavors by shamans always took place in public contexts. Illness that resulted in external signs such as skin rashes, boils, and "sores" was often treated with plant-based medicines and sweating, which had little effect against plague, smallpox, and syphilis (Simmons 1976).*

There is some archaeological evidence for indigenous ideas of bodiliness in southern New England. A remarkable series of large, centralized indigenous cemeteries were established in the Narragansett Bay and Taunton River drainage, tightly dated from 1620 to 1720 (McBride 1994; Welters et al. 1996; see also Howey, this volume). These cemeteries are located within the region in which the fur trade and wampum production were concentrated and where epidemic diseases had taken a great toll, although there is no clear indication that the people buried in these cemeteries died from epidemic diseases. These cemeteries are unlike earlier burials in the region both in the large number of interments and in the richness of the grave furniture (Gibson, ed. 1980; Rubertone 2001; Simmons 1970). In many cases, the bodies of the interred in these cemeteries were oriented toward the southwest and were often accompanied by grave goods such as tools, pipes, strings of wampum, glass beads, and items of metal (including trade kettles, as discussed by Howey, this volume).

Linda Welters and colleagues (1996) have also identified small numbers of fragments of imported cloth (totaling fewer than 200 fragments, some of which were probably from the same pieces of cloth) in five 17th- and early 18th-century cemeteries in southern New England, all of which also include fragments of Native textiles (Table 6.1).†

Although poor preservation conditions in the region make cloth an elusive artifact, the variety of contexts in which cloth and clothing have been discovered archaeologically may show something of its symbolic significance. Welters and colleagues (1996) report that cloth was used to wrap or cover other grave offerings, including what appear to be "medicine bundles," to line the burial pits, and to wrap the bodies themselves. They detected only a few instances in which it was possible that the bodies interred in these cemeteries were garbed in trade cloth or in ready-made articles of clothing (Welters et al. 1996:229). However, additional anecdotal evidence from other early historic period interments in the region that were looted or excavated

* The two epidemics that spread through the region have been variously interpreted. Observers noted a variety of symptoms, including rashes, sores, yellowed skin, and bleeding from the mouth and nose. Sherburne Cook (1973) diagnoses both bubonic plague and smallpox, while Arthur E. Spiess and Bruce D. Spiess (1987) suspect an infectious hepatitis. Syphilis was also noted in the region during this period (Cook 1973). All of these epidemics involved skin conditions frequently noted by Native informants.

† By far the largest number of these archaeological fragments were woolens, consistent with traders' records that state a preference among the Native people for woven woolens known as "duffels," "shag cotton," and "trading cloth." Pynchon's records also note substantial quantities of ready-made clothing, some produced by local English tailors for the Indian trade, and some imported from abroad (Bridenbaugh 1985; Thomas 1979).

TABLE 6.1. Cloth types recovered from indigenous cemeteries in the region (based on Welters et al. 1996:212)

SITE AND DATE RANGE	CLOTH TYPES RECOVERED
West Ferry (1620–1660)	metallic, native
Witford (mid-1650s)	woolens, cotton, native
RI-1000 (1650–1670)	woolens, cotton, native
Burr's Hill (1650–1675)	woolens, linen, metallic, native
Long Pond (1670–1720)	woolens, native

before the 1970s suggests that some (high status?) individuals were indeed buried in red woolen coats.*

It is difficult to discern the meaning behind these few instances of the use of cloth in mortuary ritual, but other evidence suggests that colonial period burials might have been constructed with "protection" of the body in mind. For example, a burial described by Thomas Morton includes a layered covering of the body:

> [The Natives] make some monuments, over the place where the corps is interred: But they put a greate difference between persons of noble, and of ignoble, or obscure, or inferior descent. . . . For indeed in the grave of the more noble, they put a planck in the bottom for the corps to be layed upon and on each side a plancke, and a plancke upon the top in form of a chest, before they cover the place with earth. This done, they erect some thing over the grave in the forme of a hearse cloath. . . . [T]hey hold impious, and inhumane to deface the monuments of the dead. (1947[1637]:35–36)

The horrific losses during the years that epidemics flourished in the region must have increased indigenous anxiety about bodily intrusions and invasions at the time that English settlers wrote their first descriptions of Native healing practices (Douglas 1996[1970]). It seems possible that as epidemic diseases took their toll, the adoption of non-Native clothing was seen as adding another "protective" layer to the body, especially efficacious because these garments were worn by leaders who remained unharmed by disease.

* As materials from these interments and those at the palisaded cemeteries are repatriated and reburied, opportunities to apply more modern analytical techniques for identifying cloth and clothing in these contexts are diminished.

While the archaeological and documentary evidence for mortuary use of imported cloth and clothing is limited, it is clear that they became part of the interment ceremonialism. These practices also included the deployment of other trade items, especially those of enduring materials such as ceramics, glass, and metal, as well as Native-made objects and textiles. If, as can be argued from other interpretations of indigenous ritual, grave furniture was, on the one hand, an extension of the body and, on the other hand, a "sacrifice" of wealth in support of the health of the living social body, then grave furniture was also closely tied to ideas of bodiliness—of interrelated ideas of status and hierarchy, wealth and its relationship to health. This is further explicated by a consideration of the attribution of cultural value to cloth and clothing.

Although not the subject of this chapter, it might also be argued that cloth and clothing took on a different meaning to the Native people who adopted Christianity in the mid- to late 17th century, an example of the ways in which the materialization of signification (Keane 2003:413) is subject to transformation and, possibly, changing ideas about the body among believers. Nevertheless, it appears that even converts at Natick, John Eliot's first "praying town," for example, paid homage to the Native "queen" who visited there in 1686, elaborately dressed in "a mantle of blue cloth . . . curiously wrought with white and blue beads" (Dunton 1867:217–218).

CONCLUSIONS: EMBODIMENT AND VALUATION

Most scholarship on trade cloth and clothing draws on two narratives. The first focuses on the economic, political, and ecological impacts of colonialism on indigenous peoples, that is, that cultural hegemonies were imposed on Native bodies (Comaroff and Comaroff 1997). The second identifies new or altered identities among Native people as individuals: elite, gendered, colonized, and ethnic. Wishing to avoid interpretations that focus only on voluntaristic behavior or on the individual as understood in Western terms, I propose that the use of imported cloth and ready-made clothing in a period of great social change might also be understood as a mark of active material engagement in "cultural work," that is, in the ways in which Native leaders in particular, with their own bodies, reproduced, explained, and transformed experience through clothing. An important component of this argument has to do with value and the process of valuation.

European cloth and clothing were important elements of exchange. In fact, they formed a kind of currency that linked historically to the period of the early fur trade and the great wealth acquired by some families due to the supremacy (for a period) of wampum as a medium of exchange. Wearing European cloth or clothing was thus like wearing money or wealth, crucial over many decades in rituals associated with periods of critical change, on which the health of the body and the body politic depended.

Part of this argument also has to do with the symbolic role that Native leaders played as literal embodiments of their communities and as advocates for community (bodily) health and well-being (Bragdon 2009; Williamson 2003). Other factors include the contexts in which non-Native clothing was worn: in diplomacy (Little 2001) and in rituals preceding battle (Bragdon n.d.). A third argument comes from *how* the garments were worn, almost always in combination with wampum belts and/or coins used as decoration. It has previously been suggested that clothing in the context of the fur trade was a kind of currency (Thomas 1979) equivalent to wampum and English money, and this Native dress often incorporated multivalent representations of wealth and health.

Since Native leaders adopted European clothing along with wampum and English coins, their symbolic equivalence and historicity are central to the dynamics of the period in which Native leaders such as Ousamequin lived. When Ousamequin first encountered the Pilgrims, he was clothed in his own skin, adorned with wampum, copper, and a stone knife, all items readable in a precolonial Native context. When "clothed" by English settlers, he was adding other "value" to his appearance, reflecting his diplomatic power and relevance, his role as principal advocate, and his ability to give important gifts or sell them for additional goods to others. In this reading, embodiment does not entail the action on or absorption of "outside" elements on or into the bodies of leaders, an understanding of embodiment that reifies some of the dichotomies the phenomenological perspective is meant to break down (Csordas 1990). Instead, cloth and clothing came to index diplomatic potency, leadership, wealth, and health, on the one hand, and may have provided "protection" against further invasion at both the social and the bodily levels, on the other. Thus, imported cloth and clothing, beyond being consumables, came to figure in the work of cultural reproduction and transformation. In short, although trade cloth and clothing can be studied from a number of standpoints, including in their role as signs and indices, a phenomenological perspective allows us to ask more questions about the ways in which a newly colonized people engaged material culture in the lived world. This association between cloth, wealth, health, and the body social survived as the frontier moved westward to be adopted and further elaborated by Native peoples elsewhere in the Americas.

NEGOTIATING POLITICAL AND SPIRITUAL WORLDS

7

THE OLIVE JAR IN THE SHRINE

Situating Spanish Objects within a 15th- to 17th-Century Maya Worldview

MAXINE OLAND

On the frontier of the Spanish empire, the colonization of Maya populations was experienced unevenly, sporadically, and often indirectly as Spaniards ceded administrative duties to existing Maya leadership. Spanish conquistadors and priests distributed European goods to indigenous people as gifts when attempting to win cooperation and conversion, and these artifacts are often the only way to locate and identify colonial Maya sites on the frontier (Pendergast et al. 1993). Yet this region is well known for its resistance to Spanish colonization and for rebellious acts in which Spaniards were killed, churches burned, and bells discarded (Chamberlain 1948:238–241; Jones 1989).

The lens of consumption allows us to focus on the changing cultural meanings of objects as they move from the context of production for the market economy into the hands of the eventual user or consumer who received them through exchange (McCracken 1986; Mullins 2011b). Paul Mullins argues that consumption is a practice by which we "confirm, display, accent, mask, and imagine who we are and who we wish to be" within the constraints of structural processes (2011b:135). Colonialism presented new structural constraints, as well as new opportunities for the cultural transformation of indigenous and European peoples, and the construction of new identities (see Cipolla, introduction, this volume). Yet in many cases, indigenous identities remained intact, while indigenous users transformed the foreign material culture itself. Attention to the context of consumption can reveal the ways foreign things were accepted into existing indigenous categories and used for indigenous purposes and in indigenous ways (Dietler 2005).

There are several examples across the Americas and in this volume of indigenous peoples transforming European things into indigenous objects. Sometimes European materials were physically transformed—from ceramic plates into beads, glass into arrow points, copper kettles into ornaments (Conte and Romero 2008; Gallivan 2007; Lightfoot 2005; Turgeon 1997). Other times, objects remained intact but were used in indigenous ways according to indigenous ontological categories (Cipolla, introduction, this volume).

In the Maya area along the frontier of the Spanish colony, Spaniards distributed mass-produced European goods as tools of pacification in order to encourage cooperation with new Spanish policies. These goods were then sometimes traded along existing Maya exchange routes. The uneven nature of colonial control on the frontier yielded opportunities for Maya residents to creatively consume and interpret Spanish objects. For example, Elizabeth Graham (2011) argues that the Maya of Lamanai and Tipu interpreted Christianity and its material accompaniments through a Maya worldview. While they may have called themselves Christian and buried their dead in Christian fashion with European goods, their understandings of Christian symbols were filtered through a Maya cultural lens (as were Spanish friars' understandings of Maya rituals and objects). Timothy Pugh (2009) argues that the Maya elites of Zacpetén transformed European goods into inalienable objects within the Maya world. They cached particular European objects within elite house floors in order to contain the dangerous pollution of these objects, as well as to harness the power of the Spaniards.

This chapter employs a consumption perspective in order to build on these Maya studies while situating the Maya acquisition, curation, and use of European objects as active choices within a long history of Maya consumption. Maya archaeologists have studied local and foreign (also known as exotic or long-distance) consumption for decades within the traditions of household archaeology, Classic period elite exchange systems, and Maya participation in a Postclassic Mesoamerica-wide system of market exchange (Chase and Chase 1992; Gonlin 2012; Kepecs 1999; Masson 2000, 2003a; Masson and Freidel 2002; McAnany 1989, 2010). Most Maya studies do not explicitly engage with theories of consumption as discussed by Mullins (2011b) and the contributors to this volume. Nonetheless, to remember that the Maya had always made economic choices about incorporating foreign objects frees us from ascribing primacy to the colonial experience as the sole agent of Maya cultural change. The archaeological record at Progresso Lagoon reveals that select Maya elites used goods obtained from Spaniards to further Maya political goals and to enable Maya political relationships—much as Maya elites had done for centuries in this community (see similar discussions in Creese and in Shephard and Gallivan, this volume).

Most relevant to this case study are comparative colonial situations in which indigenous people already ascribed value to things "from away" and those in which exotic objects were used to display rank or status. One example is the Iroquois value system, in which things from far away were more valuable because they were thought to come from the "World's Rim," a mythical place at the edge of the world where the sun originated each day. George Hamell (1992) argues that European trade beads were desired because they fit into the category of powerful and exotic objects from the edge of the world and that the properties of beads and other trade goods complemented or replaced indigenous exotics such as shell and local copper.

When exotic objects were used in processes of defining and identifying indigenous rank, European objects were often easily adapted to elite purposes. In chiefdoms of the southeastern United States, chiefs eagerly sought out and allied with Spanish soldiers in order to acquire foreign European items (Beck et al. 2011). Another example is the chiefs of the Powhatan, who desired European copper and other materials from the settlers of Jamestown. The archaeological remains, however, show that copper kettles and other artifacts were reworked into ornaments that would signify rank and status (Gallivan 2007; see also Shephard and Gallivan and Cobb and Stephenson, this volume). These examples illustrate how European objects were used to maintain indigenous political systems and identities in situations of colonial entanglement where colonists did not overtly control indigenous people (Jordan 2009).

At the Maya community of Chanlacan, on the western shore of Progresso Lagoon (Figure 7.1), most households did not consume Spanish artifacts or show any change in material culture after colonization (Oland 2009). Household data reveal that most residents were struggling with indigenous political and economic changes that occurred in the 15th century, nearly a century before the arrival of Spaniards in the region (see the discussion of time and temporality in Cipolla, introduction, this volume). Colonization surely exacerbated these struggles but did not significantly alter the daily life of Chanlacan's residents. Only the primary elite Maya household consumed European objects, and these objects were used in practices of Maya ritual and status display.

For the elite leader at Chanlacan, the consumption of Spanish artifacts was part of an active process of self-definition. European objects did mark the community's leader as elite, but not because he was more Spanish.* Nor, as might be assumed, does their presence indicate an acceptance of colonialism by the leadership. Instead, Spanish artifacts marked the elite leader as "other," a status that was long coveted by Maya elites at Progresso Lagoon and throughout the Maya world (Restall 2006; see also Pugh 2009). The use of Spanish artifacts in Maya ritual and display allowed the leader

* We can assume the elite leader was male, because after Chanlacan rebelled in 1546, Juan de Aguilar pacified the town with "the gifts and good treatment that he gave them, and because he gave the cacique [leader] his wife who had been in prison at the time as she had been taken in other entradas" (Jones 1989:46).

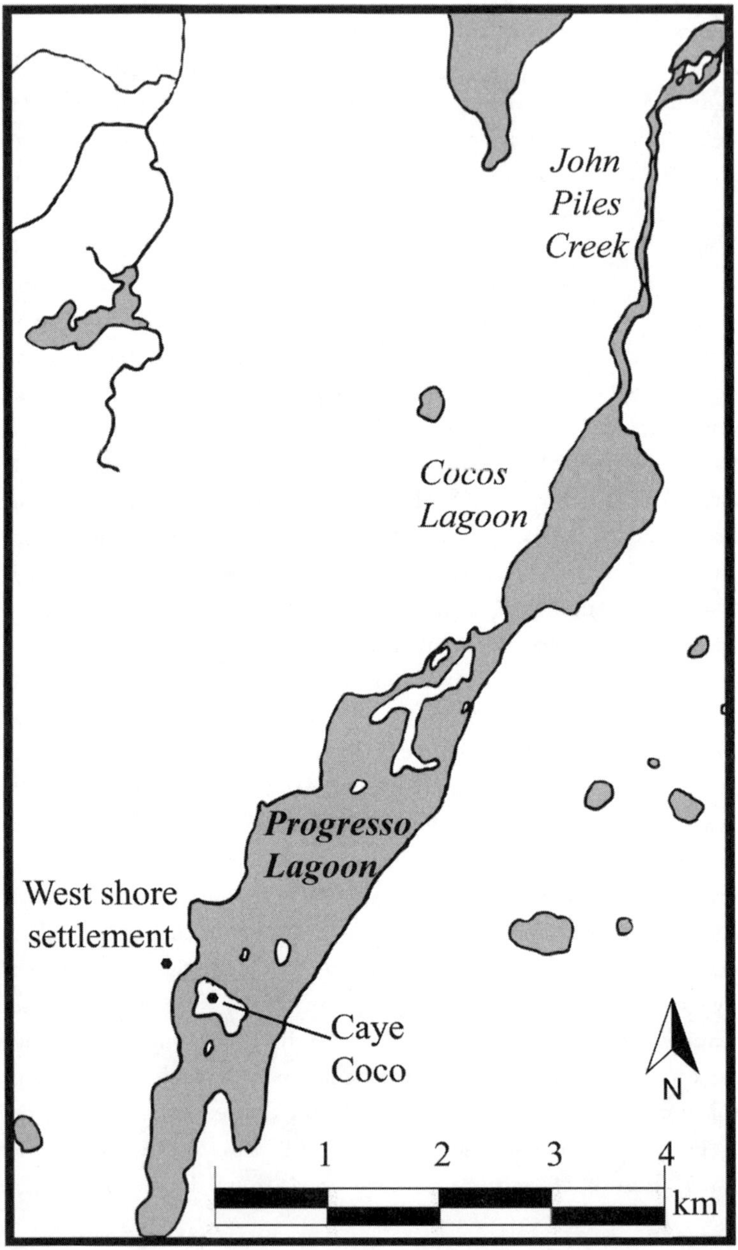

FIGURE 7.1. Map of Progresso Lagoon, Belize, showing the relationship between the island of Caye Coco and the west shore settlement.

to claim legitimacy at a time when elites were struggling to justify their position in the regional hierarchy. When situated within a Maya worldview and ontology and a long-term history of place, the consumption of Spanish goods can be seen as the continuation of elite Maya practices of marking authority and nobility through the consumption of foreign goods and symbols. These practices existed alongside colonialism and were entangled with Spanish actions and goals, but they indicate a continued desire for relevance in the Maya world.

SITUATING SPANISH ARTIFACTS IN TIME AND PLACE

Progresso Lagoon is most likely the Maya community of Chanlacan, known from Spanish records as an encomienda (grant of Native labor and tribute to a Spanish encomendero) founded during the 1544 conquest of the Belize region (Jones 1989:284). Grant Jones (1989) refers to this region as a colonial frontier: beyond full Spanish colonial control and a refuge for Maya fleeing oppressive conditions in northern Yucatán. It was far from Mérida, the Spanish capital of Yucatán, and farther still from the primary Spanish colonial capitals at Mexico City and Lima. It was administered by a small group of Spaniards from the outpost of Salamanca de Bacalar, a community known for its ill health, poverty, smuggling, and harsh violence against the uncooperative Maya population (Jones 1989:64–91).

The 1544 conquest was led by Melchor Pacheco and his cousin Alonso López Zarco after two earlier attempts by other Spaniards failed to conquer the region (Jones 1989:41–44; Lopéz de Cogolludo 1688:bk. 3, chap. 15). After receiving permission from the colonial authorities in Mérida, they went to Mexico City to obtain supplies, and we can assume that at least some of the European goods found in archaeological contexts in Belize were obtained during this trip. The conquest was notorious for its cruelty and uncharacteristic violence toward the local population and sparked a series of Maya rebellions that would continue until the Spanish lost control of the territory to the British in the late 17th or early 18th century.

The community of Chanlacan is known primarily for a single act of violence against Spanish authorities when in 1546 its residents killed their Spanish encomendero (Jones 1989:46). The murder was part of the first widespread Maya rebellion against Spanish leadership that spread across the Maya lowlands in a coordinated attack. Regional rebellions continued throughout the Spanish colonial period, and Jones (1989:14–15) calculates that they occurred roughly every twenty years, at the midpoint of the Maya *k'atun* cycle (a ~20-year cycle of the Maya calendar associated with political transition). His most recent interpretation of these rebellions is that they were encouraged (or even carried out) by emissaries of the unconquered Petén Itzá Maya kingdom, who threatened cooperative Maya missions along the Belize frontier (Jones 1998, 2005).

Chanlacan produced only small amounts of tribute and was not on a major inland waterway leading to the interior. It therefore received little attention from Spanish officials, and there are few references to the community in the historic record. Chanlacan is listed on a 1584 list of *visita* missions (Scholes et al. 1938), suggesting that it would have had a church (and occasional visiting priest), but no church structure has yet been located archaeologically. No Spaniards lived at Chanlacan, and encomenderos depended on indirect rule by local Maya leaders for the maintenance of order and the collection of tribute. This gave communities such as Chanlacan tremendous freedom to interpret the constraints and conditions of colonialism, unlike the tightly controlled congregated settlements of northern Yucatán.

Consequently, the Maya political system did not end with the arrival of Spaniards. Maya polities were based on personal relationships of hierarchical subordination (Okoshi-Haradi 2012; Quezada 2014). These relationships were fluid, contested, and negotiated, and they existed roughly at the level of neighborhood, village, and province (although some neighborhood leaders owed allegiance to elites from other villages). Leaders facilitated relations within the community, with other communities in the region, and with gods and ancestors. Yet Maya leaders also cultivated foreign and celestial origins to justify power. After the arrival of Spaniards in the region, the economic and political motivations of Maya leaders were entangled with new foreign people and objects.

FOREIGNNESS: MATERIALIZING THE EXOTIC

Matthew Restall (2006) argues that we can apply Mary Helms's (1988) ideas about foreignness to the colonial Maya—that elite status is conferred through associations with things and ideas from far away. He relates this to the colonial Maya chronicles, or *chilam balams*—Maya lineage histories written in order to justify a particular lineage's claims to power and authority. In these histories, which are recorded according to phases of the Maya calendar, elites make claims that their ancestors originated in "West Zuyua," somewhere vaguely in central Mexico. Restall argues that, far from the "Toltec invasion" imagined by early Mayanists, lineage elites cultivated mysterious origins as the basis for their status. Archaeologists have had to adjust their understandings of Mexican iconography and material culture to understand them as commercial interactions with central Mexico, political influence, and elite claims to otherness, rather than as a military conquest of Yucatán.

An analogous situation is seen in the way archaeologists have understood the interactions between Classic period Maya elites and the state of Teotihuacan. The presence of Teotihuacan iconography and styles led some archaeologists to theorize that Teotihuacan warriors had militaristically colonized Early Classic Maya centers in Guatemala for their rich resources (see Proskouriakoff 1993; Stuart 2000). Other scholars suggest that Teotihuacan imagery was actively manipulated by Maya elites to legitimate their rule (see Braswell 2003; Englehardt 2011; Taube 1992). The latter explanation is particularly convincing by the Late Classic period, when Teotihuacan had fallen, but Maya elites continued to employ Teotihuacan imagery to emphasize the disconnection between elites and commoners (Stone 1989; Stuart 2000).

At Progresso Lagoon, elites relied on foreign connections to justify and centralize leadership during the Terminal Classic and Late Postclassic periods. Between the ninth and 11th centuries, elites at Progresso Lagoon referenced the northeastern Yucatecan capital of Chichén Itzá when they erected a round temple dedicated to the "cult of Quetzalcoatl" (Rosenswig and Masson 2003). These round temples are found throughout the Maya lowlands (see Harrison-Buck 2012; Harrison-Buck and McAnany 2013; McAnany 2007) and are thought to be part of a ritual program dedicated to the investiture of local elites by overlords (Ringle 2004). The ideology of Chichén Itzá materially linked local elites to the larger political hierarchy and set them apart from the general population of the community.

Between the 13th and 15th centuries, elites from Progresso Lagoon engaged with the culture style of the Yucatecan capital of Mayapán (Masson 2003b). Elites converted the round shrine to a rectangular lineage council house (Rosenswig and Masson 2003) and sponsored the new *chen mul incensario* cult, which originated at Mayapán (Masson 1999, 2000). The new ritual paraphernalia was tightly controlled by Progresso Lagoon's elites, conferring special access to the gods/ancestors embodied within the incense burners by elite practitioners. Mayapán-style calendrical ritual also linked elites to neighboring communities, facilitating power-sharing agreements and competitive feasting events (Masson 2000). Thus, at the time of the Spanish conquest, there was a well-established elite pattern of cultivating "foreignness" and "otherness" at Progresso Lagoon using the ritual symbolism of distant Maya capitals.

THE ARCHAEOLOGICAL RECORD AT 15TH- TO 17TH-CENTURY CHANLACAN

Archaeological research on the western shore of Progresso Lagoon was conducted as part of a larger project investigating the Postclassic Maya communities of northern Belize (Masson 1999, 2003a, 2003b). The island of Caye Coco was the center of the Progresso Lagoon community beginning in the 13th century. Excavations on the shore of the lagoon show significant development of the western shore at the end of the 15th century (Oland 2009). I have interpreted this to mean that the political center moved to the western shore of the lagoon in the 15th century and remained there throughout the period of Spanish colonialism (Oland 2009, 2012). The comparison between the settlement on Caye Coco and the settlement on the western shore allowed for a diachronic analysis of change between the two settlements.

Survey and test excavations revealed that the 15th- to 17th-century occupation of the western shore was approximately 11 hectares, and neighborhood clusters of commoner houses were stretched along the bluff above the shore of the lagoon (Oland 2009). The site center was located on the shoreline and consisted of a large elite household, its associated ritual shrine building, and at least one other ritual structure, which had been bulldozed. Test excavations were conducted on 43 different domestic and ritual structures, with horizontal exposures on six of these.

As I have summarized elsewhere (Oland 2009, 2012), the 15th century was a time of significant indigenous transition at Progresso Lagoon and across the region. In the mid-15th century, the Maya lowlands were shaken by the collapse of Mayapán, a political and economic capital in northwestern Yucatán. Significantly, colonial period Maya lineage histories (chilam balams) focus on this collapse as a defining moment in the history of the Maya rather than on the Spanish conquest. The period was defined by tension between rival lineages, a struggle to redefine hierarchical relationships and tribute arrangements, and the collapse of power-sharing agreements (Quezada 2014; Restall 1998, 2001).

At Progresso Lagoon, changes in material and practice indicate that the 15th-century transition was fraught with conflict and a lack of regional connectedness. A huge increase in the use and production of small side-notched projectile points indicates that internecine and regional violence had reached the community (Oland 2012, 2013). Artifact assemblages from the western shore community reflect a decrease in engagement in regional festivals and feasts, a decrease in access to long-distance and regional products from market, and a corresponding decrease in market production (Oland 2009, 2012). Additionally, a change in the distribution of ritual objects suggests decentralization in local leadership and ritual practice at this time.

In over 700 square meters of excavation, Spanish artifacts were found only at the site center, in and around the elite household and ritual shrine (Oland 2009, 2012, 2014). In other parts of the site there was no change in material culture or practice that would distinguish the precolonial period from the era of colonialism. In fact, for most of the population, there was far more change in the mid-15th century than there was with the introduction of Spanish colonialism. Why, then, would Spanish artifacts be clustered at the elite household in the site center? Accounts indicate that the 1544 conquest was brutal, and we know that Chanlacan participated in at least one uprising against the Spanish authority. In some accounts, uprisings involved the destruction of European objects (Chamberlain 1948:238–241). Yet it appears that the elite leader of this community curated Spanish goods, displayed them to followers, and utilized them in Maya rituals (see a similar use of foreign goods by Powhatan leaders in Shephard and Gallivan, this volume).

I suggest that Chanlacan's elite leaders used Spanish objects to cultivate a sense of "otherness" to legitimate their position of authority and nobility in the difficult political and economic conditions of the 15th century. Archaeological and historic sources show that indicators of foreignness, real or imagined, were long used by Maya elites to justify their status and leadership and that these symbols, religious rituals, and other referents were kept away from the general population. Spanish artifacts were consumed in elite contexts and ritual deposits at sites across the colonial Maya frontier (Oland 2014). I argue that, far from having a novel reaction to colonial power, local elites had a very Maya response to a crisis of indigenous leadership.

SPANISH ARTIFACTS AS ELITE EXOTICS ALONG THE BELIZE FRONTIER

Spanish artifacts at Progresso Lagoon were used by elites in ways that echo earlier Maya efforts to distinguish themselves as different from commoners. Nearly all Spanish artifacts were found at the site center, at the elite residence and its associated ritual structure (Oland 2009, 2012). The elite residential mound was larger than any recorded at the western shore site and was notable in several ways in addition to its size. First, it had an adjacent household shrine with a circular altar made of burned cobblestones and the fragmented remains of a red-painted plaster floor and walls. Second, the household had several exotic items not present in any other household, or only in very low numbers. These exotics included several indigenous copper alloy celts or axes, a Preclassic diadem pendant, a hematite bead, and marine shell beads and other ornaments (Figure 7.2). Finally, the household had the densest deposit of animal bones from the site, suggesting that its residents regularly hosted feasts. Compared with other household deposits at the site, this elite household consumed more large mammals (deer and peccary), better cuts of meat, and some marine animals not found elsewhere at the site (e.g., shark and rays) (Oland 2009).

These data suggest that the elite household was the residence of a *batab* (local Maya leader), sometimes referred to as a cacique in Spanish accounts, who hosted feasts and rituals for his followers. The Spanish artifacts found at this household are items commonly distributed by Spanish conquistadors in the frontier region and may have been given to the household residents as gifts or traded along the frontier (Oland

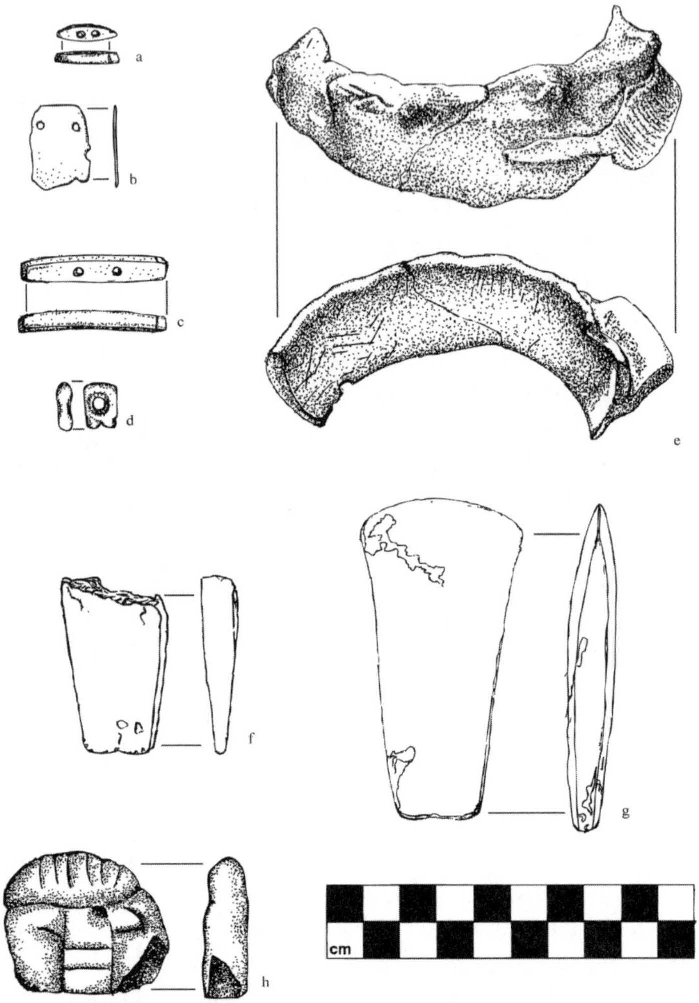

FIGURE 7.2. Indigenous exotic objects found at the primary elite residence on the west shore of Progresso Lagoon. a–e: marine shell beads and bracelet; f–g: bronze copper celts; h: Preclassic diadem pendant, with a failed attempt to drill through the forehead. Drawings by Peter Vamosy.

2014). They include glass beads, a glass ornament shaped like a bivalve shell, sherds of olive jars and majolica dishes, and assorted small metal objects (see Figure 7.3).

Similar patterns are seen at other sites across the frontier. At Lamanai, Tipú, and Cedar Bank (in present-day Belize), Spanish artifacts were primarily found only in elite contexts or in and around Spanish churches (Graham 1991, 2011; Morandi

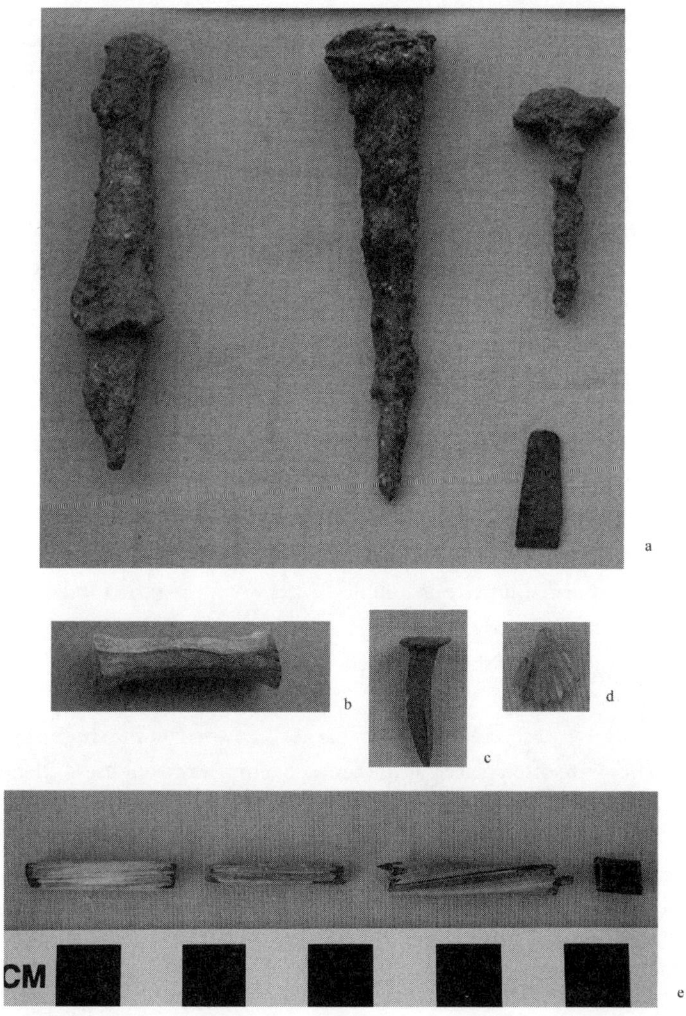

FIGURE 7.3. European artifacts found at the primary elite residence on the west shore of Progresso Lagoon. a: iron artifacts; b: bronze rivet; c: bronze tack; d: glass shell ornament; e: glass beads. Photographs by Maxine Oland.

2010; Pendergast 1991). At the Kowoj Maya site of Zacpetén and the Itzá capital at Tayasal (in present-day Petén, Guatemala), Timothy Pugh (2009; Pugh et al. 2012) has found European artifacts used in elite ritual contexts. This region was not conquered until 1697, and Spanish visits to the region were often met with fierce resistance. Pugh (2009) has theorized that European artifacts were restricted or avoided by most Kowoj because of their negative associations with colonizing others, but they were valued by Kowoj elites, who hoped to appropriate the knowledge of the distant "other."

SPANISH ARTIFACTS AS MAYA RITUAL OBJECTS: SMASHING AND CACHING

At sites with limited contact from Spaniards, such as Progresso Lagoon and Zacpetén, there was more room for elites to creatively appropriate Spanish objects into indigenous value systems. At both of these sites, elites used Spanish artifacts in Maya rituals, caching them in meaningful locations or breaking them and scattering the pieces. Both caching and smashing were ways to dispose of powerful and contaminating objects, such as ceremonial offerings or effigies of gods that had completed their cycle of use (Chase 1988; Pugh 2009; Tozzer 1941).

Caches were also "earth offerings" (see Becker 1993), in which objects were ritually deposited in the ground in order to animate or "ensoul" a space (Mock 1998; Pugh 2009:378). At Progresso Lagoon, a large sherd from an olive jar was cached beneath the circular altar of the elite shrine at the site center (Figures 7.4, 7.5). This altar was a raised circle of burned limestone cobbles. After excavating the top layers of rock, a clearly defined feature of darker soil was visible (circular and ~30 cm in diameter) (Oland 2003). The olive jar sherd was cached at the bottom of the feature to animate the shrine.

This was only one of several dedicatory caches recovered on the shore of Progresso Lagoon. Caches were often placed at the center or entryway of houses (Oland 2009). Most analogous to the elite shrine was a small cobble altar feature associated with a dirt-floor house, within which a single greenstone bead had been cached. Like the greenstone bead, the olive jar buried beneath the elite altar was an exotic material associated with distant peoples and places. And while greenstone beads were very rare at this site (N = 2), they were available to commoners, whether through trade or as heirlooms. The sherd of olive jar, in contrast, was a new exotic that was *only* available to the elite leader.

At Zacpetén, iron tools and other European objects such as a white clay smoking pipe stem and a cow mandible were used in ritual caches in place of indigenous exotic materials such as bronze (Pugh 2009). These caches were used to animate structures

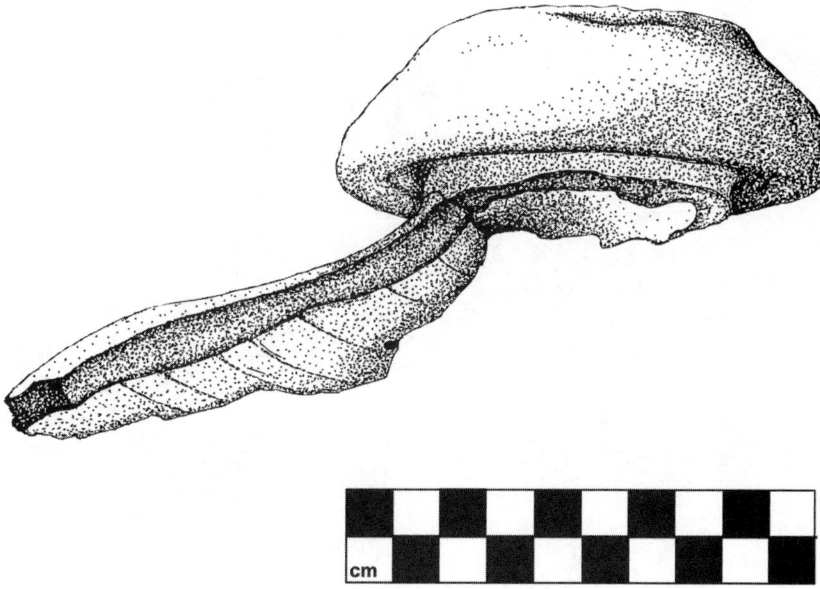

FIGURE 7.4. Olive jar neck and shoulder found at the primary elite residence on the west shore of Progresso Lagoon. Drawing by Peter Vamosy.

but also to contain the negative power of the objects. Pugh (2009) argues that both bronze and iron were associated with the sun god and that the accumulation of these powerful metal objects could be spiritually dangerous. He suggests that European artifacts, while coveted as exotics, were also associated with a negative power. Caches were a way to contain the power of both metal and European goods.

The pattern is different at Progresso Lagoon, where both indigenous bronze objects and Spanish goods were found outside of caches and around the home of the elite leader. Nonetheless, it appears that olive jars were treated in a way analogous to powerful ritual Maya objects. Large olive jar sherds were recovered from the top of the elite household shrine structure at the site center. The structure was fairly clean, and it seemed that the sherds were intentionally scattered there alongside large pieces of Maya incense burners and redware dishes.

Many ritual objects, such as Mayapán-style effigy incense burners, were thought to hold the spirit of the god/ancestor that was represented in the effigy (Chuchiak 2009), and it was traditional to break and discard these effigies to release their power after they had served their purpose (Chase 1985, 1988). Some discarded effigy censer sherds were then used for other purposes. On the shore of Progresso Lagoon, sherds

FIGURE 7.5. Circular shrine and olive jar sherd from the west shore of Progresso Lagoon. Photographs by Maxine Oland.

of censers were placed above a burial and left as offerings on the altar of a lineage ancestor shrine.

Censer sherds were also used to terminate (i.e., ritually kill) household structures upon their abandonment (see a similar discussion of termination in Cobb and Stephenson, this volume). Nearly every house structure on the shore of Progresso Lagoon had effigy censer sherds scattered across its ruins. At other sites in northern Belize, pilgrims brought effigy sherds to older ruins and left them as offerings to the gods and ancestors (Hammond and Bobo 1994; Walker 1990). I suggest that the olive jars were intentionally broken and scattered over the elite shrine structure, most likely in an act of termination.

A combination of caching and smashing practices can be seen in the deposition of Spanish objects in caves along the colonial frontier. As openings into the earth, caves represented sacred liminal spaces between the human world and the supernatural (Brady and Scott 1997; Prufer and Brady 2005). Throughout Maya history, they were used to make offerings and to deposit ritual objects (Moyes 2007). Archaeologists have found a Spanish sword (Awe and Helmke 2015) and whole olive jars and olive jar sherds cached in caves and cenotes at Xcaret in Quintana Roo (Andrews and Andrews 1975), in central and western Belize (Awe and Helmke 2015; Peterson 2006), and on Cozumel (López 2008). On Cozumel and in western Belize, the olive jars had "kill holes," or holes punctured through the bottom of the vessel in order to terminate it and release its power (Awe and Helmke 2015). These examples show that Spanish olive jars were spiritually powerful objects, used in ways completely outside of their intended utilitarian purposes.

DISCUSSION AND CONCLUSION

In both colonial and Classic period Maya contexts, elites relied on foreign associations with real or mythical places to create "social distance between rulers and ruled" (Restall 2010:397). Elites had access to symbols and rituals that commoners did not and used these to achieve alterity—a state in which they would become "other," even as they asserted their rightful place at the center of the community (Pugh 2009; Restall 2001, 2006). Restall (1998, 2006) points out that some Maya elites adopted the Spanish surname Montejo (after Francisco de Montejo, the conquistador of Yucatán), Spanish dress (Jones 1998:208–209), or the title of *indio hidalgo* (noble Indian). Taking on the guise of "Maya conquistadors" allowed them to "distance themselves from the Maya masses and to appropriate the Conquest as a way of inverting defeat and maintaining status" (Restall 2006:281).

Elites needed exotic and ritual objects to animate and terminate structures at Progresso Lagoon. European goods existed along a continuum of exotic materials but could not be accessed by the general population. The elite Maya consumption of Spanish artifacts was a conscious act rather than a reaction—a way of referencing powerful others in order to justify and consolidate power among one's followers. This was particularly important following the collapse of Mayapán and the breakdown of economic and political cooperation in the region.

One could make the case that the Spanish colonial empire represented a fundamentally different kind of foreign power from Teotihuacan, Chichén Itzá, or Mayapán. But how different did it seem to the Maya of the frontier? Indirect rule meant that local elites stayed in power and continued to conduct political and economic affairs. At frontier communities like Chanlacan, where visits from Spanish encomenderos and clerics were infrequent, the effects of colonialism were felt very differently from communities in the core of the colony or even those en route to the interior. Moreover, like Chichén Itzá and Mayapán, the Spanish colonial capital at Mérida was known through its emissaries, symbols, and material culture but probably never visited by any locals from Progresso Lagoon.

By insisting that Spanish objects indicate defeat, conquest, or cultural change by Spaniards (or even the inverse: that they are used in ritual as objects of resistance), we echo externalist theories that the prehistoric Maya were dominated by outside power centers. It is clear from the archaeological record that the community at Progresso Lagoon was already changing before the arrival of the Spaniards and that elite decisions were guided by the unstable conditions of the time and a desire to maintain political power. Utilitarian Spanish artifacts were consumed as elite Maya had always consumed exotic objects and symbols from afar, and they were transformed, through elite Maya practices, into ritual objects to legitimize elite rule.

ACKNOWLEDGMENTS

This research was made possible by the Belize Institute of Archaeology and the villages of Progresso and San Estevan, Belize. The work was funded by the Belize Postclassic Project and the University at Albany—SUNY Archaeological Field School, Northwestern University, a National Science Foundation Dissertation Improvement Grant (#0315331), and a dissertation grant from the Wenner-Gren Foundation for Anthropological Research (#7055).

8

COSMIC DEBT AND RELATIONAL CONSUMPTION

CHARLES R. COBB AND KEITH D. STEPHENSON

ECONOMISTS ATTRIBUTED MUCH OF THE LASSITUDE in the U.S. economy following the Great Recession of 2008 C.E. to an unhealthy accrual of personal debt. With an uncertain job market, maxed-out credit cards, and underwater mortgages, Americans refrained from the unbridled consumption patterns that had promoted a decade of unparalleled circulation of wealth prior to the recession. In contrast to this notion of debt as a pathological condition, there has been a robust history of anthropological research demonstrating that credit and debt are powerful inducements for the circulation of goods and privileges that, in turn, underlie networks of social interaction and reciprocity, as well as exploitation (Appadurai 1986; Graeber 2011; Mauss 1990[1954]; Peebles 2010; Sahlins 1972). We extend this argument to suggest that public feasting—and the materiality of those events—could play a prominent role in the accumulation and discharge of credit and debt.

A number of researchers (e.g., Blitz 1993; Hudson 1976; Kassabaum 2013; Van Derwarker 1999; Wallis and Blessing 2015) have described a widespread pattern of feasting among the late prehistoric Mississippian chiefdoms of the American Southeast (ca. 1000–1500 C.E.). Some of this work has a functional and instrumental cast in that the communal sharing of food and the gifting of objects are portrayed as displays of conspicuous consumption that cement horizontal social ties and/or foster social inequality. The traditional archaeological sine qua non of Mississippian feasting has been, not surprisingly, large accumulations of animal bone in special contexts (e.g., on or near platform mounds where elites resided). In these deposits we can see that feasting is intimately related to consumption in its most literal sense.

Not all Mississippian feasting activities were alike, however. If we examine in more detail the variety of durable goods in addition to the comestibles represented, it is apparent that the use of nonlocal and exotic substances and objects was also integral to some feasts. In this light, we borrow a term from Julie Chu (2010), "cosmic debt," to make the argument that some feasts were "cosmo-political" projects. They were intended to discharge debts to supernaturals in exchange for productivity and harmony on the secular plane. From our perspective, consumption surrounding a cosmic feast assumes multidimensional qualities that transcend space, time, and corporeality. Initially, consumption for the feast is about accumulation. It entails a welter of complex activities to draw in comestibles, substances, and objects from both near and far to, in effect, create a temporary hoard. Although the process may involve a number of strategies, its ultimate goal is largely material. However, in some cases this hoard may be ritually transferred into another realm of consumption, one that centers on redistribution through the celebration of a feast with cosmic overtones. This may involve activities we associate with traditional notions of consumption, such as a communal meal, but it also involves the manipulation or destruction of material culture as a means of engaging with the spiritual world. Finally, a cosmic feast continues to radiate outward even after the physical act itself is completed. There is a notion of delayed return on debt, where hosts anticipate that feast participants will in the future in some way repay their invitations, repayments that engage other forms of accumulation and consumption. This complexity leads us to argue for a relational model of consumption, where ontological borders between things, between entities, and between things and entities may dissolve in the act of the feast.

This perspective on consumption also broadens our notion of who constitutes a consumer. At the most obvious level, the consumers are those tangible individuals in attendance at the cosmic feast. Joining them, however, were ancestors and other otherworldly beings whose participation was integral to a sense of spiritual harmony.

Our arguments for the nature of the cosmic feast rest largely on two central pillars. First, drawing inspiration from a recent alternative perspective on the remains found in Mississippian feasting contexts (Wallis and Blessing 2015), we employ the notion of relational ontologies to address the materiality of the feast. In this framework, objects that may seem to be ontologically disparate (e.g., deer bone and pottery) assume a linkage based not only on depositional context but also on the logic of the feasting activity itself. And, as we will argue, exotic or imported things played a prominent role in activating that linkage. Second, we maintain that discharging debts usually requires some kind of documentation (which can be social as well as legal) to the effect that incurred obligations have been cleansed. For feasting, this often falls into the realm of public performance, an arena that provides broad first-hand testimony that reciprocity has been actualized.

THE MISSISSIPPIAN FEAST: A NORMATIVE PERSPECTIVE

The Mississippian world of the southeastern United States represented an apogee of cultural complexity brought down by the arrival of Europeans in the 1500s C.E. (Figure 8.1). A first generation of explorers from Spain, France, and England encountered sizable towns dominated by earthen mounds that were platforms for chiefly structures, temples, and charnel houses; sizable agriculture fields dominated by maize; and relatively powerful chiefs serving in central ritual and religious roles, as military leaders, and as arbiters of civic life. These patterns are all reflected in the archaeological record as a lifeway established around 1000–1100 C.E. (Blitz 2010; Cobb 2003).

FIGURE 8.1. Mississippian sites referred to in text.

FIGURE 8.2. Depiction of a late 16th-century southeastern feast from an engraving by Theodor de Bry. Courtesy of the P. K. Yonge Library of Florida History, Special and Area Studies Collections, George A. Smathers Libraries.

As described by European and Euro-American chroniclers, feasts of various sorts were held by Native American communities throughout southeastern North America (Figure 8.2). Perhaps the best known of these feasts are those related to the busk or green corn ceremony. This event was held in summer to celebrate the ripening of the corn. Although busk ceremonies varied in detail from one group to another, they did share in common connotations of purification, where past debts and misdeeds were expunged through events such as fasting and the dousing of ceremonial fires that had remained lit throughout the year. Communal feasts signaled the closure of purification. To provide one example, the Chickasaw of Mississippi marked the end of the busk and the fasting period by igniting new fires in their houses, followed by a major feast, during which people consumed large quantities of meat, fish, oil, corn, beans, pumpkins, and wild fruit (Adair 2005[1775]).

Despite the attention given to the feast itself, it must be kept in mind that the acts of consumption surrounding the event represent just one segment of a larger continuum of social credit and debt. In many cases around the world, large-scale feasts were just one particularly momentous point in a longer cycle of negotiations over the transfer and return of goods and services (Dietler 2001; Hayden 1996; Jennings et al. 2005; Spielmann 2002). The process of accumulation leading up to the feast could be drawn out and socially complex, involving a series of protracted production struggles accompanied by a spiral of indebtedness. The feast itself was a culmination of a preparation cycle and often involved a strong element of theatricality as debts were repaid and new forms of credit extended through an event of ostentatious consumption. Then a period of dissemination followed, representing an outward ripple of new debt ensuing from the feast, sustained as feasting recipients repaid their obligations to former hosts, often in the form of new rounds of feasting.

Archaeological studies of feasting in Mississippian contexts have tended to emphasize food remains. There are numerous accounts of large pits containing large volumes of bone, particularly prime cuts of white-tailed deer; concentrations of maize, nuts, and other botanical remains; and inordinate amounts of pottery vessels (e.g., Blitz 1993; Jackson and Scott 1995; Kelly 1972; Kelly 1997; Van Derwarker 1999; Wallis and Blessing 2015). By and large, this evidence has been used to support a dual model for Mississippian feasting. "Potluck" feasts were of modest size, involved relatively mundane food items and objects, and were oriented toward community cohesion. "Community" feasts were sponsored by elites and may have serviced either the public at large or a more restricted group of elites, but in either case they served as a means of status aggrandizement for the host.

THE COSMIC FEAST

These interpretations of feasting are not necessarily wrong, but they are limited in the view that sponsors of feasts primarily targeted three groups: friends or relatives participating in a spirit of conviviality; work parties or other groups that are being thanked for some public task; or prestigious peers. The ethnohistoric literature strongly supports the notion, however, that in many cases guests from the spiritual world also had a seat at the feasting table. Furthermore, although feasts revolved around production and consumption, they were also strongly invested in transformation (see Vivieros de Castro 2004:475–478), specifically the metamorphosis of feast participants that in turn allowed them to commune with spiritual guests. Many of the exotic goods found in feasting assemblages were integral to this transformation.

An association with gods or ancestors was often embedded in Native American feasting (Hudson 1976; Knight 1986). Despite variation in the green corn ceremony, it was widely held to be a rite of thanksgiving to supernatural beings. In alignment with the cleansing and purification associated with the new or holy fire that inaugurated a new agricultural year, pure actions would be rewarded with health, rain, and victory in conflict. The feast itself appears to have been a way of cleansing a debt of gratitude following a good year, or, alternatively, a way to ward off the possibility of a bad one. According to James Howard's observations, these dimensions of the feast were epitomized among the Creek Indians: "It seems quite likely that, bound to agriculture as it was, the entire Creek ceremonial cycle developed as a technique to secure from the Powers Above fertility for the crops and a beneficial rainfall. Perhaps the strong emphasis on peace and the high moral tone of the ceremonies were not so much virtue for virtue's sake but rather were designed to oblige the Master of Breath to insure good crops" (1968:7).

These kinds of feasting transactions were not limited to busks. Among some southern Siouan groups, for instance, wealthier lineages held preferential access to the gods by virtue of their ability to host major feasts outside of the green corn cycle (Brown 2006:203). Wallis and Blessing's (2015) study of a Mississippian feasting pit in northern Florida suggests that it may have been a metaphorical sacred bundle. Native American bundles (which could contain a variety of items, from clothing to precious objects) had transhistorical, cosmological connotations that referenced and interlinked people, things, qualities, and powers (Pauketat 2013; Zedeño 2008; see also Shephard and Gallivan, this volume). Bundling metaphors thus could confer a powerful ritual dimension to the feast.

We will not provide a comprehensive inventory of Mississippian feasting events. However, we will offer enough examples to demonstrate that, despite the variability in feasting throughout the Southeast, there are some important commonalities related to the notion of cosmic feasts. In particular, we argue that while feasting may imply eating, certain Mississippian feasting assemblages consistently contain the remains of exotic and foreign objects or substances in conjunction with food remains (Table 8.1). While there has been a tendency to analyze these in a unidimensional, categorical way (e.g., bird bones may equate with feather mantles, copper with prestigious adornments), we believe that many of these things are intimately related to one another in a form of relational ontology (Hill 2011; Wallis 2013; Zedeño 2008, 2009). In other words, many of these items were important in tandem for working to open thresholds to the spiritual world during the celebration of the feast, the very kinds of openings necessary to discharge cosmic debts.

A constant theme running throughout this volume is the reliance on Paul Mullins's (2011b) conception of consumption as a process of socialization through goods or things. This is, of course, a broad portfolio, since "socialization" encompasses so many activities and processes. Nonetheless, this perspective dovetails nicely with the theoretical reorientation toward materiality in archaeology, which not only emphasizes how things make society but also leads us to focus on the objects themselves, the

TABLE 8.1. Artifacts and materials commonly found in Mississippian feasts*

	CAHOKIA	TOWOSAHGY	WINTERVILLE MOUND COMPLEX	PARNELL MOUND	ETOWAH MOUND COMPLEX	KINZEY'S KNOLL AT SHIELDS MOUND	MOUNDVILLE MOUND COMPLEX	LUBBUB CREEK MOUND	CARTER ROBINSON
Quartz crystal	√	√	√	√					
Mineral pigment	√	√	√	√	√	√	√	√	
Foreign or exotic pottery	√	√	√		√	√	√		√
Avian fauna	√						√	√	
Cosmological iconography	√					√			
Copper	√					√	√		
Shell	√					√			√
Tobacco seeds	√								
Datura	√								
Red cedar	√								
Mica		√						√	
Cannel coal									√

*Given the disparity in recovery methods between sites, additional study of these assemblages (especially botanical remains) could increase the representation in categories.

ways in which they may be ontologically heterogeneous, and how their intertwined properties as assemblages may contribute to the formation of social fields (cf. Hodder 2012; Miller 2005b; Meskell 2005).

Although not all of the materiality advocates are on the same theoretical page, there does seem to be one theme that they hold in common: in the same way that Alfred Gell (1998) argues for distributed personhood, objects and substances can have a distributed materiality (for examples in this volume see Creese, Shephard and Gallivan). Indeed, from the vantage point of materiality this quality is a truism—the fact that we have material "culture" implies that this stuff will be constitutive of, a product of, and an index of the partibility of the social being. Whereas many of the studies on relational ontology focus on the constellation of varied objects and beings, it must also be kept in mind that an object or being in itself can embody multiple latent ontologies, any one of which may be called into prominence by certain events or activities. Moreover, in what may seem like a paradox for a consideration of consumption, one aspect of a partible materiality is an immateriality—a quality tied to "the need to objectify, to abstract[,] and our embodied practices in the spheres of magic and making" (Meskell 2005:3; see also Hodder 2012; Walker 2008). In this conception, humans, animals, and objects contain spiritual essences that can be activated via special objects and/or ceremonies. A closer look at Mississippian feasting suggests that some of the imported objects found in the assemblages seem to have had this triggering capability, which in turn provided the means for opening a portal between the worlds of the material and the immaterial.

MISSISSIPPIAN FEASTING AND THE CONSUMPTION OF DEBT

One of the best-known Mississippian examples of the remains of feasting derives from a vast pit filled with refuse at Cahokia in west-central Illinois, the largest town known north of central Mexico (Pauketat et al. 2002). Recovered remains comprise a veritable inventory of foods and objects known from the ethnohistoric record to be sacred among Native Americans of the Southeast, such as quartz crystals, tobacco seeds, datura, and red cedar. A somewhat similar assemblage was recovered from the "temple dump" at Towosahgy in southeastern Missouri, including quartz crystal, mica, fluorspar, limonite, red ocher, and lumps of white kaolin clay (Price and Fox 1990). In addition, there was broken pottery representing foreign types, such as negative-painted bottles likely from either Indiana or Tennessee (Figure 8.3).

Cahokia and Towosahgy are located in the Central Mississippi Valley, a region that many consider to be the hearth of the Mississippian phenomenon (Anderson

FIGURE 8.3. Examples of objects related to Mississippian ritual activities. a: beakers that have yielded biomarker evidence for the ritually important Black Drink (Crown et al. 2012); b: a figurine associated with a complex of house and pit features possibly related to the busk ceremony (Jackson et al. 1992). Figures courtesy of the Illinois State Archaeological Survey, University of Illinois.

1999; Pauketat 1994). Nevertheless, the materials and practices reflected at those sites are pervasive throughout the Southeast. For example, on the southerly fringe of the Mississippian culture region, the 13th-century Parnell Mound in northern Florida contained an off-mound subsurface roasting pit or earth oven that yielded a large volume of animal remains and pottery, along with hematite and quartz crystal fragments (Wallis and Blessing 2015) and vessel types specific to feasting (Hall 2013:38).

At the Etowah Mound complex in northwestern Georgia, one of the major Mississippian sites, indications of ceremonial activity occurring during the 11th century A.D. included several extensive borrow pits filled with large quantities of faunal material, exotic pottery with effigy adornos, chunky stone discoidals, and mineral pigments (King 2001:34–36, 2003:114–115). Another example of feasting assemblages with exotic materials is found at Kinzey's Knoll, a rise that is ceremonially related and in direct proximity to the flat-topped mound on the Shields Mound site in northeastern Florida (Ashley 2003:326–328, 2005). The midden formation at Kinzey's Knoll is interpreted as an accretional by-product of feasting and ritual activities. Besides an abundance and diversity of food remains within the midden, there are mineral pigments, copper artifacts, numerous bone and shell tools, and exotic pottery (Ashley and Rolland 2014). Particularly noteworthy is the presence of a bone pin engraved with an eye motif—iconography indicative of the three levels of spiritual worlds (discussed further below) collectively linked by four cosmic cords, symbolizing Muskogean cosmology (Ashley 2005:292–293).

Assemblages from Mounds B and C at the Winterville mound complex in the Yazoo-Mississippi River Delta basin illustrate the close association of feasting remains and sacred objects (Brain 1989; Jackson and Kowalski 2010). The high quantity of faunal material indicates food consumption on a large scale on Mound C. Also present are animal-head-rim adornos that would have decorated special vessels of pottery, a chunky stone discoidal, and mineral pigments. Evidence for large food-serving events atop Mound C is further supported on the basis of vessel morphology (Geiger 2014). The comparative absence of ceramic, lithic, and bone debris suggests that Mound B was not commonly used for daily activities and may have supported a temple structure given the high concentration of burned daub. The presence of a yellow quartz crystal suggests it served as a sacred place (Burkes 2014:24–25).

Many of the noncomestible items described here were imports that entered into various kinds of local consumptive patterns (see Table 8.1). Some objects, like quartz crystal, were likely regionally available for sites near the Appalachian or Ozark regions but were presumably traded to towns away from rock-rich areas; others, such as negative-painted vessels (primarily made at sites in the Ohio Valley or northern Tennessee), would have traveled from at least 150 kilometers or so away to reach sites like

Towosahgy in Missouri and Etowah in Georgia. Likewise, copper and marine shell in most cases traveled hundreds of kilometers to reach sites in the interior Southeast.

Many of these feasting goods are also of interest because they had "magico-religious" connotations and were particularly important for facilitating passage to the so-called Upper World, in the Native American tripartite conception of Upper, Lower, and This Worlds (Pauketat et al. 2002:272–274). Upper World is the terrain inhabited by spirits, ancestors, and deities (Hudson 1976:120–132). In fact, among the wide variety of things and materials found in feasting contexts, there is a recurrence of some items that suggests that there may be some form of "index objects" in this regard—items that are important for "animating objects and places around them" (Zedeño 2009). Categories that seem to occur with particular regularity include imported pottery, quartz crystals, and minerals associated with pigments, tobacco, and datura (Table 8.1). These materials were seemingly important for enacting spiritual passages. Quartz crystals and other translucent or reflective materials such as mica were commonly used in ritual ceremonies dedicated to spirit beings and were often included in medicine bundles. Substances like limonite and ocher may have promoted this transition, too, since they were traditionally used to manufacture pigments, and body painting was an important means of transformation allowing individuals to assume other personae or qualities. As James Knight has pointed out, "pigment use is profoundly associated with elite behavior at Moundville, thus there does seem to be a link between paints and persons of special status" (2004:309). It is possible that certain individuals at feasts may have added social–spiritual skins via pigments to assume a temporary identity that could commune with the Upper World—very much an idea in line with Gell's (1998) ideas on distributed personhood.

According to the oft-cited work of Mary Helms (1988, 1993), it is possible that the power of index objects in ritual and ceremonialism was a complex combination of their intrinsic qualities (e.g., color) and/or the fact that they derived from distant sources. Yet it is noteworthy that many of the locally available goods found in feasting contexts could also be used to commune with the Upper World. For example, datura and tobacco are well known for their psychoactive properties. Red cedar was considered sacred because of its aromatic qualities, and it was frequently burned at ritual events.

The transformative power of local, "mundane" items from feasting contexts could extend to food as well (Figure 8.4). In traditional societies in the southeastern United States and elsewhere, certain species may have been eaten because of the qualities they could confer on humans (Fausto 2007; Jackson and Scott 1995; Vivieros de Castro 2004). To Native Americans, deer meat encouraged fleetness and dogs encouraged bravery, while bears (often found in feasting pits) were held in particular regard

FIGURE 8.4. Feasting remains traditionally associated with eating and drinking activities from Parnell Mound site, Florida: bear bone (*upper left*); ceramics (*central*); deer bone (*right*) (courtesy Neill Wallis, Florida Museum of Natural History).

because they could rise on their hind legs and were viewed as hybrid creatures that could transcend human and animal realms (Hudson 1976). Thus, the presence of animal bones in feasting deposits was not merely about eating; as ethnohistoric records show, one purpose of the busk ceremony "was to propitiate the spiritual counterparts of various animal and bird species. These animals and birds included not only those which were hunted, and used for meat, hides, and feathers . . . but also those non-game species the spirits of which might help or hinder the tribesmen in their endeavors" (Howard 1968:82).

Although the qualities of animals could be imparted through ingestion, the wielding of certain body parts could also confer special powers and capabilities. Notably, bird elements provided the ability to travel to the Upper World. In an intriguing discovery from the Lubbub Creek mound site in Alabama, bones from a feast-preparation deposit included bird species that were known to be valued for their plumage, such as Carolina parakeets, blue jays, and cardinals (Blitz 1993). Among southeastern tribes, feathers were endowed with great spiritual power and agency, and birds were revered for the ability to transcend worldly boundaries (Jackson and Scott 1995:106; Levine 1991). In another provocative example of the importance of birds to feasting, swan constituted over 50 percent of the bird bone in one of the deposits in the large Cahokia feasting pit, yet no wing elements were found (Pauketat et al. 2002). Swan wings were considered particularly important ceremonial items among southeastern Native Americans.

The Cahokia and Lubbub Creek faunal assemblages seem to reflect the idea that feasts did not come prepackaged. In other words, the processing of materials (in this case, animals) oftentimes seems to have occurred alongside or just prior to the feasting activities. Other examples of this pattern are common. The Sponemann site near Cahokia was found to contain a cluster of structures and large, debris-filled features that have been interpreted as evidence for both processing for and consumption at busk ceremonies (Jackson et al. 1992). The pits contained large amounts of food remains and ceramic sherds, and unusual objects (or the fragments thereof), such as flint clay figurines (see Figure 8.3b), were scattered throughout the houses and pits. At the 13th-century frontier mound center of Carter Robinson in southwestern Virginia, excavation revealed portions of a large single-set post building with two features that appear to have been interior hearths (Meyers 2011:319–336). The presence of cannel coal fragments and shell debris as by-products of bead and pendant manufacture in this structure implies nonutilitarian craft production. That this was not a regular surface structure is suggested by its location near the mound, its size, the evidence of nonutilitarian goods, and, in particular, the presence of a large number of bowls as serving vessels. The building seemingly was a public space where large numbers of people gathered for singular feasting events.

The question of "large numbers of people gathered for singular feasting events" does underscore some differences of opinion over what constitutes a feast (cf. Dietler 1996; Spielmann 2002; Twiss 2007). Whereas for some it seems to imply a very large gathering, our definition is somewhat looser and incorporates the notion of an important occasion that transcends the family unit and is tied to important places and activities, such as renewal and busk ceremonies. In contrast, Knight (2004:309) has documented intriguing patterns of craft production and culinary habits on earthworks at Moundville that he does not view as feasts because they do not seem to fit a scalar criterion. However, the activities he records at Mounds G and Q at Moundville (Knight 2004, 2010:301; see also Jackson and Scott 2010:346–347) seem to reflect important eating and ceremonial events that we think can be construed as feasts, even if modest. For example, there is evidence for the transport of choice elements of deer alongside such "delicacies" as passenger pigeon, as well as carnivores that may have had "symbolic as well as culinary importance" (Knight 2004:309). There are also signatures of the crafting of imported goods, including copper working, the manufacture of greenstone celts and chisels, and the production of drills and perforators from a distinctive chert type found 200 kilometers to the north (Knight 2004:309). In Megan Kassabaum's (2013) conception of Mississippian feasting, Mounds G and Q would probably fall in her category of "competitive events with limited attendance."

Timothy Pauketat (1997) at one time criticized Mississippian prestige goods models for, among other reasons, their emphasis on foreign finished objects. He argued that foreign materials or substances were oftentimes charged with greater power if they could be shaped to local traditions, in effect becoming hybrid objects of foreign materials and homegrown styles. As we have shown, many of the feasting contexts we describe do show a strong reliance on the local crafting of imported materials. Perhaps ritually charged and recently completed objects were "unveiled" and displayed during occasions of feasting to symbolically communicate a capacity to evoke ethereal entities. Although this idea is speculative, the widespread evidence in the Mississippian world of craft-production debris surrounding feasts is provocative.

Given the range of data we have presented, we propose that there was a complex spiritual duality intrinsic to the objects we find in certain Mississippian feasting contexts that comprised both the material and the immaterial. First, the conviviality of the event itself, with associated sharing of food and related activities, constituted acts of thanksgiving or supplication to the Upper World—an argument largely drawn by ethnohistoric analogy but for which there are ample archaeological data. Second, opening a passage between This World and the Upper World may have facilitated these acts of thanksgiving. It is for this reason, we argue, that feasting assemblages contain artifacts that are indexical. They reference the subject of transformation, where key individuals passed into a liminal status by ingesting psychotropic substances; by swathing or surrounding themselves with accoutrements of spiritual passage such as feathers, body paint, and cedar smoke; and by relying on magical objects like quartz crystals. Despite the archaeological taxonomic differences between the remains of birds, quartz crystals, pigments, tobacco seeds, and so on, the nominal essences of these categories dissipate if we view them as parts of an assemblage required to create a cosmic feast. This is very similar to the ways in which objects for the Iroquoian Wendat served to perform "emotion-work" and make connections to absent family and the dead (Creese, this volume). From this perspective, there may be little distinction between foreign and local, exotic and mundane.

One unexplained aspect of Mississippian feasting debris is the intentional breakage of what were presumably intact and valued objects, such as exotic ceramic vessels and stone figurines. This pattern is widely seen throughout the Southeast. Why destroy that which is intended as a gift? As Maxine Oland (this volume) observes for the colonial Maya region, "caching and smashing" may have been a way to get rid of powerful and contaminating objects. This practice may also be consistent with Susanne Küchler's (2002) model of the sacrificial economy: "killed" objects are often gifts to spiritual beings or ancestors, and the destruction of objects materializes renewal and self-creation. In this sense, destruction is also production; it is an act that activates new qualities in a thing and allows it to enter a new arena of interobject relations. It may be that it is not the pottery itself that is spiritually activated but the liquids and foods contained in the bowls, jars, and bottles. Unfortunately, we lack data for the contents of such vessels, but ongoing strides in absorbed residue analysis may help inform on this important element of feasting comestibles. As one notable example, organic residues from unusual beakers from Cahokia and nearby sites (Figure 8.3a) have yielded biomarkers typical of *Ilex* spp., a form of holly described from ethnohistoric accounts as being used in the preparation of the ritually important Black Drink and a plant whose native range is far to the south of Cahokia (Crown et al. 2012).

THE DRAMA OF DEBT

A number of studies have demonstrated that feasts were often performances of consumption, very theatrical and geared toward an audience (Mills 2007; Mullins 2011b:138; Weissner 2001). Likewise, their association with elevated platform mounds and other venues largely visible to the surrounding community, particularly the plaza, presumably heightened the social potency of certain Mississippian feasts (Jackson and Scott 1995:108; Knight 2001; Smith and Williams 1994). Platform mounds were particularly important because, in addition to their use as stages for feasting dramas, their construction was integrally related to world renewal ceremonialism. This is manifested by the steady accretion of platform mounds in a series of stages, as previous occupations were often burned or otherwise erased to be replaced by a new mantle and a new structure. It may be that the size of these feasts was relatively modest, as was the audience, given the limited space on mound summits, but, as we have maintained, it is less the scale that is important for defining the cosmic feast and more a matter of contents. Although the immediate audience and public-performance reach of these events may have been relatively limited, we suggest that the drama was nonetheless heightened by the elite nature of the spectators and the sacred space in which the feast took place.

The larger contexts (by size of depositional context and volume of remains) for cosmic feasts tend to occur in or to abut plazas at the bases of mounds. These variables indicate that such feasts had larger attendances, as well as a larger scope of performance. A strong case has been made that plazas were central integrating spatial features of the physical, social, and ceremonial life of the Mississippian town (Holley 1999; Kidder 2004; Lewis and Stout 1998). Plazas served as a template for the ritual orientation of a community, as well as the basis of town planning. Moreover, as has been argued for Mesoamerica and South America, plazas were also central to the theatrical events sponsored by elites that were viewed and attended by a larger spectrum of society than one would anticipate on a mound top (e.g., Inomata 2006; Moore 1996).

Although many of these studies see theatricality in an aggrandizing way (i.e., elites using spectacle as a way to leverage power), there may also be a link between public performance and the discharge of debt. Elevating the visibility of consumption allowed feasting to serve as a mnemonic device for important events (Hamilakis 2008) and to confirm to the community at large that a social debt had been paid. Polly Weissner (2002) demonstrates this point in her ethnographic work in New Guinea, where she documented a pattern of "borrowing" pigs on credit to finance marriages and other social transactions. This debt was publicly repaid at feasts in a form of conspicuous visual affirmation that social-fiscal obligations were being met.

The tallying of debt in small-scale societies is much more nuanced than the modern spreadsheet and relies on a complex balance of social memory and citational practices. In this calculus, location and visibility may have been integral to activating the agentive qualities of the objects necessary to the performance of the cosmic feast and for convincing the community that harmony between secular and spiritual worlds was assured. Just as importantly, because the feast was part of a longer, repeating cycle rather than an isolated event, the public performance of the discharge of debt provided a means of closure to one stage of that cycle so that another could begin.

SURPLUS AND RELATIONAL CONSUMPTION

Brian Hayden, surely one of the key figures in feasting studies, has observed in his avowedly ecological perspective that "feasting in traditional societies was predicated on the production and use of surplus resources. Without surpluses, feasts would simply be unthinkable" (2014:6). In this materialist view, the potential for large-scale consumption and attendant social complexity becomes possible only when societies have marshaled the means to intensify subsistence practices (primarily via plant and animal domestication) above those required for biological reproduction. Although there is certainly some truth to this reasoning, it also references an age-old debate in economic anthropology over the nature of surplus and the views espoused by Marvin Harris in that exchange (cf. Dalton 1960; Harris 1959; Pearson 1957). In our opinion, the idea that social evolution is dependent on increasingly large, opportunistic surpluses that can be funneled toward cultural activities after everyone has eaten oversimplifies what surplus is. Practically speaking, all societies produce some kind of surplus, and a portion of that is always reserved for activities viewed as socially necessary (Dalton 1960; Pearson 1957). So the compelling issue for us is not whether a society produces some generic volume of output above that putatively required for survival. Instead, we are drawn more to the questions of what objects and materials constitute a surplus and why. What are the meanings attached to those things, why can only certain individuals or groups appropriate them, and how are they consumed in the context of a feast?

This perspective leads us toward a model of relational consumption: What are the objects and materials that must be gathered in an assemblage for a form of consumption that may have ends other than—or at least in addition to—biological survival and/or the political and economic leverage accrued through sharing a food surplus? Ian Hodder (2012:93) has argued that our engagements with materiality must take a relational perspective that considers not only the amplifying dimension of articulations but also how humans and things can constrain and entrap one another through their physical connections. Through the course of time and over extensive distances, the biographies of things can assume almost a snowball-rolling-downhill effect in their accumulation of social relations and ties with other things. Through this drawn-out process we become dependent on objects—they enable but are also contingent (pencils are useful for communication, but we do have other means available); and we develop dependencies with objects—interactions between humans and things that oblige us to pursue certain courses of action (the North American investment in road infrastructure and dispersed living has made automobiles, and all that they require, almost indispensable).

The materiality of Mississippian feasts embodies all of these dependences and dependencies. Feasting behaviors have a lengthy history preceding the Mississippian period in southeastern North America (e.g., Carder et al. 2004; Knight 1990; Mainfort 1988; Milanich et al. 1997; Pluckhahn 2003; Pluckhahn et al. 2006; Seeman 1979). Knight (2001) observes that in the earlier Woodland period (ca. 200–1000 C.E.), preagricultural feasts oftentimes included exotics in addition to food remains, took place in special locations, and were dedicated to world-renewal ceremonialism—much like the green corn ceremonies of later times. His implication is that many of the features of green corn ceremonial feasting evolved from earlier feasting practices. Mississippian peoples did not develop this practice *sui generis*; they were relying on a deep history of established dependences between objects and places that were modified with the adoption of agriculture and that eventually became synonymous with the success of the fall harvest.

The commitment to agriculture entailed a series of constraining dependencies. Societies became tethered to new forms of material and social prerequisites for their literal survival whereby, as some have noted, humans domesticated (i.e., entrapped) themselves (Hodder 1990; Wilson 1988). Mississippian agriculture required a commitment to planning and to the landscape that engendered a materiality quite different from that of earlier times (Cobb and Nassaney 2002). This materiality was manifested in a relational dependency that was regional in scope and involved imported objects both within and outside of the feast. Notably, stone agricultural digging implements from only a few source areas were widely traded throughout the upper and mid-South (Cobb 2000; Winters 1981). Although the remains of these hoes are abundant at, for example, Cahokia and the surrounding American Bottom region, they do not occur in the famous feasting deposit at Cahokia (Pauketat et al. 2002). Nevertheless, their usefulness for planting means that they cannot be divorced from the remains associated with busk ceremonies. In this regard, Mississippian feasts were a particularly visible example of how ontologically different objects (and objects with multiple ontologies) drawn from throughout the Southeast and related to world renewal and otherworldly beings became enmeshed in local projects of consumption (see also Creese, this volume).

CONCLUSIONS

To invert Hayden's argument that surpluses make feasts thinkable, we could argue that the need for special consumption events to satisfy debts (personal and social, as well as cosmological) made certain kinds of surplus labor thinkable. Examples from around the world demonstrate that the labor invested in feasts was considerable and had far-reaching effects in terms of indebtedness and consumption. For one noteworthy example, the *ani shrëati* feast among the South American Shipibo-Conibo tribe, which celebrated the coming of marriageable age of girls, could take two to three years of preparations (DeBoer 2001). These kinds of labor commitments were inevitably tied up in a range of debt obligations. In the Philippines, coastal chiefdoms raided the interior for captive women, who provided much of the labor required to produce the goods to sponsor feasts (Junker 2008). This labor also supported many of the specialists who crafted objects used to participate in external exchange networks that returned exotics and prestige goods to chiefs—exotics that played a prominent role in ritual feasts that attracted numerous warriors.

These kinds of feasts and the consumption practices associated with them may have had an aura of cultural inevitability because they were ritually and socially necessary and because they had been celebrated since time immemorial in terms of human reckoning. Likewise, the lengthy history of feasting in southeastern North America indicates that Mississippian peoples were participating in and reproducing a kind of structural history surrounding these practices, one that had been set in motion by preceding Woodland peoples and that had defined many of the parameters adopted during the Mississippian period. The tradition of consuming finished objects and substances from distant places was embedded in this structural history. Mississippian societies adopted this practice from earlier times and, in some cases at least, rephrased Woodland feasts into world renewal ceremonies associated with fertility and agriculture. The complex interplay of materiality of these events was essential for mediating the ritual relations with the otherworld necessary to release obligations to spirits.

9

SYMPATHETIC MAGIC AND INDIGENOUS CONSUMPTION OF KETTLES DURING EARLY COLONIAL ENCOUNTER IN THE NORTHEAST

MEGHAN C. L. HOWEY

WITH A NEAR-CONSTANT MYRIAD of material objects acquired and exchanged, valued and destroyed, produced and consumed during the 16th and 17th centuries, the Northeast region forms a robust venue for archaeologies of consumption, defined broadly as the acquisition and socialization of "foreign" things (following Mullins 2011b; Cipolla, introduction, this volume). In this chapter, I use the interpretive frame of consumption to explore the subjectivities arising from interaction with foreign goods and the negotiations of object value within indigenous ontologies (Joyce 2014). In particular, I examine some of the ways that European-made kettles, an especially popular item in the fur trade, were assigned value within indigenous ontologies. I focus on the importance of sympathetic magic in these transformations, specifically, contagious magic. Contagious magic is based on the idea that things that have once been in contact with each other continue to act on each other even at a distance (Frazer 1951[1922]:13; see also Gell 1998). While Sir James George Frazer's classic study of sympathetic magic positioned magic as a naive impulse, I approach magic instead as something indigenous groups used to effectively register their desires within the changing world of colonial encounter, which, in turn, shaped the emergent market economy of the 16th and 17th centuries in the Northeast.

EMERGENT AND AMBIGUOUS CONSUMPTION IN THE NORTHEAST

Before the northeastern Atlantic seaboard was renamed by colonists as "the Maritimes" and "New England," the region was known to the indigenous communities there quite simply yet profoundly as "our land," the place "to which we belong" (Figure 9.1; Brooks 2013:724). The indigenous communities of the Northeast were drawn into colonial encounter early, as Basque whalers and fishers and, soon after, French traders arrived in the 1500s, followed by English Puritans in the early 1600s (Prins 2002; Salisbury 1996; Whitehead 1993). Almost immediately the fur trade came to be a dominating conduit for cultural contact between Native Americans and Europeans across the region (Wagner 1998:430). Informal trading for furs began as early as the 1520s in the Maritimes and on the coast of Maine (Salisbury 1996:452), and formalized trading accelerated along the Atlantic seaboard and in the Gulf and Estuary of St. Lawrence after the mid-1500s, when demand for fancy furs began to increase in Europe (Fitzgerald et al. 1993).

The period of early colonial encounter in the Northeast (ca. A.D. 1500–1680) was a time during which both indigenous peoples and colonial Europeans were becoming something that had never existed before: "New World People" (Reid 1995:74). Exactly what this would look like, what this meant, was not yet clear, nor was if and how becoming something new would obfuscate what they had been before. It was a time, then, of identity negotiation as "Self" and "Other" were intertwined into a "third space" (*sensu* Bhabha 1994). The indigenous and colonial ontologies of "Self" and "Other" brought into this third space differed in significant ways, particularly as the indigenous peoples of the Northeast understood everything in the universe as filled with an animating spirit called *manit* (also variously *mantu*, *manitou*; Crosby 1988; see also Creese; Shephard and Gallivan, this volume). This third space held a material grip on the bodies and minds of both indigenous and European peoples (Gosden 2004:3). The grip was manifest in the practice of the fur trade whereby the exchange of material goods became *the* mode by which contact with other human beings was mediated during early colonial encounter (Reid 1995:74). The exchange of material goods was important for facilitating economic relationships, but it did not become such a critical conduit for intercultural interaction on this basis alone; exchange became the mode for contact because it provided a tangible way of navigating the uncertainties caused by the differences, or alterity, that lay at the heart of both indigenous and European experience during colonial encounter (Reid 1995:74; see also Fitzgerald et al. 1993; Rubertone 1989; Salisbury 1996; White 1999).

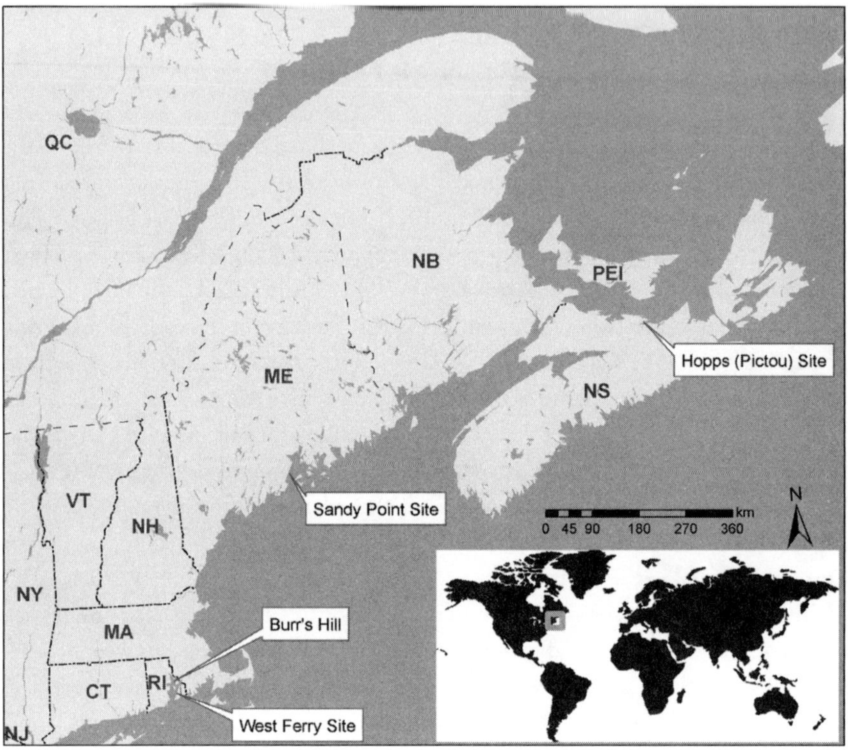

FIGURE 9.1. Locations of examined early contact burial sites.

Uncertainties were not only a defining feature of early colonial encounter on the North American side of the Atlantic; the 16th century was also the time when concepts of "consumer" and "commodity" began acquiring their contemporary associations in Europe with the rise of the European bourgeoisie (Belisle 2003). It was only in 1460 that the first written use of the word "commodity" to describe a thing produced for use or sale appeared (Belisle 2003:184). Before the 1500s, Europeans understood the term "consume" to mean "destruction by fire," but with the colonial expansions of the 16th century, "consume" became regularly used to describe the acquisition, use, and destruction of material goods (Belisle 2003:183).

As economic exchange defined much of intercultural interaction during the 16th and 17th centuries in the Northeast, this initial phase of the fur trade created numerous opportunities for indigenous communities to direct and even expand their socioeconomic systems—opportunities that largely closed by the end of the 17th century and were never paralleled again (White 1999). This early period of encounter was unique and distinct, then, for its becoming and its dynamism, with a lack of defined prescripts for how indigenous peoples had to act as consumers of European goods or, inversely, how Europeans had to act as producers and suppliers of commodities (a time when there was not a clear binary between production and consumption; see Cipolla, introduction, this volume). Indigenous peoples of the Northeast found themselves ever more involved in a market economy during this period, but this economy was itself an emergent and ambiguous entity (see Creese's discussion of "economies of affect," this volume).

Negotiations of material object value occurred not in defined markets but in the interstices of colonial understandings and misunderstandings (Loren 2013a:152). Within this context, indigenous communities across the Northeast were frequently able to ascribe value to European-made objects within their own frames of reference, including kettles, one particularly popular trade item. Understanding the import of a specific trade item, such as the kettle, is not possible by looking at the immediacy of exchange; instead, it requires an examination of how trade objects became embedded in the lives of regional indigenous communities and of the meaning and resonance they came to hold (Loren 2013a:159). Indigenous consumption of European-made kettles during early colonial encounter in the Northeast was not straightforward, and it generated, as Daniel Miller (2005a:286) has described for consumption broadly, diverse personhoods, social relations, and communities in everyday life (and also, I would add for this case, the afterlife).

KETTLES: COMMODITIES OF SPIRIT

Copper and copper-colored kettles were *essential* items in the trade networks being established between Europeans and indigenous peoples of the Northeast (Martin 1975; Trigger 1976; Turgeon 1997; van Dongen 1996). As colonial encounter and exchange began in the 1500s, European explorers and traders quickly recognized that there existed a widespread demand among the indigenous groups of the Northeast for copper kettles (Groce 1980:108). Initially, traders responded to this demand by trading the high-quality iron-banded "red copper" kettles they had access to as products used in their home countries (Fitzgerald et al. 1993). As demand accelerated over the course of the 1500s, high-quality copper kettles were replaced in French and English trade repertoires with a less complex, more economical, rolled-rim variety with folded-over copper alloy lugs often made of brass; these kettles are referred to as "trade kettles" (Ehrhardt 2005:73; Fitzgerald et al. 1993; Turgeon 1997). Trade kettles were standardized in form and mass-produced in Europe specifically for wide distribution among indigenous communities in North America (Figure 9.2; Bradley 1987;

FIGURE 9.2. Image of a standardized copper trade kettle used by the French during early contact (ca. 17th century). This well-preserved kettle was excavated at the Place Royale in Quebec City, which Samuel de Champlain began constructing in 1608. Image and permission to reproduce it from Aurélie Desgens 2015, © Ministère de la Culture et des Communications.

van Dongen 1996; Howey 2011). They remained chief items in the fur trade from the late 16th century through at least the third quarter of the 17th century (Bradley 1987:197).

The trajectory of European production of kettles illustrates the ways the market economy on the European side of the Atlantic during the early phases of colonial encounter was, as it was in North America, in the process of becoming and defining. At the outset of colonial encounter, European traders, recognizing, although not fully understanding, the strong demand by indigenous groups for copper kettles, responded by bringing the kettles they had available to them, their own locally used products, to trade with indigenous communities in the Northeast. As demand for kettles continued to increase over the course of the 1500s and early 1600s, Europeans responded by commoditizing kettles, creating trade kettles as items specifically removed from, and never intended for, European daily life but rather designed for markets—markets composed of indigenous consumers and intended to generate producer profit (see the discussion of iron trade axes, Cipolla, introduction, this volume).

While Europeans responded to the popularity of kettles in the early fur trade, it was driven by indigenous negotiations of their own ontologies and ascriptions of value. Europeans valued kettles as cooking utensils, but, in fact, earthenware pottery continued to form the main indigenous subsistence cooking technology across much of the Northeast until the middle of the 17th century (Bradley 1987; van Dongen 1996). During early contact, then, the popularity of trade kettles among indigenous groups was not related to any kind of "advance" in cooking technology. Rather, the popularity of kettles stemmed in part from copper's preexisting highly charged value among indigenous peoples of the Northeast. Native copper had been used from the Archaic period (ca. 8000–800 B.C.E.) onward for highly charged symbolic purposes; for example, its color was cognitively linked to a "metaphysics of light" (Childs 1994; Ehrhardt 2005; Hamell 1983; Miller and Hamell 1986; see also Shephard and Gallivan, this volume).

Laurier Turgeon furthers our understanding of the kettle's significant value when he informs us that, in fact, European copper's singularity, coming in the form of something novel and virtually irreproducible (kettles), led it to be invested with "statutory and symbolic power" exceeding even the power of local copper in prehistory (1997:9–10). As Mary Helms (1993) detailed, it is common for political and ideological symbolism to be attributed to geographically distant peoples, places, and things in non-Western Native cosmologies. Qualities or values of such items are not and cannot be understood solely in utilitarian terms (Helms 1993:95). The trade kettle's origin with the "Other" who had entered the social, economic, and ideological spheres of northeastern indigenous communities combined with its material connection to a Native medium that had held symbolic significance for millennia prior to colonialism resulted in kettles' primary place in early contact trade (Howey 2011).

Accordingly, we see that throughout the early period of intercultural contact, indigenous groups did not acquire kettles to cook with, as Europeans used them, but instead incorporated kettles into symbolically, ceremonially, and socially charged activities. Two of these primary activities included cutting kettles apart as sheet metal to make sacred jewelry or ornaments, which sometimes served as grave goods, and including whole kettles as grave goods themselves (see Howey 2011 for more on the research on nonutilitarian kettle use).

Indigenous groups did not trade for kettles as economic commodities. In fact, if we can understand them as commodities of any kind, they were likely commodities of spirit, objects ascribed with manit, an animating spirit. As mentioned above, the concept of manit was pervasive across the indigenous Northeast. This concept was frequently extended to European materials by indigenous peoples during colonial encounter, and this was the case for kettles too (Crosby 1988; Martin 1975; Turgeon 1997).

KETTLES IN EARLY CONTACT BURIALS, A.D. 1500–1680

Prior to contact, burials were furnished with very few grave goods. This changed during the earliest phases of contact when burial practices shifted in the Northeast and indigenous internments became frequently furnished with large amounts of grave goods, especially European items. A combination of whole or fragmentary copper or copper-colored kettles introduced by Europeans and/or other artifacts made from these metals permeated many of these burials, so much so that these burials have been referred to by some as "copper-kettle burials" (Petersen et al. 2004:2). Kettles and kettle-derived objects are one of the only grave goods in early contact period indigenous graves to show any kind of overlap in male and female graves or to occur across age groups (Bushnell 1920).

Indigenous groups placed kettles and/or kettle artifacts in burials across the Northeast, especially in the Maritimes and southern New England (Brenner 1988; Petersen et al. 2004; Whitehead 1993). Of note, a few kettle-rich burials have been found outside the Northeast, as far south as Maryland and as far inland as western Ontario (Petersen et al. 2004).

Well-furnished burials often included kettles or kettle-derived objects; this was a prevalent practice from the 1500s through 1680 (Gibson 1980; Loren 2013a; Petersen et al. 2004; Rubertone 2001; Trigger 1976). The time span of these burials indicates that they were specific to the liminality of early colonial encounter with its emergent market economy. That is, well-furnished, mixed-trade-good burials begin when ambiguity was the norm, when both indigenous peoples and Europeans were becoming "New World People" and experiencing the uncertainties of colonial encounter. These burial practices end after ca. 1680, after which the various impacts of colonial encounter, including disease, religious conversion, economic stress, and militarism, had rendered the outcome of colonialism across the Northeast much less ambiguous. This time frame marks the moments after the end of King Phillip's War, a conflict that dealt the indigenous communities of southern New England significant losses and left them clearly subject to the authority of the English colonial government; this conflict had widespread ramifications across the Northeast and beyond (Crosby 1988:187). At the close of the 17th century, it was clear that structural power lay with colonial entities all along the Northeast Atlantic seaboard.

EARLY CONTACT PERIOD BURIALS

Most early contact period burials were "dug" during the 1800s and early 1900s by landowners and/or interested locals.* The unsystematic nature of the majority of these excavations has left only a sketchy archaeological record, an outline of which I present here. Thirteen "copper-kettle" burial sites have been recorded in Nova Scotia and New Brunswick, which are Mi'kmaq and Maliseet traditional homelands (protohistoric sites date here to ca. 1500–1630; see Whitehead 1993). Of these, only one was somewhat systematically excavated and recorded: the Hopps or Pictou site, dug and published by J. R. Harper (1956, 1957). Moving down through Wabanaki, the Passamaquoddy traditional homelands of central Maine, the Sandy Point site and the Walker's Pond site included burials with copper kettles or kettle artifacts and, while not systematically excavated, have more recently had their collections analyzed (Petersen et al. 2004).

In southern New England, a variety of early contact period sites with Native American burials containing kettles and/or kettle artifacts have been found, primarily through accidental spot finds and/or avocational activities during the 1800s and 1900s. Elise Brenner (1988) provided a thorough survey of late 16th- and 17th-century burial sites in southern New England, inventorying seven in Massachusetts and six in Rhode Island, Massachusetts, and Wampanoag and Narragansett traditional homelands (see also Bragdon, this volume). Of these, Burr's Hill, a large Wampanoag burial ground in Warren, Rhode Island, had its excavations partially recorded and has been the subject of a thorough reanalysis (Gibson, ed. 1980). In addition, the West Ferry site, a Narragansett burial ground on Conanicut Island in Narragansett Bay, Rhode Island, was excavated professionally in the 1960s (Simmons 1970). Of note, RI-1000, another Narragansett burial ground, was also excavated professionally in a salvage situation involving the Narragansett after Brenner's inventory (Rubertone 2001).

Despite the shortcomings in the record, I focus on the extant data from four of the more well-documented sites to start to develop a picture of the ways copper or copper-colored kettles were included in early contact indigenous burials across the broad geographic and tribal range of the Northeast: from Nova Scotia (Hopps or Pictou site in Mi'kmaq territory) to Maine (Sandy Point in Passamaquoddy territory) to southern New England (Burr's Hill, a Wampanoag cemetery, and the West Ferry

* In order to respect the wishes of descendant communities and repatriation processes, I do not include any pictures from sites of the bodies or goods.

site, a Narragansett cemetery). These data sets provide an opportunity to rethink how indigenous ontologies reshaped and redefined kettles.

Kettles appear in burials from this era in three main patterns: (1) as whole or partial kettles that were damaged, sometimes extensively, and included as grave furniture next to the body or bodies; (2) as whole intact kettles that were often inverted and placed in contact with human remains, including being placed over the skull of the deceased; and (3) as dismembered kettle metal refigured into nonkettle forms, such as jewelry, other body ornamentation, or grave lining, placed on and/or in contact with the body (Brenner 1988; Groce 1980; Harper 1956, 1957; Martin 1975; Petersen et al. 2004; Rubertone 2001; Simmons 1970; Whitehead 1993).

THE HOPPS (PICTOU) SITE, NOVA SCOTIA

At the best-documented Maritime copper-kettle burial site, Hopps (Pictou), kettles were used in all three ways described above (Harper 1956, 1957). Two burial pits were excavated avocationally at this site (Table 9.1). Burial pit one had two sections. In the first section, three intact copper kettles were "placed with their bottoms upwards" on a painted animal skin, and beneath each kettle was a black layer of decayed organic material that contained human remains, including many skull parts (Harper 1956:40–41). In the second section of the pit, there were six kettles, all of which were mutilated and inverted; only one had a black layer under it. For the most part, these damaged kettles were not in contact with burials (Harper 1956:42).

Burial pit 2 had three distinct strata (Harper 1957:13). The lowest stratum was lined with deconstructed kettle sheet metal and birch bark, with the skeletal remains of three or four individuals placed on the lining. A compact mass of grave goods lay next to, but not in contact with, these bodies; this mass of grave goods included eight copper kettles that were "crushed or completely smashed" (Harper 1957:14). In the second stratum were two inverted intact copper kettles, both of which covered human remains. The third stratum had the remains of two fires (Harper 1957:16).

At Hopps (Pictou) we see a striking dichotomy in terms of the inclusion of whole kettles in graves. Damaged kettles were kept out of contact with human remains, while intact kettles were always inverted and placed in contact with bodies, forming a kind of protective armor over the human remains, including over skulls.

THE SANDY POINT SITE, MAINE

The Sandy Point site is located near Penobscot Bay (Petersen et al. 2004:3). The site was excavated avocationally over the course of one week in 1914; what is known about the context of the site comes only "in the form of sketchy field notes" (Petersen

TABLE 9.1. Distribution of kettles and kettle-derived objects from the Hopps Site (A.D. 1550–1630), based on Harper (1956, 1957)

BURIAL PIT	SECTION OR STRATUM	WHOLE KETTLE	KETTLE-DERIVED OBJECT	DESCRIPTION
1	1	Yes	No	3 intact, inverted kettles; black humus layer beneath each with human bones, including skull parts
1	2	Yes	No	4 inverted, crushed kettles; one lay over a black humus layer (no bones)
2	Lowest stratum	Yes	Yes	3 or 4 bodies lay on grave floor lined with kettle-derived copper sheeting; 10 inverted, crushed kettles scattered throughout stratum (not in contact with bones)
2	Middle stratum	Yes	No	2 inverted copper kettles; 1 lay over human skull parts and several long bone fragments; the other lay on black humus layer (no bones)
2	Upper stratum	No	No	Ash layer from fire, no objects or bodies

et al. 2004:3) and through mention by Warren Moorehead (1922). Site materials were stored at the Robert S. Peabody Museum of Archaeology, where professionals reanalyzed them prior to repatriation (Petersen et al. 2004).

In reanalysis, James Petersen and colleagues (2004) determined there were at least 17 individuals grouped in nine burials. In his early discussion of the site, Moorehead

(1922) noted whole iron fitted copper kettles placed over the heads of two burials (these higher-quality kettles date the site to ca. 1580–1600). No whole kettles ended up in the collection at the Peabody Museum. Petersen and colleagues (2004:41–43) were able to determine that one of the nine burial groups included an individual—a six-and-a-half- to seven-and-a-half-year-old female—buried with a kettle inverted over the head (Table 9.2). They were not able to confirm which of the other burial groups was associated with the second kettle.

Four other burial groups at the site had bodies showing copper staining on the bones, and their grave good inventories included copper objects likely made from kettles (Petersen et al. 2004:16). The copper-stained bones indicate that copper objects were included in direct contact with the bodies of the interred. One of the most interesting of these grave goods was a serrated copper band with animal fur that formed a copper headband placed on a child burial (Petersen et al. 2004:44). Of note, none of the burials were associated with purposefully damaged kettles (Table 9.2).

This site shows a similar pattern to the one found at Hopps: when intact, whole kettles and kettle-derived objects were included in graves, and they were placed in direct contact with the bodies of the dead. The kettle inverted and placed over one child's skull and a copper headband wrapped around the skull of another child suggest that contact with the skull was a distinct aspect of these funerary practices.

Age and sex data from the site provide suggestive patterning to the kettle or copper objects. The individual buried with a kettle inverted over her head was a female child. The four burial groups showing copper staining with copper objects include adult females and male and female children but no adult males. Adult males occur in the other four burial groups at the site (but not exclusively; they are with adult females and children of both sexes). The unsystematic excavations at this site make conclusive statements hard, but the lack of kettle or copper objects in burial groups containing adult males is still striking. This is also unlike patterns at other sites examined here, where kettles occur across sexes, suggesting local variation. Given that multiple tribal communities occupied the Northeast, distinct traditions were certainly incorporated in burial practices, creating local variation within broad regional trends.

SOUTHERN NEW ENGLAND WAMPANOAG: BURR'S HILL, RHODE ISLAND

Burr's Hill is a 17th-century Wampanoag cemetery on the eastern shore of the Warren River between Warren and Bristol, Rhode Island (Gibson 1980:9). Warren and Bristol were both critical places for the Wampanoag, respectively forming the principal village for sachem Massasoit and the headquarters of Massasoit's son Metacomet, or King Phillip (Gibson 1980:9).

TABLE 9.2. Distribution of kettle and kettle-derived objects at the Sandy Point Site (A.D. 1580–early 1600s), based on Peterson et al. (2004:9–12, 41–52)

BURIAL GROUP	WHOLE KETTLE	KETTLE-DERIVED OBJECT	DESCRIPTION	NUMBER OF INTERMENTS AND AGE AND SEX COMPOSITION
198	No	Yes	Copper beads; staining	1: child, 2–3 years
199	No	No		5: 2 newborns; child 1 year; older child; adult male; adult female
200	No	No		2: adult male, 35–45 years; adult, sex indeterminate, 35 years
201/3	No	No		1: adult male, 37–42
202	No	No		1: female, 10–11
204	No	Yes	Copper beads; staining	1: female, 25–35
205	No	Yes	Copper headband; staining	3: children, ranging in age from newborn to 3 years
206	No	Yes	Copper beads; staining	2: children, ranging in age from 4–5 years
207	Yes	No	Kettle inverted over head; staining	1: female, 6.5–7.5 years

Accidental finds of bodies in the area began in the 1800s during gravel mining; graves were subsequently looted. In 1913 Charles Read Carr, the librarian in Warren, undertook the only somewhat systematic excavations both to salvage remaining graves and to collect materials for an exhibit at the library (Gibson 1980:9). He never published his work, but his notes and all known materials from Burr's Hill were assembled and reanalyzed by the Haffenreffer Museum of Anthropology (Gibson, ed. 1980).

Carr unearthed 42 burials in 1913. Prior to this, ten other burials were "excavated" (Gibson 1980:21). Just after Carr's excavations, John Drown "excavated" several additional burials. Drown only twice noted the association of grave goods with bodies and otherwise just provided a list of goods from an unknown number of total graves (Gibson 1980:21). The burials unearthed from these varied activities at the site produced numerous funerary objects of Native American and European manufacture (Loren 2013a:159; Table 9.3).

Of the 42 burials excavated by Carr, almost half (20, or 47.6 percent) included kettles or kettle-derived objects. Of these 20, 16 included whole, intact kettles, while one included intentionally damaged kettles, and three included kettle-derived objects. Only one of the ten burials "excavated" prior to 1913 produced a kettle. The only two graves for which Drown provided specific notes both had whole kettles. This totals 23 graves from Burr's Hill documented to have kettle or kettle objects. Of these, 19 had intact whole kettles; this was clearly the predominant way kettles were included at Burr's Hill.

Looking at the inclusion patterns of the 19 intact whole kettles, we see some interesting trends (Table 9.3). First, whole kettles were often inverted when included as grave goods (10 out of 19). Second, kettles were frequently included in intimate contact with the bodies of the deceased (11 out of 19; but note that the other eight cases of whole kettles did not have location information, so we do not know definitively that these whole kettles were not also in contact with bodies). The most common form of intimate contact was the placement of inverted kettles over the head of the deceased (8 out of 19), but there were other intimate poses as well. In Carr's Burial #11, the largest multiple burial at the site, seven kettles were included. Two were in close contact with the dead: one was "full of small (human) bones," and one was "over (human) femurs and 1 humerus" (Gibson 1980:17). In Carr's Burial #36, a baby and kettle were wrapped together in a blanket (Gibson 1980:20). The ways kettles were included in direct contact with bodies here—over the skull, cradling the bones of the dead, bundled with the body of a baby—echo patterns seen also at Hopps and Sandy Point, where kettles were used in intimate and protective poses with the deceased.

SOUTHERN NEW ENGLAND NARRAGANSETT: WEST FERRY SITE, RHODE ISLAND

The West Ferry site is a 17th-century Narragansett cemetery site located on Conanicut Island in Narragansett Bay (Figure 9.1; Simmons 1970:4). Loam removal from the Watson farm in 1936 first revealed this site (Simmons 1970:7). One burial "excavated" at this time came to be called the Chief's Burial and was partially recorded; the remaining graves are undocumented (Simmons 1970:8). In 1966–67 Simmons conducted

TABLE 9.3. Distribution of kettles and kettle-derived objects at the Burr's Hill Site (A.D. 1650–1680), based on Gibson (1980:17–21)

BURIAL NUMBER	BURIAL COMPOSITION	WHOLE KETTLE	KETTLE-DERIVED OBJECT	LOCATION OF KETTLE OR KETTLE-DERIVED OBJECT
1	Adult	Yes	No	2 kettles: copper kettle on head; iron kettle at feet
3	Adult	Yes	No	Iron kettle on head
7	Adult	Yes	No	2 kettles: small kettle on head; large kettle over small kettle
9	Adult	Yes	No	2 kettles: large kettle over head to shoulders; small kettle, location not given
10	One adult, one infant	Yes	No	3 kettles, no location given: small brass kettle; kettle with patch of blanket or matting adhered; brass kettle
11	Multiple mixed burials	Yes	No	7 kettles: kettle full of small bones; kettle over femura and 1 humerus; 4 small brass kettles; brass kettle, bark, matting, etc. (pouch was under upside-down kettle; feathers on bottom)
14	Unknown	Yes	Yes	1 kettle: brass kettle (shell and glass beads on bottom and inside); copper segment
16	Adult	No	Yes	Brass kettle fragments
17	Adult	Yes	No	2 kettles: small kettle over head; large kettle adjacent
18	Adult	Yes	No	3 kettles: copper kettle on head; 2 iron kettles, location not given

continued

TABLE 9.3. *(continued)*

BURIAL NUMBER	BURIAL COMPOSITION	WHOLE KETTLE	KETTLE-DERIVED OBJECT	LOCATION OF KETTLE OR KETTLE-DERIVED OBJECT
22	Likely adult	Yes	No	1 kettle: kettle near head with iron spoon in it
25	Unknown	Yes	Yes	3 kettles: 3 brass kettles, all damaged, location not given; copper beads
28	Likely adult	Yes	No	1 kettle: iron kettle, location not given
30	Likely adult	No	Yes	brass tube; copper or brass fragments
31	Unknown	Yes	No	1 kettle: brass kettle, location not given
35	Double grave	Yes	No	2 kettles: 2 brass kettles, locations not given
36	One adult, one infant	Yes	No	1 kettle: infant in blanket with kettle
38	One adult, one infant	No	Yes	Copper beads around neck
39	Likely adult	Yes	Yes	1 kettle: small brass kettle, location not given; 3 brass kettle ears; kettle handle; brass kettle fragment
42	Likely adult	Yes	No	Small brass kettle
Pre-1913 burial	Unknown	Yes	Unknown	2 kettles: copper kettle, location not given; iron kettle, location not given
Drowned 1913	Likely adult	Yes	Unknown	1 kettle: three-legged iron kettle over head
Drowned 1913	Likely adult	Yes	Unknown	1 kettle: copper kettle over head

Note: Few burials were aged, and no skeletons were sexed.

systematic excavations at the landowners' request, uncovering 58 early contact period graves; with the Chief's Burial, that makes 59 17th-century graves documented (grave goods date the site to ca. 1620–1660; Simmons 1970:42). The burials included a fair amount of funerary objects of European manufacture and some of Native American manufacture.

Of the 59 burials (Table 9.4), four included whole kettles, and five produced kettle-derived objects (15.25 percent). Three burials had kettles inverted and placed immediately near the head of the deceased (not directly over the skull but in direct contact). The other burial with whole kettles had two nested kettles kept upright and placed approximately 40 centimeters from the head (Simmons 1970:95). In the five burials with kettle-derived objects, all objects appear in contact with the bodies of the dead, including underlying the head of the so-called Chief's Burial. This again matches the patterns noted at the other sites, with whole kettles and kettle-derived objects being included in graves in intimate contact with the bodies of the dead, often near the head.

This site, owing to its relatively recent excavation, has age and sex data for most burials (Simmons 1970). The distribution of kettles and objects does not pattern with sex; instead, it crosscuts these categories (Table 9.4). Of note, this differs from RI-1000 (another Narragansett early contact burial site subject to professional excavation more recently), where kettles were only found with adult females (Rubertone 2001). At West Ferry, however, there is a pattern in age distribution: no kettle or kettle-derived object was recovered from a child burial. Furthermore, four child burials have what I suggest is a purposeful transposing of Native-made ceramic vessels for European-origin kettles in the grave repertoire. These burials have pots placed on or right next to the child's face or skull, the same pattern of kettle placement observed in adult burials.

While children at other sites had kettles included with them, here the local community found it important to keep children from kettle objects while also marking some children in a similar logic to adults with kettles but using Native-made pots instead. At RI-1000 kettles were also only associated with adult females, a pattern interpreted as a reflection of the responsibilities of becoming or being a gendered adult female in Narragansett society (Rubertone 2001:152). The pattern at the West Ferry site's Narragansett community burial is also likely related to rites of passage and the responsibilities of adulthood (or the inverse, the protection of childhood). Were children unprepared for the power of European-made kettles? Or were they being protected from colonial tainting? The specific ontologies expressed in this practice deserve a separate investigation, one combined with descendant communities.

TABLE 9.4. Distribution of kettles and kettle-derived objects at West Ferry Site (A.D. 1610–1660), based on Simmons (1970)

BURIAL NUMBER	BURIAL COMPOSITION	WHOLE KETTLE	KETTLE-DERIVED OBJECT	LOCATION OF KETTLE OR KETTLE-DERIVED OBJECT
3	Female (50 years)	Yes	No	Small overturned brass kettle in front of forehead
5 (2)	Male (55–59 years); infant (0–4 years)	Yes	No	2 kettles with adult male: 1 overturned near skull; 1 overturned (in bad repair) about 40 cm from adult's feet (a short section of large mammal long bone underneath)
6	<4 years	Pot	No	No kettle, but a clay pot placed upside down before the child's face
8	Female (30–49 years)	Yes	No	2 brass kettles: one inside the other and right side up, located about 40 cm from skull
13	Female (30 years)	No	Yes	Tiny copper shred in western edge of pit and staining from a copper item on bone
14	Male (40 years)	No	Yes	Shred of copper near wrists
16	4–5 years	Pot	No	Clay pot cascaded over child's face
17	6–8 years	Pot	No	Clay pottery on its side or upside down before child's face
18	Female (15–19 years)	Yes	No	Brass kettle debris sprawled in an ample area before face
23	Male (30 years)	No	Yes	Brass waist plate with copper and brass fashioned objects in it
47	Unknown	No	Yes	No bones left in burial; copper shred found near where the head had been

TABLE 9.4. *(continued)*

BURIAL NUMBER	BURIAL COMPOSITION	WHOLE KETTLE	KETTLE-DERIVED OBJECT	LOCATION OF KETTLE OR KETTLE-DERIVED OBJECT
53	5–9 years	Pot	No	Burial 53 associated with "Chief's burial" (number 59); the pot was most likely associated with the chief
59	Adult male	No	Yes	"Chief's burial" recorded as having head set upon a large square sheet of brass (dug 1936)

SYMPATHETIC MAGIC AND INDIGENOUS KETTLE VALUATION

This brief survey of four well-documented early contact burial sites from across the broad geographic and tribal range of the Northeast shows local variation in terms of the inclusion of kettles or kettle-derived objects, including the presence of more damaged kettles at Hopps than at any other site, the exclusion of kettles from adult male burials at Sandy Point, the predominance of whole intact kettles at Burr's Hill, and the exclusion of kettles from child burials (and transposition with Native-made ceramic vessels) at the West Ferry site. Strikingly, it also reveals significant shared trends across the region. In particular, patterns of kettle inversion and bodily contact were observed across sites.

With inversion, we see that when kettles were included in burials as whole vessels (both fragmented and whole), there was a strong tendency for them to be inverted. All of the kettles at the Hopps site and Sandy Point site were inverted (Tables 9.1 and 9.2). At Burr's Hill, ten out of 19 were inverted, as were three out of four at the West Ferry site (Tables 9.3 and 9.4). For many societies, death reflects an inversion of the living world (Ovsyannikov and Terebikhin 2013:54). Among the tribal communities of the Northeast during early contact, death as an inversion may explain in part the inversion of kettles in graves in addition to context-specific layers of meaning. For those communities of the Northeast, the world of the living was being inverted before their eyes through their interactions with the people who brought kettles. A kettle's utilitarian function as a cooking pot requires the kettle to be upright; inverting it eradicated the utilitarian function and value instilled in it by Europeans (see discussions of ritual killing by Oland and by Cobb and Stephenson, this volume). As discussed above, kettles were ascribed with manit, an animating spirit, by indigenous people of the Northeast, and these practices of inversion helped transform these objects into indigenously meaningful and controlled items, a transformation that extended into the afterlife. Inverted in burials, kettles were passed on with the dead in distinctly non-European form, perhaps as offerings for a reinversion of the world in the next life.

Considering bodily contact, we see that both whole intact kettles and kettle-derived objects were routinely placed in contact with the bodies of the dead (of note, damaged kettles, it seems, were rarely placed in contact with the dead). Frequently, the contact is specifically with the face or skull of the deceased. At the Hopps site, there were five intact whole kettles recovered across the two burial pits, four of the five definitively (and one potentially) inverted over human bones. All of these were associated with fragmentary bones that included many skull parts. The kettle-derived grave lining had three to four bodies laid in direct contact with it at Hopps as well (Table 9.1). At Sandy Point the kettle and kettle-derived artifacts were all in contact with bodies. One kettle covered a child's skull, and there was a copper headband on another child (Table 9.2). At Burr's Hill, in 11 of the 19 burials with whole kettles, the kettles were in direct contact with bodies, and in eight of these cases, kettles were inverted over the skull like a helmet (Table 9.3). At West Ferry three of the four burials with kettles had the kettles placed directly next to and in contact with, but not over, skulls. In all five of the burials with kettle-derived objects, the objects were in contact with the dead, including brass sheets underlying the skull of the Chief's Burial (Table 9.4).

I suggest that the practice of including kettles and kettle-derived objects in contact with human remains was a material expression of sympathetic magic used purposefully and thoughtfully to register indigenous desires about the changing world of early colonial encounter.

Frazer explores sympathetic magic in detail in his classic work *The Golden Bough* (1951[1922]). The essence of sympathetic magic is a belief that persons or things can exert a sympathetic influence on each other from a distance (Frazer 1951[1922]:25). Sympathetic magic has two branches: imitative magic and contagious magic. Imitative magic is based on the idea that like produces like, or that effect resembles its cause (Frazer 1951[1922]:13). Contagious magic is based on the idea that things that have once been in contact with each other continue to act on each other even at a distance (Frazer 1951[1922]:13). Both assume that things act on each other at a distance through a secret sympathy (Frazer 1951[1922]:14).

Contagious magic asserts the power of physical contact to transcend time and space: that which was in contact with one person or object is able to convey impressions from this person or object to another through contact with it even if long disconnected from the original person or object (Frazer 1951[1922]:43). I suggest that indigenous groups of the Northeast were materializing concepts of contagious magic in their inclusion of whole intact kettles and kettle-derived objects in contact with the bodies of the dead in their funerary practices. The contact of kettles and kettle-derived objects appears often in a protective pose in these interments, with the kettles over the skulls almost like armored helmets on the dead and the cases of grave linings or kettles holding bones as encasements. The protective power of these kettles or kettle-objects was about more than the physical protection of human remains; it was about the power inherent in kettles from both their origin in contact with Europeans and their indigenously ascribed animating spirit (manit). The power of these objects was transferred to the dead through these acts of contagion.

Again, the kettle was a trade item that was instantly popular and remained in high demand throughout the 16th and 17th centuries. Kettles became so popular in part because they were tied to long-established precolonial indigenous value systems around copper, and they were therefore readily incorporated into the indigenous ontology of a universe filled with animating spirit. The kettle acquired further symbolic charge in early contact because indigenous peoples always experienced it as an irreproducible good with an origin in contact with the "Other" (Turgeon 1997:9–10).

By placing kettles and kettle-derived objects in direct contact with the bodies of the dead, sympathetic magic could relay the power inherent in kettles from both their original contact with Europeans and their indigenously ascribed animating spirit to the dead. The dead would then be able to take the kettle, which was irreproducible by them in this world, and the power it held from its foreignness, as well as from its indigenous manit, with them into the next world. As an indigenous leader in the Maritimes explained to Jesuit missionaries in the early 1600s, they buried the dead with kettles because the dead "have need of it since it is among us a utensil of new introduction, and with which the other world cannot yet be furnished" (Denys 1908[1672]:440). Kettles, experienced as an irreproducible good in the world of contact, would, through contagion, become available to the indigenous peoples of the Northeast in the afterworld. Unlike the experience of colonial encounter in their earthly life, in this afterlife they would already have kettles with them as a spiritual and physical resource to protect them from another inversion of indigenous space.

Although he provided a classic analysis, Frazer nevertheless perceived of magic as a product of crude intelligence, of primitive peoples, stating that to them, "magic is always an art and never a science" (1951[1922]:13). Rather than interpreting magic as a naïve impulse of "primitive" peoples, as Frazer and other early anthropologists did, I suggest it is more constructive to see this use of sympathetic magic in the consumption of European-made goods as sophisticated, meaningful, and functional. As Alfred Gell (1998:101) proposes, the causality behind sympathetic magic is quite practical (not mystical), as it is based on intent; the likelihood of something happening is directly related to one's desire for it to happen. Magic registers and publicizes the strength of desire. During the 16th and 17th centuries across the Northeast, the colonial project, based on territorial dispossession, militarism, and religious conversion of indigenous peoples, was expanding. As they placed kettles in contact with their dead, indigenous communities registered their desires to have access to the power of Europeans but also to be able to reformulate this power for their use and protection in an exclusively indigenous next world.

CONCLUSIONS

Within the context of the alterity and ambiguity of early colonial encounter, between A.D. 1500 and 1680, indigenous communities across the Northeast developed new burial practices that involved furnishing graves with large amounts of European-origin goods, as well as with some Native-origin goods. These burials reflect one of the ways indigenous groups expressed in material form the ongoing negotiation of their coexisting identities in this period—that of being indigenous and of being "New World People" (Reid 1995:89). During this period, being indigenous did not negate the reality of being entrenched in a colonial world, but neither did being "New World People" negate the notion of humanity contained in being indigenous (Reid 1995:89). This complex duality was expressed in the dynamic inclusion of kettles in early contact indigenous burials.

Kettles were transformed into objects that disavowed colonial reality and replaced it with the materialization of indigenous desires (Bhabha 1994:130). Kettles, in whole or partial form, were rarely included in burials in a form that acknowledged their European-valued utilitarian function. Whole kettles were crushed and/or inverted in burials, purposefully marking them as nonutilitarian. Kettle-derived objects were also nonutilitarian, coming from kettles whose use as a functional vessel was gone (as they were cut into sheet metal to make objects). By consistently including these items in burials in ways that avoided, if not mocked, the European value ascribed to kettles, indigenous groups placed their own valuation systems on these goods. One of these was sympathetic magic, specifically contagious magic. By placing kettles and kettle-derived objects in direct contact with the bodies of the dead, indigenous groups materialized contagious magic and its assertion of the power of physical contact to transcend time and space. Through kettle–body contagion in burial rites, indigenous communities endowed their loved ones with both the manit they ascribed to these objects and the power that these objects inhered from their origin with Europeans in the afterlife, sending the dead off, as it were, prepared for and protected against similar encounter, trauma, and inversion in the next world.

During early colonial encounter in the broader Northeast, indigenous groups deployed sympathetic magic in their consumption of kettles. When we consider this in light of the fact that the inclusion of kettles in graves in the Northeast during this period was so frequent and significant that it was actually a driving force behind the persistent cumulative demand for kettles in the fur trade (Martin 1975:114), it becomes clear that it was indigenous frames of reference, and not European ones, that drove the supply and valuation of kettles in the market-based economy of early contact.

RESISTING AND ENDURING

10

INDIGENOUS VAQUEROS IN COLONIAL CALIFORNIA

Labor, Identity, and Autonomy

LEE M. PANICH

AS THE CHAPTERS IN THIS VOLUME DEMONSTRATE, Native people incorporated introduced objects or new materials into existing cultural traditions and emerging practices, some of which eventually became deeply ingrained in their economic livelihoods and cultural identities. A classic case of the latter is Native American horse culture, which has deep historical roots and continued contemporary importance, particularly on the Great Plains (e.g., Sargent 2014); yet indigenous groups in California also quickly and widely incorporated the horse and associated material culture into localized practices. The indigenous vaqueros, or cowboys, of colonial California offer an intriguing example of how Native people used foreign animals and associated material culture in ways that both articulated with precontact traditions and provided innovative strategies for the negotiation of Euro-American colonialism. With a primary focus on the Spanish colonial period, broadly defined, I explore four examples of how Native Californians used material culture to forge vaquero identities, as well as how, in some cases, knowledge of horse handling facilitated indigenous autonomy from the early colonial period into modern times.

Any discussion of indigenous vaqueros necessarily entails a consideration of labor. Archaeologists and historians focusing on Native labor in colonial California have shown how indigenous people were able to turn certain aspects of the colonial labor regime to their favor. Stephen Silliman (2001), for example, suggests that although the labor system established by Franciscan missionaries posed very real constraints, it also provided certain opportunities for achieving relative status or autonomy within the mission community. George Harwood Phillips (2010) demonstrates how Native workers in southern California capitalized on colonial labor systems both during and after the mission period. His analysis acknowledges the difficulties of missionization and the far-reaching changes it wrought for Native Californians, but he also traces common threads of the daily practice of labor from precontact times into the missions and the postmission rancho economy. Steven Hackel criticizes some previous scholars for their essentialist view of Native labor, stating that, "ironically, in much of this scholarship, Indians are ascribed the power to reject the Franciscans' labor regime but denied the ability to incorporate aspects of it selectively to their own lives" (1997:124).

I take up these issues by bridging a concern for Native labor and agency in colonial California with recent archaeological discussion about using consumption as an analytical framework for understanding how people "socialize material goods" (Mullins 2011b; see also Dietler 2010; Cipolla, introduction, this volume). As applied to the archaeology of colonial contexts, a consumption framework challenges long-standing views of Native people as static or ahistorical (Beaudoin, this volume) but also allows that indigenous people did not necessarily employ foreign objects to signal identities in a commonsense, representationalist manner (Creese, this volume). Consumption can thus be viewed as the active use of foreign (new or nonlocal) objects within localized but diachronic understandings and strategies. To tease out the "complexities of consumption" (Silliman and Witt 2010), archaeologists must closely examine the context of how foreign goods were acquired, used, and ultimately deposited in the archaeological record. As the chapters in this volume demonstrate, indigenous people drew on particular worldviews to mobilize new materials in the negotiation of changing circumstances, often incorporating foreign items into their personal adornment (Loren, this volume; Bragdon, this volume) and ceremonial practices (Howey, this volume; Oland, this volume) in ways that differed significantly from the uses imagined or intended by Euro-American colonists.

Here I examine how indigenous people in California actively integrated horses (a totally foreign animal) and their material trappings (novel pieces of material culture) into evolving local and regional traditions (see Anderson 2004; Mitchell 2015). This analysis requires two interrelated steps: an examination of how new things were acquired, as well as how they were ultimately used and understood. Although a thorough accounting of the supply of horses and associated objects is outside the scope of this chapter, where possible I provide information on the social processes that gave Native people access to horses and the material goods related to animal handling. The second consideration necessitates the examination of how foreign objects—in this case, animals—were incorporated into existing and/or emerging practices. These issues are explored across the colonial landscape, from mission establishments to contemporaneous secular ranchos to Native homelands (Figure 10.1). Using multiple lines of evidence from different regions of Alta and Baja California, I outline two patterns related to

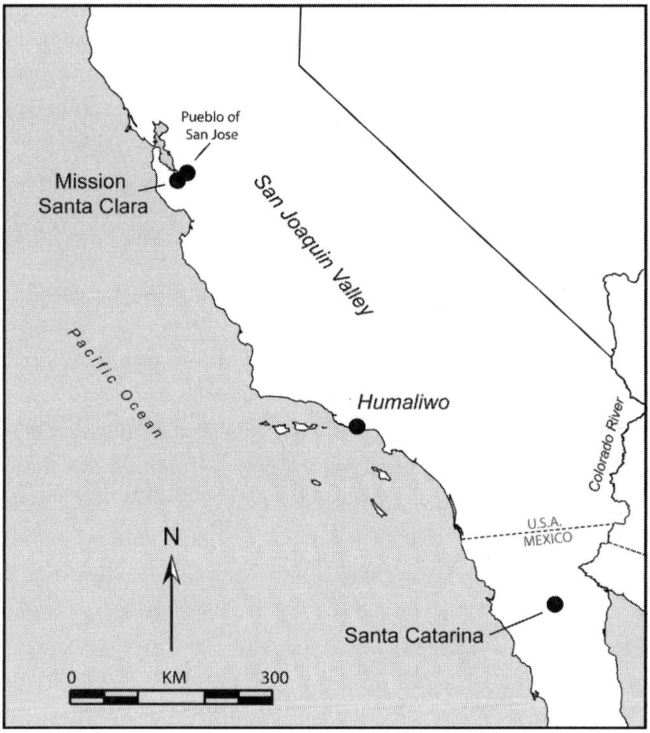

FIGURE 10.1. Map of portions of California and Baja California showing places mentioned in text.

the role of horses and related material culture in Native California. First, I argue that vaquero labor and socially meaningful use of associated equipment may have given some individuals unprecedented paths to social status. Second, I suggest that knowledge of horse handling, learned in the missions and other colonial settlements, may have paradoxically facilitated the persistence of indigenous autonomy in some parts of the broader region.

INDIGENOUS VAQUEROS IN SPANISH CALIFORNIA

During the late 18th and early 19th centuries, Spanish officials implemented a three-pronged plan to extend colonial control over the coastal strip of Alta California. In addition to four presidios and three pueblos that were established by military and secular colonists, Franciscan missionaries founded 21 missions in Alta California over the course of the colonial period (ca. 1769-1840s). Although many Native individuals did develop ties to the presidios and pueblos, the missions were designed to be the primary institution through which California's diverse array of indigenous groups would be converted to Catholicism and Euro-American lifeways. A primary component of this enculturation program was the teaching of agricultural practices to the various hunter-gatherer-fisher people who joined the missions, whom the missionaries collectively termed "neophytes."

The use of horses by Native Californians, however, provoked fear in most Spanish colonial administrators, who hoped to avoid the creation of independent mounted raiders like those who plagued Spanish colonial settlements in the North American interior (Hackel 2005:338–339). Spanish colonial policy held that Native people in California, including mission neophytes, should be prohibited from having horses or even the materials necessary for riding them. As early as 1782, Felipe de Neve instructed that halters and ropes carried by Native Californians, either "heathen or Christian," should be confiscated on the grounds that such equipment would only be used to steal livestock (Beilharz 1971:160). In 1818 and 1819 colonial officials issued declarations restricting indigenous use of horses to approved mission-based vaqueros. Any Native people in violation were subject to lashing (Hackel 2005:338–339; and see Haas 2014:39).

Although the role of Native Californians in the mission era stock-raising enterprise appears to have been a source of worry and antagonism between missionary, military, and secular officials, the vast numbers of livestock—including cattle, horses, sheep, and others—in Alta California precipitated a need for Native workers to manage them. By 1805 California was home to some 95 thousand cattle and 21 thousand horses (Hackel 1997:116), and at the end of the mission period, in the mid-1830s, an estimated 500 thousand cattle were kept in the region (Peelo 2009:596). The herds were so large that most missions maintained multiple outlying cattle ranches or other agricultural outstations that were staffed by neophytes. In 1795 Fermín Francisco de Lasuén, father president of the Alta California missions, wrote that although the missionaries wished to prevent Native Californians from acquiring horses, the growing mission herds required vaqueros, and "these have to be Indians, for there are no others" (quoted in Phillips 2010:72). Such sentiments were shared by some military officials and secular settlers, who themselves employed unmissionized Native Californians for various labor tasks that involved riding horseback—often in violation of colonial policy.

The indigenous vaqueros of colonial California, whom Lasuén reluctantly argued were necessary for the success of the mission enterprise, were distinguished through a unique material assemblage. This included specialized equipment, such as saddles, spurs, and bits, as well as boots, hats, leather jackets, and other items of personal adornment that probably resembled those of colonial Californio horsemen (Lacson 2015:216; Lightfoot 2005:70–71). Account books kept in Mexico for individual mission and presidio establishments contain records of the purchases of hardware and other items—saddles, spurs, bits, etc.—required for vaquero labor in Alta California (e.g., Perissinotto 1998; Skowronek et al. n.d.). Although the details of their production largely escaped notice in colonial era documents, quantities of horse hardware were also produced in the blacksmith shops that were eventually established at the missions and presidios of Alta California (Simmons and Turley 1980).

The involvement of Native people in the social, economic, and material relationships of horse handling offered opportunities for men who worked as vaqueros to gain prestige and autonomy across colonial California. Mission-based indigenous vaqueros typically held elevated status in the ostensibly communal social world of the Franciscan missions. They were also more likely to reside outside of the mission quadrangle, where they may have enjoyed increased mobility, as well as the opportunity to live away from the watchful eyes of the padres (Lightfoot 2005). Less is known about Native vaqueros who rode for secular ranchos during the Spanish period, but these establishments relied heavily on indigenous laborers to manage their herds. It may be that secular ranchos offered an appealing alternative to the strict social controls of the California missions. Both types of vaquero labor—in the missions and at early secular ranchos—likely provided unprecedented avenues of physical and social mobility for Native men. Horses and associated knowledge also quickly spread into the interior of Alta California, where groups who already had well-established regional trade connections incorporated horse raiding into their economic repertoire. The mobility and influence of these mounted groups helped stave off Spanish colonial expansion into the interior and offered yet another alternative for Native people fleeing or avoiding the coastal missions. In the following sections, I provide brief examples of each of these three points in the broader landscape of colonial California.

MISSION VAQUEROS: SANTA CLARA DE ASÍS

Archaeological and documentary evidence from Mission Santa Clara de Asís offers insight into the social worlds of indigenous vaqueros in the heart of the mission system. Founded in 1777 near the southern margin of San Francisco Bay, Santa Clara was home to a diverse group of Native people, including individuals of Ohlone and Yokuts descent. The mission's herds, though variable in size, were a source of both food and economic power; for most of the mission's existence it held between three thousand and six thousand cattle and one thousand and two thousand horses. In 1828 the mission reported 14,500 head of cattle, perhaps reflecting the growing importance of cattle ranching and the hide and tallow trade after Mexican independence (Shoup and Milliken 1999:52).

Few accounts describe indigenous vaqueros at Mission Santa Clara, but the documentary record is not entirely silent on the subject. Writing in 1814 in response to a questionnaire, or *interrogatorio*, sent by colonial administrators, Fathers Magín Catalá and José Viader provided a brief list of male labor roles at Santa Clara, including "cowboys, shepherds, shoemakers, stonemasons, carpenters, blacksmiths, tanners, teamsters, etc." (Geiger and Meighan 1976:131). The mission's sacramental records include a handful of references to indigenous vaqueros, including an entry marking the death of Cosme, an Ohlone man who died after falling from his horse in late August 1808 (Huntington Library 2006:SCL Death No. 3848). Cosme was one of as many as 25 indigenous vaqueros who worked at Mission Santa Clara during the early 19th century, according to Nasario Galindo, whose father was the mission's *mayordomo del campo* (Galindo et al. 1959). The presence of vaqueros is also revealed by the more than 100 pairs of spurs, as well as dozens of saddles and horse bits listed in the mission's account book between the time of the mission's founding and 1810 (Skowronek et al. n.d.). Despite the fears of some colonial officials about the dangers associated with indigenous people's access to such materials, the missionaries at Santa Clara appear to have outfitted neophyte vaqueros with the full complement of horse-related hardware.

While direct archaeological evidence of vaquero labor at Mission Santa Clara is scant, multiple recently excavated pit features within Mission Santa Clara's Native *ranchería* have included spurs and other objects associated with horse handling (Figure 10.2). The initial functions of these features likely varied, but I argue that at least three features represent either the destruction of an individual's property following his or her death or the remnants of annual mourning ceremonies, both of which were common practices among the Ohlone and Yokuts groups who joined the neophyte community at Santa Clara (Panich 2014, 2015). Indeed, Alfred Kroeber (1925) noted that the destruction, through burning and/or burial, of the deceased's property was ubiquitous across Native California, while variations on the annual mourning ceremony—to commemorate all of the previous year's dead—were practiced throughout southern and central California and often involved the destruction of personal property. In addition to the horse-related items present in all three features, these pits each exhibited various forms of *in situ* burning and contained thousands of shell beads, as well as other valuable items. These features, moreover, were all discovered near adobe barracks, residences that were typically reserved for long-tenured or high-status neophytes.

The largest feature (Feature 5) was excavated in 2012 during an archaeological field school, during which approximately 25 percent of the feature was exposed (Panich

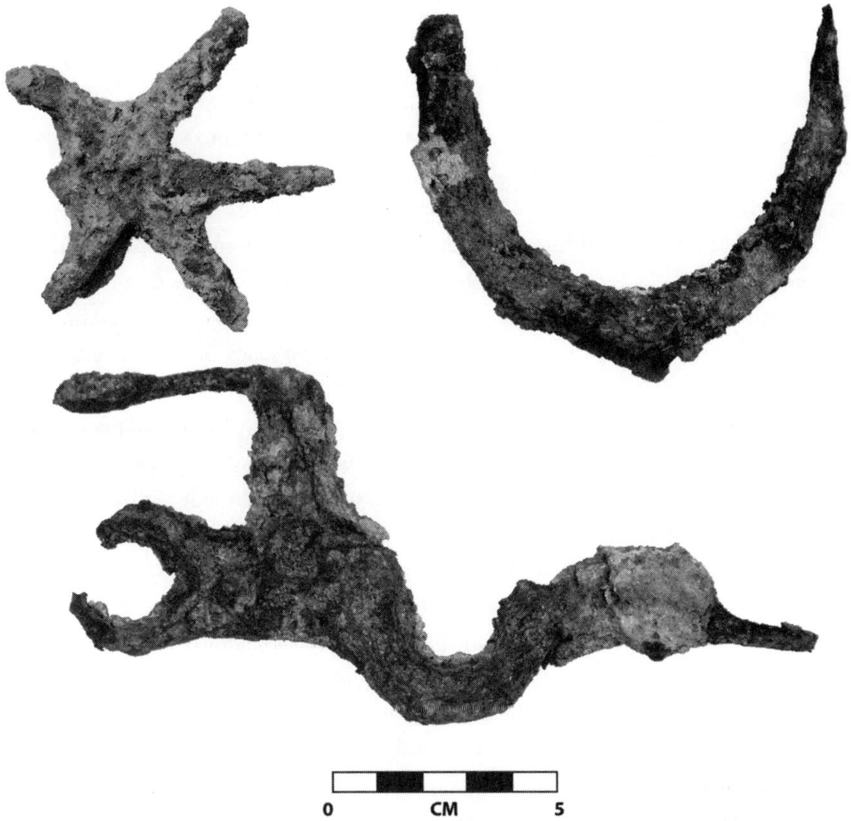

FIGURE 10.2. Vaquero equipment recovered from pit features within the Native *ranchería* at Mission Santa Clara. *Clockwise from top left*: spur rowel, heel band for boot spur, and fragment of a spade bit (shank and portion of mouthpiece).

et al. 2014). With regard to vaquero gear, the excavated portion of the pit contained a single iron spur rowel, as well as other heavily oxidized metal objects. The feature also yielded many items of personal adornment, including more than 1,800 shell beads, 30 glass beads, and an assortment of other items such as a brass finger ring. Approximately 2,500 tobacco (*Nicotiana* sp.) seeds were recovered via flotation. The feature, which dates to the 1810s or later, also contained large quantities of mission roof tile, as well as faunal remains. Two similar features were excavated in 2004 (Allen et al. 2010). Feature 63 contained the heel band of an iron boot spur, as well as portions of a spade bit for a horse. Excavation of the feature also yielded nearly 2,200 shell beads, 35 glass beads, a *Haliotis* pendant, an obsidian projectile point, and additional items. Feature 64 also contained the heel band of an iron boot spur, as well as more than 1,200 shell beads, 32 glass beads, and two *Haliotis* pendants, among other objects. Features 63 and 64 were discovered adjacent to one another, and both have a post-1800 date.

Together, these three features provide a unique window onto vaquero labor and identity within the mission community. Many of the constituents of these features—items such as shell and glass beads, as well as shell pendants—are typical of grave goods found in Native California. Similar items have also been recovered from two mission cemeteries at Santa Clara, although it is important to note that the deposition of grave goods would have been officially prohibited by Catholic teachings at the time (Panich 2015). In the case of Feature 5, the presence of large quantities of tobacco seeds further suggests that at least some of the materials in the feature were ceremonially deposited. Many California archaeologists view beads and pendants as objects associated with individual persona in life, while their deposition in mortuary contexts presented opportunities for the living to assert and memorialize the status of the deceased (Milliken et al. 2007; Robinson 2013). Like the thousands of beads with which they were deposited, the bit and spur fragments were not casually cast off. Rather, they were valuable objects intentionally deposited during times of mourning, possibly as part of the destruction of the property of deceased individuals.

The inclusion of vaquero gear—portions of spurs and horse bits—in features that appear to have been part of indigenous mourning ceremonies suggests that such items were actively incorporated into not only established mortuary practices but also evolving sensibilities regarding the role of new forms of labor and concomitant social identities within the mission community. Social status among the indigenous population at Mission Santa Clara likely involved an individual's position within the mission labor regime and political hierarchy, as well as in the often-clandestine social world of the ranchería (Panich et al. 2014). The spurs and other horse trappings in these three features do not reflect a simple process of acculturation. Instead, they were found in association with thousands of shell beads, as well as other artifacts and ecofacts that have direct antecedents in precontact Native Californian understandings of mourning and social status. Contextual evidence from other mission sites in California includes many spurs that have been recovered from adobe neophyte barracks, residences that were often reserved for high-status individuals and families within the mission community (e.g., Allen 1998; Bertrando 1997). It may be, even, that mission vaqueros, through their more geographically mobile occupation with the mission estate, had greater access to important materials available only from outside of the mission walls. These patterns suggest that indigenous vaqueros at Mission Santa Clara likely enjoyed positions of high social standing not only in the eyes of the missionaries but also within the mission's large indigenous community.

INDIGENOUS VILLAGES AND SECULAR SETTLEMENTS: HUMALIWO

In colonial California, cattle ranching grew in importance over time, eventually dominating the region's economy under Mexican rule. During the Spanish period (1769–1821), stock raising was largely limited to ranches run by the missions, although secular settlers also established roughly 30 private grazing enterprises in Alta California. In many cases, secular ranches competed directly with the missions for land and often for indigenous laborers (Farris 2014). While the large ranchos associated with Mexican California employed former neophytes after the closing of the California missions in the 1830s and 1840s, the Spanish period ranches typically employed unmissionized Native workers, including men who worked as vaqueros. Accordingly, these early ranchos may have offered an alternative to the missions for Native people caught in a rapidly changing social and ecological context. The details of secular ranches varied across the province, but in some cases Native laborers were able to maintain close ties to their ancestral villages (Reddy 2015). The example of Humaliwo offers insight into how certain Native people were able to capitalize on economic ties to secular ranches both to avoid the missions and perhaps to enhance their social standing.

The Chumash settlement of Humaliwo, within the modern city of Malibu, was a large coastal village near the Santa Monica Mountains. Archaeological work at Humaliwo has identified extensive archaeological deposits dating from precontact and colonial times. While no substantive residential areas from the colonial period were identified during excavations in the 1960s and 1970s, a large, discrete, historic era cemetery, totaling 136 burials, was completely excavated in 1972. Based on bead types, the cemetery appears to have been in use from 1775 to 1805 (Bickford 1982; Gamble 2008). Lynn Gamble and colleagues (2001) synthesized information from prehistoric and historic era burials at Humaliwo to understand the genesis of ranked society among the Chumash, who are thought to have had relatively complex social, political, and ritual hierarchies partially reinforced through material wealth. By examining data regarding grave goods, grave depth, and population structure at Humaliwo, Gamble and colleagues (2001) found that certain families enjoyed high rank and material wealth relative to commoners living at the village and that this social status was symbolically reinforced through the offering of grave goods, a practice that persisted into the Spanish period.

Historical documentation of the Chumash inhabitants of Humaliwo indicates that nearly 120 individuals from the village were baptized at nearby Spanish missions, largely San Fernando Rey and San Buenaventura, where at least two men went on to become mission vaqueros (Lacson 2015:221). But most baptisms of individuals from Humaliwo did not occur until the early 19th century, when the historic era cemetery was already falling into disuse. Based on ethnohistorical evidence, Gamble (2008:205–206) argues that the village, at least in the early years of the colonial period, was more closely associated with nearby secular ranching activities. She identifies the Rancho Topanga Malibu Sequit, established by 1801, as a likely source of employment for Chumash living at Humaliwo.

Several artifacts related to horse handling were recovered from the historic era cemetery at Humaliwo (Bickford 1982). These include an iron *concho*, a metal ornament commonly worn by vaqueros; five *higos*, small decorative metal objects that were hung from saddle skirts; a headstall plate, a type of metal ornament incorporated into a bridle; and a spur rowel and heel band similar to those recovered from Mission Santa Clara. Metal knives, buttons, and fragments of firearms were also found in the cemetery. While the exact depositional associations for some of the metal artifacts are unclear, all of the objects were found either with burials, within caches of beads and other artifacts, or underneath rock cairns and can be seen collectively as burial offerings. These metal items were not the only grave goods present in the cemetery, which additionally contained thousands of shell beads and over 15 thousand glass beads. Many of the burials with sizable bead lots were also associated with fragments of asphaltum or redwood, materials that are indicative of redwood-plank canoes or canoe fragments. Only certain people in Chumash society had the knowledge required to build plank canoes—members of the hereditary Brotherhood of the Tomol—and the 11 individuals found with canoe remains at Humaliwo were likely either of high rank and/or members of canoe-owning families (Gamble et al. 2001:198–199).

Interestingly, canoe remains and vaquero gear do not co-occur within particular features or grave lots within the historic era cemetery at Humaliwo, pointing toward differential use of material goods to reinforce or forge social status in changing circumstances. While the presence of shell and glass beads along with horse trappings in the possible mourning features at both Mission Santa Clara and the historic era cemetery at Humaliwo is notable, the complex social ranking of Chumash society differed from that of the Ohlone and Yokuts groups who joined Mission Santa Clara. At Humaliwo, the plank canoe remains suggest not just the persistence of hereditary social ranking but also the importance of labor (in the form of canoe making) and perhaps mobility (in the form of watercraft) for social identity. The metal objects from the cemetery similarly relate to indigenous labor and mobility in colonial California, supporting the idea that vaquero labor was one avenue for Native people to achieve relative autonomy within the colonial system and relative status within their own community. That the canoe remains and objects associated with horses are mutually exclusive may further indicate that Chumash men working as vaqueros were not originally from highly ranked families. These items, acquired through economic ties to colonial establishments, were deposited in ways that used enduring cultural practices to solidify evolving social identities.

NATIVE HOMELANDS: CALIFORNIA'S SAN JOAQUIN VALLEY

While the horse was a central component of mission and rancho labor regimes, its use also extended unchecked into the interior of California, where various Native groups lived outside of direct colonial control. California's San Joaquin Valley was home to numerous Native groups who evaded missionization and made their living partly by raiding the livestock of the coastal missions, pueblos, and ranchos. The San Joaquin Valley and adjacent Sierra Nevada foothills were originally home to diverse Yokuts groups who in precontact times facilitated the flow of goods between the resource-rich regions of the Pacific Coast and Sierra Nevada. In the colonial era, the political economy of the valley was restructured as groups coalesced and were joined by people fleeing the missions (Cook 1962; Honig 2003; Phillips 1993). Knowledge of horses spread out from colonial centers, carried by fugitive neophytes, mission Indians on leave, or unmissionized rancho laborers. Horses themselves were typically stolen from colonial establishments, and horse raiding by valley people began as early as the 1780s (Arkush 1993). As discussed by Albert Hurtado (1990), the developments in the San Joaquin Valley intimately linked indigenous labor and raiding.

By the early to mid 19th century, horse raiding was one of the primary pursuits of the dynamic, multiethnic groups of the San Joaquin Valley who often included former mission neophytes. In 1828 and 1829, for example, large numbers of Yokuts people left the missions of the southern San Francisco Bay region under the leadership of two Native rebels, Estanislau from Mission San José and Cipriano from Mission Santa Clara. While the role of indigenous vaqueros in these events is unclear, the insurgents certainly had knowledge of horses, as they took many animals from missions and other settlements (Haas 2014:146–147). Similar raids continued unabated into the 1830s, with Native raiders making off with nearly all the horses from the Pueblo of San José by middecade (Phillips 1993:109–110). One estimate puts the total number of horses stolen from colonial establishments in central California from 1825 to 1845 at 100 thousand animals (Arkush 1993:629). An account from 1830 underscores the importance of the horse for the Native people of the San Joaquin Valley: "There is not a village which does not have horses" (José Berreyesa, quoted in Cook 1962:187).

The influx of introduced animals and associated knowledge offered several opportunities to Native people in the region. Yokuts groups successfully used the animals to open new avenues of trade to the east, while horses and associated knowledge also became important status symbols. As described by Lisbeth Haas (2014:38–40), Native leaders appropriated the horse as a symbol of prestige within and outside of their own villages, with particular leaders anticipating that their horses would elicit respect from missionaries and other colonial officials. Fugitive neophytes, for their part, brought horses with them to the interior to ease social tensions with their unmissionized kin (Phillips 1993:96). Within the dynamic context of interior California, even the gendered nature of mission and rancho-based labor roles appears to have broken down. In 1819 Father President Mariano Payeras wrote, "In the Tulares all ride, even the women" (quoted in Lacson 2015:215). Native people also used horses for hunting elk, though historical accounts indicate that horses themselves became an important source of food for many Native groups living in the San Joaquin Valley. Phillips (1993:105) presents several eyewitness accounts describing large piles of butchered horse bones encountered by early Anglo-American explorers in the region.

Nevertheless, the determination of Yokuts people to accumulate horses and to resist Spanish colonization made these villages targets for increasing violence, as Spanish and Mexican officials sent expeditions into the interior to capture fugitive neophytes and to punish horse thieves. Colonial officials were fearful that the Yokuts' fondness for horses could lead to the creation of a new Apachería, sentiments that echoed earlier attempts to keep Native Californians from acquiring horses (Haas 2014:39–40; Heizer 1941:104–105; Zappia 2014:95). With the growth of foreign exploration of the San Joaquin Valley, Native raiders expanded beyond the coastal missions and other settlements founded by the Spanish. Valuable manufactured goods and woolen items were available via trade connections to the east, while Anglo-American fur-trapping parties offered further possibilities of trading and raiding, although the latter often ended in ruthless violence against Native people (Phillips 1993).

Interestingly, little archaeological evidence exists that could be used to illuminate the role of horses within the dynamic Native societies of the Central Valley during the Spanish and Mexican periods. An early review of historic era sites in the region by Robert Heizer (1941) mentions glass beads but no artifacts specifically related to horse handling. It may be that indigenous horse raiders made do without specialized gear; indeed, an image of a Native horseman from the San Joaquin Valley produced in 1854 shows him riding bareback and barefoot, using a simple rope hackamore (Koppel 1854; Panich and Schneider 2015:Fig. 5). Despite the numerous historical observations of valley groups butchering and eating horses, Heizer (1941) concluded that archaeological evidence for such practices was largely lacking (but see Moratto 1984:323).

The horse was the key to indigenous autonomy in the San Joaquin Valley during the colonial period (Mitchell 2015:204–212). Knowledge of horses also allowed many neophytes to seek alternatives to the mission system as either fugitives or raiders, or both. While the interior region never developed into a full-fledged Apachería, as some colonial officials feared it would, Native people were able to quickly incorporate horses into evolving patterns of residential mobility, subsistence, and trading. Few archaeological deposits are known to exist that could illuminate the intimate negotiations of labor and identity like those that unfolded at places like Mission Santa Clara and Humaliwo, but the broader patterns of independence of—and resistance to—Spanish and Mexican colonialism amply demonstrate how Native people were able to incorporate foreign animals into emerging local practices.

INDIGENOUS VAQUEROS FROM THE MISSIONS TO THE MODERN DAY

After the secularization of the Franciscan missions, much of California's coastal strip was granted to private individuals, and Native Californians were alienated from their ancestral territories and former mission lands. Yet some Native people were able to successfully weather the period's political and economic turmoil based on the skills they had acquired at the missions. With the expansion of California's ranching economy, based in large part on the trade of cattle hides and tallow, vaquero skills remained in high demand (see Silliman 2004:22–31 for an overview of Native American labor in the ranchos of California). For example, Phillips suggests that the continuity of labor tasks made Native vaqueros the "least affected of all the neophytes by the breakup of the missions" (1993:108). In a later work, Phillips (2010) demonstrates the value of horse handling to some indigenous groups in southern California where the ranchos offered opportunities for Native people to use the knowledge gained in the missions to achieve relative autonomy.

Even in the American period, knowledge of horses remained one way for indigenous people to maintain a measure of independence and to continue what was by then an important cultural tradition. As detailed by L. Frank Hogeland and Kim Hogeland (2007:36–41), Native people across California drew on cowboy skills for their economic livelihoods—and recreation in the form of rodeos—throughout the late 19th and 20th centuries.

SANTA CATARINA, BAJA CALIFORNIA

As in Alta California, the Native inhabitants of northern Baja California acquired knowledge of horses during the Spanish colonial period, and these groups have since incorporated the animals and associated skills into important aspects of their economic and cultural practices. Here I briefly consider the long-term implications of horse handling for the indigenous community of Santa Catarina in Baja California, Mexico, where I conducted an archaeological and ethnohistorical investigation of the Dominican mission of Santa Catalina (1797–1840). Historical and ethnographic information from the region gives context to the enduring importance of the horse in local understandings of both status and labor. Prior to the establishment of the mission, for example, one local indigenous leader was dubbed "Capitan de la Yegua" (Captain Mare). His mount was apparently obtained from Native groups living along the Colorado River (Arrillaga 1969:30), suggesting that Native people in the region valued horses and horse handling even in advance of Spanish missionization. In 1870, 30 years after Mission Santa Catalina was destroyed in a Native uprising, a newspaper account notes that 80 people continued to live around the ruins of the former mission and that many had skills necessary for working on nearby ranchos (Shipek 1965:27).

Today, horse handling is still valued in Santa Catarina, a multiethnic community that includes members of the Paipai, Ko'alh/Kumeyaay, and Kiliwa ethnolinguistic groups (Panich 2010). In 2008 I interviewed 11 tribal elders in Santa Catarina, and although the semistructured interviews were not specifically designed to elicit information regarding horses, many of my consultants mentioned the importance of vaquero labor for local economic and social relationships. For example, one consultant worked for 18 years as a vaquero on a Mexican ranch. He explained how ranches provided much-needed jobs for the community, where work was—and still is—hard to come by. Another consultant described how he worked as a vaquero in the mid-20th century, work that took him to many of the major indigenous communities in the region. He stated that he worked with other men from Santa Catarina but that the job also allowed them to visit friends and relatives from other villages. This sentiment was shared by a third consultant, who described how her father, also a vaquero, was constantly coming and going from Santa Catarina.

The importance of the horse and of vaquero identity was best articulated by one of my primary Paipai consultants, a community leader and unofficial tribal historian. He linked the persistence of vaquero knowledge to the establishment of Mission Santa Catalina in 1797. He readily acknowledged the negative outcomes of missionization but also stated that the Paipai of Santa Catarina and neighboring communities worked many of the changes wrought by colonialism to their advantage. In particular, he said that knowledge of horseback riding and cattle ranching were two of the primary contributions of the mission and that since colonial times the Paipai have been known as the best vaqueros in the region. He stated that Paipai vaqueros were sought after by ranchers for their knowledge of riding and for their ability to rope and drive cattle (Figure 10.3).

What is particularly salient about the last account is that my consultant directly links modern vaquero culture with the mission period, underscoring how local Native people were able to rearticulate the changes of the colonial period within locally situ-

FIGURE 10.3. Vaquero near Santa Catarina, Baja California, 1926. Photo by E. H. Davis. © San Diego History Center.

ated economic and social relationships. Indeed, the skills that Native people learned at the mission have endured despite the relatively minor role of the mission itself in regional developments (Panich 2010). The mission's herds probably never exceeded 1,000 cattle (partly due to stock raiding by unmissionized Native people), and three field seasons of archaeological research, focused primarily on indigenous residential spaces outside of the mission walls, yielded no materials directly related to mission era vaqueros (Meigs 1935; Panich 2009). Yet the importance of the horse to Native people in Santa Catarina and neighboring communities is obvious. As described by an ethnographer who worked in the region in the mid-20th century: "In this country a horse or a mule is a necessity, and almost every male adult Indian has his favorite mount; individuals who are fairly well off, or working as vaqueros for some neighboring Mexican ranch, will have more than one horse" (Hohenthal 2001:130).

CONCLUSION

Since the onset of colonialism, Native people in California have incorporated horses and associated material culture into a range of economic and social practices. The four examples provided here offer glimpses into how these varied processes unfolded in particular geographic and temporal settings. Across colonial California, introduced animals and associated materials were incorporated into emerging indigenous labor practices, local expressions of identity and status, and bids for relative autonomy under colonialism. Consumption is an inherently diachronic process, and the Native Californian use of horses and related materials has evolved through the Spanish period, through the Mexican and early American periods, and into the present day. Within this chapter's primary focus on the Spanish period, the incorporation of horse handling unfolded at different scales and at different nodes in the colonial landscape, from the missions to secular ranches to the vast interior of Alta California.

Close to colonial centers, such as at Mission Santa Clara and Humaliwo, access to horses no doubt enabled certain individuals to physically move between colonial establishments and ancestral landscapes. Archaeological evidence, moreover, demonstrates how the material trappings of vaquero labor were used for social differentiation at the time of death. Unlike glass beads (which were simultaneously foreign and familiar for the occupants of both sites), a direct functional antecedent for vaquero gear did not exist in precontact California. Yet these items were deposited at Santa Clara and Humaliwo in ways that made sense within established Native mortuary practices. The bit and spur fragments from Santa Clara were deposited during times of mourning alongside other items that were likely symbols of relative status within the social structure of the California missions. At Humaliwo, similar horse-related artifacts were used as grave goods in the same manner as plank canoes, items associated with social ranking, as well as with labor and mobility in Chumash society (Gamble 2008). These patterns can be compared with the San Joaquin Valley, where knowledge about horses provided novel economic and social opportunities. The material trappings may have been harder to acquire and less visible archaeologically, but the animals themselves also gave Yokuts raiders enhanced mobility—a powerful tool for avoiding missionization or resisting colonialism (Scheiber and Finley 2011). With the closing of the missions and with the establishment of the modern nation-states of Mexico and the United States, the knowledge of horse handling remained an important skill for many Native people who continue to work as vaqueros into the present day.

Over the course of the past 250 years, the indigenous groups of California and Baja California have incorporated horses and their associated material culture into a range of practices. By examining these processes through the vantage point of consumption, it is possible to more clearly see these developments as the direct results of Native action. Rather than discontinuity or passive acculturation, indigenous use of horses involved the active reinterpretation of local traditions. As the examples presented here demonstrate, Native Californians socialized horses and associated goods in ways that made sense within local cultural, political, and economic circumstances.

ACKNOWLEDGMENTS

I thank the members of the community of Santa Catarina who participated in the oral history project. John Grafton provided information regarding bits and spurs in colonial California. The chapter was enhanced by the insightful comments of Craig Cipolla, Martin Gallivan, Maxine Oland, Christopher Shephard, and two anonymous reviewers.

11

ARCHAEOLOGIES OF NATIVE PRODUCTION AND MARKETING IN 19TH-CENTURY NEW ENGLAND

PATRICIA E. RUBERTONE

HISTORICAL AND ARCHAEOLOGICAL RESEARCH on Native Americans' consumption of European objects has emphasized transactions in which Native peoples were mostly suppliers of raw materials and consumers of European commodities who became increasingly dependent on these foreign goods and mired in cycles of debt. Despite recent thinking that has reevaluated Native peoples' "consumer choices" in the early colonial period by focusing on their appropriation, transformation, display, and reexchange of newly introduced things, whether somewhat familiar or strange, there has been relatively little attention paid to Native peoples' production and marketing of goods for non-Native clientele, especially during later centuries. This marginalization of indigenous production underscores the pervasiveness of dependency theory, which situates Native peoples at the receiving end of consumer culture, as well as cultural premises in Euro-American society that question Indians' initiative. Reversing the analytical gaze toward their roles as producers and sellers allows us to explore how they navigated the colonized landscape's geographies of consumption and to contribute to destabilizing dominant ideologies that underestimate Native peoples' participation in the practices and materialities of the marketplace in 19th-century America. The production and marketing of herbal medicine by an Indian doctress in urban New England serves to illustrate Native American entrepreneurship, strategic engagement with modernity, dual signification in advertising, and self-awareness that defies victimhood.

MAKING AND SELLING INDIAN MEDICINE

In 18th- and 19th-century New England, many Native Americans made and sold herbal medicines, baskets, and other utilitarian goods, as well as art commodities or souvenirs, to tourists to supplement their incomes (Lester 1987; Mandell 2008; Phillips 1998). The marketing of both types of products, utilitarian and art, was economically important to Native peoples' creative survival. However, their marketability depended on the abilities of indigenous producers to meet the needs of non-Native consumers and to reimagine their products and themselves in terms of popular conventions of Indianness held by the wider society. Indian medicine, remedies that drew on the therapeutic properties of plants in the Native pharmacopeia, filled such a niche among Euro-Americans because of a widespread distrust of the scientific erudition of the medical profession, the appeal of commonsense cures, and the paucity of health-care options in rural and marginalized urban neighborhoods. Coupled with increasing mortality rates, concerns about contagion, water contamination, and work-related hazards connected to industrial capitalism, Indian medicine offered alternative cures for people seeking to find remedies for their illnesses or to boost or protect their health (Beck 1992; Bellin 2006; Brunton 2014; McBride and Prins 1996; Paynter et al. 1994). Successful marketing also required good product recognition that employed stereotypes of Indianness to convince consumers that Native herbal medicines were pure, natural, and effective. In turn, the consumption of these remedies answered the desires of American nativists and recent immigrants to identify with Native Americans and assert their place on the indigenous landscape (Phillips 1998; Simmons 2002).

The healing properties of plants, as well as the methods of preparing and administering them as medicine, are well documented in the indigenous knowledge of northeastern Indians and, more broadly, eastern Algonquian tribes. According to Frank Speck, the practical use of herbs as medicines is "a fundamentally primitive idea" that has survived despite changes in the details and ritualized beliefs surrounding the cultural practice over time (1917:303). Awareness of the healing qualities of herbs most likely developed by relying on the smell, color, taste, and texture of a plant to indicate its application and through trial-and-error experimentation. This repertoire of indigenous knowledge, which may have begun with the simple idea that a certain herb had a specific effect in counteracting a bodily ailment and evolved into the practice of mixing multiple herbs into a single medicine to treat a complex disorder or achieve overall wellness, was passed down generationally (Speck 1917). Such stores of knowledge about the healing properties of plants as well as the methods for preparing and administering them as medicine were entrusted mostly to women but also to men whom tribal elders considered worthy of the right to minister to their kindred. Gladys

Tantaquidgeon (1977), a Mohegan woman who began as a little girl in the early 1900s to accompany her grandmother to nearby fields and wooded areas to gather plants to be used as medicine, compiled extensive information on medicinal plants collected by older members of her community and by elders at Mashpee and Gay Head in Massachusetts into the late 1930s.

As with most folk medicine passed down orally and by example within families, there were rules for gathering, handling, and preparing herbs for use in healing. For example, Mohegan herbalists were told not to gather medicinal plants during the dog days of late summer, presumably because of attitudes linking astrological events and illness that were widespread in folk medicine. Herbalists were also advised to exercise restraint, a theme common in New England Indian folklore (Simmons 1986), by not picking the first plant they spotted of a species desired for a certain medicine but instead to leave it and walk a short distance away, where they would "find many plants." They then should collect only as many plants as they needed and leave the rest in reserve (Tantaquidgeon 1977:69). Other protocols involved drying the herbs in the sun before gathering them into bunches or bundles and bringing them indoors to be stored for later use on the belief that the sun added to their potency, and avoiding the use of metal implements when crushing or grinding the herbs to prepare the medicines (Tantaquidgeon 1977:69).

Many Native healers, women as well as men, gained a reputation that spread not only among their communities but also among white families who frequently sought their cures, if not their expertise, to improve their own knowledge about the medicinal virtues of plants. During the early 19th century, Molly Ockett, a legendary Pigwacket Abenaki woman with an extensive knowledge of herbal remedies, traveled from Vermont to Maine to treat whites who turned to her for help (McBride and Prins 1996). Another Abenaki doctor, Louis Watso, traveled in 1837 with members of his community from Canada to Deerfield, Massachusetts, where he shared his knowledge of plants with Dr. Stephen West Williams, whom Watso guided in collecting specimens for Williams's herbarium. Despite his interest in the Abenaki's medical practices, Williams refused Dr. Watso's offer to treat his heart palpitations with one of their prepared medicines, since it contained a large amount of snakeroot (Bruchac 1998). Presumably, Williams's reticence was due to the belief that the plant, while used to decrease the heart rate and treat other ailments such as snakebites, also could be poisonous.

Others were not at all hesitant about taking Indian cures. Hannah Dexter of Natick, a Massachusetts town that a local historian in the 1830s described as teeming with Indian physicians and doctresses, gained such fame for her skills with roots and herbs that the sick from wealthy sections of Boston and Cambridge sent their carriages to bring her to their homes so that she could treat them (Mandell 2008; Simmons

1986; Ulrich 2001). Rhoda Rhoades, whose father was white and mother was Mahican, is remembered as a successful physician who ministered to patients in western Massachusetts towns and as far south as Hartford, Connecticut. She made house calls but also had "many genteel folks" under her care stay at her house for extended periods of time. Among them was a minister from Springfield who spent a week in her home as a young theological student after he "had been around the world in a vain search for health." Helped by her, he returned the following season and stayed the entire winter (Bruchac 1998). Much like other proficient Indian doctresses whose experience taught them to have more faith in the efficacy of certain herbs than others, Rhoda Rhoades became known for an herbal medicine called The Extract. Assisted by her son, she made the medicine by boiling down large quantities of medicinal herbs, which she grew in her garden and collected from the roadsides and along a stream on her property, in a large potash kettle to a tar-like consistency and sold in clam-shell-sized doses at two dollars each that were meant to be diluted for use (Bruchac 1998).

The Mitchell sisters, Melinda and Charlotte, were well-known Wampanoag healers in rural and urban southeastern Massachusetts during the late 19th century. They were raised and educated in Abington and Cambridge apart from known Native communities and had moved to the family's remaining ancestral land at Betty's Neck in Plymouth County with their mother, Zerviah Mitchell, in 1879. Zerviah, who also had attended schools in Abington and Boston and taught for a while at a private school in Boston, apparently had entrusted them with medicinal knowledge that had been passed down to her through her maternal relatives (Simmons 2002). The Mitchell sisters' great-grandmother Lydia Tuspaquin of Betty's Neck "claimed great skill in the healing art, and was in the act of gathering herbs for medical purposes when she fell from a high bank into the Assowamsett Pond and was drowned" in 1812 (Peirce 1878:215–216). Charlotte Mitchell's diary covering the period from January 2 through March 15, 1896, comments on her and her sister's work as healers, which they did along with making baskets, telling fortunes, selling eggs, and performing routine farm activities to support themselves.

Several entries in Charlotte's diary track the process of refilling an order for two bottles of the same medicine that Melinda had previously prepared for a client in New Bedford (Simmons 2002:134, 135). One of the ingredients in the medicine was wormwood (an herb in the Native pharmacopeia used as a vermifluge to treat intestinal parasites), which Charlotte picked up for Melinda in Middleborough along with a box of headache tablets (Tantaquidgeon 1977:70). In another entry, she again mentioned going to Middleborough, where she "got some herbs for Lin's medicine and Alcohol" and "2 doz tin boxes for Salve" from the local apothecary (Simmons 2002:134). What emerges from the diary is that while the Mitchells relied on traditional indigenous knowledge about the healing properties of plants and sometimes gathered plants available on their land at Betty's Neck (such as plantain, whose leaves they mashed into a poultice to treat the ulcerated foot of a white child who boarded with them for a few years), their medicinal practices were subject to innovation and tied to the market economy. Their purchases at a local apothecary indicate that they also took advantage of the inventory of supplies of herbs, alcohol, and tin boxes typically carried by pharmacies in the 19th century for making and packaging medicines that they sold to their patients. That Charlotte bought tin boxes for salve also raises questions about whether traditional rules about avoiding contact with metals when processing herbs into medicine, which did not anticipate packaging these medicines for sale, were strictly followed. Much like glass bottles, the use of tin boxes represents a material innovation that allowed healers to dispense their medicines more efficiently in response to consumer demands.

Although some Indian healers worked from their homes, others continued to "walk the medicine line" as itinerant doctors, selling their services and medicines into the late 19th and early 20th centuries "on the unmarked trail through the liminal zone between oppositional cultures" (McBride and Prins 1996:322). Dr. Ben Nokay (Noka), a Narragansett, traveled from the reservation in Charlestown, Rhode Island, often stopping at the houses of other Indians that served as gathering spots where itinerant healers, basket sellers, and other Indians in transit could rest and visit. Mrs. Sarah Ciscoe Sullivan, a Nipmuc from Grafton, Massachusetts, recalled that Dr. Noka frequently stayed at her family's house, sometimes for days because of deep snow, and would use the time to make a batch of medicines for the next lap of his journey before gathering up his gear, remedies, and pamphlets advertising his medicines (Redwing 1935). Similarly, Dr. William Perry, a Wampanoag, continued to live on the Fall River Reservation and travel the countryside to minister to Indians across southern New England and to some white families that called on him for help (Simmons 1986:102–104). However, other Native healers increasingly gave up life on the traveling medical circuit and moved to cities where growing populations offered the possibilities of a steady flow of patients and earning income. For example, Rebecca Davis, a Punkapoag, moved to Boston, where she sold a salve that she prepared from herbs according to the prescription of some ancient medicine man and used the money she earned to visit her ancestral community every year (Mandell 2008:32).

Rather than simply a continuation or an invention of a tradition, the manufacture and selling of herbal medicine drew on ancestral and Euro-American knowledge to reorder practical activities in ways that enabled Native peoples to assert their independence and help cover the expenses of everyday necessities, as did making baskets, scrubs, and souvenir arts (Phillips 1998; Simmons 2002). In New England, Native peoples' reliance on consumer goods had escalated steadily since 1700 due to the reduction of their land base, impoverished agricultural conditions on Indian reservations, migration, soldiering, and wage labor. The need to purchase clothing and food (which typically comprised the bulk of their expenditures), household goods, and building materials and pay for funerals and rents contributed to mounting expenses, as well as increasing debts (Baron et al. 1996; Johnson 2009; Silliman and Witt 2010; Silverman 2001; White 2011). To cover expenses and spiraling debts, Native consumers offered their labor in exchange for credit, sold off parcels of their remaining land, or confronted their economic predicament by marshaling traditional indigenous knowledge such as the practice of herbal medicine and adapting it to the marketplace. More than just a way of "making do," making and selling herbal medicines situates Native Americans squarely in the production and marketing spaces of 19th-century economic life and comments on resourcefulness and entrepreneurship rarely associated with Indians.

As an option available to Native people struggling to make ends meet during the 19th century, producing and dispensing herbal medicine also fulfilled broad cultural assumptions about the relationship between race, gender, and labor in Euro-American society (e.g., Mullins 1999; McClintock 1995). It reinforced stereotypes about Indian doctors and doctresses as anachronisms who lived "off the beaten track" in remote and impoverished rural areas and missed out on modernity as witches with diabolical powers or as drunkards who spent their profits on rum (McBride and Prins 1996; Simmons 1986; Ulrich 2001). That Native physicians lived in and marketed their expertise in both cities and rural areas confounded societal expectations about being Indian and modern but also posed the added contradiction of being urban (Deloria 2004; Rubertone 2013; Thrush 2007). As was true for Native practitioners who were country people, making herbal medicines in cities was not merely a vestige of an ancestral way of life that persisted in a few isolated pockets from earlier times. Instead, it was a skill that Native people brought with them when they moved from their ancestral communities to cities and marketed with the hope of establishing footholds in the urban economy. For Native women who lived in New England's cities during the 19th century, manufacturing and selling herbal medicine was an alternative to working as a domestic or a laundress or in some other low-skilled occupation as a way to meet economic challenges, affirm their independence as providers, and, paradoxically, conform to and contradict expectations about the region's Indians. Consequently, manufacturing and selling herbal medicine is not just about Native survival or subsistence. Rather, it is a practice of survivance in which Native people asserted their presence, persevered, and renounced "dominance, detractions, obtrusions, the unbearable sentiments of tragedy, and the legacy of victimry" (Vizenor 2008:1).

SARAH BAXTER, AN INDIAN DOCTRESS IN AN URBAN HOMELAND

During the 19th century, Providence increasingly became home to Native people, who mostly went unnoticed in written accounts of its urban history. Underrepresented and notoriously misidentified in census schedules and other documentary records, they had migrated to find jobs and make better lives for themselves and their families. Some men found more or less steady work as day laborers, dockworkers, and teamsters; women, as mentioned, found work outside of the home as domestics and laundresses. For others, the city offered not only the promise of jobs but also a market for Native products. For instance, a family of Passamaquoddy identified as "basket makers" from Maine "pitched their tents" on the city's outskirts in the 1860s, presumably with the expectation of finding consumers for their fancy baskets or of selling utilitarian wood-splint baskets to fishing, shipping, and wholesale businesses in need of inexpensive and lightweight containers. There was a high urban demand for both that created economic opportunities for Native producers, so much so that Melinda Mitchell told a newspaper reporter around 1902 that she and her sister, Charlotte, who also made and sold herbal medicine, "used to send 400 or 500 [baskets] every year to firms in Boston, and seldom were any returned" (Simmons 2002:134–135).

An Indian doctress named Sarah Baxter, born in Nantucket sometime in the late 1700s or early 1800s, was living in Providence by at least 1840. Her race or color was recorded in censuses as Indian, mulatto, black, and colored, which was not altogether uncommon, since individuals were often given different labels during their lifetime. In contrast, the tag "Indian doctress," which combined a racial designation with the work she performed, remained relatively constant in public documents from the late 1850s to the early 1880s. This practice of identifying individual Indians by the work they performed and their race had become common in New England during the 18th century, when European colonists considered these attributes Indians' most significant characteristics (Silverman 2001:653), and persisted into later centuries for an occupation such as Indian doctor (or doctress), considered to be quintessentially "Indian."

Little is known about Sarah Baxter's early life or about her route from Nantucket to Providence. She was born after the Indian Sickness, an epidemic that is estimated to have devastated the island's Native population in the 1760s (Little 1990). Her parents' names are unknown, except for a single reference on Sarah's death record to what may be her mother's surname. Although the surname does appear in lists of the family names of survivors of the Indian Sickness, I suspect that her mother was a Nantucket Indian, probably Wampanoag, and that her father was African American or possibly some other ethnicity. Intermarriage and coresidence were facts of life on the island because of

FIGURE 11.1. Sarah Baxter's home and laboratory were located on the site of the American Screw Company's Bay State Mill at Stevens and Bark Streets (1873). Courtesy of the Rhode Island Historical Society, ink on paper, RHi 17 1716.

the epidemic and Indians' involvement in seafaring, which employed them from "Nova Scotia to the Mississippi" and brought sailors from mainland and foreign ports to the island, where they intermingled with the indigenous population (Crèvecoeur quoted in Silverman 2001:645). On Nantucket, where "whaling wives" often ran households and shops while men were away at sea, independent and enterprising women would have been role models who gave Sarah Baxter the incentive to apply her practical knowledge in ways that allowed her to live and work against modernity (Hudson 2003).

From the 1850s into the 1870s, Sarah made and sold medicinal remedies, most notably Mrs. Baxter's Indian Healing Balm and Indians Bitters, that were marketed in Rhode Island and Massachusetts. Unlike many Indian doctresses who made house calls to their clients, Sarah consulted from a home she rented from the American Screw Company, a two-story house (or laboratory) where she had an office and bedroom on the lower floor and two bedrooms, a parlor, and a sitting room on the floor above (Figure 11.1). The rental property also had a separate kitchen house. Her business was built on claims to years of experience and discoveries made in treating patients who had sought her care both "day and night" and on "all diseases." Nestled among factory buildings, she confronted and embraced modernity by offering natural cures for the physical and emotional illnesses of 19th-century urban life and by marketing her own brand of salves, tinctures, and syrups, as well as her services. These contradictions between rural–urban and traditional–modern are evident in a series of advertisements for the brand that appeared in Providence city directories during the 1860s and 1870s.

THE MARKETING AND MATERIALITY OF MRS. BAXTER'S BRAND

The earliest advertisement, published in 1867, was for Mrs. Baxter's Healing Balm, an "Internal and External Remedy, for the cure of Asiatic Cholera, Rheumatism, Neuralgia, Sore Throat, or Diphtheria, and other Diseases," along with a liver syrup and a cough or croup remedy. The copy claims that all these medicines were purely vegetable and were prepared and sold only by Mrs. Baxter. The accompanying image shows a woman who is partially dressed with long flowing hair cascading to her knees and holding a sprig of herbs in her left hand (Figure 11.2). The image, which loosely resembles John White's watercolors of Algonquian Indians from the 16th century, presents the romanticized stereotype of the Indian as a "noble savage" living in close harmony with nature that was popular in the Euro-American imagination (Marcellus 2008). As a marketing tool, the image connects Mrs. Baxter and her herbal remedies to nature and deep stores of knowledge passed down by generations of Indian healers. It sells tradition as an antidote to modernity and its afflictions in a way that would not have threatened the imaginative security of non-Native consumers (Steele 1996).

An advertisement for the same products was published in the 1870 city directory with a different image (Figure 11.3). The symbol for the brand is also an "Indian"

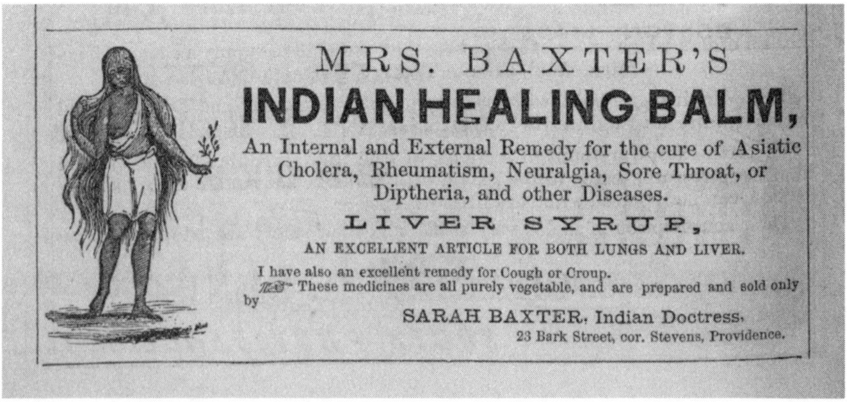

FIGURE 11.2. 1867 advertisement for Mrs. Baxter's Indian Medicines, Providence city directory. Courtesy of the Rhode Island Historical Society, ink on paper, RHi X17 1699.

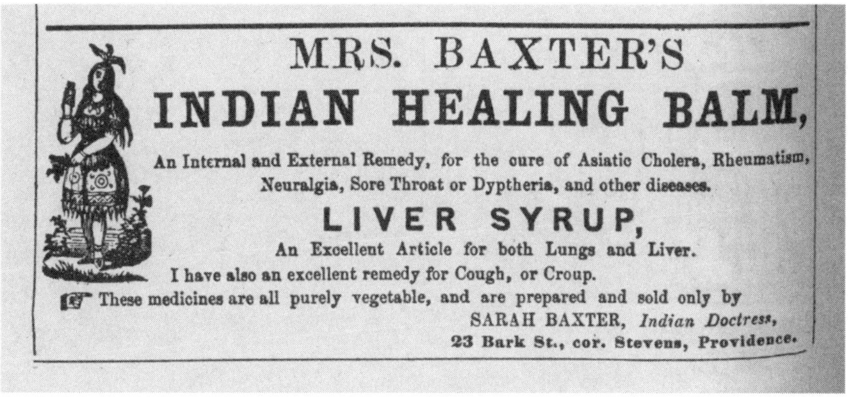

FIGURE 11.3. 1870 advertisement for Mrs. Baxter's Indian Medicines, Providence city directory. Courtesy of the Rhode Island Historical Society, ink on paper, RHi X17 1701.

woman, but one who is shown wearing a fringed dress, a necklace decorated with what appear to be bear-claw pendants, bracelets, feather plumes at the back of her head, and moccasins. She holds a medicine bottle upright in her right hand, and her left hand, which is extended downward across her body, clutches a bunch of herbs. The skirt of the dress is faced with circular designs resembling Plains Indian sun symbols. Except for some minor variations, the manner of dress depicted in the advertisement resembles imagery that evoked a broad set of mainstream cultural expectations about American Indians that were more familiar to Euro-Americans in the 19th century than those suggested by White's watercolors. Here both the dress and the woman's quaint demeanor recall the trope of the "Indian princess," a reductive image symbolizing Indian women that in various iterations and distortions has been widely used in advertising to serve the white imagination rather than historical or contemporary reality (Mithlo 2009).

In 1874 a new product called Indian Bitters was marketed under the Mrs. Baxter's brand along with her healing balm, tea syrup for the lungs, and cough and croup syrup. The copy for her Indian Bitters stated that it was generally superior to similar products on the market for invigorating the body and eradicating disease. "As a general Spring and Summer medicine" and as a remedy for a range of aliments from headaches, dizziness, chest pain, indigestion, pains all over the body, and stomach problems, it could not be surpassed. The face of the brand in the advertisement was neither reminiscent of Native women in John White's drawings nor a stereotype of the Indian princess but a person of color, a term for Native Americans, African Americans, and those of mixed ancestry. She is uncannily characteristic of Sarah Baxter herself (Figure 11.4).

FIGURE 11.4. 1874 advertisement for Mrs. Baxter's Indian Medicines, including her Indian Bitters, Providence city directory. Courtesy of the Rhode Island Historical Society, ink on paper, RHi X17 1702.

She wears a dark-colored dress with a white ruffled collar and bow typical of a widow's dress in the 1870s. Her hair is short and curled at the ends with a fringe of bangs combed to either side of her face. From her hooded lids, her gaze is reassuring, exuding wisdom, reliability, and confidence. As the brand symbol, she is neither the exotic "other" in the ads of the 1860s nor the pretty Indian princess of 1870. Instead, she represents herself as the person behind the brand—a woman of color of a certain age, strong and knowing, who would have no substitutes.

Although I cannot say for certain whether the image is absolutely that of Sarah Baxter, multiple strands of evidence, including shared similarities, strongly suggest that it is. In commodity racism, in which racial or ethnic stereotypes are used in branding, images of African Americans, while found on ads for many products, were not used to sell medicine during the 19th century (Marcellus 2008:796). Additionally, details of Sarah Baxter's life from documentary records correlate with the copy and pictographic information in the advertisement. The Bark Street address noted in the advertisement was listed as her home since the 1850s, though she had possibly lived there with her husband as early as 1840. The image, which has a quality of photographic realism from leggotyping that is not apparent in the earlier advertisements, is also age appropriate, based on estimates of Sarah Baxter's age at the time. Finally, she had been widowed in 1855, which makes the style of dress depicted in the advertisement fitting to her state in life and the time period, in contrast to a buckskin dress or a mere apron-like skirt.

Despite the widespread industrial and urban growth that filled much of Providence's open space with buildings, it was "an unusually spacious city" (Ihlder n.d.) where many plants with curing properties that could have been used in preparing medicines would have been available. These plants would have grown wild in vacant lots, along the banks of the Moshassuck River and the Cove Lands near Sarah's home, in other swampy areas, in small patches of land sheltered by buildings, and even in cracks in the city's sidewalks. A survey of specimens in Brown University's Herbarium collected from various locales in Providence from the mid-19th to the early 20th century indicates that many plants in the pharmacopeia of northeastern Indians, particularly of the Mohegan (Speck 1917; Tantaquidgeon 1977), are represented. For example, yarrow (*Achillea millefolium*) and wild plum (*Prunus americana*), both used by Mohegan practitioners for liver and kidney disorders, could well have been ingredients in the liver syrup that Sarah Baxter prepared and subsequently sold as a treatment for these ailments. The bark, roots, and leaves of plants such as maple (*Acer saacharum*), pigweed (*Amaranthus retroflexus*), jack-in-the-pulpit (*Arisaema triphyllum*), canker lettuce (*Pyrola elliptica*), spikenard (*Smilacina racemosa*), white clover (*Trifolium repens*), and American elm (*Ulmus americana*), all used to treat sore throats, hoarseness, and coughs, could have been used in making her "excellent remedy for cough, or croup."

As with Mrs. Baxter's other medicines, the formula for her Indian Bitters, a spring or summer tonic for invigorating the body, is unknown, which is not surprising, since the exact composition of patent medicines was meant to be kept secret. However, Speck (1917:320), who drew on information given to him by Gladys Tantaquidgeon, reported that the Mohegan made a spring tonic by steeping together a dozen different plants, the majority of which—wild cherry (*Prunus serotina*), sassafras (*Sassafras officinale*), sweet flag (*Acorus calamus*), spikenard (*Smilacina racemosa*), white daisy (*Chrysanthemum leucanthemum*), boneset (*Eupatorium perfoliatum*), motherwort (*Leonurus cardiaca*), and black birch (*Betula lenta*)—were part of botanical life in Providence during the decades when Sarah Baxter was making and marketing her medicines (Figure 11.5). Tantaquidgeon described a similar recipe for a spring tonic that her grandmother prepared "from as many as ten plants" (1977:68). Of the 11 plants listed (Tantaquidgeon 1977:77), seven are the same as those listed above that were available historically in Providence. The only exception is white daisy. Dandelion, which the Mohegan used in their spring tonic, while not among the specimens preserved in the collections of the Brown Herbarium, is a common species that would have thrived almost anywhere in the city.

Floral remains from archaeological features associated with 19th-century domestic sites once located in the largely Native and African neighborhood where Sarah Baxter

FIGURE 11.5. Sweet flag (*Acorus calamus*). Image provided by the Brown University Herbarium [BRU], accessed through the Consortium of Northeastern Herbaria website, www.neherbaria.org, May 22, 2015.

lived and just a few blocks south of her home and laboratory on Bark Street included species known for their curative purposes among New England Indians, which further suggests the local availability of plants used in preparing herbal medicines (Artemel et al. 1984). Among the seeds recovered were jimson weed (*Datura stramonium*), considered a "powerful plant" in the Mohegan pharmacopeia; dock (*Rumex crispus*), which purified the blood; sorrell (*Rumex acetosella*), which was good for the stomach; grape (*Vitacea vitis* sp.), which relieved pain; and blackberry (*Rubus* sp.), which was administered as a cure for dysentery (Tantaquidgeon 1977).

Like other Indian herbal doctors, however, Sarah Baxter would not have gathered only those medicinal plants growing wild on the urban landscape or that she or friends possibly cultivated in their gardens. She would also have purchased them along with other medical supplies from apothecaries (e.g., Brunton 2014; Simmons 2002). Her postmortem inventory indicates that among her debts were those she owed for unspecified "medical supplies." Although the entries are ambiguous and possibly were related to charges for her own medical care rather than for the services and remedies she provided, they nevertheless point to her links in the expanding and increasingly diversified network of medical practitioners and suppliers in 19th-century Providence, including physicians who cared for her during her "last sickness."

The question is why Sarah Baxter appeared as the trademark for the brand in 1874, the final advertisement for her products printed in city directories. At the time, many New Englanders had long been convinced that the region's Indians had become irreparably mixed because of intermarriage and dismissed the validity of their Native lineage. A "real" Indian doctress would not look like Indian women drawn by John White or the ones that conformed to stereotypes of "Indian princesses." With the Civil War ended and Rhode Island on the brink of implementing popular ideas about Native American decline and assimilation by legislating the Narragansett Nation, the state's principal tribal entity, out of existence, Mrs. Baxter, a woman of color, emerged from behind the guises of what can be called "strategic essentialism" in which conventional representations of Indianness were pragmatically employed to communicate to consumers (Mithlo 2009). Whether the brand's new face was a personal decision or a clever marketing strategy to differentiate her products from the glut of similar cures available to consumers or both, it underwrote her claims of "authenticity" and "purity" in which she asserted that the remedies were made by her and were entirely natural. Given that the advertisement was printed at a time when expectations about what "authentic" and "pure" meant for Americans and their particular histories were being both redefined and contested, Sarah Baxter stood behind her products by revealing herself as a woman of color typical in appearance to many of the region's Indians because of historical conditions that contributed to intermarriage with other ethnic groups.

With an expanding market for medicines in the 19th century, Indian medicine, which consumers could obtain as part of a consultation or could purchase directly from practitioners, experienced a boom in popularity. It competed with medicines composed by druggists or prescribed by physicians, as well as cures offered by Euro-Americans who attempted to take over Indian medicine by playing the Indian doctor. The phenomenon of Euro-American individuals marketing their pills, potions, and powders—as well as themselves as experts—under the banner of Indian healing assumed the proportions of a full-fledged craze, ironically at a time that coincided with the rhetoric of Manifest Destiny in the United States and with deliberate legal and ideological projects of Native American erasure in New England. But not all Indian doctors were charlatans. Vine Deloria Jr., critiquing the endless parade of "white Indians" in the 19th century, lamented that the market for Indian medicine has been so glutted and muddied by substitutes that "when a real Indian stands up and speaks the truth at any given moment, he or she is not likely to be believed, but will probably be contradicted and 'corrected' by the citation of some non-Indian and totally inaccurate 'expert'" (quoted in Bellin 2006:6). I argue that Sarah Baxter was neither merely playing the Indian doctress nor just a brand name. She was a real person who was a practitioner of herbal medicine and the creative force behind an Indian balm, syrup, and bitters and their marketing whose life experiences comment on struggles over the definition and control of Indian medicine and, more importantly, Indian identity in 19th-century New England. She died insolvent at the age of 90 in 1882, two years after her name, address, and the tag "Indian doctress" appeared for the last time in a city directory. After her death, "Mrs. Baxter's" medicines were no longer manufactured.

Similar to other Native people considered marginal who often insinuated themselves into Euro-American society by nudging notions of indigeneity in directions they found useful, Sarah Baxter sometimes "played Indian" in the commonplace imaginings of non-Indians in the 19th century (Deloria 1998:8). At other times, she challenged these fantasies by overtly rejecting Indian playing. However, even her use of Native stereotypes might not have been employed for the same ends as those of non-Natives who used conventional, if not damaging, representations of Indians in their advertisements. Critical theorists have argued that the latter is an example of continuing colonialism that denies political, social, and economic rights, whereas the use of these stereotypes by Native peoples themselves might aim at challenging these inequities (Mithlo 2009:16). At the very least, the proactive use of these essentialized images by individuals who were victimized by them was a way to maneuver in a hostile environment such as a competitive marketplace. In the context of 19th-century consumerism, the advertisements for Mrs. Baxter's medicines sometimes appropriated these essentialized, stereotypical images of Indianness to appeal to, if not parody, white consumer demands for authentic Indian remedies. Yet in the 1874 advertisement she employed an entirely different image that more accurately represented her, as well as registering the realities of other Native people, particularly in urban, pan-tribal New England, than those of Indians in white American consciousness. Rather than simply a matter of product marketability, the images reveal the multiple ways in which Sarah Baxter deftly navigated the seemingly conflicting quandary of being both Indian and modern. Expressions of her identity in the ads, similar to definitions of her identity in official records and her own self-identity, were not static but were instead subject to refashioning amid continued colonialism. From this perspective, art resembled life in the advertisements for Mrs. Baxter's medicines—the life that she made for herself in Providence, where her knowledge and marketing of traditional healing were as much prescriptions for her own survival as they were for those who sought her care.

Other than the printed images in city directories, little else is directly known about the materiality and marketing of Mrs. Baxter's herbal medicine. The house she rented and the surrounding factory buildings have long been razed and replaced with new construction, precluding the possibility of uncovering archaeological evidence that might shed light on the specific plants she used in her medicines or whether she followed the protocols of traditional practices for maintaining their purity by avoiding contamination with metal objects. An initial inspection of glass bottles reported from 19th-century archaeological contexts in Providence has not identified any bottles marked with Mrs. Baxter's imprint in which she would have dispensed her syrups and "Indian bitters." Limited excavation, sketchy diagnostic information, bottle reuse, and consumer preferences for other patent medicine brands could account for their absence, though local brands are well represented in the assemblages (see, e.g., Mullins 1999). However, a bottle for Dr. Baxter's Indian Bitters (a.k.a. Mrs. Baxter), the new product she advertised in 1874, is described on a website for bottle collectors. Unlike many other bottles for Indian bitters in the 1870s that promised an Indian cure to Euro-American consumers, it was not molded in the shape of an iconic "Indian princess." Instead, the bottle, rectangular in shape, aqua colored, embossed on three sides with the words "DR. BAXTER'S INDIAN BITTERS, PROV, RI," and 9.25 inches high, similar to the picture of the woman in the 1874 advertisement, exhibited no flagrant Indian imagery.

BEYOND CONSUMPTION: REPRESENTING NATIVE PRODUCTION AND SURVIVANCE

Despite the marginalization of their involvement in the production of commodities for non-Native consumers and Euro-Americans' appropriation of the manufacturing and marketing of goods they considered distinctively Indian, Native people participated in the 19th-century American economy as both producers and sellers. Notwithstanding the alleged cures of bogus white entrepreneurs claiming to be Indian, Native healers' herbal remedies found a market among Euro-Americans who sought alternatives to modern medicine and for whom products symbolizing the essence of indigeneity in the collective imaginary provided a connection to a mythical past of vanished Indians they claimed as their own during a time of increasing foreign immigration and urbanization (Bellin 2006; Cangany 2012; Simmons 2002). In branding these medicines, some Native healers, like white impostors, used ingrained American images of Indians in print ads and in packaging to make these products recognizable to consumers. However, herbal healers from New England's Indian communities were not shadowy figures from a vanishing world or simply pretenders. Rather, they were individuals who harnessed ancestral knowledge to Euro-American desire by marketing their healing skills in ways that both conformed and contradicted expectations about the region's Indians.

In making and marketing herbal medicines, Sarah Baxter embraced both tradition and modernity and showed that being Indian and urban are not mutually exclusive categories. Her participation in the 19th-century marketplace comments on the complex entanglement among the disparate groups of producers, sellers, and consumers that archaeologists have variously explored. However, studies of consumption focusing on Indigenous peoples tend to emphasize their consumption of mass-produced goods. While shedding new light on these objects' blurring of ethnic, class, and racial lines, the limits of consumer agency, and the dimensions of cultural translation, little attention has been paid to Native entrepreneurship, which simultaneously flourished alongside consumption. More than purely a matter of economic opportunism that they seized to fill a niche in the marketplace and help cover their own expenses as consumers, Native peoples' production and marketing of indigenous goods such as herbal medicines were means for them to assert themselves and make their presence known. In doing so, they adroitly navigated the complicated terrain of commodity racism by sometimes pragmatically employing popular images of Indianness in the wider society to sell their products, but perhaps also to critique white assumptions about Indians. At other times, they defied these conventions by opting instead for more realistic images of New England Indianness, as Sarah Baxter did to represent herself and the brand she guaranteed to be "pure" and "authentic."

That the vernacular urban experiences of Native peoples are often difficult to trace does not mean that they did not happen or that methodological problems are insurmountable (Rubertone 2012; Thrush 2013). Future research will require archaeologists to stretch their imaginings of what it meant to be Indian in 19th-century New England and what it entailed, particularly for Native peoples who engaged in the "maelstrom of urban life" (Miller 2013), where they struggled to come to terms with modernity perhaps more so than on reservations. Such repositioning means continuing to challenge notions of Native peoples as passive victims and instead looking at how they attempted to secure better lives for themselves as consumers and also as producers. Theorizing Indigenous production and marketing, as I have argued, requires giving more attention to evidence preserved in material, environmental, spatial, visual, and ethnographic records that is too often overlooked to break the silence about how Native producers may have negotiated urban geographies of consumption. Their decisions about how to market products and the subjective choices they made in advertising suggest that these images, as well as the commodities they extolled, may be interpreted as a demand for inclusion as producers in the American marketplace and as citizens in American democratic society. Not in the least, Native peoples' control over and manipulation of the imagery in the advertisements for their products are key to understanding their responses to the more widespread use of Indian stereotypes in product advertising in the 19th century and today (e.g., Mihm 2014), in which real Indians and the diversity of their lived experiences are made invisible.

Confronted with these images, Native producers appropriate and subvert them to reverse commodity racism. Similar to Sarah Baxter, some boldly embrace realism to challenge their invisibility in public consciousness and the failure to acknowledge their colonial circumstances. With Native peoples increasingly entering the marketplace in the 21st century as a source of consumer goods that appeal to Euro-Americans' desire for alternative, if not healthy and hand-crafted, products and as purchasers with disposable income comprising an emerging new market for advertisers, they have unprecedented opportunities to influence "Indian labeling" in ways that can promote their economic success, disconfirm stereotypes, and declare their agency and self-awareness as Indians to the wider world. Understanding the complex signification of product imagery for Sarah Baxter's medicines and Native peoples' empowerment through production, marketing, and consumption is not just a matter of scholarly debate or wishful thinking. Both have important and far-reaching implications for ongoing struggles by individuals and groups in New England and elsewhere over claims to indigenous identity and the ways that it is judged in arenas of federal, state, and local recognition within Indian communities.

POSTSCRIPT

Postcolonial Archaeology in the Age of Things

CRAIG N. CIPOLLA

Objects, in short, make very convenient subaltern subjects.
FOWLES (2016:23)

THE METAPHORICAL BEDROCK OF AMERICAN ARCHAEOLOGY is certainly vibrant these days. Many of us feel the related rumblings of the turn toward things and recent questions concerning ontologies. These movements threaten to shake up and perhaps radically transform our worlds. Evidence of their growing momentum is seen in a host of new banners and frameworks, including "symmetrical archaeology" (Webmoor and Witmore 2008; Witmore 2007; Witmore and Olsen 2015), "new materialism" (Fowler and Harris 2015), "entanglement" theory (Hodder 2012), "archaeology 'after' interpretation" (Jones and Alberti 2013), and archaeology as "the discipline of things" (Olsen et al. 2012). These new theories present sharp challenges to archaeology as a whole, particularly when it comes to the larger pragmatic project of decolonization. According to Severin Fowles (2016:22), the idea of making archaeology or anthropology part of "a human political project" is anthropocentric from these new theoretical vantage points and thus perhaps defunct in the age of things. I am not convinced that all would agree with this notion. For instance, Jane Bennett's (2010) work takes a new materialist approach to argue for more sustainable ways of living in the world. Before focusing on this tension between intellectual and practical problems, I first lay out a brief summary of how these recent theoretical stances relate to *Foreign Objects*.

Chris Pinney (2005) provided some early thoughts on the "thingly" revolution in anthropology. He critiqued materiality studies that emphasize the coconstitution of people and things. Pinney, taking a symmetrical approach inspired by sociologist of science Bruno Latour, acknowledged the important contributions of thinkers like Arjun Appadurai and Nicholas Thomas (introduction, this volume) but ultimately classified such approaches as "purifications" that reify dualisms between subjects and objects. Latour (1993) used the term *purification* in his oft-cited *We Have Never Been Modern*, where he argued that "modernity" involves artificially separating out things from people, objects from subjects, and different spheres of our world, such as economics, science, religion, and social relations. According to him, we are dealing with an old set of Cartesian dualisms hidden beneath a cloak of modernism. The lie of purification, he argued, denies that these entities are forever entangled in dense networks to the point where they are inseparable and hybridized. The more we insist that these entities exist apart from one another, the more we facilitate their admixture.

According to Pinney, Appadurai's (1986) *The Social Life of Things* makes objects into "quasihumans." The "social life" metaphor, when applied to things, assumes that nonhumans possess human-like agency (Joyce 2015). Yet, Chris Gosden (2004, 2005) contradicted such assumptions by noting distinct qualities in nonhumans, such as their abilities to "outlive" humans and give shape to the world for much longer periods of time. Pinney critiqued Thomas's use of the term *entanglement* (1991) because it valued things only insofar as they served as the medium for human social relations, symbolism, and culture. Pinney asked, "Must we forever remain imprisoned in the dichotomous tautologies of purification, or can we imagine alternative ways of encountering materiality?" (2005:267). This crucial question challenged materiality studies of the last decade or so, including those using objectification (Miller 2005b) or dialectical models of any kind. Timothy Webmoor and Christopher Witmore (2008:55) critiqued such materiality studies as anthropocentric. They rejected materiality's fixation on cultural constructs of reality rather than on the world "out there," namely, the world of things. According to Webmoor and Witmore, in attempting to transcend subject–object dualisms through dialectical models, materiality studies reify the same old dualisms (see also Jones and Alberti 2013:23). As the argument goes, materiality studies assume that people make things and things make people; the two realms are mutually constituted. However, according to materiality's critics, the starting point for such an analysis already assumes major distinctions between subjects and objects. Following this logic, these entities are potentially mixed, and we should never assume that they are ontologically distinct.

These arguments remind us that nonhuman agency is enacted in many different ways, some of which can be quite distinct from the ways that people are agentive. More pressing than this point, however, is the fact that nonhumans are more than just passive vehicles for human meaning and use. Things shape our worlds, and they do so in ways that are beyond our comprehension or control. More than that, things are us (Webmoor and Witmore 2008) in the sense that the human lineage has been entangled with nonhumans for many millions of years. To heed this warning, we must turn back to things themselves. These thinkers argue that we cannot make assumptions about the capabilities of humans versus nonhumans in any given situation. We must begin on "symmetrical" ground, as they say. This use of "symmetry" is important to highlight here, since some tend to read the call for a symmetrical archaeology as a call for making humans and nonhumans universally equivalent in terms of their capabilities (Witmore and Olsen 2015). In reality, the argument for symmetrical archaeology is about leveling the starting points of our analyses with no set ideas of how humans, nonhumans, and/or hybrids relate to or contrast with one another.* This notion goes against what I referred to above as assuming that subjects and objects are fundamentally (ontologically) distinct.

Among these critiques, we also hear of the ontological turn or the new animism (Alberti 2014; Alberti and Bray 2009; Alberti and Jones 2013; Alberti and Marshall 2009; Alberti et al. 2011; Henare et al. 2007), which is built on a bedrock of Eduardo Vivieros de Castro's work (e.g., 2004). Simply put, this perspective critiques standard anthropological approaches that seek out the worldviews of non-Western peoples. Those approaches, according to thinkers like Benjamin Alberti (2014) and Yvonne Marshall (Alberti and Marshall 2009), assume that we occupy *one* world, best knowable through the Western scientific perspective. When an indigenous person tells an anthropologist that she can transform into a jaguar, the anthropologist tends not to believe her. The anthropologist assumes that this notion of turning into a jaguar is a different (and flawed) view of the world. The ontological turn asks about the possibilities for *multiple* worlds (Alberti et al. 2011). This perspective, in its most extreme form, urges anthropologists to push beyond recording indigenous peoples' "worldviews," to assume that they—the anthropologists—must not fully understand the world described. This approach takes moments of alterity (e.g., a person reporting on turning into a jaguar) and expands upon them. In this instance, the ontologist asks more about the *type* of world where people transform into animals. For archaeologists, this entails looking at the objects that we study as more than just *representations* or *materializations* of worldviews. Alberti (2014; Alberti and Marshall 2009) pioneered this new approach with his interpretation of "body-pots" from first-millennium A.D. Argentina. As their name implies, body-pots are ceramic vessels that have elements resembling parts of humans and animals. Instead of assuming that body-pots are pots that *represent* bodies, he treats them as a single entity (body-pots) and asks about the world in which they existed. This approach attempts to turn back to things and promises to move beyond the postprocessual fixation on representation and interpretation (Jones and Alberti 2013).

* This certainly applies to the first iteration of arguments for symmetrical approaches in archaeology (see Webmoor and Witmore 2008; Witmore 2007).

I tend to agree with critics of this approach (e.g., Fowles's section in Alberti et al. 2011; Fowles 2016); this take on ontologies seems to colonize difference, emphasizing radical alterity and glossing over elements that "Western" and "non-Western" people might share. This is a particular danger when dealing with colonial contexts in which continuities between colonists and colonized are quite important (see the discussion of Matthews 2010 in the introduction). Without recognizing these continuities, we run the risk of steering back toward the well-trodden and rejected grounds of acculturation (introduction, this volume), where relations between objects (e.g., a European-made pot versus an indigenous-made pot) are taken to stand in for relations between peoples and/or cultural essences (e.g., Europeanness versus indigeneity).

The purpose of this postscript, however, is not to outline these new ideas in any further detail. I leave that to you, the reader. Instead, I focus on the relationship (or lack thereof) between these new directions in theory and what we might refer to as a general "postcolonial" archaeology. Here I ask if these two areas of theory stand to benefit from closer dialogue with one another. But let me be frank: my aim is not "symmetrical" whatsoever. I begin with some strong opinions of the two, and I see one side of this encounter as more important than the other. To be sure, I argue that the turn toward things in archaeology needs postcolonialism, not the other way around. Having noted this asymmetry, postcolonial archaeologies still stand to benefit from a new regard for things and serious questions about ontologies as long as they keep their focus on the political and pragmatic goals of decolonizing. Perhaps this statement is naive and automatically disqualifies postcolonial archaeologies from ever truly taking up the turn toward things' war on dualisms (discussed further below). At the very least, however, this postscript encourages more positive dialogue across the current rift separating postcolonialism and "thingly" matters.

Practitioners with an ear to the ground are aware of the widening gap that characterizes our archaeological terrain in the new millennium. On one side of this rift we hear of postcolonial concerns, of decolonizing archaeological knowledge production, and of experimenting with new forms of archaeological practice, some of which involve indigenous peoples as the archaeologists or as partners in archaeological projects. As with this volume, many studies of this general type attempt to challenge Eurocentric aspects of our discipline. These transformations parallel postcolonial literary critics' scrutiny of the Eurocentric and colonial nature of Western representations of "Others," or subalterns (e.g., Bhabha 1994; Said 1978; Spivak 1988). Postcolonial theory is concerned with how the West portrays colonized subjects as radically different (often "finding" alterity) and as antithetical to Western "progressive" societies and cultures. Within archaeology this movement began taking on serious momentum at the start of the new millennium (e.g., Watkins 2000), and it continues to spread and grow (e.g., Atalay 2012; Lydon and Rizvi 2010; Silliman 2006). There are critics (e.g.,

La Salle 2010; McGhee 2008) and practitioners who view postcolonial archaeologies as a work in progress (Cipolla and Quinn 2016), but it seems that this area of scholarship is here to stay. I argue that much of this "staying power" relates to the abilities of postcolonial archaeologies to make differences in the world beyond academia (e.g., Cipolla 2015; Mrozowski et al. 2009) and make archaeological knowledge production more democratic (Cipolla and Quinn 2016).

The turn toward things and the ontological approach outlined above sit on the other side of this rift. At first the message appeared deceptively similar to the postcolonial critique. Bjørnar Olsen warned us that "archaeologists should unite in a defence of things, a defence of those subaltern members of the collective that have been silenced and 'othered' by the imperialist social and humanist discourses" (2003:100). As we hear and read more about this critique (Olsen 2010, 2012; Olsen et al. 2012; see also Fowles 2010b, 2016 for discussions of this movement), it becomes strikingly clear that it actually sits on ground very different from that of postcolonialism. As the argument goes, things are now in need of liberation. We gasp to think that the medicine bundles and bottles of this book are a new type of subaltern! For many of us working with indigenous communities, Olsen's postcolonial rhetoric simply does not work. How are we to bring this critique to the table when it comes to working with indigenous and local communities? As we work collaboratively on reservations with *actual* colonized peoples, how are we to explain that—from our perspective—the time of liberating people has passed, and it is now time to decolonize things? To say the least, the way Olsen chose to frame this new problem leaves much to be desired; and this narrative has the potential to become quite dangerous if left unchecked or adopted uncritically.

In this volume, most contributors look to objects in order to help explain *cultural* history, *social* transformation, or *human* perseverance. Yet some chapters reveal the complexities of identifying subjects and objects in foreign cultural territories; the ways in which foreign objects became extensions of persons are perfect examples (Creese, Shephard and Gallivan, Bragdon, this volume). In other cases, contributors explore how foreign objects led to new "hybridized" and entangled forms, perhaps showing the fallacy of certain notions of purification. Most of the contributors also deal with indigenous ontologies, though none claim to shed their Western perspective and appropriate indigenous philosophy as archaeological theory (see Alberti and Marshall 2009). Instead they offer a milder version that is more in line with archaeologists such as Maria Zedeño (2009), who incorporates knowledge of indigenous world*views* into archaeological epistemologies. In spite of these convergences with "thingly" and ontological critiques, I am certain that there is ample evidence for anthropocentrism and dualisms in these pages, usually framed as the main culprits in crimes of purification.

Indeed, the turn toward things warns us to do away with intellectual dualisms that restrict our thinking and our practice (much as I did in the introduction, this volume). For a long time now, these dualisms have been under attack. We see this war waged in discussions of practice, agency, object agency, object biography, various types of phenomenology, materiality, and even semiotics (Harris and Cipolla 2017). Ian Hodder (2012, 2014) recently argued that this fixation on binaries is problematic. For me (and not necessarily for Hodder), the war on binaries becomes dangerous when it forces us to lose sight of other important issues in our work and, more importantly, in our world. If we decide that intellectual binaries are our only and biggest foe, perhaps we need to stroll back to the windows of our ivory towers and look outside. Out there, it seems that people have other problems. Think back to the brief mention of collaboration above. It is possible (and I would venture to say likely) that many of our indigenous colleagues and collaborators have other issues on their mind than dualisms. To reiterate, Latour (1993) pointedly argued that the more we insist on the separateness of categories in our world (religion, science, social relations), the more they become entangled. Inversely, it seems that the more we wage a war against intellectual binaries in archaeological theory, the deeper we drive the wedge between us and the rest of the world. In eradicating modernist binaries, we increase the breadth of the widening chasm between intellectual archaeology and the real world. In describing their move "beyond" interpretation, Andrew Jones and Benjamin Alberti argue, "Interpretation involves understanding the interconnections between archaeological remains, tools of archaeological excavation, survey, and recording (trowels, total stations, etc.), and the archaeologists themselves, rather than positing either the archaeologists or the past human subject as the primary site of interpretation" (2013:21). I fully agree, but I would add to this list the *other people* surrounding the archaeologist, her tools, and the archaeological remains. This list must not skip over descendant and local communities tied to that landscape. To privilege them or their problems is, of course, anthropocentric, but perhaps an anthropocentrism worth keeping. So we must ask if there is a way to engage some of these new ideas while also continuing to mind and close the gap between academics, indigenous communities, and the general public. Witmore and Olsen (2015) recently responded to some of their critics, explaining that symmetrical archaeology does not preclude engaging in ethical issues. No matter the intellectual sacrifices involved in making the following claim, I still feel that this is *not* enough; we need to privilege contemporary social issues, asking pragmatic questions about the differences that archaeological work might make in the world.

What differences, then, does *Foreign Objects* make in the real world? This book explored different cultural ontologies and the ways in which they reacted with and to "foreign objects." It did not set out to identify the masks behind which capitalism was allowed to do its dirty work involving the creation and maintenance of gross inequalities (Matthews 2010), perhaps inviting critique from our Marxist colleagues. It did, however, attempt to move beyond the Eurocentric frameworks of capitalism by exploring some relatively new territory for consumption studies. I do not see this project as completely separate from the "real-world" problems of indigenous peoples of the Americas. In fact, I argue that the complex and varied perspectives that contributors provide could in fact serve to further decolonize our shared world by challenging popular and public narratives of colonialism and indigenous authenticity (Cipolla 2013a, 2013b, 2015). These, of course, are part of the ideology masking or naturalizing colonial inequality.

But the pragmatic project is far from complete. A chasm still remains between archaeological knowledge production and the world out there. I was reminded of this gap when I received a peer review of the proposal for this volume. Suggesting that I steer away from certain arguments related to acculturation theory, the reviewer chided, "That paradigm has not been operative for more than 10–15 years. Cipolla doesn't need this 'straw man' to validate these essays." If we judge the cases explored in this volume only in intellectual terms, I largely agree with the reviewer. In this sense, we could have pronounced the death of acculturation at some point in the 1990s. The case studies in this volume certainly demonstrate that the days of European-to-Native artifact ratios are behind us, while critical approaches to indigenous consumption (and its long-term history) are here.

To ponder acculturation's metaphorical death even further, I turn to the writings of philosopher Charles Sanders Peirce.[†] His notion of death is not so simple. He argued that beyond biological death there existed a social consciousness, "by which a man's spirit is embodied in others, and which continues to live and breathe and have its being very much longer than the superficial observers think" (Peirce Edition Project 1998:3). For Peirce, people's semiotic mediation in the world made death a complicated and challenging problem to think through. Could we not say the same for the death of a concept? If acculturation's spirit is gone from the ivory tower, does it exist elsewhere in the world? A superficial consideration of indigenous struggles in the present and public representations of indigeneity and colonial history might give us cause for concern. Think of recent debates concerning sports mascots or the public reaction to the renaming of Mount McKinley as Denali. These current tensions lay bare contested grounds of authenticity and narratives of colonial triumphs versus vanished Indians! The point is that narratives taken as "straw men" in our intellectual worlds are anything but in a world where xenophobe Donald Trump is set to become the forty-fifth president of the United States of America. The chapters in this

[†] Perhaps the metaphor of "social life" simply breaks down for nonorganic entities, as suggested recently by Rosemary Joyce (2015) in her argument for object "itineraries."

volume represent positive directions for the ways in which we think through the foreign objects we find and classify at archaeological sites. I can only hope that we continue these discussions with nonacademics and find new ways of communicating the complexities of these arguments to those who share our worlds. The turn toward things and the ontological turn could be valuable additions to our theoretical repertoires if they take pragmatic and political problems of the "real world" seriously rather than forcing us into further intellectual exile.

REFERENCES CITED

Adair, James. 2005[1775]. The History of the North American Indians. K. E. Holland Braund, ed. Tuscaloosa: University of Alabama Press.

Adams, William Hampton, and Sarah Jane Boling. 1989. Status and Ceramics for Planters and Slaves on Three Georgia Coastal Plantations. Historical Archaeology 23(1):69–96.

Agamben, Giorgio. 1998. Homo Sacer: Sovereign Power and Bare Life. Stanford: Stanford University Press.

Alberti, Benjamin. 2014. Designing Body-Pots in the Formative La Candelaria Culture, Northwest Argentina. *In* Making and Growing: Anthropological Studies of Organisms and Artefacts. Elizabeth Hallam and Tim Ingold, eds. Pp. 107–125. London: Ashgate.

Alberti, Benjamin, and Tamara L. Bray. 2009. Animating Archaeology: Of Subjects, Objects and Alternative Ontologies. Cambridge Archaeological Journal 19(3):337–343.

Alberti, Benjamin, Severin Fowles, Martin Holbraad, Yvonne Marshall, and Christopher Witmore. 2011. "Worlds Otherwise": Archaeology, Anthropology, and Ontological Difference. Current Anthropology 52(6):896–912.

Alberti, Benjamin, Andrew M. Jones, and Joshua Pollard, eds. 2013. Archaeology after Interpretation: Returning Materials to Archaeological Theory. Walnut Creek, CA: Left Coast Press.

Alberti, Benjamin, and Yvonne Marshall. 2009. Animating Archaeology: Local Theories and Conceptually Open-Ended Methodologies. Cambridge Archaeological Journal 19(3): 344–356.

Allen, Rebecca. 1998. Native Americans at Mission Santa Cruz, 1791–1834: Interpreting the Archaeological Record. Perspectives in California Archaeology, 5. Institute of Archaeology, University of California Los Angeles.

Allen, Rebecca, R. Scott Baxter, Linda Hylkema, Clinton Blount, and Stella D'Oro. 2010. Uncovering and Interpreting History and Archaeology at Mission Santa Clara. Report to Santa Clara University by Past Forward, Inc., Santa Clara University Archaeology Research Lab, and Albion Environmental, Inc.

Anders, Martha B. 1989. Wamanga Pottery: Symbolic Resistance and Subversion in Middle Horizon Epoch 2 Ceramics from the Planned Wari Site of Azángaro (Ayacucho, Peru). *In* Cultures in Conflict: Current Archaeological Perspectives. Diana Claire Tkaczuk and Brian C. Vivian, eds. Pp. 7–18. Proceedings of the Twentieth Annual Chacmool Conference. Calgary: University of Calgary Series.

Anderson, David G. 1999. Examining Chiefdoms in the Southeast: An Application of Multiscalar Analysis. *In* Great Towns and Regional Polities in the Prehistoric American Southwest and Southeast. Jill E. Neitzel, ed. Pp. 215–241. Amerind Foundation New World Study Series, 3. Albuquerque: University of New Mexico Press.

Anderson, Virginia DeJohn. 2004. Creates of Empire: How Domestic Animals Transformed Early America. Oxford: Oxford University Press.

Andrews, E. Wyllys, and Anthony P. Andrews. 1975. A Preliminary Study of the Ruins of Xcaret, Quintana Roo, Mexico: With Notes on Other Archaeological Remains on the Central East Coast of the Yucatan Peninsula. Vol. 40. New Orleans: Middle American Research Institute, Tulane University.

Anselmi, Lisa M., Martha A. Latta, and R. G. V. Hancock. 1997. Instrumental Neutron Activation Analysis of Copper and Brass from the Auger Site (BdGw-3), Simcoe County, Ontario. Northeast Anthropology 53:47–59.

Appadurai, Arjun. 1986. Introduction: Commodities and the Politics of Value. *In* The Social Life of Things: Commodities in Cultural Perspective. Arjun Appadurai, ed. Pp. 3–63. Cambridge: Cambridge University Press.

Appadurai, Arjun, ed. 1986. The Social Life of Things: Commodities in Cultural Perspective. Cambridge: Cambridge University Press.

Arkush, Brooke S. 1993. Yokuts Trade Networks and Native Culture Change in Central and Eastern California. Ethnohistory 40:619–640.

Arnn, John Wesley, III. 2012. Land of the Tejas: Native American Identity and Interaction in Texas, A.D. 1300–1700. Austin: University of Texas Press.

Arrillaga, José Joaquín. 1969. José Joaquín Arrillaga: Diary of His Surveys of the Frontier, 1796. Froy Tiscareno, trans., John W. Robinson, ed. Baja California Travels Series, 17. Los Angeles: Dawson's Book Shop.

Artemel, Janice G., Edward J. Flanagan, Elizabeth Crowell, and Louise Akerson. 1984. Providence Cove Lands Phase III Report. On file at Rhode Island Historical Preservation and Heritage Commission, Providence, RI.

Ashley, Keith H. 2003. Interaction, Population Movement, and Political Economy: The Changing Social Landscape of Northeastern Florida (A.D. 900–1500). Ph.D. dissertation, Department of Anthropology, University of Florida, Gainesville. Electronic document, http://etd.fcla.edu/UF/UFE0002312/ashley_k.pdf.

———. 2005. Toward an Interpretation of Shields Mound (8Du12) and the Mill Cove Complex. Florida Anthropologist 58:287–299.

Ashley, Keith H., and Vicki Rolland. 2014. Ritual at the Mill Cove Complex: Realms beyond the River. *In* New Histories of Pre-Columbian Florida. Neill J. Wallis and Asa R. Randall, eds. Pp. 262–282. Gainesville: University Press of Florida.

Atalay, Sonya. 2012. Community-Based Archaeology: Research with, by, and for Indigenous and Local Communities. Berkeley: University of California Press.

Atkins, Ashley L., Christopher J. Shephard, and Martin D. Gallivan. 2010. Memory and Social Reproduction in the Algonquian Chesapeake. Paper presented at the Annual Meeting of the Society of American Archaeology, St. Louis, April 17.

Awe, Jaime, and Christophe Helmke. 2015. The Sword and the Olive Jar: Material Evidence of Seventeenth-Century Maya-European Interaction in Central Belize. Ethnohistory 62(2): 333–360.

Bailyn, Bernard. 1955. New England Merchants in the Seventeenth Century. Cambridge, MA: Harvard University Press.

Bamann, Susan, Robert Kuhn, James Molnar, and Dean Snow. 1992. Iroquoian Archaeology. Annual Review of Anthropology 21:435–460.

Bangs, Jeremy. 2002. Indian Deeds: Land Transactions in Plymouth Colony, 1620–1691. Boston: New England Historical Genealogical Society.

Barash, Vladimir. 2011. The Dynamics of Social Contagion. Ph.D. dissertation, Department of Information Science, Cornell University.

Barnes, Linda L., and Susan S. Sered, eds. 2004. Religion and Healing in America. Oxford: Oxford University Press.

Baron, Donna Keith, J. Edward Hood, and Holly V. Izard. 1996. They Were Here All Along: The Native American Presence in Lower-Central New England in the Eighteenth and Nineteenth Centuries. William and Mary Quarterly 53(3):561–586.

Bauer, Alexander. 2013. Objects and Their Glassy Essence: Semiotics of Self in Early Bronze Age Black Sea. Signs in Society 1(1):1–31.

Baumgarten, Linda. 1975. The Textile Trade in Boston 1650–1700. *In* Arts of the Anglo-American Community in the Seventeenth Century. Ian M. G. Quimby, ed. Pp. 219–273. Charlottesville: University of Virginia Press.

———. 2002. What Clothes Reveal: The Language of Clothing in Colonial and Federal America. New Haven, CT: Yale University Press for the Colonial Williamsburg Foundation.

Bayman, James M. 1996. Shell Ornament Consumption in a Classic Hohokam Platform Mound Community Center. Journal of Field Archaeology 23(4):403–420.

Beauchamp, William M. 1901. Wampum and Shell Articles Used by the New York Indians. New York State Museum Bulletin, 41. Albany: New York State Museum.

Beaudoin, Matthew A. 2013. De-essentializing the Past: Deconstructing Colonial Categories in 19th-Century Ontario. Ph.D. dissertation, Department of Anthropology, University of Western Ontario.

———. 2016. Archaeologists Colonizing Canada: The Effects of Unquestioned Categories. Archaeologies: Journal of the World Archaeological Congress 12(1):7–37.

Beck, Jane C. 1992. Traditional Folk Medicine in Vermont. *In* Medicine and Healing. Peter Benes, ed. Pp. 34–43. Seminar for New England Folklife Annual Proceedings 1990. Boston: Boston University.

Beck, Robin A., Jr., Christopher B. Rodning, and David G. Moore. 2011. Limiting Resistance: Juan Pardo and the Shrinking of Spanish La Florida, 1566–1568. *In* Enduring Conquests: Rethinking the Archaeology of Resistance to Spanish Colonialism in the Americas. Matthew Liebmann and Melissa Murphy, eds. Pp. 19–39. Santa Fe, NM: School for Advanced Research Press.

Becker, Marshall Joseph. 1993. Earth Offering among the Classic Period Lowland Maya: Burials and Caches as Ritual Deposits. *In* Perspectivas antropológicas en el mundo maya. María Josefa Iglesias Ponce de León and Francisco de Asis Ligorred Perramón, eds. Pp. 45–72. Publicaciones de la S.E.E.M.

———. 2005. Matchcoats: Cultural Conservatism and Change in One Aspect of Native American Clothing. Ethnohistory 52(4):727–787.

Beilharz, Edwin A. 1971. Felipe de Neve, First Governor of California. San Francisco: California Historical Society.

Belisle, Donica. 2003. Toward a Canadian Consumer History. Labour / Le Travail 52:181–206.

Bell, Robert E. 1947. Trade Materials at Spiro Mound as Indicated by Artifacts. American Antiquity 12(3):181–184.

Bellin, Joshua David. 2006. Taking the Indian Cure: Thoreau, Indian Medicine, and the Performance of American Culture. New England Quarterly 79(1):3–36.

Bennett, Jane. 2005. The Agency of Assemblages and the North American Blackout. Public Culture 17(3):445–465.

———. 2010. Vibrant Matter: A Political Ecology of Things. Durham, NC: Duke University Press.

Beranek, Christa M. 2009. Beyond Consumption: Social Relationships, Material Culture, and Identity. *In* The Materiality of Individuality: Archaeological Studies of Individual Lives. Carolyn L. White, ed. Pp. 168–183. New York: Springer.

Bernardini, Wesley, and Matthew A. Peeples. 2015. Sight Communities: The Social Significance of Shared Visual Landmarks. American Antiquity 80(2):215–235.

Bertrando, Luther. 1997. Mission San Antonio de Padua Archaeological Field School Excavations of 1993, 1994, and 1996. Pacific Coast Archaeological Society Quarterly 33(4):57–91.

Beverley, Robert, and Louis B. Wright. 1947[1705]. The History and Present State of Virginia. Chapel Hill: University of North Carolina Press.

Bhabha, Homi K. 1994. The Location of Culture. New York: Routledge.

Bickford, Virginia. 1982. European Artifacts from a Chumash Cemetery, CAL-LAN-264. M.A. thesis, Department of Anthropology, California State University Long Beach.

Binford, Lewis R. 1962. Archaeology as Anthropology. American Antiquity 28(2):217–225.

———. 1983. In Pursuit of the Past: Decoding the Archaeological Record. Berkeley: University of California Press.

Birch, Jennifer. 2010. Coalescence and Conflict in Iroquoian Ontario. Archaeological Review from Cambridge 25(1):29–48.

———. 2012. Coalescent Communities: Settlement Aggregation and Social Integration in Iroquoian Ontario. American Antiquity 77(4):646–670.

Blakeslee, Donald J. 1981. The Origin and Spread of the Calumet Ceremony. American Antiquity 46(4):759–768.

Blanton, Dennis B., and Carter C. Hudgins. N.d. Archaeological Evidence for Native Prestige Commodity Devaluation: An Example from the Chesapeake Associated with the Jamestown Colony. Unpublished MS.

Blanton, Dennis B., Stevan C. Pullins, Veronica L. Deitrick, and Gwenyth Duncan. 1999. The Potomac Creek Site (44ST2) Revisited. Research Report Series, 10. Richmond: Virginia Department of Historic Resources.

Blitz, John. 1993. Big Pots for Big Shots: Feasting and Storage in a Mississippian Community. American Antiquity 58(1):80–96.

———. 2010. New Perspectives in Mississippian Archaeology. Journal of Archaeological Research 18(1):1–39.

Bloomfield, Leonard. 1941. Proto-Algonquian *-i·t-* 'Fellow'. Language 17(4):292–297.

———. 1946. Algonquian. *In* Linguistic Structures of Native America. Harry Hoijer and Cornelius Osgood, eds. Pp. 85–129. Viking Fund Publications in Anthropology, 6. New York: Wenner-Gren Foundation.

Borck, Lewis. 2012. Patterns of Resistance: Violence, Migration, and Trade in the Gallina Heartland. M.A. thesis, School of Anthropology, University of Arizona.

———. 2016. Lost Voices Found: An Archaeology of Contentious Politics in the Greater Southwest, A.D. 1100–1450. Ph.D. dissertation, School of Anthropology, University of Arizona.

———. 2017. Sophisticated Rebels: Meaning Maps and Settlement Structure as Evidence for a Social Movement in U.S. Southwestern Deep History. *In* Social Identity in Frontier and Borderland Communities of the North American Southwest. Karen G. Harry and Sarah Herr, eds. Boulder: University Press of Colorado. In review.

Borck, Lewis, Barbara J. Mills, Matthew A. Peeples, and Jeffery J. Clark. 2015. Are Social Networks Survival Networks? An Example from the Late Pre-Hispanic U.S. Southwest. Journal of Archaeological Method and Theory 22(1):33–57.

Bourdieu, Pierre. 1977. Outline of a Theory of Practice. Cambridge: Cambridge University Press.

———. 1984. Distinction: A Social Critique of the Judgment of Taste. R. Nice, trans. Cambridge, MA: Harvard University Press.

———. 1990. The Logic of Practice. Stanford, CA: Stanford University Press.

Bradford, William. 1892. History of Plymouth Plantation. Boston: Dover Books.

Bradley, James W. 1987. Evolution of the Onondaga Iroquois: Accommodating Change 1500–1655. Syracuse, NY: Syracuse University Press.

———. 2007. Before Albany: An Archaeology of Native-Dutch Relations in the Capital Region 1600–1664. Albany: New York State Museum.

Bradley, James W., and S. Terry Childs. 2007. Basque Earrings and Panther's Tails: The Form of Cross-Cultural Contact in Sixteenth Century Iroquoia. *In* Archaeology of the Iroquois. Jordan Kerber, ed. Pp. 290–305. Syracuse, NY: Syracuse University Press.

Brady, James E., and Ann Scott. 1997. Excavations in Buried Cave Deposits: Implications for Interpretation. Journal of Caves and Karst Studies 59:15–21.

Bragdon, Kathleen J. 1996. Native People of Southern New England 1500–1650. Norman: University of Oklahoma Press.

———. 2009. Native People of Southern New England, 1650–1775. Norman: University of Oklahoma Press.

———. 2015. Knowledge Production, Identity Formation and Mortuary Ritual in Colonial Native New England: A View from Native Language Documents. *In* Native Wills from the Colonial Americas: Dead Giveaways in a New World. Mark Christianson and Jonathan Truitt, eds. Pp. 158–181. Salt Lake City: University of Utah Press.

———. N.d. Conspicuous Consumption as a Trope in Native Southern New England. *In* Gender in Archaeology. Susan Kus and Kimberly Kasper, eds. Gainesville: University Press of Florida. In review.

Brain, Jeffrey P. 1979. Tunica Treasure. Papers of the Peabody Museum of Archaeology and Ethnography, 71. Cambridge, MA: Harvard University Press.

———. 1988. Tunica Archaeology. Papers of the Peabody Museum of Archaeology and Ethnography, 78. Cambridge, MA: Harvard University Press.

———. 1989. Winterville: Late Prehistoric Culture Contact in the Lower Mississippi Valley. Archaeological Report, 23. Jackson: Mississippi Department of Archives and History.

Brandt, Elizabeth A. 1994. Egalitarianism, Hierarchy, and Centralization in the Pueblos. *In* The Ancient Southwest Community: Models and Methods for the Study of Prehistoric Social Organization. Wirt H. Wills and Robert D. Leonard, eds. Pp. 9–24. Albuquerque: University of New Mexico Press.

Braswell, Geoffrey E. 2003. Introduction: Reinterpreting Early Classic Interaction. *In* The Maya and Teotihuacan: Reinterpreting Early Classic Interaction. Geoffrey E. Braswell, ed. Pp. 1–43. Austin: University of Texas Press.

Braudel, Fernand. 1980. On History. Chicago: University of Chicago Press.

Braun, Gregory V. 2012. Petrography as a Technique for Investigating Iroquoian Ceramic Production and Smoking Rituals. Journal of Archaeological Science 39:1–10.

Brenner, Elise. 1988. Sociopolitical Implications of Mortuary Ritual Remains in 17th-Centry Native Southern New England. *In* The Recovery of Meaning: Historical Archaeology in the Eastern United States. M. Leone and P. Potter, eds. Pp. 147–182. Washington, DC: Smithsonian Institution Press.

Bridenbaugh, Carl. 1985. The Pynchon Papers: Selections from the Account Books of John Pynchon. Charlottesville: University of Virginia Press.

Brittain, Marcus, and Oliver J. T. Harris. 2010. Enchaining Arguments and Fragmenting Assumptions: Reconsidering the Fragmentation Debate in Archaeology. World Archaeology 42(4):581–594.

Brooks, Lisa. 2013. Turning the Looking Glass on King Phillip's War: Locating American Literature in Native Space. American Literary History 25(4):718–750.

Brose, David S., C. Wesley Cowan, and Robert C. Mainfort, eds. 2001. Societies in Eclipse: Archaeology of the Eastern Woodlands Indians, A.D. 1400–1700. Washington, DC: Smithsonian Institution Press.

Brown, James A. 2006. Where's the Power in Mound Building? An Eastern Woodlands Perspective. *In* Leadership and Polity in Mississippian Society. Brian M. Butler and Paul D. Welch, eds. Pp. 197–213. Occasional Paper, 33. Carbondale: Southern Illinois University, Center for Archaeological Investigations.

Brown, Jennifer S. 2006. Fields of Dreams: Revisiting A. I. Hallowell and the Berens River Ojibwe. *In* New Perspectives on Native North America: Cultures, Histories, and Representations. Sergei A. Kan and Pauline T. Strong, eds. Pp. 17–41. Lincoln: University of Nebraska Press.

Brown, Michael F. 1991. Beyond Resistance: A Comparative Study of Utopian Renewal in Amazonia. Ethnohistory 38(4):388–413.

Bruchac, Margaret M. 1998. In Search of the Indian Doctress. http://pvhn2.wordpress.com/1800-2/rhoda-rhoades/, accessed May 26, 2015.

Brumfiel, Elizabeth M. 2000. On the Archaeology of Choice: Agency Studies as a Research Stratagem. *In* Agency in Archaeology. Marcia-Anne Dobres and John Robb, eds. Pp. 249–255. New York: Routledge.

Brunton, Deborah. 2014. Health and Wellness in the 19th Century. Santa Barbara, CA: Greenwood.

Bruseth, James E., and Toni S. Turber. 2004. From a Watery Grave: The Discovery and Excavation of La Salle's Shipwreck, La Belle. College Station: Texas A&M University Press.

Burkes, Caitlyn E. 2014. Religious and Ceremonial Microartifacts from the Winterville Archaeological Site (22WS500). B.A. honors thesis, Department of Anthropology and Sociology and Department of Religion, University of Southern Mississippi, Hattiesburg. Electronic document, http://aquila.usm.edu/cgi/viewcontent.cgi?article=1208&context=honors_theses/.

Burley, David V. 2000. Creolization and Late 19th Century Métis Vernacular Log Architecture on the South Saskatchewan River. Historical Archaeology 34(3):49–56.

Burt, Ronald S. 1987. Social Contagion and Innovation: Cohesion versus Structural Equivalence. American Journal of Sociology 92(6):1287–1335.

———. 1992. Structural Holes: The Social Structure of Competition. Cambridge, MA: Harvard University Press.

Burwell, Lewis. 1833. Field Note Book—Survey of Brant County. Archived material, Brant County Archives, Brantford, ON.

Bushnell, David. 1920. Native Cemeteries and Forms of Burial East of the Mississippi. Bulletin 71. Washington, DC: Bureau of American Ethnology.

Cameron, Catherine M. N.d. How Diffusion Happens. *In* Social Networks in the Ancient Southwest. Karen Harry and Barbara Roth, eds. Boulder: University Press of Colorado. In review.

Cangany, Catherine. 2012. Fashioning Moccasins: Detroit, the Manufacturing Frontier, and the Empire of Consumption, 1701–1835. William and Mary Quarterly 69(2):265–304.

Carder, Nanny, Elizabeth J. Reitz, and J. Matthew Compton. 2004. Animal Use in the Georgia Pine Barrens: An Example from the Hartford Site (9PU1). Southeastern Archaeology 23:25–40.

Carr, Christopher. 1995a. Building a Unified Middle-Range Theory of Artifact Design. *In* Style, Society, and Person: Archaeological and Ethnological Perspectives. Christopher Carr and Jill E. Neitzel, eds. Pp. 151–170. New York: Plenum Press.

———. 1995b. A Unified Middle-Range Theory of Artifact Design. *In* Style, Society, and Person: Archaeological and Ethnological Perspectives. Christopher Carr and Jill E. Neitzel, eds. Pp. 171–258. New York: Plenum Press.

Carson, James T. 2005. Sacred Circles and Dangerous Peoples: Native American Cosmology and the French Settlement of Louisiana. *In* French Colonial Louisiana and the Atlantic World. Bradley G. Bond, ed. Pp. 65–82. Baton Rouge: Louisiana State University Press.

Casella, Eleanor C., and Chris Fowler. 2005. The Archaeology of Plural and Changing Identities. New York: Kluwer Academic.

Casella, Eleanor, and Barbara L. Voss, eds. 2012. The Archaeology of Colonialism: Intimate Encounters and Sexual Effects. Cambridge: Cambridge University Press.

Ceci, Lynn. 1982. The Value of Wampum among the New York Iroquois. Journal of Anthropological Research 38(1):97–107.

———. 1990. Native Wampum as a Peripheral Resource in the Seventeenth Century World System. *In* The Pequots in Southern New England: The Fall and Rise of an American Indian Nation. Laurence Hauptman and James Wherry, eds. Pp. 48–64. Norman: University of Oklahoma Press.

Certeau, Michel de. 1984. The Practice of Everyday Life. Berkeley: University of California Press.

Cessford, Craig. 2012. Life in a "Cathedral of Consumption": Corporate and Personal Material Culture Recovered from a Cellar at the Robert Sayle Department Store in Cambridge, England, ca. 1913–21. International Journal of Historical Archaeology 16(4):784–808.

Chamberlain, Robert S. 1948. The Conquest and Colonization of Yucatan, 1517–1550. Washington, DC: Carnegie Institution of Washington.

Chapman, John. 2000. Fragmentation in Archaeology. London: Routledge.

Chase, Arlen F., and Diane Z. Chase. 1992. Mesoamerican Elites: Assumptions, Definitions and Models. *In* Mesoamerican Elites: An Archaeological Assessment. Diane Z. Chase and Arlen F. Chase, eds. Pp. 3–17. Norman: University of Oklahoma Press.

Chase, Diane Z. 1985. Ganned but Not Forgotten: Late Postclassic Archaeology and Ritual at Santa Rita Corozal, Belize. *In* The Lowland Maya Postclassic. Arlen F. Chase and Prudence M. Rice, eds. Pp. 104–125. Austin: University of Texas Press.

———. 1988. Caches and Censerwares: Meaning from Maya Pottery. *In* A Pot for All Reasons: Ceramic Ecology Revisited. Charles C. Kolb and Louana M. Lackey, eds. Pp. 81–104. Philadelphia: Special Publication of Cerámica de Cultura Maya et al., Laboratory of Anthropology, Temple University.

Cheek, Charles D. 1998. Massachusetts Bay Foodways: Regional and Class Influences. Historical Archaeology 32(3):153–172.

Childs, S. Terry. 1994. Native Copper Technology and Society in Eastern North America. *In* Archaeometry of Pre-Columbian Sites and Artifacts. D. A. Scott and P. Meyers, eds. Pp. 229–253. Los Angeles: Getty Conservation Institute.

Chu, Julie Y. 2010. Cosmologies of Credit: Transnational Mobility and the Politics of Destination in China. Durham, NC: Duke University Press.

Chuchiak, John F., IV. 2009. De Descriptio Idolorum: An Ethnohistorical Examination of the Production, Imagery, and Functions of Colonial Yucatec Maya Idols and Effigy Censers, 1540–1700. *In* Maya Worldviews at Conquest. Leslie G. Cecil and Timothy W. Pugh, eds. Pp. 135–158. Boulder: University Press of Colorado.

Church, Benjamin. 1827[1716]. The Entertaining History of King Philip's War: which began in the month of June, 1675; as also of expeditions more lately made against the common enemy, and Indian rebels, in the eastern parts of New-England; with some account of the divine providence towards Col. Benjamin Church. Boston: Press unknown.

Cipolla, Craig N. 2008. Signs of Identity, Signs of Memory. Archaeological Dialogues 15(2):196–215.

———. 2013a. Becoming Brothertown: Native American Ethnogenesis and Endurance in the Modern World. Tucson: University of Arizona Press.

———. 2013b. Native American Historical Archaeology and the Trope of Authenticity. Historical Archaeology 47(3):12–22.

———. 2015. Colonial Consumption and Community Preservation. *In* Rethinking Colonialism: Comparative Archaeological Approaches. Craig N. Cipolla and Katherine H. Hayes, eds. Pp. 17–39. Gainesville: University Press of Florida.

Cipolla, Craig N., and Katherine H. Hayes, eds. 2015. Rethinking Colonialism: Comparative Archaeological Approaches. Gainesville: University Press of Florida.

Cipolla, Craig N., and James Quinn. 2016. Field School Archaeology the Mohegan Way: Reflections on Twenty Years of Community-Based Research and Teaching. Journal of Community Archaeology and Heritage, in press.

Clark, Jeffery. 2001. Tracking Prehistoric Migrations: Pueblo Settlers among the Tonto Basin Hohokam. Anthropological Papers of the University of Arizona, 65. Tucson: University of Arizona Press.

Clark, Jeffery J., Deborah L. Huntley, J. Brett Hill, and Patrick D. Lyons. 2013. The Kayenta Diaspora and Salado Meta-identity in the Precontact U.S. Southwest. *In* Hybrid Material Culture: The Archaeology of Syncretism and Ethnogenesis. Jeb J. Card, ed. Pp. 399–424. CAI Occasional Paper, 40. Carbondale: Center for Archaeological Investigations, Southern Illinois University.

Clark, Jeffery J., and Patrick D. Lyons, eds. 2012. Migrants and Mounds: Late Prehistoric Archaeology of the Lower San Pedro Valley. Anthropological Papers, 45. Tucson: Archaeology Southwest.

Cobb, Charles R. 2000. From Quarry to Cornfield: The Political Economy of Mississippian Hoe Production. Tuscaloosa: University of Alabama Press.

———. 2003. Mississippian Chiefdoms: How Complex? Annual Review of Anthropology 32:63–84.

Cobb, Charles R., ed. 2003. Stone Tool Traditions in the Contact Era. Tuscaloosa: University of Alabama Press.

Cobb, Charles R., and Michael S. Nassaney. 2002. Domesticating Self and Society in the Woodland Southeast. *In* The Woodland Southeast. Robert C. Mainfort and David G. Anderson, eds. Pp. 525–539. Tuscaloosa: University of Alabama Press.

Cobb, Charles R., and Stephanie Sapp. 2015. Imperial Anxiety and the Dissolution of Colonial Space and Practice at Fort Moore, South Carolina. *In* Rethinking Colonial Pasts through Archaeology. Neal Ferris, Rodney Harrison, and Michael V. Wilcox, eds. Pp. 212–232. Oxford: Oxford University Press.

Cogley, Richard W. 1999. John Eliot's Mission to the Indians before King Philip's War. Cambridge, MA: Harvard University Press.

Comaroff, John L., and Jean Comaroff. 1990. Goodly Beasts, Beastly Goods: Cattle and Commodities in a South African Context. American Ethnologist 17(2):195–216.

———. 1997. Of Revelation and Revolution, vol. 1: Christianity, Colonialism and Consciousness in South Africa. Chicago: University of Chicago Press.

Comaroff, Jean, and John L. Comaroff. 2006. Beasts, Banknotes and the Colour of Money in Colonial South Africa. Archaeological Dialogues 12(2):107–132.

Conte, Ignacio, and Facundo Romero. 2008. Microwear Analysis of Retouched Glass Fragments from Fortlet Miñana, Azul, Argentina, 1860–1863. International Journal of Historical Archaeology 12(3):248–262.

Cook, Lauren J., Rebecca Yamin, and John P. McCarthy. 1996. Shopping as Meaningful Action: Toward a Redefinition of Consumption in Historical Archaeology. Historical Archaeology 30(4):50–65.

Cook, Sherburne F. 1962. Expeditions to the Interior of California, Central Valley, 1820–1840. University of California Anthropological Records, 20:151–213.

———. 1973. The Significance of Disease in the Extinction of the New England Indians. Human Biology 45(3):485–508.

Cooke, David G. 1989. Adena Related Burials: Glastonbury, Connecticut. Bulletin of the Archaeological Society of Connecticut 62:7–15.

Cooke, David G., and Barbara Jordan. 1972. An Adena-Like Burial at East Windsor Hill. Archaeological Society of Connecticut Bulletin 37:47–51.

Coward, Fiona. 2013. Grounding the Net: Social Networks, Material Culture and Geography in the Epipalaeolithic and Early Neolithic of the Near East (~21,000–6,000 cal BCI). *In* Network Analysis in Archaeology: New Approaches to Regional Interaction. Carl Knappett, ed. Pp. 181–202. Oxford: Oxford University Press.

Creese, John L. 2011. Deyughnyonkwarakda—"At the Wood's Edge": The Development of the Iroquoian Village Southern Ontario, A.D. 900–1500. Ph.D. dissertation, Department of Anthropology, University of Toronto.

———. 2012. The Domestication of Personhood: A View from the Northern Iroquoian Longhouse. Cambridge Archaeological Journal 22(3):365–386.

———. 2016a. Emotion Work and the Archaeology of Consensus: The Northern Iroquoian Case. World Archaeology 48(1):14–34.

———. 2016b. Making Pipes and Social Persons at the Keffer Site: A Life History Approach. *In* Perspectives on the Archaeology of Pipes, Tobacco and Other Smoke Plants in the Ancient Americas. Elizabeth Bollwerk and Shannon Tushingham, eds. Pp. 27–49. New York: Springer.

Crook, Penny. 2000. Shopping and Historical Archaeology: Exploring the Contexts of Urban Consumption. Australasian Historical Archaeology 18:17–28.

Crosby, Constance A. 1988. From Myth to History, or Why King Philip's Ghost Walks Abroad. *In* The Recovery of Meaning: Historical Archaeology in the Eastern United States. Mark P. Leone and Parker B. Potter, eds. Pp. 183–210. Washington, DC: Smithsonian Institution Press.

Crossland, Zoe. 2010. Embodiment and Materiality. *In* The Oxford Handbook of Material Culture Studies. Dan Hicks and Mary C. Beaudry, eds. Pp. 386–405. Oxford: Oxford University Press.

Crossley, Nick. 2001. The Social Body: Habit, Identity, and Desire. Thousand Oaks, CA: Sage.

Crown, Patricia L. 1994. Ceramics & Ideology: Salado Polychrome Pottery. Albuquerque: University of New Mexico Press.

Crown, Patricia L., Thomas E. Emerson, Jiyan Gu, W. Jeffrey Hurst, Timothy R. Pauketat, and Timothy Ward. 2012. Ritual Black Drink Consumption at Cahokia. PNAS 109(35):13944–13949.

Cruikshank, Ernest Alexander. 1929. Records of Niagara, 1784–9.Collected and Edited by Brig. General E. A. Cruikshank. Niagara: Niagara Historical Society.

Csordas, Thomas. 1990. Embodiment as a Paradigm for Anthropology. Ethos 18:5–47.

———. 1996. Embodiment and Experience: The Existential Ground of Body and Self. Cambridge: Cambridge University Press.

Dalton, George. 1960. A Note of Clarification on Economic Surplus. American Anthropologist 62(3):483–490.

Deagan, Kathleen A. 2002. Artifacts of the Spanish Colonies of Florida and the Caribbean, 1500–1800, vol. 2: Personal Portable Possessions. Washington, DC: Smithsonian Institution Press.

Dean, Jeffrey S., ed. 2000. Salado. Albuquerque: University of New Mexico Press.

DeBoer, Warren R. 2001. The Big Drink: Feast and Forum in the Upper Amazon. *In* Feasts: Archaeological and Ethnographic Perspectives on Food, Politics, and Power. Michael Dietler and Brian Hayden, eds. Pp. 215–239. Washington, DC: Smithsonian Institution Press.

DeLanda, Manuel. 2006. A New Philosophy of Society. London: Continuum.

Deloria, Philip J. 1998. Playing Indian. New Haven, CT: Yale University Press.

———. 2004. Indians in Unexpected Places. Lawrence: University Press of Kansas.

Den Ouden, Amy. 2005. Beyond Conquest: Native Peoples and the Struggle for History in New England. Lincoln: University of Nebraska Press.

Denys, Nicholas. 1908[1672]. Description géographique et historique des costes de l'Amérique septentrionale: Avec l'histoire naturelle du païs. Toronto: Champlain Society.

Dietler, Michael. 1996. Feasts and Commensal Politics in the Political Economy: Food, Power and Status in Prehistoric Europe. *In* Food and the Status Quest: An Interdisciplinary Perspective. Polly Wiessner and Wulf Schiefenhövel, eds. Pp. 87–125. Providence, RI: Berghahn Books.

———. 1998. Consumption, Agency, and Cultural Entanglement: Theoretical Implications of a Mediterranean Colonial Encounter. *In* Studies in Culture Contact: Interaction, Culture Change and Archaeology. James G. Cusick, ed. Pp. 288–315. Carbondale: Southern Illinois University Press.

———. 2001. Theorizing the Feast: Rituals of Consumption, Commensal Politics, and Power in African Contexts. *In* Feasts: Archaeological and Ethnographic Perspectives on Food, Politics, and Power. Michael Dietler and Brian Hayden, eds. Pp. 65–114. Washington, DC: Smithsonian Institution Press.

———. 2005. The Archaeology of Colonization and the Colonization of Archaeology: Theoretical Challenges from an Ancient Mediterranean Colonial Encounter. *In* The Archaeology of Colonial Encounters: Comparative Perspectives. Gil J. Stein, ed. Pp. 33–68. Santa Fe, NM: SAR Press.

———. 2010. Archaeologies of Colonialism: Consumption, Entanglement, and Violence in Ancient Mediterranean France. Berkeley: University of California Press.

Dillon, Phyllis. 1980. Trade Fabrics. *In* Burr's Hill: A 17th Century Wampanoag Burial Ground in Warren, Rhode Island. Susan Gibson, ed. Pp. 100–107. Providence, RI: Brown University Press.

DiPeso, Charles C. 1958. Western Pueblo Intrusion into the San Pedro Valley. Kiva 23(4):12–16.

Douglas, John E., and Carol Kramer. 1992. Interaction, Social Proximity, and Distance: A Special Issue. Journal of Anthropological Archaeology 11(2):103–110.

Douglas, Mary. 1996[1970]. Natural Symbols: Explorations in Cosmology. New York: Routledge.

Douglas, Mary, and Baron Isherwood. 1979. The World of Goods. New York: Basic Books.

Doyel, David E. 1976. Introduction. Kiva 42(1):1–4.

Doyel, David E., and Emil W. Haury. 1976. Summary of Conference Discussion. Kiva 42:127–134.

Drooker, Penelope B. 2004. Pipes, Leadership, and Interregional Interaction in Protohistoric Midwestern and Northeastern North America. *In* Smoking and Culture: The Archaeology of Tobacco Pipes in Eastern North America. Sean Rafferty and Rob Mann, eds. Pp. 73–123. Knoxville: University of Tennessee Press.

Dumont de Montigny, Jean-François-Benjamin. 2012. The Memoir of Lieutenant Dumont, 1715–1747: A Sojourner in the French Atlantic. Gordon M. Sayre and Carla Zecher, eds. Chapel Hill: University of North Carolina Press.

Dungan, Katherine Ann. 2015. Social Boundaries and Religious Architecture in the Mogollon Highlands. Ph.D. dissertation, School of Anthropology, University of Arizona.

Dunton, John. 1867. John Dunton's Letters from New England [1686]. Boston: Publications of the Prince Society.

Du Poisson, Paul. 1900. Letter from Father du Poisson, Missionary to the Akensas, to Father * * *. Dated Oct 3, 1727. *In* The Jesuit Relations and Allied Documents, vol. 67. Rueben Gold Thwaites, ed. Pp. 276–326. Cleveland: Burrows Brothers.

Ehrhardt, Kathleen. 2005. European Metals in Native Hands: Rethinking the Dynamics of Technological Change 1640–1683. Tuscaloosa: University of Alabama Press.

Elson, Mark D. 1998. Expanding the View of Hohokam Platform Mounds: An Ethnographic Perspective. Anthropological Papers of the University of Arizona, 37. Tucson: University of Arizona Press.

Emerson, Thomas E., Kristin M. Hedman, and Mary L. Simon. 2005. Marginal Horticulturalists or Maize Agriculturalists? Archaeobotanical, Paleopathological, and Isotopic Evidence Relating to Langford Tradition Maize Consumption. Midcontinental Journal of Archaeology 30(1):67–118.

Emerson, Thomas E., and Timothy R. Pauketat. 2002. Embodying Power and Resistance at Cohokia. *In* Dynamics of Power. Maria O'Donovan, ed. Pp. 105–125. Carbondale: Southern Illinois University Press.

Englehardt, Joshua. 2011. The King Is Dead, Long Live the King: Mimesis and Identity in the Cultural Projects of the New Order at Tikal. *In* Identity Crisis: Archaeological Perspectives on Social Identity. Proceedings of the 42nd (2010) Annual Chacmool Archaeology Conference. Lindsay Amundsen-Meyer, Nicole Engel, and Sean Pickering, eds. Pp. 199–210. Calgary, AB: University of Calgary.

Entwistle, Joanne. 2000. Fashion and the Fleshy Body: Dress as Embodied Practice. Fashion Theory 4:323–348.

Evans, Helen. 2002. The Syncretic Continuum: The Incorporation of European Goods at a 17th Century Huron Village. St. John's: Copetown Press.

Farris, Glenn J. 2014. Depriving God and the Kind of the Means of Charity: Early Nineteenth-Century Missionaries' Views of Cattle Ranchers near Mission La Purísima, California. *In* Indigenous Landscapes and Spanish Missions: New Perspectives from Archaeology and Ethnohistory. Lee M. Panich and Tsim D. Schnieder, eds. Pp. 135–153. Tucson: University of Arizona Press.

Fausto, Carlos. 2007. Feasting on People: Eating Animals and Humans in Amazonia. Current Anthropology 484(4):497–530.

Feest, Christian F. 1983. Powhatan's Mantle. *In* Tradescant's Rarities: Essays on the Foundation of the Ashmolean Museum, 1683, with a Catalogue of the Surviving Early Collections. Arthur Macgregor, ed. Pp. 130–135. Oxford: Oxford University Press.

Feinman, Gary M., Linda M. Nicholas, and Helen R. Haines. 2006. Socioeconomic Inequality and the Consumption of Chipped Stone at El Palmillo, Oaxaca, Mexico. Latin American Antiquity 17(2):151–175.

Ferguson, Leland. 1991. Struggling with Pots in Colonial South Carolina. *In* The Archaeology of Inequality. Randall H. McGuire and Robert Paynter, eds. Pp. 28–39. Oxford: Blackwell Publishers.

Ferguson, T. J. 2002. Dowa Yalanne: The Architecture of Zuni Resistance and Social Change during the Pueblo Revolt. *In* Archaeologies of the Pueblo Revolt: Identity, Meaning, and Renewal in the Pueblo World. Robert W. Preucel, ed. Pp. 85–98. Albuquerque: University of New Mexico Press.

Ferris, Neal. 2006. In *Their* Time: Archaeological Histories of Native-Lived Contact and Colonialisms, Southwestern Ontario, A.D. 1400–1900. Ph.D. dissertation, Department of Anthropology, McMaster University.

———. 2009. The Archaeology of Native-Lived Colonialism: Challenging History in the Great Lakes. Tucson: University of Arizona Press.

Ferris, Neal, Rodney Harrison, and Matthew A. Beaudoin. 2015. Introduction. *In* Rethinking Colonial Pasts through Archaeology. Neal Ferris, Rodney Harrison, and Michael V. Wilcox, eds. Pp. 1–36. Oxford: Oxford University Press.

Fesler, Garrett, David Givens, and Matthew Laird. 2001. Phase III Data Recovery at Site 44SK11, Suffolk, Virginia: 42" Water Line Replacement, along the Nansemond River, for the City of Norfolk, Virginia. Technical Report. Williamsburg: James River Institute for Archaeology, Inc.

Finch, Martha L. 2010. Dissenting Bodies: Corporealities in Early New England. New York: Columbia University Press.

Fish, Suzanne K., and Marcia Donaldson. 1991. Production and Consumption in the Archaeological Record: A Hohokam Example. Kiva 56(3):255–275.

Fitzgerald, William R. 1990. Chronology to Culture Process: Lower Great Lakes Archaeology 1500–1650. Ph.D. dissertation, Department of Anthropology, McGill University.

Fitzgerald, William R., and Peter G. Ramsden. 1988. Copper Based Metal Testing as an Aid to Understanding Early European-Amerindian Interaction: Scratching the Surface. Canadian Journal of Archaeology 12:153–162.

Fitzgerald, William R., R. H. Whitehead, J. W. Bradley, and L. Turgeon. 1993. Late Sixteenth Century Basque Banded Copper Kettles. Historical Archaeology 27:44–57.

Flexner, James. 2014. The Historical Archaeology of States and Non-states: Anarchist Perspectives from Hawai'i and Vanuatu. Journal of Pacific Archaeology 5(2):8197.

Fontana, Bernard. 1965. On the Meaning of Historic Sites Archaeology. American Antiquity 31(1):61–65.

Foster, Michael K. 1985. Another Look at the Function of Wampum in Iroquois-White Councils. *In* The History and Culture of Iroquois Diplomacy. Francis Jennings, William N. Fenton, Mary A. Druke, and David R. Miller, eds. Pp. 99–114. Syracuse, NY: Syracuse University Press.

Foucault, Michel. 1981. The Order of Discourse. *In* Untying the Text: A Post-structuralist Reader. Robert J. C. Young, ed. Pp. 48–78. Boston: Routledge.

———. 1995. Discipline and Punish: The Birth of the Prison. Alan Sheridan, trans. New York: Vintage Books.

Fowler, Chris. 2004. The Archaeology of Personhood: An Anthropological Approach. New York: Routledge.

Fowler, Chris, and Oliver J. T. Harris. 2015. Enduring Relations: Exploring a Paradox of New Materialism. Journal of Material Culture 20(2):127–148.

Fowles, Severin. 2010a. A People's History of the American Southwest. *In* Ancient Complexities: New Perspectives in Pre-Columbian North America. Susan Alt, ed. Pp. 183–204. Provo: University of Utah Press.

———. 2010b. People without Things. *In* An Anthropology of Absence: Materializations of Transcendence and Loss. Mikkel Bille, Frida Hastrup, and Tim Floher Soerensen, eds. Pp. 23–41. New York: Springer.

———. 2013. An Archaeology of Doings: Secularism and the Study of Pueblo Religion. Santa Fe, NM: School for Advanced Research.

———. 2016. The Perfect Subject (Postcolonial Object Studies). Journal of Material Culture 21(1):9–27.

Fox, William. 2002. Thaniba Wakandagi among the Ontario Iroquois. Canadian Journal of Archaeology 26(2):130–151.

Frazer, James G. 1951[1922]. The Golden Bough: A Study in Magic and Religion. New York: Macmillan Company.

Frink, Lisa, and Karen G. Harry. 2008. The Beauty of "Ugly" Eskimo Cooking Pots. American Antiquity 73(1):103–118.

Galindo, Nasario, Cristina Alviso Chapman, and Keith Ponsford. 1959. Early Days at Mission Santa Clara: Recollections of Nasario Galindo. California Historical Society Quarterly 38(2):101–111.

Gallivan, Martin D. 2007. Powhatan's Werowocomoco: Constructing Place, Polity, and Personhood in the Chesapeake, C.E. 1200–C.E. 1609. American Anthropologist 109(1):85–100.

———. 2016. The Powhatan Landscape: An Archaeological History of the Algonquian Chesapeake. Gainesville: University Press of Florida.

Gallivan, Martin, Buck Woodard, and Christopher Shephard. 2008. Chesapeake Frontiers and Algonquian Community Construction before and after Contact. Paper presented at the Conference on Social Archaeology of the Southeastern Colonial Frontiers, South Carolina Institute for Archaeology and Anthropology, Columbia, May 15.

Galloway, Patricia. 1998. Savage Medicine: Du Pratz and Eighteenth-Century French Medical Practice. *In* France in the New World. David Buisseret, ed. Pp. 108–109. East Lansing: Michigan State University Press.

Gamble, Lynn H. 2008. The Chumash World at European Contact: Power, Trade, and Feasting among Complex Hunter-Gatherers. Berkeley: University of California Press.

Gamble, Lynn H., Phillip L. Walker, and Glenn S. Russell. 2001. An Integrative Approach to Mortuary Analysis: Social and Symbolic Dimensions of Chumash Burial Practices. American Antiquity 66(2):185–212.

Geiger, Amy C. 2014. Pottery and Differential Foodways: An Evaluation of Social Stratification at the Winterville Site (22WS500). B.A. honors thesis, Department of Anthropology and Sociology and Department of Religion, University of Southern Mississippi, Hattiesburg. Electronic document, http://aquila.usm.edu/honors_theses/235/.

Geiger, Maynard J., and Clement W. Meighan. 1976. As the Padres Saw Them: California Indian Life and Customs as Reported by the Franciscan Missionaries, 1813–1815. Santa Barbara: Santa Barbara Mission Archive Library.

Gell, Alfred. 1998. Art and Agency: An Anthropological Theory. Oxford: Oxford University Press.

Gibson, Susan. 1980. Introduction. *In* Burr's Hill: A 17th Century Wampanoag Burial Ground in Warren, Rhode Island. Susan Gibson, ed. Pp. 9–24. Providence, RI: Haffenreffer Museum of Anthropology, Brown University.

Gibson, Susan, ed. 1980. Burr's Hill: A 17th Century Wampanoag Burial Ground in Warren, Rhode Island. Providence, RI: Haffenreffer Museum of Anthropology, Brown University.

Gladwin, Winifred, and Harold Gladwin. 1935. The Eastern Range of the Red-on-Buff Culture. Medallion Papers. Globe, AZ: Gila Pueblo.

Gleach, Frederic W. 1997. Powhatan's World and Colonial Virginia: A Conflict of Cultures. Lincoln: University of Nebraska Press.

Goddard, Ives, and Kathleen J. Bragdon. 1988. Native Writings in Massachusetts. Philadelphia: American Philosophical Society.

Golub, Benjamin, and Matthew O. Jackson. 2012. How Homophily Affects the Speed of Learning and Best-Response Dynamics. Quarterly Journal of Economics 127(3):1287–1338.

Gonlin, Nancy. 2012. Production and Consumption in the Countryside: A Case Study from the Late Classic Maya Rural Commoner Households at Copán, Honduras. *In* Ancient Households of the Americas: Conceptualizing What Households Do. John G. Douglass and Nancy Gonlin, eds. Pp. 79–116. Boulder: University Press of Colorado.

González-Ruibal, Alfredo. 2014. An Archaeology of Resistance: Materiality and Time in an African Borderland. Lanham, MD: Rowman & Littlefield.

Goodby, Robert G. 1998. Technological Patterning and Social Boundaries: Ceramic Variability in Southern New England, A.D. 1000–1675. *In* The Archaeology of Social Boundaries. Miriam T. Stark, ed. Pp. 161–182. Washington, DC: Smithsonian Institution Press.

Gosden, Chris. 2004. Archaeology and Colonialism: Culture Contact from 5000 BC to the Present. Cambridge: Cambridge University Press.

———. 2005. What Do Objects Want? Journal of Archaeological Method and Theory 12(3):183.

Gosden, Chris, and Yvonne Marshall. 1999. The Cultural Biography of Objects. World Archaeology 31(2):169–178.

Graeber, David. 2001. Toward an Anthropological Theory of Value: The False Coin of Our Own Dreams. New York: Palgrave.

———. 2011. Debt: The First 5,000 Years. Brooklyn: Melville House.

Graham, Elizabeth A. 1991. Archaeological Insights into Colonial Period Maya Life at Tipu, Belize. *In* Columbian Consequences: The Spanish Borderlands in Pan-American Perspective. David Hurst Thomas, ed. Pp. 319–335. Washington, DC: Smithsonian Institution Press.

———. 2011. Maya Christians and Their Churches in Sixteenth-Century Belize. Gainesville: University Press of Florida.

Gramsci, Antonio. 1971. Selections from the Prison Notebooks. New York: International Publishers.

Grand River Heritage Mines Society. 2003. Herons and Cobblestones: A History of Five Oaks and the Bethel Area of Brantford Township, County of Brant. Paris, ON: Grand River Heritage Mines Society.

Gray, Leslie. 1954. From Bethlehem to Fairfield, 1798, Diary of the Brethren John Heckewelder and Benjamin Mortimer. Ontario History 46:107–131.

Graymont, Barbara. 1991. The Six Nations Indians in the Revolutionary War. *In* Sweet Promises: A Reader on Indian-White Relations in Canada. J. R. Miller, ed. Pp. 93–104. Toronto: University of Toronto Press.

Grayson, Donald K. 1970. Statistical Inference and Northeastern Adena. American Antiquity 35(1):102–104.

Groce, Nora. 1980. Ornaments of Metal: Rings, Medallions, Combs, Beads, and Pendants. *In* Burr's Hill: A 17th Century Wampanoag Burial Ground in Warren, Rhode Island. Susan Gibson, ed. Pp. 108–117. Providence, RI: Haffenreffer Museum of Anthropology, Brown University.

Haas, Lisbeth. 2014. Saints and Citizens: Indigenous Histories of Colonial Missions and Mexican California. Berkeley: University of California Press.

Hackel, Steven W. 1997. Land, Labor, and Production: The Colonial Economy of Spanish and Mexican California. *In* Contested Eden: California before the Gold Rush. Ramón A. Gutiérrez and Richard J. Orsi, eds. Pp. 111–146. Berkeley: University of California Press.

———. 2005. Children of Coyote, Missionaries of Saint Francis: Indian-Spanish Relations in Colonial California, 1769–1850. Chapel Hill: University of North Carolina Press for the Omohundro Institute of Early American History and Culture.

Haefeli, Evan. 2007. On First Contact and Apotheosis: Manitou and Men in North America. Ethnohistory 54(3):407–443.

Hall, Kristen C. D. 2013. Reexamining Suwannee Valley Pottery: A Typological and Formal Analysis of Pottery in Feature 1 at Parnell Mound. B.A. honors thesis, Department of Anthropology, University of Florida, Gainesville. Electronic document, https://anyflip.com/hezt/lkhr.

Hallowell, Irving. 1960. Ojibwa Ontology, Behavior, and World View. *In* Culture in History: Essays in Honor of Paul Radin. Stanley Diamond, ed. Pp. 17–49. New York: Columbia University Press.

Hamell, George R. 1983. Trading in Metaphors: The Magic of Beads, Another Perspective upon Indian-European Contact in Northeastern North America. *In* Proceedings of the 1982 Glass Trade Bead Conference. C. Hayse, ed. P. 528. Rochester, NY: Rochester Museum and Science Center.

———. 1992. The Iroquois at the World's Rim: Speculations on Color, Culture, and Contact. American Indian Quarterly 16:451–469.

Hamilakis, Yannis. 2008. Time, Performance, and the Production of a Mnemonic Record: From Feasting to an Archaeology of Eating and Drinking. *In* The Aegean Feast. Louise A. Hitchcock, Robert Laffineur, and Janice I. Crowley, eds. Pp. 3–17. Leuven, BE: Peeters Publishers.

Hammond, Norman, and Matthew R. Bobo. 1994. Pilgrimage's Last Mile: Late Maya Monument Veneration at La Milpa, Belize. World Archaeology 26(1):19–34.

Hamor, Ralph, Thomas Dale, Alexander Whitaker, and John Rolfe. 1615. A Trve Discovrse of the Present Estate of Virginia, and the Successe of the Affaires there Till the 18 of Iune.

1614 Together: With a Relation of the Seuerall English Townes and Forts, the Assured Hopes of that Countrie and the Peace Concluded with the Indians: The Christening of Powhatans Daughter and Her Mariage with an English-Man. London: John Beale.

Hamilton, Scott, and B. A. Nicholson. 2007. The Middleman Fur Trade and Slot Knives: Selective Integration of European Technology at the Mortlach Site (DiMe-23). Canadian Journal of Archaeology 31(3):137–162.

Handsman, Russell G. 1988. Algonquian Women Resist Colonialism. Artifacts 16(3–4):29–31.

Hansen, Karen Tranberg. 2004. The World in Dress: Anthropological Perspectives on Clothing, Fashion, and Culture. Annual Review in Anthropology 33:369–392.

Hansen, Thomas B., and Finn Stepputat. 2006. Sovereignty Revisited. Annual Review of Anthropology 35:295–315.

Hantman, Jeffrey L. 1990. Between Powhatan and Quirank: Reconstructing Monacan Culture and History in the Context of Jamestown. American Anthropologist 92(3):676–690.

Hantman, Jeffrey L., and Deborah Gold. 2002. The Woodland in the Middle Atlantic: Ranking and Dynamic Political Stability. *In* The Woodland Southeast. David Anderson and Robert Mainfort, eds. Pp. 270–291. Tuscaloosa: University of Alabama Press.

Hariot, Thomas. 1588. A Briefe and True Report of the New found Land of Virginia. London.

Harmon, James M. 1999. Archaeological Investigations at the Posey Site (18CH281) and 18CH282, Indian Head Division, Naval Surface Warfare Center Charles County, Maryland. Jefferson Patterson Park and Museum Occasional Papers, 7. St. Leonard: Maryland Archaeological Conservation Laboratory.

Harper, J. R. 1956. Portland Point, Crossroads of New Brunswick History (Appendix A). New Brunswick Museum, Historical Studies, 9.

———. 1957. Two Seventeenth Century Micmac "Copper-Kettle" Burials. Anthropologica 4:11–36.

Harris, Marvin. 1959. The Economy Has No Surplus? American Anthropologist 61(2):185–198.

Harris, Oliver J. T. 2014. (Re)assembling Communities. Journal of Archaeological Method and Theory 21(1):76–97.

Harris, Oliver J. T., and Craig N. Cipolla. 2017. Archaeological Theory in the New Millennium: An Introduction. New York: Routledge. In review.

Harris, Oliver J. T., and John E. Robb. 2012. Multiple Ontologies and the Problem of the Body in History. American Anthropologist 114(4):668–679.

Harris, Oliver J. T., and Tim Flor Sorensen. 2010. Rethinking Emotion and Material Culture. Archaeological Dialogues 17(2):145–163.

Harrison, Rodney. 2004. Contact Archaeology and the Landscapes of Pastoralism in the North-West of Australia. *In* The Archaeology of Contact in Settler Societies. Tim Murray, ed. Pp. 109–143. Cambridge: Cambridge University Press.

———. 2014. Shared Histories: Rethinking "Colonized" and "Colonizer" in the Archaeology of Colonialism. *In* Rethinking Colonial Pasts through Archaeology. N. Ferris, R. Harrison, and M. V. Wilcox, eds. Pp. 37–56. Oxford: Oxford University Press.

Harrison-Buck, Eleanor. 2012. Architecture as Animate Landscape: Circular Shrines in the Ancient Maya Lowlands. American Anthropologist 114(1):64–80.

Harrison-Buck, Eleanor, and Patricia A. McAnany. 2013. Terminal Classic Circular Architecture in the Sibun Valley, Belize. Ancient Mesoamerica 24(2):295–306.

Hart, John P. 2001. Maize, Matrilocality, Migration, and Northern Iroquoian Evolution. Journal of Archaeological Method and Theory 8(2):151–182.

Haury, Emil W. 1945. The Excavation of Los Muertos and Neighboring Ruins in the Salt River Valley, Southern Arizona. Papers of the Peabody Museum of American Archaeology and Ethnology, 24(1). Cambridge, MA: Harvard University.

———. 1958. Evidence at Point of Pines for a Prehistoric Migration from Northern Arizona. *In* Migrations in New World Culture History. Raymond H. Thompson, ed. Pp. 1–6. Tucson: University of Arizona Press.

———. 1989. Point of Pines, Arizona: A History of the University of Arizona Archaeological Field School. Anthropological Papers of the University of Arizona, 50. Tucson: University of Arizona Press.

Hayden, Brian. 1996. Feasting in Prehistoric and Traditional Societies. *In* Food and the Status Quest: An Interdisciplinary Perspective. Polly Wiessner and Wulf Schiefenhövel, eds. Pp. 127–146. Providence, RI: Berghahn Books.

———. 2014. The Power of Feasts: From Prehistory to the Present. Cambridge: Cambridge University Press.

Hayes, Katherine H. 2015. Colonialism and the Classification of Displacement. *In* Rethinking Colonialism: Comparative Archaeological Approaches. Craig N. Cipolla and Katherine H. Hayes, eds. Pp. 54–75. Gainesville: University Press of Florida.

Heath, Dwight, ed. 1963[1622]. Mourt's Relation: A Journal of the Pilgrims at Plymouth. New York: Corinth Books.

Heizer, Robert F. 1941. The Direct-Historical Approach in California Archaeology. American Antiquity 7(2):98–122.

Helms, Mary W. 1988. Ulysses' Sail: An Ethnographic Odyssey of Power, Knowledge, and Geographical Distance. Princeton, NJ: Princeton University Press.

———. 1993. Craft and the Kingly Ideal: Art, Trade, and Power. Austin: University of Texas Press.

Henare, Amiria, Martin Holbraad, and Sari Wastell, eds. 2007. Thinking Through Things: Theorising Artefacts Ethnographically. London: Routledge.

Hill, Erica. 2011. Animals as Agents: Hunting Ritual and Relational Ontologies in Prehistoric Alaska and Chukotka. Cambridge Archaeological Journal 21(3):407–426.

Hill, J. Brett, Matthew A. Peeples, Deborah H. Huntley, and H. Jane Carmack. 2015. Spatializing Social Network Analysis in the Precontact U.S. Southwest. Advances in Archaeological Practice 3(1):63–77.

Hochschild, Arlie R. 1979. Emotion Work, Feeling Rules, and Social Structure. American Journal of Sociology 85(3):551–575.

Hodder, Ian. 1980. Trade and Exchange: Definitions, Identification and Function. *In* Models and Methods in Regional Exchange. SAA Paper, 1. Robert E. Fry, ed. Pp. 151–156. Washington, DC: Society for American Archaeology.

———. 1990. The Domestication of Europe: Structure and Contingency in Neolithic Societies. Oxford: Basil Blackwell.

———. 2012. Entangled: An Archaeology of the Relationships between Humans and Things. Malden, MA: Wiley-Blackwell.

———. 2014. The Asymmetries of Symmetrical Archaeology. Journal of Contemporary Archaeology 1(2):228–230.

Hodge, Christina. 2013. Consumerism and Control: Archaeological Perspectives on the Harvard College Buttery. Northeast Historical Archaeology 42(1):54–74.

———. 2014. Consumerism and the Emergence of the Middle Class in Colonial America. Cambridge: Cambridge University Press.

Hogeland, L. Frank, and Kim Hogeland. 2007. First Families: A Photographic History of California Indians. Berkeley: Heyday Books.

Hohenthal, William D. 2001. Tipai Ethnographic Notes: A Baja California Indian Community at Mid-Century. Thomas C. Blackburn, ed. Ballena Press Anthropological Papers, 48. Novato, CA: Ballena Press.

Holley, George. 1999. Late Prehistoric Towns in the Southeast. *In* Great Towns and Regional Polities in the Prehistoric American Southwest and Southeast. Jill E. Neitzel, ed. Pp. 22–38. Albuquerque: University of New Mexico Press.

Honig, Sasha. 2003. Yokuts, Spaniards, and Californios in the Southern San Joaquin Valley, 1772–1824. Boletín: The Journal of the California Mission Studies Association 20(1):50–62.

Hoopes, James, ed. 1991. Peirce on Signs: Writings on Semiotics. Chapel Hill: University of North Carolina Press.

Horsfall, Sue, and Gary Warrick. 2003. The Davisville 2 Site (AgHb-242): Report on 2001 Archaeological Excavations. Report on file with the Ontario Ministry of Tourism and Culture, Toronto.

Hoskins, Janet. 2006. Agency, Biography and Objects. *In* Handbook of Material Culture. Christopher Tilley, Webb Keane, Susanne Küchler, Mike Rowlands, and Patricia Spyer, eds. Pp. 74–84. London: Sage Publications.

Hosmer, William, ed. 1864. Autobiography of Reverend Alvin Torry, First Missionary to the Six Nations and the Northwestern Tribes of British North America. Auburn: William J. Moses.

Howard, James H. 1968. The Southeastern Ceremonial Complex and Its Interpretation. Memoir no. 6. Missouri Archaeological Society. Columbia: University of Missouri.

Howey, Meghan. 2011. Colonial Encounters, European Kettles, and the Magic of Mimesis in the Early Sixteenth and Late Seventeenth Century Indigenous Northeast and Great Lakes. International Journal of Historical Archaeology 15(3):329–357.

Hoy, David Couzens. 2004. Critical Resistance: From Poststructuralism to Post-critique. Cambridge, MA: MIT Press.

Hudson, Charles. 1976. The Southeastern Indians. Knoxville: University of Tennessee Press.

Hudson, Lynn M. 2003. The Making of "Mammy Pleasant," a Black Entrepreneur in Nineteenth-Century San Francisco. Urbana: University of Illinois Press.

Huntington Library. 2006. Early California Population Project Database. Electronic document, http://www.huntington.org/information/ECPPmain.htm, accessed August 25, 2014.

Hurtado, Albert L. 1990. California Indians and the Workaday West: Labor, Assimilation, and Survival. California History 69(1):2–11.

Hyman, Herbert H., and Paul B. Sheatsley. 1947. Some Reasons Why Information Campaigns Fail. Public Opinion Quarterly 11(3):412–423.

Ihlder, John. N.d. The Houses of Providence, a Study of Present Conditions and Tendencies, with Notes on the Surrounding Communities and Some Mill Villages. Providence, RI: Snow and Farnham Co. Printers (reprinted by General Books).

Ingold, Tim. 2007. Materials against Materiality. Archaeological Dialogues 14(1):1–16.

Inomata, Takeshi. 2006. Plazas, Performers, and Spectators: Political Theaters of the Classic Maya. Current Anthropology 47(5):805–842.

Jackson, Douglas K., Andrew C. Fortier, and Joyce A. Williams. 1992. The Sponeman Site 2: The Mississippian and Oneota Occupations. American Bottom Archaeology FAI-270 Site Reports, 24. Urbana: University of Illinois Press.

Jackson, H. Edwin, and Jessica Kowalski. 2010. Chronology and Function of Mound C at Winterville: A Report on the 2009 Season. Paper presented at the 2010 Joint Annual Meeting of the Louisiana Archaeological Society and the Mississippi Archaeological Society, West Monroe, LA.

Jackson, H. Edwin, and Susan L. Scott. 1995. The Faunal Record of the Southeastern Elite: The Implications of Economy, Social Relations, and Ideology. Southeastern Archaeology 14:103–119.

———. 2010. Zooarchaeology of the Moundville Elite. *In* Mound Excavations at Moundville: Architecture, Elites, and Social Order. Vernon J. Knight, Jr., ed. Pp. 326–347. Tuscaloosa: University of Alabama Press.

Jennings, Justin, Kathleen L. Antrobus, Sam J. Atencio, Erin Glavich, Rebecca Johnson, German Loffler, and Christine Luu. 2005. "Drinking Beer in a Blissful Mood": Alcohol Production, Operational Chains, and Feasting in the Ancient World. Current Anthropology 46(2):275–303.

Jirikowic, Christine A. 1999. Final Report on the 1990, 1991, and 1994 Excavations at the Hughes Site (18MO1). Washington, DC: American University Potomac River Archaeology Survey.

Johnson, Laura E. 2004. "Goods to Clothe Themselves": Native Consumers, Native Images on the Pennsylvania Trading Frontier, 1712–1760. Ph.D. dissertation, University of Delaware.

———. 2009. "Goods to Clothe Themselves": Native Consumers and Native Images on the Pennsylvania Trading Frontier 1712–1760. Winterthur Portfolio 43(1):115–140.

Johnston, Charles M. 1994. The Six Nations in the Grand River Valley, 1784–1847. *In* Aboriginal Ontario: Historical Perspectives on the First Nations. E. S. Rogers and D. B. Smith, eds. Pp. 167–181. Toronto: Dundurn Press.

Johnston, Charles M., ed. 1964. The Valley of the Six Nations: A Collection of Documents on the Indian Lands of the Grand River. Toronto: Champlain Society.

Johnston, Richard B. 1979. Notes on Ossuary Burial among the Ontario Iroquois. Canadian Journal of Archaeology 3:91–104.

Jones, Andrew M., and Benjamin Alberti (with contributions from Chris Fowler and Gavin Lucas). 2013. Archaeology after Interpretation. *In* Archaeology after Interpretation: Returning Materials to Archaeological Theory. Benjamin Alberti, Andrew M. Jones, and Joshua Pollard, eds. Pp. 15–35. Walnut Creek, CA: Left Coast Press.

Jones, Grant D. 1989. Maya Resistance to Spanish Rule: Time and History on a Colonial Frontier. Albuquerque: University of New Mexico Press.

———. 1998. The Conquest of the Last Maya Kingdom. Stanford, CA: Stanford University Press.

———. 2005. Ethnohistorical Knowledge and Interdisciplinary Research: Rethinking Colonial "Resistance" on the Colonial Frontiers of Yucatán. *In* A Catalyst for Ideas: Anthropological Archaeology and the Legacy of Douglas W. Schwartz. Vernon L. Scarborough, ed. Pp. 287–316. Santa Fe, NM: School of American Research Press.

Jordan, Kurt A. 2008. The Seneca Restoration, 1715–1754: An Iroquois Local Political Economy. Gainesville: University Press of Florida.

———. 2009. Colonies, Colonialism, and Cultural Entanglement: The Archaeology of Postcolumbian Intercultural Relations. *In* International Handbook of Historical Archaeology. Teresita Majewski and David Gaimster, eds. Pp. 31–49. New York: Springer.

———. 2015. Pruning Colonialism: Vantage Point, Local Political Economy, and Cultural Entanglement in the Archaeology of Post-1415 Indigenous People. *In* Rethinking Colonial Pasts through Archaeology. Neal Ferris, Rodney Harrison, and Michael V. Wilcox, eds. Pp. 103–122. Oxford: Oxford University Press.

Joyce, Rosemary A. 2005. Archaeology of the Body. Annual Review in Anthropology 34:139–158.

———. 2014. Comments on Indigenous People and Foreign Things: Archaeologies of Consumption in the Americas. Paper presented at the Annual Meeting of the Society for American Archaeology, Austin, TX.

———. 2015. Things in Motion: Itineraries of Ulua Marble Vases. *In* Things in Motion: Object Itineraries in Anthropological Practice. Rosemary A. Joyce and Susan D. Gillespie, eds. Pp. 21–38. Santa Fe, NM: School for Advanced Research.

Joyce, Rosemary A., and Susan D. Gillespie. 2015. Making Things Out of Objects That Move. *In* Things in Motion: Object Itineraries in Anthropological Practice. Rosemary A. Joyce and Susan D. Gillespie, eds. Pp. 3–20. Santa Fe, NM: School for Advanced Research.

Joyce, Rosemary A., and Susan D. Gillespie, eds. 2015. Things in Motion: Object Itineraries in Anthropological Practice. Santa Fe, NM: School for Advanced Research.

Junker, Laura L. 2008. The Impact of Captured Women on Cultural Transmission in Contact Period Philippine Slave-Raiding Chiefdoms. *In* Invisible Citizens: Captives and Their Consequences. Catherine M. Cameron, ed. Pp. 110–137. Salt Lake City: University of Utah Press.

Kassabaum, Megan. 2013. First, We Eat: Conceptualizing Feasting at Feltus. Paper presented at the 70th Annual Meeting of the Southeastern Archaeological Conference, Tampa Bay, FL.

Keane, Webb. 2001a. An Interview with Anthropologist Webb Keane: On Language, Ritual and Social Change. Journal of the International Institute 8(3). Electronic document, http://quod.lib.umich.edu/j/jii/4750978.0008.304?view=text;rgn=main.

———. 2001b. Money Is No Object: Materiality, Desire, and Modernity in an Indonesian Society. *In* The Empire of Things: Regimes of Value and Material Culture. Fred R. Myers, ed. Pp. 65–90. Santa Fe, NM: School of American Research Press.

———. 2003. Semiotics and the Social Analysis of Material Things. Language and Communication 23:409–425.

Kearsley, Ronald G. 1997. Pinched-Face Human Effigy Pipes: The Social Mechanisms That Conditioned Their Manufacture and Use in Seventeenth Century Iroquoia. M.A. thesis, Department of Anthropology, Trent University.

Kelley, Robin D. G. 1992. An Archaeology of Resistance. American Quarterly 44(2):292–298.

Kelly, A. R. 1972. The 1970–71 Field Seasons at Bell Field Mound, Carters Dam. Laboratory of Archaeology Series, 40. Athens: University of Georgia.

Kelly, John E. 1997. Stirling Phase Socio-political Activity at East St. Louis and Cahoka. *In* Cahokia: Domination and Ideology in the Mississippian World. Timothy R. Pauketat and Thomas E. Emerson, eds. Pp. 141–166. Lincoln: University of Nebraska Press.

Kelsay, Isabel Thompson. 1984. Joseph Brant, 1743–1807: Man of Two Worlds. Syracuse, NY: Syracuse University Press.

Kelso, William M., Beverly Straube, and Daniel Schmidt. 2012. 2007–2010 Interim Report on the Preservation Virginia Excavations at Jamestown, Virginia. Jamestowne Rediscovery, Jamestown.

Kenyon, Ian. 1985. The Onondaga Settlement at Middleport. KEWA 85(3):4–23.

———. 1987. Levi Turkey and the Tuscarora Settlement on the Grand River. KEWA 87(1): 20–25.

———. 1997. "Weeds Uprising Where the Hearth Should Be": Rural House Abandonment in Southern Ontario. Ontario Archaeology 64:39–55.

Kenyon, Ian, and Neal Ferris. 1984. Investigations at Mohawk Village, 1983. Arch Notes 84(1):19–50.

Kenyon, Ian T., and William R. Fitzgerald. 1986. Dutch Glass Beads in the Northeast: An Ontario Perspective. Man in the Northeast 32:1–34.

Kenyon, Ian T., and Thomas Kenyon. 1982. Social Dimensions of Ceramic Use in Southwestern Ontario, 1814–1867. Paper presented at the Society for Historical Archaeology, Philadelphia, PA.

———. 1986. Echo the Firekeeper: A Nineteenth Century Iroquois Site. KEWA 86(2):4–27.

Kenyon, Walter A. 1982. The Grimsby Site: A Historic Neutral Cemetery. Toronto: Royal Ontario Museum.

Kepecs, Susan M. 1999. The Political Economy of Chikinchel, Yucatan, Mexico: A Diachronic Analysis from the Prehispanic Era through the Age of Spanish Administration. Ph.D. dissertation, University of Wisconsin, Madison.

Kidd, Kenneth E. 1953. The Excavation and Historical Identification of a Huron Ossuary. American Antiquity 18(4):359–379.

———. 1954. Trade Goods Research Techniques. American Antiquity 20(1):1–8.

Kidder, Tristram R. 2004. Plazas as Architecture: An Example from the Raffman Site, Northeast Louisiana. American Antiquity 69(3):514–532.

King, Adam. 2001. Excavations at Mound B, Etowah: 1954–1958. Laboratory of Archaeology Series Report, 37. Department of Anthropology, University of Georgia, Athens.

———. 2003. Etowah: The Political History of a Chiefdom Capital. Tuscaloosa: University of Alabama Press.

Klein, Michael, and Douglas Sanford. 2004. Analytical Scale and Archaeological Perspectives on the Contact Era in the Northern Neck of Virginia. *In* Indian and European Contact in Context: The Mid-Atlantic Region. Dennis B. Blanton and Julia A. King, eds. Pp. 47–73. Gainesville: University Press of Florida.

Knappett, Carl. 2006. Beyond Skin: Layering and Networking in Art and Archaeology. Cambridge Archaeological Journal 16(2):239–251.

Knappett, Carl, and Lambros Malafouris, eds. 2008. Material Agency: Towards a Non-anthropocentric Approach. New York: Springer.

Knight, Vernon James, Jr. 1986. The Institutional Organization of Mississippian Religion. American Antiquity 51(4):675–687.

———. 1990. Excavation of the Truncated Mound at the Walling Site: Middle Woodland Culture and Copena in the Tennessee Valley. Division of Archaeology, Report of Investigations, 56. Tuscaloosa: Alabama State Museum of Natural History.

———. 2001. Feasting and the Emergence of Platform Mound Ceremonialism in Eastern North American. *In* Feasts: Archaeological and Ethnographic Perspectives on Food, Politics, and Power. Michael Dietler and Brian Hayden, eds. Pp. 311–333. Washington, DC: Smithsonian Institution Press.

———. 2004. Characterizing Elite Midden Deposits at Moundville. American Antiquity 69(2):304–321.

———. 2007. Identification of a Moth/Butterfly Supernatural in Mississippian Art. *In* Ancient Objects and Sacred Realms: Interpretations of Mississippian Iconography. F. Kent Reilly and James F. Garber, eds. Pp. 136–151. Austin: University of Texas Press.

———. 2010. Mound Excavations at Moundville: Architecture, Elites, and Social Order. Tuscaloosa: University of Alabama Press.

Koppel, Charles. 1854. Plain between the San Joaquin and Kings Rivers. Bancroft Library, University of California Berkeley. Electronic document, http://content.cdlib.org/ark:/13030/tf8v19p5gv/?order=1, accessed August 8, 2014.

Kopytoff, Igor. 1986. The Cultural Biography of Things: Commoditization as Process. *In* The Social Life of Things: Commodities in Cultural Perspective. Arjun Appadurai, ed. Pp. 64–91. Cambridge: Cambridge University Press.

Krauss, Bertram S. 1944. Acculturation, a New Approach to the Iroquoian Problem. American Antiquity 9(3):302–318.

Kroeber, Alfred L. 1925. Handbook of the Indians of California. Bureau of American Ethnology Bulletin, 78. Washington, DC: Smithsonian Institution.

Küchler, Susanne. 2002. Malanggan: Art, Memory and Sacrifice. Oxford: Berg.

Kuhn, Robert. 1986. Indications of Interactions and Acculturation through Ceramic Analysis. *In* The Mohawk Valley Project: 1983 Jackson-Everson Excavations. Robert Kuhn and Dean R. Snow, eds. Pp. 75–92. Albany: State University of New York.

———. 1987. Trade and Exchange among the Mohawk-Iroquois: A Trace Element Analysis of Ceramic Smoking Pipes. North American Archaeologist 8(4):305–315.

Kuhn, Robert, and Martha Sempowski. 2001. A New Approach to Dating the League of the Iroquois. American Antiquity 66(2):301–314.

Lacson, Paul Albert. 2015. "Born of Horses": Missionaries, Indigenous Vaqueros, and Ecological Expansion during the Spanish Colonization of California. Journal of San Diego History 60(3):207–229.

Landon, David B. 1996. Feeding Colonial Boston: A Zooarchaeological Study. Historical Archaeology 30(1):1–153.

———. 2008. Seasonal Slaughter Cycles and Urban Food Supply in the Colonial Chesapeak. *In* Case Studies in Environmental Archaeology. 2nd edition. E. J. Reitz, C. M. Scarry, and S. J. Scudder, eds. Pp. 375–390. New York: Springer.

Lapham, Heather A., and William C. Johnson. 2002. Protohistoric Monongahela Trade Relations: Evidence from the Foley Farm Phase Glass Beads. Archaeology of Eastern North America 30:97–120.

La Salle, Marina J. 2010. Community Collaboration and Other Good Intentions. Archaeologies: Journal of the World Archaeological Congress 6(3):401–422.

Latour, Bruno. 1993. We Have Never Been Modern. Cambridge, MA: Harvard University Press.

———. 2005. Reassembling the Social: An Introduction to Actor-Network-Theory. Oxford: Oxford University Press.

Latta, Martha A. 1976. The Iroquoian Cultures of Huronia: A Study of Acculturation through Archaeology. Ph.D. dissertation, Department of Anthropology, University of Toronto.

Lattanzi, Gregory D. 2007. The Provenance of Pre-contact Copper Artifacts: Social Complexity and Trade in the Delaware Valley. Archaeology of Eastern North America 35:125–137.

Lavin, Lucianne. 2013. Connecticut's Indigenous Peoples: What Archaeology, History, and Oral Traditions Teach Us about Their Communities and Culture. New Haven, CT: Yale University Press.

Le Page du Pratz, Antoine S. 1975. The History of Louisiana. English reprint of the 1774 original edition. Baton Rouge: Louisiana State University Press.

Le Petit, Mathurin. 1730. Letter from Father Mathurin Le Petit, Missionary, to Father d'Avaugour, Procurator of the Missions in North America, July 12, 1730. *In* The Jesuit Relations and Allied Documents, vol. 68. Reuben Gold Thwaites, ed. Pp. 120–223. Cleveland: Burrows Brothers.

Lepore, Jill. 1998. The Name of War: King Philip's War and the Origins of American Identity. New York: Vintage Books.

Lester, Joan. 1987. "We Didn't Make Fancy Baskets Until We Were Discovered": Fancy Basket-Making in Maine. *In* A Key into the Language of Woodsplint Baskets. Ann McMullen and Russell G. Handsman, eds. Pp. 38–59. Washington, CT: American Indian Archaeological Institute.

Lesure, Richard. 2005. Linking Theory and Evidence in Archaeology of Human Agency: Iconography, Style, and Theories of Embodiment. Journal of Archaeological Method and Theory 12(3):237–255.

LeVine, Robert A. 1990. Enculturation: A Biosocial Perspective on the Development of Self. *In* The Self in Transition: Infancy to Childhood. Dante Cicchetti and Marjorie Beeghly, eds. Pp. 99–117. Chicago: University of Chicago Press.

Levine, Victoria Lindsay. 1991. Feathers in Southeast American Indian Ceremonialism. Expedition 33(2):3–9.

Lewis, R. Barry, and Charles Stout. 1998. The Town as Metaphor. *In* Mississippian Towns and Sacred Spaces: Searching for an Architectural Grammar. R. Barry Lewis and Charles B. Stout, eds. Pp. 227–242. Tuscaloosa: University of Alabama Press.

Liebmann, Matthew. 2002. Signs of Power and Resistance: The (Re)creation of Christian Imagery and Identities in the Pueblo Revolt Era. *In* Archaeologies of the Pueblo Revolt: Identity, Meaning, and Renewal in the Pueblo World. Robert W. Preucel, ed. Pp. 132–144. Albuquerque: University of New Mexico Press.

———. 2012. The Rest Is History: Devaluing the Recent Past in the Archaeology of the Pueblo Southwest. *In* Decolonizing Indigenous Histories: Exploring Prehistoric/Colonial Transitions in Archaeology. M. Oland, S. M. Hart, and L. Frink, eds. Pp. 19–44. Tucson: University of Arizona Press.

Lightfoot, Kent G. 1995. Culture Contact Studies: Redefining the Relationship between Prehistoric and Historical Archaeology. American Antiquity 60(2):199–217.

———. 2005. Indians, Missionaries, and Merchants: The Legacy of Colonial Encounters on the California Frontiers. Berkeley: University of California Press.

Lightfoot, Kent, and Antoinette Martinez. 1995. Frontiers and Boundaries in Archaeological Perspective. Annual Review of Anthropology 24:471–492.

Lightfoot, Kent G., Antoinette Martinez, and Ann M. Schiff. 1998. Daily Practice and Material Culture in Pluralistic Social Settings: An Archaeological Study of Culture Change and Persistence from Fort Ross, California. American Antiquity 63(2):199–222.

Lightfoot, Kent G., Lee M. Panich, Darren Modzelewski, Theresa Molino, and Elliot H. Blair. 2013. The Study of Indigenous Political Economies and Colonialism: Implications for Contemporary Tribal Groups and Federal Recognition. American Antiquity 78(1):89–103.

Lilley, Ian. 2004. Diaspora and Identity in Archaeology: Moving beyond the Black Atlantic. *In* A Companion to Social Archaeology. Lynn Meskell and Robert W. Preucel, eds. Pp. 287–312. Malden, MA: Blackwell.

———. 2006. Archaeology, Diaspora, and Decolonization. Journal of Social Archaeology 6(1):28–47.

Lindman, Janet M., and Michele L. Tarter, eds. 2001. A Centre of Wonders: The Body in Early America. Ithaca, NY: Cornell University Press.

Little, Ann M. 2001. Shoot That Rogue, for He Hath an Englishman's Coat On! Cultural Cross-Dressing on the New England Frontier 1620–1760. New England Quarterly 74(2): 238–273.

Little, Elizabeth A. 1990. The Nantucket Indian Sickness. *In* Papers of the Twenty-First Algonquian Conference. William Cowan, ed. Pp. 181–196. Ottawa: Carleton University.

López, Luis Alberto Martos. 2008. Underwater Archaeological Exploration of the Mayan Cenotes. Museum International 60(4):100–110.

López de Cogolludo, Diego. 1688. Historia de Yucatán. Madrid: J. García Infanzón.

Loren, Diana. 2008. In Contact: Bodies and Spaces in the Sixteenth- and Seventeenth-Century Eastern Woodlands. Lanham, MD: AltaMira Press.

———. 2009. Material Manipulations: Beads and Cloth in the French Colonies. *In* The Materiality of Individuality: Archaeological Studies of Individual Lives. Carolyn L. White, ed. Pp. 109–124. New York: Springer.

———. 2010a. The Archaeology of Clothing and Bodily Adornment in Colonial America. Gainesville: University Press of Florida.

———. 2010b. The Exotic in Daily Life: Trade and Exchange in Historical Archaeology. *In* Trade and Exchange: Archaeological Studies from History and Prehistory. C. D. Dillian and C. L. White, eds. Pp. 195–204. New York: Springer.

———. 2011. Fear, Desire, and Material Strategies in Colonial Louisiana. *In* The Archaeology of Colonialism: Intimate Encounters and Sexual Effects. Barbara L. Voss and Eleanor Casella, eds. Pp. 105–121. Cambridge: Cambridge University Press.

———. 2013a. Considering Mimicry and Hybridity in Early Colonial New England: Health, Sin and the Body "Behung with Beades." Archaeological Review from Cambridge 28(1): 151–168.

———. 2013b. The Illusion of Imperium: Visual and Material Perspectives of Colonial Louisiana. World Art 3(1):83–99.

———. 2015. Casting Identity: Sumptuous Action and Colonized Bodies in Seventeenth-Century New England. *In* Rethinking Colonial Pasts through Archaeology. Neal Ferris, Rodney Harrison, and Michael V. Wilcox, eds. Pp. 251–267. Oxford: Oxford University Press.

Luard, Peter D. 1966. Oxen, Candles and Homespun. *In* A Glimpse of the Past: A Centennial History of Brantford and Brant County. Pp. 10–21. Brantford, ON: Brant Historical Society.

Lucas, Gavin. 2005. The Archaeology of Time. New York: Routledge.

Luccketti, Nicholas M., Mary Ellen N. Hodges, and Charles T. Hodges. 1994. Paspahegh Archaeology: Data Recovery Investigations of Site 44JC308 at the Governor's Land at Two Rivers, James City County, Virginia. Williamsburg: James River Institute for Archaeology, Inc.

Lydon, Jane, and Uzma Z. Rizvi, eds. 2010. Handbook of Postcolonial Archaeology. Walnut Creek, CA: Left Coast Press.

Lyons, Patrick D., and Jeffery J. Clark. 2011. Irrigation Communities and Communities in Diaspora. *In* Movement, Connectivity, and Landscape Change in the Ancient Southwest. Margaret C. Nelson and Colleen Strawhacker, eds. Pp. 375–401. Boulder: University Press of Colorado.

Lyons, Patrick D., J. Brett Hill, and Jeffery J. Clark. 2008. Demography, Agricultural Potential, and Identity among Ancient Immigrants. *In* The Social Construction of Communities in the Ancient Southwest. Mark D. Varien and James M. Potter, eds. Pp. 191–213. Lanham, MD: AltaMira Press.

Lyons, Patrick, and Alexander J. Lindsay. 2006. Perforated Plates and the Salado Phenomenon. Kiva 72(1):5–54.

Mackenzie, James Bovell. 1896. The Six Nations Indians in Canada. Toronto: Hunter, Rose Company Ltd.

Mainfort, Robert C., Jr. 1988. Middle Woodland Ceremonialism at Pinson Mounds, Tennessee. American Antiquity 53(1):158–173.

Majewski, Teresita, and Michael B. Schiffer. 2009. Beyond Consumption: Toward an Archaeology of Consumerism. *In* International Handbook of Historical Archaeology. Teresita Majewski and David Gaimster, eds. Pp. 191–207. New York: Springer.

Mallios, Seth W. 2006. The Deadly Politics of Giving: Exchange and Violence at Ajacan, Roanoke, and Jamestown. Tuscaloosa: University of Alabama Press.

Mallios, Seth, and Shane Emmett. 2004. Demand, Supply, and Elasticity in the Copper Trade at Early Jamestown. Journal of the Jamestown Rediscovery Center 2:1–5.

Mandell, Daniel R. 2008. Tribe, Race, and History: Native Americans in Southern New England, 1780–1880. Baltimore, MD: Johns Hopkins University Press.

Mann, Rob. 2004. Smokescreens: Tobacco, Pipes, and the Transformational Power of Fur Trade Rituals. *In* Smoking and Culture: The Archaeology of Tobacco Pipes in Eastern North America. Sean M. Rafferty and Rob Mann, eds. Pp. 165–183. Knoxville: University of Tennessee Press.

———. 2008. From Ethnogenesis to Ethnic Segmentation in the Wabash Valley: Constructing Identity and Houses in Great Lakes Fur Trade Society. International Journal of Historical Archaeology 12(4):319–337.

———. 2015. Persistent Pots, Durable Kettles and Colonialist Discourse: Aboriginal Pottery Production in French Colonial Basse. *In* Rethinking Colonial Pasts through Archaeology. Neal Ferris, Rodney Harrison, and Michael V. Wilcox, eds. Pp. 268–289. Oxford: Oxford University Press.

Marcellus, Jane. 2008. Nervous Women and Noble Savages: The Romanticized "Other" in Nineteenth-Century US Patent Medicine Advertising. Journal of Popular Culture 41(5): 784–808.

Marsden, Paul. 1998. Memetics and Social Contagion: Two Sides of the Same Coin. Journal of Memetics—Evolutionary Models of Information Transmission 2(2):171–185.

Martelle, Holly A. 2002. Huron Potters and Archaeological Constructs: Researching Ceramic Micro-stylistics. Ph.D. dissertation, Department of Anthropology, University of Toronto.

Martin, Calvin. 1975. The Four Lives of a Micmac Copper Pot. Ethnohistory 22(2):111–133.

Marx, Karl. 1990[1867]. Capital. New York: Penguin.

Mason, Carol I. 2003. Jesuit Rings, Jesuits, and Chronology. Midcontinental Journal of Archaeology 28(2):233–257.

Mason, Ronald. 2002. Great Lakes Archaeology. Caldwell, NJ: Blackburn Press.

Masson, Marilyn A. 1999. Postclassic Maya Communities at Progresso Lagoon and Laguna Seca, Northern Belize. Journal of Field Archaeology 26(3):285–306.

———. 2000. In the Realm of Nachan Kan: Postclassic Maya Archaeology at Laguna de On, Belize. Boulder: University Press of Colorado.

———. 2002. Ancient Maya Political Economies. Walnut Creek, CA: Altamira.

———. 2003a. Laguna de On and Caye Coco: Economic Differentiation at Two Postclassic Island Communities in Northern Belize. *In* Perspectives on Ancient Maya Rural Complexity. Giles Iannone and Samuel V. Connell, eds. Pp. 119–130. Los Angeles: Cotsen Institute of Archaeology, University of California.

———. 2003b. The Late Postclassic Symbol Set in the Maya Area. *In* The Postclassic Mesoamerican World. Michael E. Smith and Frances F. Berdan, eds. Pp. 194–200. Salt Lake City: University of Utah Press.

Masson, Marilyn A., and David A. Freidel, eds. 2002. Ancient Maya Political Economies. Walnut Creek, CA: Altamira.

Mathews, Zena P. 1976. Huron Pipes and Iroquoian Shamanism. Man in the Northeast 12: 15–31.

Mathien, Frances Joan. 2001. The Organization of Turquoise Production and Consumption by the Prehistoric Chacoans. American Antiquity 66(1):103–118.

Matthews, Christopher N. 2010. The Archaeology of American Capitalism. Gainesville: University Press of Florida.

Mattingly, David J. 2013. Imperialism, Power, and Identity: Experiencing the Roman Empire. Princeton, NJ: Princeton University Press.

Mauss, Marcel. 1973. Techniques of the Body. Economy and Society 2(1):70–89.

———. 1990[1954]. The Gift. New York: Routledge Press.

McAnany, Patricia A. 1989. Stone-Tool Production and Exchange in the Eastern Maya Lowlands: The Consumer Perspective from Pulltrouser Swamp, Belize. American Antiquity 54(2):332–346.

———. 2007. Culture Heroes and Feathered Serpents: The Contribution of Gordon R. Willey to the Study of Ideology. *In* Gordon R. Willey and American Archaeology: Contemporary Perspectives. Jeremy A. Sabloff and William L. Fash, eds. Pp. 209–232. Norman: University of Oklahoma Press.

———. 2010. Ancestral Maya Economies in Archaeological Perspective. Cambridge: Cambridge University Press.

McBride, Bunny, and Harald E. L. Prins. 1996. Walking the Medicine Line: Molly Ockett, a Pigwacket Doctor. *In* Northeastern Indian Lives, 1632–1816. Robert S. Grumet, ed. Pp. 321–347. Amherst: University of Massachusetts Press.

McBride, Kevin A. 1990. The Historical Archaeology of the Mashantucket Pequot. *In* The Pequots: The Fall and Rise of an American Indian Nation. Laurence Hauptman and James Wherry, eds. Pp. 96–116. Norman: University of Oklahoma Press.

———. 1994. The Source and Mother of the Fur Trade: Native-Dutch Relations in Eastern New Netherland. *In* Enduring Traditions: The Native Peoples of New England. Laurie Weinstein, ed. Pp. 31–51. Westport, NY: Bergin & Garvey.

———. 2008. Pequot Medicine Bundle. *In* Early Native Literacies in New England: A Documentary and Critical Anthology. Kristina Bross and Hilary E. Weiss, eds. Pp. 130–141. Amherst: University of Massachusetts Press.

McClintock, Anne. 1995. Imperial Leather: Race, Gender, and Sexuality in the Colonial Contest. New York: Routledge.

McCracken, Grant. 1986. Culture and Consumption: A Theoretical Account of the Structure and Movement of the Cultural Meaning of Consumer Goods. Journal of Consumer Research 13:71–84.

McGhee, Robert. 2008. Aboriginalism and the Problems of Indigenous Archaeology. American Antiquity 73(4):579–597.

McGuire, Randall H. 2012. Pueblo Religion and the Mesoamerican Connection. *In* Religious Transformation in the Late Pre-Hispanic Pueblo World. Donna M. Glowacki and Scott Van Keuren, eds. Pp. 23–49. Tucson: University of Arizona Press.

Meigs, Peveril, III. 1935. The Dominican Mission Frontier of Lower California. University of California Publications in Geography, 7. Berkeley: University of California Press.

Merleau-Ponty, Maurice. 1981. The Phenomenology of Perception. New York: Routledge.

Meskell, Lynn. 2004. Object Worlds in Ancient Egypt: Material Biographies Past and Present. Oxford: Berg.

———. 2005. Introduction: Object Orientations. *In* Archaeologies of Materiality. Lynn Meskell, ed. Pp. 1–17. Malden, MA: Blackwell.

Meyers, Maureen S. 2011. Political Economy of Exotic Trade on the Mississippian Frontier: A Case Study of a Fourteenth-Century Chiefdom in Southwestern Virginia. Ph.D. dissertation, Department of Anthropology, University of Kentucky.

Michelaki, Kostalina, Ronald G. V. Hancock, Gary Warrick, and Dean H. Knight. 2013. 17th Century Huron Village Life: Insights from the Copper-Based Metals of the Ball Site, Southern Ontario, Canada. Journal of Archaeological Science 40:1250–1259.

Mihm, Stephen. 2014. How Indians Became America's Favorite Marketing Tool. June 20, 2014. Electronic document, http://bloombergview.com/articles/2014–06–20, accessed March 8, 2015.

Milanich, Jerald T., Ann S. Cordell, Vernon J. Knight, Jr., Timothy A. Kohler, and Brenda J. Sigler-Lavelle. 1997. Archaeology of Northern Florida A.D. 200–900: The McKeithen Weeden Island Culture. Gainesville: University Press of Florida.

Miller, Christopher L., and George R. Hamell. 1986. A New Perspective on Indian-White Contact: Cultural Symbols and Colonial Trade. Journal of American History 73(2):311–328.

Miller, Daniel. 1987. Material Culture and Consumption. New York: Basil Blackwell.

———. 1995. Consumption and Commodities. Annual Review of Anthropology 24:141–161.

———. 2005a. Consumption Studies as the Transformation of Anthropology. *In* Acknowledging Consumption: A Review of New Studies. Daniel Miller, ed. Pp. 263–292. London: Routledge.

———. 2005b. Materiality: An Introduction. *In* Materiality. Daniel Miller, ed. Pp. 1–50. Durham, NC: Duke University Press.

———. 2006a. Consumption. *In* Handbook of Material Culture. Christopher Tilley, Webb Keane, Susanne Küchler, Michael Rowlands, and Patricia Spyer, eds. Pp. 341–354. London: Sage.

———. 2006b. Objectification. *In* Handbook of Material Culture. Christopher Tilley, Webb Keane, Susanne Küchler, Michael Rowlands, and Patricia Spyer, eds. Pp. 60–73. London: Sage.

Miller, Douglas K. 2013. Willing Workers: Urban Relocation and American Indian Initiative, 1940s–1960s. Ethnohistory 60(1):51–76.

Miller, George L. 1980. Classification and Economic Scaling of 19th-Century Ceramics. Historical Archaeology 14:1–40.

———. 1991. A Revised Set of CC Index Values for Classification and Economic Scaling of English Ceramics 1787 to 1880. Historical Archaeology 25(1):1–25.

Miller, George L., with Patricia Samford, Ellen Shlasko, and Andrew Madsen. 2000. Telling Time for Archaeologists. Northeast Historical Archaeology 29(1):1–22.

Miller, Henry M., Dennis J. Pogue, and Michael A. Smolek. 1983. Beads from the Seventeenth Century Chesapeake. *In* Proceedings of the 1982 Glass Trade Bead Conference. Charles F. Hayes III, ed. Pp. 127–144. Rochester, NY: Rochester Museum and Science Center.

Milliken, Randall T., Richard T. Fitzgerald, Mark G. Hylkema, Randy Groza, Tom Origer, David G. Bieling, Alan Leventhal, Randy S. Wiberg, Andrew Gottsfield, Donna Gillete, Viviana Bellifemine, Eric Strother, Robert Cartier, and David A. Fredrickson. 2007. Punctuated Culture Change in the San Francisco Bay Area. *In* California Prehistory: Colonization, Culture, and Complexity. Terry L. Jones and Kathryn A. Klar, eds. Pp. 99–124. Lanham, MD: Altamira Press.

Mills, Barbara. 2007. Performing the Feast: Visual Display and Suprahousehold Commensalism in the Puebloan Southwest. American Antiquity 72(2):210–239.

———. 2008. How the Pueblos Became Global: Colonial Appropriations, Resistance, and Diversity in the North American Southwest. Archaeologies: Journal of the World Archaeological Congress 4(2):218–232.

———. 2011. Themes and Models for Understanding Migration in the Southwest. *In* Movement, Connectivity, and Landscape Change in the Ancient Southwest. Margaret C. Nelson and Colleen Strawhacker, eds. Pp. 345–359. Boulder: University Press of Colorado.

Mills, Barbara J., Jeffery J. Clark, Matthew A. Peeples, W. R. Haas, John M. Roberts, J. Brett Hill, Deborah L. Huntley, Lewis Borck, Ronald L. Breiger, Aaron Clauset, and M. Steven Shackley. 2013. Transformation of Social Networks in the Late Pre-Hispanic U.S. Southwest. Proceedings of the National Academy of Sciences 110(15):5785–5790.

Mills, Barbara J., Sarah A. Herr, and Scott Van Keuren. 1999. Living on the Edge of the Rim: Excavations and Analysis of the Silver Creek Archaeological Research Project, 1993–1998. Arizona State Museum Archaeological Series, 192. Tucson: University of Arizona.

Mills, Barbara J., and Matthew A. Peeples. N.d. Reframing Diffusion through Social Network Theory. *In* Social Networks in the Prehistoric Southwest: Proceedings of the 14th Southwest Symposium. Karen Harry and Barbara Roth, eds. Boulder: University Press of Colorado. In review.

Mills, Barbara J., Matthew A. Peeples, Jr., W. Randall Haas, Lewis Borck, Jeffery J. Clark, and John M. Roberts, Jr. 2015. Multiscalar Perspectives on Social Networks in the Late Prehispanic Southwest. American Antiquity 80(1):3–24.

Mills, Barbara J., John M. Roberts, Jeffery J. Clark, William R. Haas, Deborah Huntley, Matthew A. Peeples, Lewis Borck, Susan C. Ryan, Meaghan Trowbridge, and Ronald L. Breiger. 2013. The Dynamics of Social Networks in the Late Prehispanic U.S. Southwest. *In* Network Analysis in Archaeology: New Approaches to Regional Interaction. Carl Knappett, ed. Pp. 181–202. Oxford: Oxford University Press.

Mitchell, Peter. 2015. Horse Nations: The Worldwide Impact of the Horse on Indigenous Societies Post-1492. Oxford: Oxford University Press.

Mithlo, Nancy Marie. 2009. "Our Indian Princess": Subverting the Stereotype. Santa Fe, NM: School for Advanced Research Press.

Mobley-Tanaka, Jeanette L. 2002. Crossed Cultures, Crossed Meanings: The Manipulation of Ritual Imagery in Early Historic Pueblo Resistance. *In* Archaeologies of the Pueblo Revolt: Identity, Meaning, and Renewal in the Pueblo World. Robert W. Preucel, ed. Pp. 77–84. Albuquerque: University of New Mexico Press.

Mock, Shirley Boteler. 1998. The Sowing and the Dawning: Termination, Dedication, and Transformation in the Archaeological and Ethnographic Record of Mesoamerica. Albuquerque: University of New Mexico Press.

Monckton, Stephen. 1990. Huron Palaeoethnobotany. Ph.D. dissertation, Department of Anthropology, University of Toronto.

Moore, Henrietta L. 2000. Ethics and Ontology: Why Agents and Agency Matter. *In* Agency in Archaeology. Marcia-Anne Dobres and John Robb, eds. Pp. 259–263. New York: Routledge.

Moore, Jerry D. 1996. The Archaeology of Plazas and the Proxemics of Ritual: Three Andean Traditions. American Anthropologist 98(4):789–802.

Moorehead, Warren K. 1922. A Report on the Archaeology of Maine. Andover, MA: Andover Press.

Morandi, Steven J. 2010. Xibun Maya: The Archaeology of an Early Spanish Colonial Frontier in Southeastern Yucatan. Ph.D. dissertation, Department of Archaeology, Boston University.

Moratto, Michael J. 1984. California Archaeology. Orlando: Academic Press.

Morton, Thomas. 1947[1637]. The New English Caanan, Reprinted in Tracts and Other Papers, Relating Principally to the Origin, Settlement and Progress of the Colonies of North America, from the Discovery of the Country to the Year 1776. Vol 2. Peter Force, ed. New York: Peter Smith.

Moyes, Holley. 2007. Ancient Maya Drought Cult: Late Classic Cave Use in Belize. Research Reports in Belizean Archaeology 4:43–54.

Mrozowski, S. A., H. Herbster, D. Brown, and K. L. Priddy. 2009. Magunkaquog Materiality, Federal Recognition, and the Search for a Deeper History. International Journal of Historical Archaeology 13(4):430–463.

Mullins, Paul R. 1999. Race and Affluence: An Archaeology of African America and Consumer Culture. New York: Kluwer Academic / Plenum Publishers.

———. 2009. Consuming Individuality: Collective Identity along the Color Line. *In* The Materiality of Individuality: Archaeological Studies of Individual Lives. C. L. White, ed. Pp. 207–219. New York: Springer.

———. 2011a. The Archaeology of Consumer Culture. Gainesville: University Press of Florida.

———. 2011b. The Archaeology of Consumption. Annual Review of Anthropology 40:133–144.

Mullins, Paul R., and Nigel Jeffries. 2012. The Banality of Gilding: Innocuous Materiality and Transatlantic Consumption in the Gilded Age. International Journal of Historical Archaeology 16(4):745–760.

Mullins, Paul R., and Timo Ylimaunu. 2015. The Materiality of Colonial Inequality and Marginalization. *In* Rethinking Colonialism: Comparative Archaeological Approaches. Craig N. Cipolla and Katherine H. Hayes, eds. Pp. 40–53. Gainesville: University Press of Florida.

Munn, Nancy D. 1986. The Fame of Gawa: A Symbolic Study of Value Transformation in a Massim (Papua New Guinea) Society. London: Duke University Press.

Nadeau, Jaclyn, and Nicholas F. Bellantoni. 2004. Lithic Artifact and Bio-archaeological Analysis of a Possible Adena Burial Site (CT84-51) in Milford, Connecticut. Bulletin of the Archaeological Society of Connecticut 66:3–15.

Nassaney, Michael S. 2004. Native American Gender Politics and Material Culture in Seventeenth-Century Southeastern New England. Journal of Social Archaeology 4(3):334–367.

Nelson, Ben A., and Steven A. LeBlanc. 1986. Short Term Sedentism in the American Southwest: The Mimbres Valley Salado. Albuquerque: University of New Mexico Press.

Netting, Robert McC. 1993. Smallholders, Householders: Farm Families and the Ecology of Intensive, Sustainable Agriculture. Stanford, CA: Stanford University Press.

Nichols, Deborah, Christina Elson, Leslie G. Cecil, Nina Eivens de Estrada, Michael D. Glascock, and Paula Mikkelsen. 2009. Chiconautla, Mexico: A Crossroads of Aztec Trade and Politics. Latin American Antiquity 20(3):443–472.

Nietzsche, Friedrich Wilhelm. 2007[1887]. On the Genealogy of Morality. Carol Diethe, trans. New York: Cambridge University Press.

Noble, William C. 1971. The Sopher Celt: An Indicator of Early Protohistoric Trade in Huronia. Ontario 16:42–47.

Okoshi-Haradi, Tsubasa. 2012. Postclassic Maya "Barrios" in Yucatán: An Historical Approach. *In* The Neighborhood as a Social and Spatial Unit in Mesoamerican Cities. M. Charlotte Arnauld, Linda R. Manzanilla, and Michael E. Smith, eds. Pp. 286–303. Tucson: University of Arizona Press.

Oland, Maxine. 2003. Continued Colonial Maya Excavations at the Avila Site (PR 9), Progresso Lagoon Shore, Belize 2002 Season. *In* Belize Postclassic Project 2002: Investigations of the Shore Settlements of Progresso Lagoon, and San Estevan. Report to the Department of Archaeology, Belmopan, Belize. Institute for Mesoamerican Studies Occasional Publication, 9. Josalyn M. Ferguson and Marilyn A. Masson, eds. Pp. 7–45. Albany, NY: University at Albany–SUNY.

———. 2009. Long-Term Indigenous History on a Colonial Frontier: Archaeology at a 15th–17th Century Maya Village, Progresso Lagoon, Belize. Ph.D. dissertation, Department of Anthropology, Northwestern University.

———. 2012. Lost among the Colonial Maya: Engaging Indigenous Maya History at Progresso Lagoon, Belize. *In* Decolonizing Indigenous Histories: Exploring Prehistoric/Colonial Transitions in Archaeology. Maxine Oland, Siobhan M. Hart, and Liam Frink, eds. Pp. 178–200. Tucson: University of Arizona Press.

———. 2013. The 15th–17th Century Lithic Economy at Progresso Lagoon, Belize. Lithic Technology 38(2):81–96.

———. 2014. "With the Gifts and Good Treatment That He Gave Them": Elite Maya Adoption of Spanish Material Culture at Progresso Lagoon, Belize. International Journal of Historical Archaeology 18(4):643–667.

Oland, Maxine, Siobhan Hart, and Liam Frink, eds. 2012. Decolonizing Indigenous Histories: Exploring Prehistoric/Colonial Transitions in Archaeology. Tucson: University of Arizona Press.

Oliver, Jeff. 2014. Native-Lived Colonialism and the Agency of Life Projects: A View from the Northwest Coast. *In* Rethinking Colonial Pasts through Archaeology. N. Ferris, R. Harrison, and M. V. Wilcox, eds. Pp. 76–102. Oxford: Oxford University Press.

Olsen, Bjørnar. 2003. Material Culture after Text: Re-membering Things. Norwegian Archaeological Review 36:87–104.

———. 2010. In Defense of Things: Archaeology and the Ontology of Objects. Lanham, MD: AltaMira.

———. 2012. After Interpretation: Remembering Archaeology. Current Swedish Archaeology 20:11–34.

Olsen, Bjørnar, Michael Shanks, Timothy Webmoor, and Christopher Witmore. 2012. Archaeology: The Discipline of Things. Berkeley: University of California Press.

Ong, Aihwa. 2006. Neoliberalism as Exception: Mutations in Citizenship and Sovereignty. Durham, NC: Duke University Press.

Orser, Charles E., Jr. 1996. A Historical Archaeology of the Modern World. New York: Plenum Press.

———. 2012. An Archaeology of Eurocentrism. American Antiquity 77(4):737–755.

Ortner, Sherry B. 1995. Resistance and the Problem of Ethnographic Refusal. Society for Comparative Study of Society and History 37(1):173–193.

Ovsyannikov, O. V., and N. M. Terebikhin. 2013. Sacred Space in the Culture of the Arctic Regions. *In* Sacred Sites, Sacred Places. D. Carmichael, J. Huber, B. Reeves, and A. Schanche, eds. Pp. 44–81. London: Routledge.

Painter, Floyd. 1980. The Great King of Great Neck: A Status Burial from Coastal Virginia. Chesopiean 18(3–6):74–76.

Panich, Lee M. 2009. Persistence of Native Identity at Mission Santa Catalina, Baja California, 1797–1840. Ph.D. dissertation, Department of Anthropology, University of California, Berkeley.

———. 2010. Missionization and the Persistence of Native Identity on the Colonial Frontier of Baja California. Ethnohistory 57:225–262.

———. 2013. Archaeologies of Persistence: Reconsidering the Legacies of Colonialism in Native North America. American Antiquity 78(1):105–122.

———. 2014. Native American Consumption of Shell and Glass Beads at Mission Santa Clara de Asís. American Antiquity 79(4):730–748.

———. 2015. "Sometimes They Bury the Deceased's Clothes and Trinkets": Indigenous Mortuary Practices at Mission Santa Clara de Asís. Historical Archaeology 49(4):110–129.

Panich, Lee M., Helga Afaghani, and Nicole Mathwich. 2014. Assessing the Diversity of Mission Populations through the Comparison of Native American Residences at Mission Santa Clara de Asís. International Journal of Historical Archaeology 18(3):467–488.

Panich, Lee M., and Tsim D. Schneider. 2015. Expanding Mission Archaeology: A Landscape Approach to Indigenous Autonomy in Colonial California. Journal of Anthropological Archaeology 40:48–58.

Panich, Lee M., and Tsim D. Schneider, eds. 2014. Indigenous Landscapes and Spanish Missions: New Perspectives from Archaeology and Ethnohistory. Tucson: University of Arizona Press.

Pauketat, Timothy R. 1994. The Ascent of Chiefs. Tuscaloosa: University of Alabama Press.

———. 1997. Specialization, Political Symbols, and the Crafty Elite of Cahokia. Southeastern Archaeology 16:1–15.

———. 2012. Bundles of/in/as Time. *In* Big Histories, Human Lives: Tackling Problems of Scale in Archaeology. John Robb and Timothy R. Pauketat, eds. Pp. 35–56. Santa Fe, NM: School for Advanced Research Press.

———. 2013. An Archaeology of the Cosmos: Rethinking Agency and Religion in Ancient America. New York: Routledge.

Pauketat, Timothy R., Lucretia S. Kelly, Gayle J. Fritz, Neal H. Lopinot, Scott Elias, and Eve Hargrave. 2002. The Residues of Feasting and Public Ritual at Early Cahokia. American Antiquity 67(2):257–279.

Paynter, Robert, Susan Hautaniemi, and Nancy Muller. 1994. The Landscapes of the W. E. B. Du Bois Boyhood Homesite: An Agenda for an Archaeology of the Color Line. *In* Race. Steven Gregory and Roger Sanjek, eds. Pp. 285–318. New Brunswick, NJ: Rutgers University Press.

Pearson, Harry. 1957. The Economy Has No Surplus: Critique of a Theory of Development. *In* Trade and Market in the Early Empires. Karl Polanyi, Conrad M. Arensberg, and Harry W. Pearson, eds. Pp. 320–341. Glencoe, IL: Free Press.

Peebles, Gustav. 2010. The Anthropology of Credit and Debt. Annual Review of Anthropology 39:225–240.

Peelo, Sarah. 2009. Baptism among the Salinan Neophytes of Mission San Antonio de Padua: Investigating the Ecological Hypothesis. Ethnohistory 56(4):589–624.

Peeples, Matthew A., and W. Randall Haas. 2013. Brokerage and Social Capital in the Prehispanic U.S. Southwest. American Anthropologist 115(2):232–247.

Peeples, Matthew A., and Barbara J. Mills. 2016. Frontiers of Marginality and Mediation in the U.S. Southwest: A Social Networks Perspective. *In* Social Identity in Frontier and Borderland Communities of the North American Southwest. Karen G. Harry and Sarah Herr, eds. Boulder: University Press of Colorado. In review.

Peers, Laura. 1999. "Many Tender Ties": The Shifting Contexts and Meanings of the S BLACK Bag. World Archaeology 31(2):288–302.
Peirce, Ebenezer W. 1878. Indian History, Biography and Genealogy: Pertaining to the Good Sachem Massasoit of the Wampanoag Tribe, and His Descendants. North Abington, MA: Z. G. Mitchell.
Peirce Edition Project, ed. 1998. The Essential Peirce: Volume 2 (1893–1913). Bloomington: Indiana University Press.
Peña, Elizabeth S. 2001. The Role of Wampum Production at the Albany Almshouse. International Journal of Historical Archaeology 5(2):155–174.
Pendergast, David M. 1991. The Southern Maya Lowlands Contact Experience: The View from Lamanai, Belize. *In* The Spanish Borderlands in Pan-American Perspective, vol. 3: Columbian Consequences. David Hurst Thomas, ed. Pp. 337–354. Washington, DC: Smithsonian Institution Press.
Pendergast, David M., Grant D. Jones, and Elizabeth Graham. 1993. Locating Maya Lowlands Spanish Colonial Towns: A Case Study from Belize. Latin American Antiquity 4(1):59–73.
Peres, Tanya M. 2008. Foodways, Economic Status, and the Antebellum Upland South in Central Kentucky. Historical Archaeology 42(4):88–104.
Perissinotto, Giorgio. 1998. Documenting Everyday Life in Early Spanish California: The Santa Barbara Presidio Memorias y Facturas, 1779–1810. Santa Barbara, CA: Santa Barbara Trust for Historic Preservation.
Petersen, James, Malinda Blustain, and James Bradley. 2004. "Mawooshen" Revisited: Two Native American Contact Period Sites on the Central Maine Coast. Archaeology of Eastern North America 32:171.
Peterson, Polly A. 2006. Ancient Maya Ritual Cave Use in the Sibun Valley, Belize. Boston University.
Pezzarossi, Guido. 2014. Camouflaging Consumption and Colonial Mimicry: The Materiality of an Eighteenth- and Nineteenth-Century Nipmuc Household. International Journal of Historical Archaeology 18(1):146–174.
Pfeiffer, Susan. 1980. Spatial Distribution of Human Skeletal Material within an Iroquoian Ossuary. Canadian Journal of Archaeology 4:169–172.
Phillips, George Harwood. 1993. Indians and Intruders in Central California, 1769–1849. Norman: University of Oklahoma Press.
———. 2010. Vineyards and Vaqueros: Indian Labor and the Economic Expansion of Southern California, 1771–1877. Norman, OK: Arthur H. Clark Company.
Phillips, Ruth B. 1998. Trading Identities: The Souvenir in Native North American Art from the Northeast, 1700–1900. Seattle: University of Washington Press; Montreal: McGill-Queen's University Press.
Pinney, Christopher. 2005. Things Happen: Or, From Which Moments Does That Object Come? *In* Materiality. Daniel Miller, ed. Pp. 256–272. Durham, NC: Duke University Press.

Plane, Ann. 2002. Colonial Intimacies: Indian Marriage in Early New England. Ithaca, NY: Cornell University Press.

Playter, George F. 1862. The History of Methodism in Canada: With an Account of the Rise and Progress of the Work of God among the Canadian Indian Tribes, and Occasional Notices of the Civil Affairs of the Province. Toronto: A. Green.

Pluckhahn, Thomas J. 2003. Kolomoki: Settlement, Ceremony, and Status in the Deep South, A.D. 350 to 750. Tuscaloosa: University of Alabama Press.

Pluckhahn, Thomas J., J. Matthew Compton, and Mary Theresa Bonhage-Freund. 2006. Evidence of Small-Scale Feasting from the Woodland Period Site of Kolomoki, Georgia. Journal of Field Archaeology 31:263–284.

Plymouth Colony. 1861. Records of the Colony of New Plymouth Vols. I, II. David Pulsipher, ed. Boston: William White.

Pomedli, Michael. 1991. Ethnophilosophical and Ethnolinguistic Perspectives on the Huron Soul. Lewiston, NY: Edwin Mellen Press.

Potter, Stephen R. 2006. Early English Effects on Virginia Algonquian Exchange and Tribute in the Tidewater Potomac. *In* Powhatan's Mantle: Indians in the Colonial Southeast. Gregory A. Waselkov, Peter H. Wood, and Thomas Hatley, eds. Pp. 215–241. Lincoln: University of Nebraska Press.

Price, James E., and Gregory L. Fox. 1990. Recent Investigations at Towosahgy State Historic Site. Missouri Archaeologist 51:1–71.

Prins, Harald. 2002. The Mi'Kmaq: Resistance, Accommodation, and Cultural Survival. Belmont, CA: Wadsworth Group.

Proskouriakoff, Tatiana. 1993. Maya History. Rosemary A. Joyce, ed. Austin: University of Texas Press.

Prufer, Keith M., and James E. Brady. 2005. Stone Houses and Earth Lords: Maya Religion in the Cave Context. Boulder: University Press of Colorado.

Pugh, Timothy W. 2009. Contagion and Alterity: Kowoj Maya Appropriations of European Objects. American Anthropologist 111(3):373–386.

Pugh, Timothy W., José Rómulo Sanchez, and Yuko Shiratori. 2012. Contact and Missionization at Tayasal, Petén, Guatemala. Journal of Field Archaeology 37(1):3–19.

Qi, Xiaoying. 2013. Intellectual Entrepreneurs and the Diffusion of Ideas: Two Historical Cases of Knowledge Flow. American Journal of Cultural Sociology 1(3):346–372.

Quezada, Sergio. 2014. Maya Lords and Lordship: The Formation of Colonial Society in Yucatán, 1350–1600. Terry Rugeley, trans. Norman: University of Oklahoma Press.

Quimby, George Irving. 1960a. Indian Life in the Upper Great Lakes, 11,000 B.C. to A.D. 1800. Chicago: University of Chicago Press.

———. 1960b. Rates of Cultural Change in Archaeology. American Antiquity 25(3):416–417.

Quimby, George Irving, and Alexander Spoehr. 1951. Acculturation and Material Culture. Fieldiana 36(6):107–147.

Rafferty, Sean M. 2004. "They Pass Their Lives in Smoke, and at Death Fall into the Fire": Smoking Pipes and Mortuary Ritual during the Early Woodland Period. *In* Smoking and Culture: The Archaeology of Tobacco Pipes in Eastern North America. Sean Rafferty and Rob Mann, eds. Pp. 1–41. Knoxville: University of Tennessee Press.

Ramsden, Peter G. 1990. The Hurons: Archaeology and Culture History. *In* The Archaeology of Southern Ontario A.D. 1650. Chris J. Ellis and Neal Ferris, eds. Pp. 361–384. Occasional Publication of the London Chapter, Ontario Archaeological Society, 5.

Reddy, Seetha N. 2015. Feeding Family and Ancestors: Persistence of Traditional Native American Lifeways during the Mission Period in Coastal Southern California. Journal of Anthropological Archaeology 37:48–66.

Redfield, Robert, Ralph Linton, and Melville J. Herskovits. 1936. Memorandum for the Study of Acculturation. American Anthropologist 38(1):149–152.

Redwing, Princess. 1935. Editorial. Narragansett Dawn 1(4):80–83. Special Collections Publications, 5 (2006). http://digitalcommons.uri.edu/sc_pubs/5, accessed May 26, 2015.

Reid, Jennifer. 1995. Myth, Symbol, and Colonial Encounter: British and Mi'kmaq in Acadia, 1700–1867. Ottawa: University of Ottawa Press.

Renfrew, Colin. 1975. Trade as Action at a Distance: Questions of Integration and Communication. *In* Ancient Civilization and Trade. C. C. Lamberg-Karlovsky and Jeremy A. Sabloff, eds. Pp. 3–59. Albuquerque: University of New Mexico Press.

———. 2001. Production and Consumption in a Sacred Economy: The Material Correlates of High Devotional Expression at Chaco Canyon. American Antiquity 66(1):14–25.

Restall, Matthew. 1998. Maya Conquistador. Boston: Beacon Press.

———. 2001. The People of the Patio: Ethnohistorical Evidence of Yucatec Maya Royal Courts. *In* Royal Courts of the Ancient Maya: Data and Case Studies. Takeshi Inomata and Stephen D. Houston, eds. Pp. 335–390. Boulder, CO: Westview Press.

———. 2006. Origin and Myth: Ethnicity, Class, and Chibal in Postclassic and Colonial Yucatan. *In* Nuevas perspectivas sobre la geografía política de los Mayas. Tsubasa Okoshi Harada, Lorrane Annette Williams-Beck, and Ana Luisa Izquierdo, eds. Pp. 269–289. Mexico City: Universidad Nacional Autónoma de México, Universidad Autónoma de Campeche, Foundation for the Advancement of Mesoamerican Studies, Inc.

———. 2010. The Mysterious and the Invisible: Writing History in and of Colonial Yucatan. Ancient Mesoamerica 21(2):393–400.

Ringle, William M. 2004. On the Political Organization of Chichén Itzá. Ancient Mesoamerica 15:167–218.

Ritchie, William A., and Don W. Dragoo. 1959. The Eastern Dispersal of Adena. American Antiquity 25(1):43–50.

Robb, John E. 2010. Beyond Agency. World Archaeology 42(4):493–520.

Robinson, David. 2013. Polyvalent Metaphors in South-Central California Missionary Processes. American Antiquity 78(2):302–321.

Roche, Daniel. 1994. The Culture of Clothing: Dress and Fashion in the Ancien Régime. Cambridge: Cambridge University Press.

Rogers, Everett M. 1973. Communication Strategies for Family Planning. New York: Free Press.

———. 2003. Diffusion of Innovations. 5th ed. New York: Simon and Schuster.

Rosenswig, Robert M., and Marilyn A. Masson. 2003. Transformation of the Terminal Classic to Postclassic Architectural Landscape at Caye Coco, Belize. Ancient Mesoamerica 13(2):213–235.

Rothschild, Nan A. 2003. Colonial Encounters in a Native American Landscape: The Spanish and the Dutch in North America. Washington, DC: Smithsonian Books.

Rountree, Helen C. 1989. The Powhatan Indians of Virginia: Their Traditional Culture. Norman: University of Oklahoma Press.

———. 1993. The Powhatan and Other Woodland Indians as Travelers. *In* Powhatan Foreign Relations, 1500–1722. Helen C. Rountree, ed. Pp. 21–52. Charlottesville: University of Virginia Press.

———. 2006. Pocahontas, Powhatan, Opechancanough: Three Indian Lives Changed by Jamestown. Charlottesville: University of Virginia Press.

Rubertone, Patricia E. 1989. Archaeology, Colonialism, and 17th Century Native America: Towards an Alternative Interpretation. *In* Conflict in the Archaeology of Living Traditions. R. H. Layton, ed. Pp. 32–45. London: Routledge.

———. 2000. The Historical Archaeology of Native Americans. Annual Review of Anthropology 29:425–446.

———. 2001. Grave Undertakings: An Archaeology of Roger Williams and the Narragansett Indians. Washington, DC: Smithsonian Institution Press.

———. 2012. Archaeologies of Colonialism in Unexpected Times and Unexpected Places. *In* Decolonizing Indigenous Histories: Exploring Prehistoric/Colonial Transitions in Archaeology. Maxine Oland, Siobhan M. Hart, and Liam Frank, eds. Pp. 267–281. Tucson: University of Arizona Press.

———. 2013. Exploring Native American Homelands in Greater Providence. Paper presented at the New England American Studies Association Annual Conference, Mashantucket, CT, September 27.

Ryan, Bryce, and Neal C. Gross. 1943. The Diffusion of Hybrid Seed Corn in Two Iowa Communities. Rural Sociology 8(1):15–24.

Sahlins, Marshall. 1972. Stone Age Economics. Chicago: Aldine-Atherton.

———. 1985. Islands of History. Chicago: University of Chicago Press.

———. 1999. Waiting for Foucault. Charlottesville: Prickly Paradigm Press.

Said, Edward. 1978. Orientalism. New York: Random House.

Sakamoto, Rumi. 1996. Japan, Hybridity and the Creation of Colonialist Discourse. Theory, Culture & Society 13(3):113–128.

Salisbury, Neal. 1996. The Indians' Old World: Native Americans and the Coming of Europeans. William and Mary Quarterly 3:435–458.

———. 1999. Waiting for Foucault. Charlottesville: Prickly Pear Press.

Sargent, Sarah. 2014. Unfulfilled Promises: Safeguarding the Horse Culture of the American Indians. Transnational Dispute Management 11(2):1–11.

Sassaman, Kenneth E. 2001. Hunter-Gatherers and Traditions of Resistance. *In* The Archaeology of Traditions: Agency and History before and after Columbus. Timothy R. Pauketat, ed. Pp. 218–236. Gainesville: University Press of Florida.

Sayre, Gordan. 1997. "Les Sauvages Américains": Representations of Native Americans in French and English Colonial Literature. Chapel Hill: University of North Carolina Press.

Scaramelli, Franz, and Kay Tarble De Scaramelli. 2005. The Role of Material Culture in the Colonization of the Orinoco, Venezuela. Journal of Social Archaeology 5(1):135–168.

Scarry, John F. 2001. Resistance and Accommodation in Apalachee Province. *In* The Archaeology of Traditions: Agency and History before and after Columbus. Timothy R. Pauketat, ed. Pp. 34–57. Gainesville: University Press of Florida.

Scheiber, Laura L., and Judson Byrd Finley. 2011. Mobility as Resistance: Colonialism among Nomadic Hunter-Gatherers in the American West. *In* Hunter-Gatherer Archaeology as Historical Process. Kenneth E. Sassaman and Donald H. Holly, Jr., eds. Pp. 167–183. Tucson: University of Arizona Press.

Scheiber, Laura L., and Mark D. Mitchell, eds. 2010. Across a Great Divide: Continuity and Change in Native North American Societies, 1400–1900. Tucson: University of Arizona Press.

Scheper-Hughes, Nancy, and Margaret M. Lock. 1987. The Mindful Body: A Prolegomenon to Future Work in Anthropology. Medical Anthropology Quarterly, n.s., 1(1):6–41.

Schmidt, Peter R., and Stephen A. Mrozowski, eds. 2013. The Death of Prehistory. Oxford: Oxford University Press.

Scholes, Frances J., Carlos R. Menéndez, J. I. Rubio Mañé, and Eleanor B. Adams, eds. 1938. La iglesia en Yucatán, vol. 2: Documentos para la historia de Yucatán. Mérida: Compañía Tipográfica Yucateca.

Schurr, Mark R. 2010. Archaeological Indices of Resistance: Diversity in the Removal Period Potawatomi of the Western Great Lakes. American Antiquity 75(1):44–60.

Schuyler, Robert L. 1970. Historical and Historic Sites Archaeology as Anthropology: Basic Definitions and Relationships. Historical Archaeology 4:83–89.

Schwartz, Saul, and William Green. 2013. Middle Ground or Native Ground? Material Culture at Iowaville. Ethnohistory 60(4):537–565.

Seeman, Eric R. 2011. The Huron-Wendat Feast of the Dead. Baltimore, MD: Johns Hopkins University Press.

Seeman, Mark F. 1979. Feasting with the Dead: Charnel House Ritual as a Context for the Redistribution of Food in Ohio Hopewell. *In* Hopewell Archaeology. David Brose and N'aomi Greber, eds. Pp. 39–46. Kent, OH: Kent State University Press.

Semple, Neil. 1996. The Lord's Dominion: The History of Canadian Methodism. Montreal: McGill-Queen's University Press.

Sharpe, Roger. 2003. The Martial Spirit: A History of the Sedentary Militia and the Six Nations Warriors of the Former Brant County Area 1784–1884. Paris, ON: Roger Sharpe.

Shea, John Gilmary, ed. 1861. Early Voyages up and down the Mississippi by Cavelier, St. Cosme, Le Sueur, Gravier, and Guignas. Albany: J. Munsell.

Shephard, Christopher J. 2009. Places of Power: The Community and Regional Development of Native Tidewater Palisades post A.D. 1200. M.A. thesis, Department of Anthropology, College of William and Mary.

———. 2015. The Materiality of Politics: Tracking the Production and Circulation of Shell Artifacts in the Algonquian Chesapeake (A.D. 900–1680). Journal of Middle Atlantic Archaeology 31:39–52.

Shipek, Florence C., ed. 1965. Lower California Frontier: Articles from the San Diego Union 1870. Baja California Travels Series 2. Los Angeles: Dawson's Book Shop.

Shoup, Laurence H., and Randall T. Milliken. 1999. Inigo of Rancho Posolmi: The Life and Times of a Mission Indian. Ballena Press Anthropological Papers, 47. Novato, CA: Ballena Press.

Shyrock, Richard H. 1960. Medicine and Society in America, 1660–1860. Ithaca, NY: Cornell University Press.

Silliman, Stephen W. 2001. Theoretical Perspectives on Labor and Colonialism: Reconsidering the California Missions. Journal of Anthropological Archaeology 20(4):379–407.

———. 2004. Lost Laborers in Colonial California: Native Americans and the Archaeology of Rancho Petaluma. Tucson: University of Arizona Press.

———. 2005. Culture Contact or Colonialism? Challenges in the Archaeology of Native North America. American Antiquity 70(1):55–74.

———. 2009. Change and Continuity, Practice and Memory: Native American Persistence in Colonial New England. American Antiquity 74(2):211–230.

———. 2014. Archaeologies of Indigenous Survivance and Residence: Navigating Colonial and Scholarly Dualities. *In* Rethinking Colonial Pasts through Archaeology. N. Ferris, R. Harrison, and M. V. Wilcox, eds. Pp. 57–75. Oxford: Oxford University Press.

———. 2015. A Requiem for Hybridity? The Problem with Frankensteins, Purées, and Mules. Journal of Social Archaeology 15(3):277–298.

Silliman, Stephen W., ed. 2006. Collaborating at the Trowel's Edge: Teaching and Learning in Indigenous Archaeology. Tucson: University of Arizona Press.

Silliman, Stephen W., and Thomas A. Witt. 2010. The Complexities of Consumption: Eastern Pequot Cultural Economics in Eighteenth-Century New England. Historical Archaeology 44(4):46–68.

Silverman, David J. 2001. The Impact of Indentured Servitude on the Society of Southern New England Indians. New England Quarterly 74(4):622–666.

Silverstein, Michael. 1976. Shifters, Linguistic Categories and Cultural Description. *In* Meaning in Anthropology. Keith Basso and Ellen Selby, eds. Pp. 11–56. Albuquerque: University of New Mexico Press.

Simmons, Marc, and Frank Turley. 1980. Southwestern Colonial Ironwork: The Spanish Blacksmithing Tradition from Texas to California. Santa Fe, NM: Museum of New Mexico Press.

Simmons, William S. 1970. Cautantowwit's House: An Indian Burial Ground on the Island of Conanicut in Narragansett Bay. Providence, RI: Brown University Press.

———. 1976. Southern New England Shamanism: An Ethnographic Reconstruction. *In* Papers of the Seventh Algonquian Conference. W. Cowan, ed. Pp. 217–256. Ottawa: Carleton University Press.

———. 1981. Cultural Bias in the New England Puritan's Perceptions of Indians. William and Mary Quarterly 38(1):56–72.

———. 1986. Spirit of the New England Tribes: Indian History and Folklore, 1620–1984. Hanover, NH: University Press of New England.

———. 2002. From Manifest Destiny to the Melting Pot: The Life and Times of Charlotte Mitchell, Wampanoag. *In* Anthropology, History, and American Indians: Essays in Honor of William Curtis Sturtevant. William Merrill and Ives Goddard, eds. Pp. 131–138. Smithsonian Contributions to Anthropology, 44. Washington, DC: Smithsonian Institution.

Skowronek, Russell K., Jelena Radovic Fanta, and Hugo Morales, eds. N.d. By All Accounts . . . The Mission Santa Clara de Asís Ledger Book, 1770–1828. Manuscript on file at the University of Texas Rio Grande Valley.

Smith, Adam T. 2011. Archaeologies of Sovereignty. Annual Review of Anthropology 40:415–432.

Smith, David G. 1992. Stylistic Variation in Middleport Smoking Pipes. *In* Proceedings of the 1989 Smoking Pipe Conference. Charles F. Hayes III, ed. Pp. 15–30. Rochester, NY: Rochester Museum and Science Center, Research Records.

Smith, Donald B. 1987. Sacred Feathers: The Reverend Peter Jones (Kahkewaquonaby) & the Mississauga Indians. Toronto: University of Toronto Press.

Smith, Gerald P. 1971. Protohistoric Sociopolitical Organization of the Nottoway in the Chesapeake Bay–Carolina Sounds Region. Ph.D. dissertation, Department of Anthropology, University of Missouri.

Smith, John. 1986a. Generall Historie of Virginia. *In* The Complete Works of Captain John Smith, vol. 2. P. L. Barbour, ed. Pp. 5–475. Chapel Hill: University of North Carolina Press.

———. 1986b. A Map of Virginia. *In* The Complete Works of Captain John Smith, vol. 1. P. L. Barbour, ed. Pp. 119–189. Chapel Hill: University of North Carolina Press.

———. 1986c. The Proceedings. *In* The Complete Works of Captain John Smith, vol. 1. P. L. Barbour, ed. Pp. 191–279. Chapel Hill: University of North Carolina Press.

———. 1986d. A True Relation. *In* The Complete Works of Captain John Smith, vol. 1. P. L. Barbour, ed. Pp. 5–117. Chapel Hill: University of North Carolina Press.

Smith, Marvin T., and Mark Williams. 1994. Mississippian Mound Refuse Disposal Patterns and Implications for Archaeological Research. Southeastern Archaeology 13:27–35.

Smith, Monica. 2007. Inconspicuous Consumption: Non-display Goods and Identity Formation. Journal of Archaeological Method and Theory 14:412–438.

Snow, Dean R. 1994. The Iroquois. Cambridge: Blackwell.

———. 1995. Mohawk Valley Archaeology: The Sites. Albany, NY: Institute for Archaeological Studies, University at Albany, SUNY.

Snyder, Gary S. 1999. Wampum: A Material Symbol of Cultural Value to the Iroquois Peoples of Northeastern North America. *In* Material Symbols: Culture and Economy in Prehistory. John E. Robb, ed. Pp. 362–381. Center for Archaeological Investigations Occasional Paper, 7. Carbondale: Southern Illinois University at Carbondale.

Snyderman, George S. 1954. The Functions of Wampum. Proceedings of the American Philosophical Society 98(6):469–494.

Speck, Frank G. 1917. Medicine Practices of the Northeastern Algonquians. *In* Proceedings of the Nineteenth International Congress of Americanists. F. W. Hodge, ed. Pp. 303–321. Washington, DC.

Spelman, Henry. 1998[1609]. Relations of Virginia, 1609. *In* Jamestown Narratives: Eyewitness Accounts of the Virginia Colony. E. W. Haile, ed. Pp. 481–495. Champlain, VA: Round-House.

Spencer-Wood, Suzanne M., ed. 1987. Consumer Choice in Historical Archaeology. New York: Plenum Press.

Spielmann, Katherine A. 2002. Feasting, Craft Specialization, and the Ritual Mode of Production in Small-Scale Societies. American Anthropologist 104:195–207.

Spielmann, Katherine A., Jeannette L. Mobley-Tanaka, and James M. Potter. 2006. Style and Resistance in the Seventeenth Century Salinas Province. American Antiquity 71(4):621–647.

Spiess, Arthur E., and Bruce D. Spiess. 1987. New England Pandemic of 1616–22: Cause and Archaeological Implications. Man in the Northeast 34:71–83.

Spivak, Gayatri C. 1988. Can the Subaltern Speak? *In* Marxism and the Interpretation of Culture. Cary Nelson and Lawrence Gossberg, eds. Pp. 271–313. Urbana: University of Illinois Press.

Sprague, Roderick. 1985. Glass Trade Beads: A Progress Report. Historical Archaeology 19(2):87–105.

Stahl, Ann Brower. 2002. Colonial Entanglements and the Practices of Taste: An Alternative to Logocentric Approaches. American Anthropologist 104(3):827–845.

———. 2010. Material Histories. *In* The Oxford Handbook of Material Culture Studies. Mary C. Beaudry and Dan Hicks, eds. Pp. 148–170. Oxford: Oxford University Press.

Stange, Marion. 2012. Vital Negotiations: Protecting Settlers' Health in Colonial Louisiana and South Carolina, 1720–1763. Goettingen: V & R Unipress.

Starna, William. 1992. The Biological Encounter: Disease and the Ideological Domain. American Indian Quarterly 16(4):511–519.

Steckley, John. 1987. An Ethnolinguistic Look at the Huron Longhouse. Ontario Archaeology 47:19–32.

Steele, Jeffery. 1996. Reduced to Images: American Indians in Nineteenth-Century Advertising. *In* Dressing in Feathers: The Construction of the Indian in American Popular Culture. S. Elizabeth Bird, ed. Pp. 45–64. Boulder, CO: Westview Press.

Stevenson, Christopher, Laure Dussubieux, and Danielle Hauck. N.d. The Acquisition of Native Copper and Copper Alloy in Prehistoric and Contact Period Virginia. Unpublished MS, School of World Studies, Virginia Commonwealth University.

Stewart, Michael R. 1989. Trade and Exchange in Middle Atlantic Region Prehistory. Archaeology of Eastern North America 17:47–78.

Stewart, Suzanne. 1991. On Longing: Narratives of the Miniature, the Gigantic, the Souvenir, the Collection. Durham, NC: Duke University Press.

Stoler, Ann Laura. 1989. Rethinking Colonial Categories: European Communities and the Boundaries of Rule. Comparative Studies in Society and History 31(3):134–161.

Stoler, Ann Laura, and Frederick Cooper. 1997. Between Metropole and Colony: Rethinking a Research Agenda. *In* Tensions of Empire: Colonial Cultures in a Bourgeois World. Frederick Cooper and Ann Laura Stoler, eds. Pp. 1–56. Berkeley: University of California Press.

Stone, Andrea. 1989. Disconnection, Foreign Insignia, and Political Expansion: Teotihuacan and the Warrior Stelae of Piedras Negras. *In* Mesoamerica after the Decline of Teotihuacan, A.D. 700–900. Richard A. Diehl and Janet Catherine Berlo, eds. Pp. 153–172. Washington, DC: Dumbarton Oaks Research Library and Collection.

Strachey, William. 1953[1612]. The Historie of Travell into Virginia Britania: Expressing the cosmographie and commodities of the country, together with the manners and customes of the people. London: Hakluyt Society.

Strathern, Marilyn. 1979. The Self in Self-Decoration. Oceania 49(4):241–257.

———. 1988. The Gender of the Gift: Problems with Women and Problems with Society in Melanesia. Berkeley: University of California Press.

———. 1999. Property, Substance & Effect: Anthropological Essays on Persons and Things. London: Athlone Press.

———. 2009. Using Bodies to Communicate. *In* Social Bodies. Helen Lambert and Maryon McDonald, eds. Pp. 148–170. New York: Berghahn Books.

Stuart, David. 2000. "The Arrival of Strangers": Teotihuacan and Tollan in Classic Maya History. *In* Mesoamerica's Classic Heritage: From Teotihuacan to the Aztecs. David Carrasco, Lindsay Jones, and Scott Sessions, eds. Pp. 465–513. Boulder: University Press of Colorado.

Swanton, John R. 1911. Indian Tribes of the Lower Mississippi Valley and Adjacent Coast of Mexico. Bureau of American Ethnology Bulletin, 43 Washington, DC: Smithsonian Institution.

Sweitz, Sam R. 2012. Consumer Strategy and Household Consumption in the Cripple Creek Mining District, Colorado, USA. International Journal of Historical Archaeology 16(1):227–266.

Taché, Karine. 2011. New Perspectives on Meadowood Trade Items. American Antiquity 76(1):41–79.

Tantaquidgeon, Gladys. 1977. Folk Medicine of the Delaware and Related Algonkian Indians. Anthropological Series, 3. Harrisburg: Pennsylvania Historical and Museum Commission.

Tarlow, Sarah. 2000. Emotion in Archaeology. Current Anthropology 41(5):713–746.

———. 2012. The Archaeology of Emotion and Affect. Annual Review of Anthropology 41:169–185.

Taube, Karl A. 1992. The Temple of Quetzalcoatl and the Cult of Sacred War at Teotihuacan. Res: Anthropology and Aesthetics 21:53–87.

Taylor, Alan. 2002. The Divided Ground: Upper Canada, New York, and the Iroquois Six Nations, 1783–1815. Journal of the Early Republic 22(1):55–75.

Taylor, Charles. 2003. Modern Social Imaginaries. Durham, NC: Duke University Press.

Tehanetorens. 1972. Wampum Belts. Onchiota, NY: Six Nations Indian Museum.

Thomas, Nicholas. 1991. Entangled Objects: Exchange, Material Culture, and Colonialism in the Pacific. Cambridge, MA: Harvard University Press.

Thomas, Peter. 1979. In the Maelstrom of Change: The Indian Trade and Cultural Process in the Middle Connecticut River Valley 1635–1655. Ph.D. dissertation, Department of Anthropology, University of Massachusetts Amherst.

Thrush, Coll. 2007. Native Seattle: Histories from the Crossing-Over Place. Seattle: University of Washington Press.

———. 2013. "Meere Strangers": Indigenous and Urban Performances in Algonquian London, 1580–1630. *In* Urban Identity and the Atlantic World. Elizabeth A. Fay and Leonard von Morzé, eds. Pp. 195–218. New York: Palgrave Macmillan.

Thwaites, Ruben G., ed. 1896–1901. The Jesuit Relations and Allied Documents. 73 vols. Cleveland: Burrows Brothers.

Tichenor, Phillip J., George A. Donohue, and Clarice N. Olien. 1970. Mass Media Flow and Differential Growth in Knowledge. Public Opinion Quarterly 34(2):159–170.

Tilley, Christopher. 2006. Objectification. *In* Handbook of Material Culture. Christopher Tilley, Webb Keane, Susanne Küchler, Michael Rowlands, and Patricia Spyer, eds. Pp. 60–73. London: Sage Publications.

Timmins Martelle Heritage Consultants, Inc. 2009. Stage 3 Archaeological Assessment, Hardy Road Historic Site, 277 Hardy Road, City of Brantford, Brant County, Ontario. Report on file with the Ontario Ministry of Tourism and Culture, Toronto.

Tozzer, Alfred M. 1941. Landa's "Relación de las cosas de Yucatán." Papers of the Peabody Museum of American Archaeology and Ethnology, Harvard University, Cambridge, MA.

Trigger, Bruce. 1976. The Children of Aataentsic: A History of the Huron People to 1660. Quebec: McGill-Queen's University Press.

———. 1985. Natives and Newcomers: Canada's "Heroic Age" Reconsidered. Montreal: McGill-Queen's University Press.

Trumbull, James Hammond. 1903. Natick Dictionary. Washington, DC: Government Printing Office.

Turgeon, Laurier. 1997. The Tale of the Kettle: Odyssey of an Intercultural Object. Ethnohistory 44(1):1–29.

———. 2006. Crossing Boundaries: Regimes of Value in Intercultural Colonial Contexts. Archaeological Dialogues 12(2):135–142.

Turner, E. Randolph. 1976. An Archaeological and Ethnohistorical Study on the Evolution of Rank Societies in the Virginia Coastal Plain. Ph.D. dissertation, Department of Anthropology, Pennsylvania State University.

———. 1992. The Virginia Coastal Plain during the Late Woodland Period. *In* Middle and Late Woodland Research in Virginia: A Synthesis. Theodore Reinhart and Mary Ellen N. Hodges, eds. Pp. 97–136. Richmond, VA: Dietz Press.

Turner, Terrence. 1995. Social Body and Embodied Subject: Bodiliness, Subjectivity, and Sociality among the Kayapo. Cultural Anthropology 10(2):143–170.

Twiss, Katheryn C. 2007. Home Is Where the Hearth Is: Food and Identity in the Neolithic Levant. *In* The Archaeology of Food and Identity. Katheryn C. Twiss, ed. Pp. 50–68. Occasional Paper, 34. Center for Archaeological Investigations, Southern Illinois University Carbondale.

Ugander, Johan, Lars Backstrom, Cameron Marlow, and Jon Kleinberg. 2012. Structural Diversity in Social Contagion. Proceedings of the National Academy of Sciences 109(16):5962–5966.

Ulrich, Laurel Thatcher. 2001. The Age of Homespun: Objects and Stories in the Creation of an American Myth. New York: Alfred A. Knopf.

Usner, Daniel H. 1992. Indians, Settlers, and Slaves in a Frontier Exchange Economy: The Lower Mississippi Valley before 1783. Chapel Hill: University of North Carolina Press.

Valente, Thomas W. 1996a. The Diffusion Network Game. Connections 19(2):30–37.

———. 1996b. Social Network Thresholds in the Diffusion of Innovations. Social Networks 18(1):69–89.

Van Derwarker, Amber M. 1999. Feasting and Status at the Toqua Site. Southeastern Archaeology 18:24–34.

van Dommelen, Peter. 2011. Postcolonial Archaeologies between Discourse and Practice. World Archaeology 43(1):1–6.

van Dongen, Alexandra. 1996. One Man's Trash Is Another Man's Treasure: The Metamorphosis of the European Utensil in the New World. Rotterdam: Museum Boymans–van Beuningen.

Van Ruymbeke, Bertrand. 2005. "A Dominion of True Believers Not a Republic for Heretics": French Colonial Religious Policy and the Settlement of Early Louisiana, 1699–1730. *In* French Colonial Louisiana and the Atlantic World. Bradley G. Bond, ed. Pp. 83–94. Baton Rouge: Louisiana State University Press.

Vaughn, Kevin J. 2004. Households, Crafts, and Feasting in the Ancient Andes: The Village Context of Early Nasca Craft Consumption. Latin American Antiquity 15(1):61–88.

Vehik, Susan C. 2002. Conflict, Trade, and Political Development on the Southern Plains. American Antiquity 67(1):37–64.

Velie, Alan. 2008. The War Cry of the Trickster: The Concept of Survivance in Gerald Vizenor's *Bear Island: The War at Sugar Point*. *In* Survivance: Narratives of Native Presence. G. Vizenor, ed. Pp. 147–162. Lincoln: University of Nebraska Press.

Vesa-Pekka, Herva, and Ristro Nurmi. 2009. Beyond Consumption: Functionality, Artifact Biography, and Early Modernity in a European Periphery. International Journal of Historical Archaeology 13(2):158–182.

Vilaça, Aparecida. 2005. Chronically Unstable Bodies: Reflections on Amazonian Corporalities. Journal of the Royal Anthropological Institute 11(3):445–464.

Vivieros de Castro, Eduardo. 2004. The Transformation of Objects into Subjects in Amerindian Ontologies. Common Knowledge 10:463–484.

Vizenor, Gerald, ed. 2008. Aesthetics of Survivance: Literary Theory and Practice. *In* Survivance: Narratives of Native Presence. Gerald Vizenor, ed. Pp. 1–24. Lincoln: University of Nebraska Press.

von Gernet, Alexander D., and Peter A. Timmins. 1987. Pipes and Parakeets: Constructing Meaning in an Early Iroquoian Context. *In* Archaeology as Long-Term History. Ian Hodder, ed. Pp. 31–42. Cambridge: Cambridge University Press.

Voss, Barbara L. 2008. The Archaeology of Ethnogenesis: Race and Sexuality in Colonial San Francisco. Berkeley: University of California Press.

———. 2010. Race, Sexuality, and Identity in Colonial San Francisco: The Archaeology of Ethnogenesis. Berkeley: University of California Press.

Wagner, Mark J. 1998. Some Think It Impossible to Civilize Them at All: Cultural Change and Continuity among the Early Nineteenth-Century Potawatomi. *In* Studies in Culture Contact: Interaction, Culture Change, and Archaeology. J. Cusick, ed. Pp. 430–456. Center for Archaeological Investigations, Occasional Paper, 25. Southern Illinois University, Carbondale.

———. 2010. A Prophet Has Arisen: The Archaeology of Nativism among the Nineteenth-Century Algonquin Peoples of Illinois. *In* Across a Great Divide: Continuity and Change in Native North American Societies, 1400–1900. L. L. Scheiber and M. D. Mitchell, eds. Pp. 107–127. Tucson: University of Arizona Press.

Walker, Debra Selsor. 1990. Cerros Revisited: Ceramic Indicators of Terminal Classic and Postclassic Settlement and Pilgrimage in Northern Belize. Ph.D. dissertation, Southern Methodist University.

Walker, William H. 2008. Practice and Non-human Social Actors: The Afterlife of Witches and Dogs in the American Southwest. *In* Memory Work: Archaeologies of Material Practices. Barbara J. Mills and William H. Walker, eds. Pp. 137–157. Santa Fe, NM: School of Advanced Research Press.

Wallace, Henry D., and William H. Doelle. 2001. Classic Period Warfare in Southern Arizona. *In* Deadly Landscapes: Case Studies in Prehistoric Southwestern Warfare. Glenn E. Rice and Steven A. LeBlanc, eds. Pp. 239–287. Salt Lake City: University of Utah Press.

Wallis, Neill J. 2013. The Materiality of Signs: Enchainment and Animacy in Woodland Southeastern North American Pottery. American Antiquity 78(2):207–226.

Wallis, Neill J., and Meggan Blessing. 2015. Ritual Prescriptions for Feasting: A Sacred Bundle of Animal Remains in Mississippi Period Florida. Cambridge Archaeological Journal 25:79–98.

Warrick, Gary. 2000. The Precontact Iroquoian Occupation of Southern Ontario. Journal of World Prehistory 14(4):415–466.

———. 2002a. Archaeological Investigation of the Davisville Community, City of Brantford, Brant County: Results of the 2000 Survey. Report on file with the Ontario Ministry of Tourism and Culture, Toronto.

———. 2002b. Davisville 2 Site: Archaeological Test Excavation of an Early 19th Century Mohawk Cabin on the Grand River. Annual Archaeological Report, Ontario 13:53–57.

———. 2004. Archaeological Investigations of the Davisville Community, City of Brantford, Brant County: Results of the 2002 Test Pit Survey, Test Excavation of Davisville 7 Site (AgHb-253) and Partial Excavation of Davisville 2 Site (AgHb-242). Report on file with the Ontario Ministry of Tourism and Culture, Toronto.

———. 2008. A Population History of the Huron-Petun, A.D. 500–1650. Cambridge: Cambridge University Press.

Waselkov, Gregory A. 2006. Indian Maps of the Colonial Southeast. *In* Powhatan's Mantle: Indians in the Colonial Southeast. Gregory A. Waselkov, Peter H. Wood, and Tom Hatley, eds. Pp. 435–502. Lincoln: University of Nebraska Press.

Watkins, Joe. 2000. Indigenous Archaeology: American Indian Values and Scientific Practice. Walnut Creek, CA: AltaMira Press.

Watts, Christopher, ed. 2013. Relational Archaeologies: Humans, Animals, Things. New York: Routledge.

Weaver, Sally M. 1978. Six Nations of the Grand River, Ontario. *In* Handbook of North American Indians: Volume 15, Northeast. Bruce G. Trigger, ed. Pp. 525–536. Washington, DC: Smithsonian Institution.

Webmoor, Timothy, and Christopher L. Witmore. 2008. Things Are Us! A Commentary on Human/Thing Relations under the Banner of a "Social" Archaeology. Norwegian Archaeological Review 41(1):53–70.

Webster, Jane. 1999. Resisting Traditions: Ceramics, Identity, and Consumer Choice in the Outer Hebrides from 1800 to the Present. International Journal of Historical Archaeology 3(1):53–73.

Weiner, Annette B. 1992. Inalienable Possessions: The Paradox of Keeping-while-Giving. Berkeley: University of California Press.

Weissner, Polly. 2001. Of Feasting and Value: Enga Feasts in a Historical Perspective (Papua New Guinea). *In* Feasts: Archaeological and Ethnographic Perspectives on Food, Politics, and Power. Michael Dietler and Brian Hayden, eds. Pp. 115–143. Washington, DC: Smithsonian Institution Press.

———. 2002. The Vines of Complexity: Egalitarian Structures and the Institutionalization of Inequality among the Enga. Current Anthropology 43(2):233–269.

Welters, Linda. 1993. From Moccasins to Frock Coats and Back Again: Ethnic Identity and Native American Dress in Southern New England. *In* Dress and American Culture. Patricia A. Cunningham and Susan Voso Lab, eds. Pp. 6–41. Bowling Green, OH: Green State University Popular Press.

Welters, Linda, Margaret Odoñez, Kathryn Tarleton, and Joyce Smith. 1996. European Textiles from Seventeenth-Century New England Cemeteries. *In* Historical Archaeology and the Study of American Culture. Lu Ann De Cunzo and Bernard L. Herman, eds. Pp. 193–232. Knoxville: University of Tennessee Press.

West, John. 1827. A Journal of a Mission to the Indians of the British Provinces, of New Brunswick, and Nova Scotia, and the Mohawks, on the Ouse, or Grand River, Upper Canada. London: L. B. Seeley and Son.

White, Bruce M. 1999. The Woman Who Married a Beaver: Trade Patterns and Gender Roles in the Ojibwa Fur Trade. Ethnohistory 46(1):109–147.

White, Carolyn L., ed. 2009. The Materiality of Individuality: Archaeological Studies of Individual Lives. New York: Springer.

White, John R. 1975. Historic Contact Sites as Laboratories for the Study of Culture Change. Conference of Historic Sites Archaeology Papers 9:153–163.

White, Leslie. 1959. The Evolution of Culture. New York: McGraw-Hill.

White, Sophie.2003. "Wearing three or four handkerchiefs around his collar, and elsewhere about him": Slaves' Constructions of Masculinity and Ethnicity in French Colonial New Orleans. Gender and History 15(3):528–549.

———. 2011. Geographies of Slave Consumption. Winterthur Portfolio 45(2/3):229–247.

———. 2013. Wild Frenchmen and Frenchified Indians: Material Culture and Race in Colonial Louisiana. Philadelphia: University of Pennsylvania Press.

Whitehead, R. 1993. Nova Scotia: The Protohistoric Period 1500–1630. Nova Scotia Museum, Curatorial Report, 75.

Whitfield, Henry. 1834. Strength out of Weakness: Or a Glorious Manifestation of the Further Progresse of the Gospel among the Indians in New England. Reprint, Collections of the Massachusetts Historical Society 35(4):149–196.

Whitthoft, John. 1967. Archaeology as a Key to the Colonial Fur Trade. *In* Aspects of the Fur Trade: Selected Papers of the 1965 North American Fur Trade Conference. R. R. Gilman, ed. Pp. 55–61. St. Paul: Minnesota Historical Society.

Wicken, William. 1993. Mi'kmaq Treaties on Trial. History, Land and Donald Marshall Junior. Toronto: University of Toronto Press.

Wilcox, Michael. 2009. The Pueblo Revolt and the Mythology of Conquest: An Indigenous Archaeology of Contact. Berkeley: University of California Press.

Wilkie, Laura A., and Kevin M. Bartoy. 2000. A Critical Archaeology Revisited. Current Anthropology 41(5):747–777.

Williams, Roger. 1936[1643]. A Key into the Language of America. Providence: Rhode Island and Providence Plantations Tercentenary Commission.

———. 1997[1643]. A Key into the Language of America. Bedford, MA: Applewood Books.

Williamson, Margaret Holmes. 2003. Powhatan Lords of Life and Death: Command and Consent in Seventeenth-Century Virginia. Lincoln: University of Nebraska Press.

Williamson, Ronald F., and Debbie Steiss. 2003. A History of Ontario Iroquoian Multiple Burial Practice. *In* Bones of the Ancestors: The Archaeology and Osteobiography of the Moatfield Ossuary. Ronald F. Williamson and Susan Pfeiffer, eds. Pp. 89–132. Gatineau, QC: Canadian Museum of Civilization.

Willoughby, Charles. 1905. Dress and Ornaments of the New England Indians. American Anthropologist 7(2):499–508.

Wilson, Gregory D. 1999. The Production and Consumption of Mississippian Fineware in the American Bottom. Southeastern Archaeology 18(2):98–109.

Wilson, Peter J. 1988. The Domestication of the Human Species. New Haven, CT: Yale University Press.

Winslow, Edward. 1910[1624]. Relation. *In* Chronicles of the Pilgrim Fathers. Pp. 267–356. Boston: Everyman's Library.

Winters, Howard D. 1981. Excavating in Museums: Notes on Mississippian Hoes and Middle Woodland Copper Gouges and Celts. Annals of the New York Academy of Sciences 376:17–34.

Witmore, Christopher L. 2007. Symmetrical Archaeology: Excerpts of a Manifesto. World Archaeology 39(4):546–562.

Witmore, Christopher L., and Bjørnar Olsen. 2015. Archaeology, Symmetry and the Ontology of Things. A Response to Critics. Archaeological Dialogues 22(2):187–197.

Wobst, H. Martin. 2005. Power to the (Indigenous) Past and Present! Or: The Theory and Method behind Archaeological Theory and Method. *In* Indigenous Archaeologies: Decolonizing Theory and Practice. Claire Smith and H. Martin Wobst, eds. Pp. 15–29. New York: Routledge.

Wood, William. 1977. New England's Prospect. Alden Vaughan, ed. Amherst: University of Massachusetts Press.

Woodward, Arthur. 1978[1937]. The Study of Historical Archaeology in America. *In* Historical Archaeology: A Guide to Substantive and Theoretical Contributions. Robert L. Schuyler, ed. Pp. 16–17. Farmingdale, NY: Baywood Publishing Company.

Wright, James V. 1966. The Ontario Iroquois Tradition. Gatineau, QC: National Museum of Canada.

Wright, Milton J. 1981. The Walker Site. Gatineau, QC: National Museum of Canada.

Wrong, George M., ed. 1939. Sagard's Long Journey to the Huron. Toronto: Champlain Society.

Wurst, LouAnn, and Randall H. McGuire. 1999. Immaculate Consumption: A Critique of the "Shop till You Drop" School of Human Behavior. International Journal of Historical Archaeology 3(3):191–199.

Zappia, Natale A. 2014. Traders and Raiders: The Indigenous World of the Colorado Basin, 1540–1859. Chapel Hill: University of North Carolina Press.

Zedeño, Maria N. 2008. Bundled Worlds: The Roles and Interactions of Complex Objects from the North American Plains. Journal of Archaeological Method and Theory 13:362–378.

———. 2009. Animating by Association: Index Objects and Relational Taxonomies. Cambridge Archaeological Journal 19:407–417.

CONTRIBUTORS

MATTHEW A. BEAUDOIN is the manager of archaeological assessment at Timmins Martelle Heritage Consultants Inc., a CRM company based out of London, Ontario, Canada, and teaches part-time at the University of Western Ontario.

LEWIS BORCK is a postdoctoral researcher in the Faculty of Archaeology at Universiteit Leiden and at Archaeology Southwest. He is interested in using the material record to study social movements and contentious politics, forms of resistance, the tension between vertical and horizontal structures of social power, and geosocial analyses.

KATHLEEN J. BRAGDON is professor of anthropology at the College of William and Mary. She is author of *Native People of Southern New England, 1500–1650* (1999, University of Oklahoma Press) and *Native Peoples of Southern New England, 1650–1775* (2009, University of Oklahoma Press).

CRAIG N. CIPOLLA is associate curator of North American archaeology at the Royal Ontario Museum and assistant professor of anthropology at the University of Toronto. Before moving to Toronto, he was lecturer in archaeology and a Marie Curie Fellow in the School of Archaeology and Ancient History, University of Leicester. He is the author of *Archaeological Theory in the New Millennium* (coauthored with Oliver Harris, forthcoming from Routledge) and *Becoming Brothertown* (2013, University of Arizona Press) and the editor of *Rethinking Colonialism* (coedited with Kat

Hayes, 2015, University Press of Florida). Craig's research interests include contemporary archaeological theory, collaborative indigenous archaeology, colonialism, and Native North America (both New England and the Great Lakes).

CHARLES R. COBB is curator and James E. Lockwood, Jr., Professor of Historical Archaeology at the Florida Museum of Natural History at the University of Florida.

JOHN L. CREESE is an assistant professor in the Department of Sociology and Anthropology at North Dakota State University. He has published on issues of personhood, power, and ritual economies in the Northeast and Great Lakes region.

DIANA DIPAOLO LOREN is a museum curator at the Peabody Museum of Archaeology and Ethnology at Harvard University. She is the author of *In Contact: Bodies and Spaces in the Sixteenth- and Seventeenth-Century Eastern Woodlands* (2007) and *The Archaeology of Clothing and Bodily Adornment in Colonial America* (2010).

MARTIN GALLIVAN is professor of anthropology in the College of William and Mary's Anthropology Department. He is author of *James River Chiefdoms* (2003, University of Nebraska Press), along with a number of book chapters and peer-reviewed articles.

MEGHAN C. L. HOWEY is associate professor of anthropology and the James H. Hayes and Claire Short Hayes Professor of the Humanities at the University of New Hampshire. She is author of *Mound Builders and Monument Makers of the Northern Great Lakes, 1200–1600* (2012, University of Oklahoma Press).

BARBARA J. MILLS is a professor in the School of Anthropology, University of Arizona, with a focus on the archaeology of the North American Southwest. Her research interests include migration, memory and materiality, colonialism and culture contact, and the application of social network analyses in archaeology.

MAXINE OLAND is the author of multiple articles and book chapters on the colonial Maya and was the lead coeditor (with Siobhan M. Hart and Liam Frink) of *Decolonizing Indigenous Histories: Exploring Prehistoric/Colonial Transitions in Archaeology* (2012, University of Arizona Press).

LEE M. PANICH is assistant professor of anthropology at Santa Clara University. He is the coeditor of *Indigenous Landscapes and Spanish Missions: New Perspectives from Archaeology and Ethnohistory* (2014, University of Arizona Press).

PATRICIA E. RUBERTONE is professor of anthropology at Brown University. She is editor of *Archaeologies of Placemaking* (2008, Left Coast Press) and author of *Grave Undertakings: An Archaeology of Roger Williams and the Narragansett Indians* (2001, Smithsonian Institution Press).

CHRISTOPHER SHEPHARD is a Ph.D. candidate in the College of William and Mary's Department of Anthropology.

KEITH D. STEPHENSON (Ph.D.) is director of the Savannah River Archaeological Research Program at the University of South Carolina.

INDEX

Page numbers in *italics* represent illustrations.

acculturation theory, 13, 19–21, 52, 55, 59, 60, 81, 113, 194, 202, 225, 228
acquisition, 4, 10, 81, 110, 188–89
agency, 9, 12, 22, 29–30, 46, 61–62, 81, 155, 188, 220–21; nonhuman, 12–13, 29, 223
Adena, 3–4
alterity, 7, 79, 141, 163, 182, 224–25
ancestors, 91, 132–33, 139–40, 144, 147, 153, 157
animism, 81–84, 93, 118–23, 139–41, 153, 163, 180–81. *See also* new animism
Appadurai, Arjun, 8, 16–17, 64, 97, 222–23
archaeological theory, 9, 226–27
authenticity, 10, 19, 53–54, 217–18, 220, 228
autonomy, 7, 187, 198–99, 202

beads, 71–72, 84, 86–88, 128–29, 138; copper, 76; glass, 93, 99, 103, 105, *106*, 121, *137*, 192–94, 196; shell, 85, 89, 108, 135, *136*, 192–94, 196. *See also* wampum
becoming, 4, 163, 165–66, 168
bear, 4, 91, 105, 153, *154*, 213
Bennett, Jane, 222
Bhabha, Homi, 6, 98
the body, 11, 13, 24, 66–67, 80, 81, 88–89, 93, 94, 99–109, 110–13, 116–24
bodiliness, 111, 115, 120–21
Bourdieu, Pierre, 34
bundles, 68–69, 78, 87, 91, 128, 138–41, 148, 174, 206. *See also* medicine bundles
burial practices. *See* mortuary contexts

caching. *See* bundles
Cape Cod, 114
capitalism, 5–8, 16–17, 21–23, 45–47, 61–63, 97, 205, 227–28
ceramics, 37–38, 50–55

ceremony, 92, 146–47, *151*, 154, 192
choice, 9, 21–23, 44–56 passim, 45–47, 53–54, 60–63, 99, 128, 155, 204, 221
circulation, of goods, *68*, 93, 143; of wealth, 143
cloth and clothing, 72, 76, 88, 99, 102–3, 105–7, 110–24 passim
colonialism, 6–8, 13–15, 55, 81–82, 94, 95–97, 123, 128, 132, 162, 187, 197–99, 201–3, 218–19, postscript; archaeologies of, 10–12, 16–17, 19–21, 44–47, 51, 54, 55, 97–102, 128–29, 162–64, 188–89
Comaroff, Jean and John, 8
commodity, 5–8, 15–17, 45, 50, 62–64, 72–78, 85–87, 94, 164–67, 204–5, 214, 219–21
commodity fetishism, 6, 64
Connecticut, 3–5, 9–10, 23, 111, 207
consumption, definitions of, 5–12, 29–30, 45–47, 60–63, 81–82, 99, 110, 127–31, 148–50, 164–65, 188, 202, ; history of term, 164–65

Davisville, 49–50, 53–55
debt, 85–86, 143–44, 146–48, 150–58, 204, 209
decolonizing, 5, 7, 56, 60, 222, 225–26, 228
descendant communities, 14, 169, 177, 227
diaspora, 10, 35–38
Dietler, Michael, 10, 45, 97–98
diffusion, 9, 31–32, 38–42, *39*
Douglas, Mary, 12, 22
dress, 88, 94, 99–100, 103, 110–24 passim, 141, 212–15

economies of affect, 59–79 passim
embodiment, 64, 99, 110–11, 123–24, 150
emotion, 59–79 passim, 156
epidemics, 66, 70, 113–18, 121–22, 210–11
exchange value, 5–6, 17, 86–87
exotics, 11, 128–29, 132–33, 135–39, 144, 147–50

feasting, 30–31, 35–37, 42, 67–70, 77, 84, 88, 133–35, 143–61 passim
fetishism, 6, 8, 20, 99, 103. *See also* commodity fetishism
foreign, 4, 10–12, 31, 45, 62–64, 81–82, 128, 132–33, 188
foreign goods: in general, 10–11, 17–18, 31. *See also* ceramics; copper and brass kettles; cloth and clothing; feasting; horse hardware; medicine; olive jars; smoking pipes; religious artifacts; Salado; and wampum
Fowles, Severin, 222
fur trade, 7–8, 65–66, 113–18, 162–64, 166–67

Gell, Alfred, 150, 153, 182
gift exchange, 16–17, 62–63, 156–57
Gosden, Chris, 17, 223

Hayes, Katherine, 10
health, 62, 76, 99, 100–101, 113, 115, 118, 120, 123–24, 205. *See also* epidemics
historical archaeology, 13–14, 21–23, 44–57 passim, 94, 204
household archaeology, 49–55, 128–29, 134–35, 138–40
Huron. *See* Wendat

identity, 19, 30, 38, 45–47, 61, 62–63, 68, 77–79, 98, 111, 163, 194, 218–19

indigeneity, 10–12, 31, 44–45
indigenous knowledge, 93, 101, 205, 209
ivory towers, 227, 228

kettles, 18, 20, 62, 76–77, 128, 129, 162–83 passim
Kopytoff, Igor, 17, 63, 64, 78

labor, 5, 86, 160, 187–203 passim, 209
Latour, Bruno, 11, 13, 222–23, 227
Lightfoot, Kent, 13–14

magic, 63, 150, 153, 156; sympathetic, 162, 179–82; contagious, 162, 179–82
manit/manitou, 21, 81, 83–86, 91, 93, 163, 167
marginality, 33, 204–5
market economy, 46, 82, 127–28, 162, 165–66, 168, 183, 204–21 passim
Marx, 5–7, 16–17, 20, 64
Marxism, 33, 62, 64, 228
Matthews, Christopher, 7–8, 225
Mauss, Marcel, 16, 62, 110. *See also* gift exchange
medicine, 100, 120–21, 204–21 passim
medicine bundles, 4, 10, 121, 153, 226
Miller, Daniel, 4, 6, 15, 165
mortuary contexts, 3–4, 68–69, 74–77, 87–88, 105–8, 111, 121–23, 139–40, 162–83, 194–96, 202
mound sites, 36, 38, 42–43, 135, 143, 145, *149*, 153–58
Mohawk Nation, 48–50, 53. *See also* Davisville, Mohawk Village, and Six Nations
Mohawk Village, 48–50, 53–55
Mullins, Paul, 8, 15, 22, 30, 45, 62, 81, 97, 127, 128, 148
multimodality, 63–64, 68

new animism, 224
New England, 3–5, 83, 110–24 passim, 162–83 passim, 204–21 passim

objectification, 111–12, 223
ontology, 5, 7, 8, 10, 13, 18, 20, 24, 31, 59, 63–66, 79, 82–83, 101, 111, 113, 128, 131, 144, 148, 150, 160, 162–63, 167, 170, 177, 181, 222–29

Pequot, 4, 10, 23, 111, 114
personhood, 7, 11, 13, 22, 24, 61, 63–64, 86, 111, 113, 119, 150, 153, 165
phenomenology, 110, 124
polychrome ceramics. *See* Salado
postcolonialism, 6, 33–34, 60, postscript
posthumanism, 4, 13, postscript
power, 9, 16, 22, 33–34, 38, 63, 80–93 passim, 97, 132, 148, 168–69, 181–82, 188
Powhatan, 81, 84–85, 92–93
Powhatan's mantle, 89–91, *90*
production, 6, 16, 21–23, 34, 81, 84, 88, 121, 127, 134, 147, 157, 165, 204, 209, 219–21

race, 22, 98–99, 209–10
racism, 22, 214, 220–21, 228–29
regimes of value, 12–13, 16, 20, 23, 64–65, 72, 76, 93
resistance, 7, 10, 32–34, 38–41, 48, 63, 95, 99, 103, 127, 138, 199,
ritual killing, 139–40, 141, 157, 180

Salado, 29–43 passim
scale, 11–12, 19, 34, 157
Silliman, Stephen W., 23, 47–48, 53, 97, 187
Six Nations (Confederacy of the Iroquois), 48, 51. *See also* Mohawk
smoking pipes, 4, 10, 24, 70–73, 138
sovereignty, 80–93 passim, 113
Strathern, Marilyn, 61, 111
subalterity, 9, 22, 34, 225–26
symmetry, 13, 222, 224–25, 227

textiles, 112–13
third space, 163
Thomas, Nicholas, 12–13, 17–19, 222–23
Trigger, Bruce, 16, 20–21, 66

use value, 5, 17, 20, 63

value. *See* exchange value and exchange value

Wahunsenacawh, 80, 82–84, 85–86, 89, 91–93
wampum, 74–76, 115–18, 121, 123–24
Wendat, 59–79 passim
worldview, 79, 82–83, 127–31, 188, 224, 226